THE SQUEAKY WHEEL:
An Unauthorized Autobiography

Brian Shaughnessy
© 2005

If you purchased this book without a cover, you should be aware that this book is stolen property. It was reported as "Unsold and destroyed" to the publisher and neither the author nor the publisher has received any payment for this "stripped book."

Copyright © 2005

All rights reserved. No part of this book may be used or reproduced in any manner whatsoever without written permission of the publisher, except in the case of brief quotations embodied in critical articles and reviews.

ISBN: 0-9708430-3-8

Printed in the United States of America
By RJ Communications, New York, New York

Without limiting the rights under copyright reserved above, no part of this publication may be reproduced, stored in or introduced into a retrieval system, or transmitted, in any form, or by any means (electronic, mechanical, photocopying, recording or otherwise), without the prior written permission of the copyright owner and publisher of this book.

To:

Amadeus Yun Chi Shaughnessy
&
Miranda Manzoline Shaughnessy
may they always keep the light in their eyes.

ACKNOWLEDGEMENTS

If I acknowledged ALL who had helped/contributed to this book I would have another book. That being said and with apologies to anyone left off, I would like to thank and acknowledge:

GOD
Nuf said

FAMILY
My parents, Steve and Lou, who loved me and taught me right; my siblings whom I've hit and hugged and have hit and hugged me: Pat, Teri, Dan, Dawn and especially Darrin for reading, responding and trying to keep me honest and not hurt anyone who didn't deserve it. My siblings' significant others, without whom, they lack significance, My Aunts, Uncles and cousins (Yes, you, Roxann) for their trips to the hospital, their prayers, gifts and support, nephew Devlin (who brought the message from heaven) and his sister Mickaylee and brother Aidan. My red-haired grandma, Nonnie, my biggest supporter who watches over me even now.

FRIENDS WHO KNEW ME WHEN
My dearest friends, Andrew Yee, Diane Jarvenpa, Don Brundage, Annie, John Mc, Tom, Tim, Wayne, and The Mikes – friends, "before," through, and forever. Those who became friends as they met me in the hospital: Avaren et al.

Mary Clark who loved, cared for me, went to hell with me and led me back.

HEALTH CARE PROFESSIONALS
Who cared more than the job requirements: Carol Opat, Jan, Julie and ALL those rehab nurses, Dr. Brock, Dr. T. and the rest.

FRIENDS WHO DIDN'T KNOW ME WHEN
Dear Dave, J.J., Kevin, Steve, Dale, Tracey, Allen, George "Jetson" O'Hanlon, Brother Brett, Belinda, Dana, Geri, Carter, Peter, Herman, Sam and Jeanie. You were/are there/here.

C. L. H. for doing the best she could and the red-headed goose.

THE APPRECIATED AIDES WHO GOT ME OUT OF BED
Jerry, Bob, Edward, Larry, Tyrone, Shawn, Roger, (what, no women?) Tato and king of all – Demitrius.

BROTHERS AND SISTERS IN DISABILITY
From whom I've learned the most, especially Jim Barton, Juan, Sterling, Halona, Glen, Kevin Kimura, Jaehn Clare, Lunsford, maybe Michelle and most definitely Christopher Reeve.

TEACHERS
Mark Medoff, Kim, Dr. James Brandon, Dennis Carol, Mike Tanigawa, Mark, Hazel, and those outside the classroom.

KOKUA
Ann Ito, Gwen, Karen, Tammy, Lanning, Candice and the cutest girl/women on campus.

THE CREW
Rita Ippoliti – who asked for and demanded more, Beth Bruno – who said, "Now it's a Book," my jacket artist and web page designer Rudolf, who never wavered in support, had the gonads to chant THAT mantra, and Annie – the Thai girl who became a woman as the camel who carried this crazy chronicle to completion.

AND AMY, The World's Best Nurse, The Woman I tricked into marrying me, the best mother for a woogedy boy. It would not have happened without you! Your magical laugh and loving eyes have delivered me from hell and shown me heaven. Thank you for risking EVERYTHING, being my best audience, making ALL possible and giving this tawdry tale a happy ending.

There is overlap in these lists. To those listed and those missed I say,

Mahalo and Aloha,

Brian

Table of Contents

Part I: STRANGER IN MY OWN LAND 1

Rainbows - 1999 2
February 2, 1983 3
As We Discussed/Disgust 7
Good Results 11
THE RUBBER STAMP ROOM 17
White Coats 31
Thou Shalt Not Covet 38
Surprise 51
Doug 54
That's Why You Don't Kill the Messenger 55
My Dinner with Andrew or Ding-dong the Witch Is Dead 58
Shunt #2 64
The First in a Long Line of Abusive Agency Workers 67
I Have Been Dismissed 71
Home Again, Home Again 74
On the Road Again 78
No Scarecrow Here 81
Nope, I'm Fine Right Here 83
What Happened to You? 88
The Unthinkable Horror 89
Carol, Jackie and Dr. Brock 91
Demerol Dreams -- Installment 1 96
That Sound 100
You Haven't Been Quadriplegic Very Long, Right? 102
Poo-Poo 2 106
Size Nine Shoes 107
Made in China 109
1984 114
Stay off the Sidewalks 116
What Happened To You... 118
Besides That, How Did You Enjoy the Show, Mr. Shaughnessy? 119
My Cover Nearly Blown 122
The Royal Scam 126

Part II: PEACE AND WAR 131

Searching for the Land of Enchantment 132
Autonomic Dysreflexia In the Real World 136
Besides That How Did You Enjoy the Play, Mrs. Lincoln? 141

You Think That's Funny?..145
So, Are You Guys Still a Couple?..147
That Sound -- Installment 2 155
Mickaylee 158
Poo-Poo Born Again...160
The Road to Outer Space Is Paved with... Black Humor...................165
Oh, What a Tangled Web...174
The Entrée of Stench..184
Black Skin 198
Dark Days in Paradise..203
Third World Dilemma..216
Dr. Yank 226
The Revenge of Dr. Friendly (Who Was Not) 245
Unexpected Guests...257
Whiner...260
Dancing and the Art of Breaking Boards...265
The Thrill Is Gone..265
Payback Can Be Sweet...273
Screenplay 280
Christmas Is for Giving of Yourself 284
Road to Tokyo...292
Letterman..296
Huffisms 302
Mission Control to Houston -- Send a Daiquiri 306
The Fight With Very Special Arts...307
Strange Brew 312
The Rainbow Coalition 314
The Greatest 318
Welcome Back, Clark..329
Greg As Emissary of Payback...333
New P.S.A...341
Lifts! 346
Bongo..349
Don Knotts vs. Mohammed Ali 351

Part III -- LAW AND DISORDER 355

But What Lovely Decorations 356
You're Going To Put That Where?...369
Feral Children and Adults 378
Mr. Cheat 379
EVERYTHING!!..392

Brian Shaughnessy

Part I: STRANGER IN MY OWN LAND

The Squeaky Wheel

Rainbows - 1999

  Rainbows float in bubbles over the heads of the wedding guests and out over the turquoise ocean. Here it is white streaked with foam and looks like rare marble. The sea is sky-blue at the next beach -- then indigo with Kokohead volcano beyond. The water at each beach in Hawaii is a different shade of blue. Past the guests and bubbles sit two regal Asian women with shoulder length hair wearing white *muumuus* and playing Elvis' "Can't Help Falling in Love" on the harp and flute. The guests are armed with disposable cameras and bubbles. As the guests arrive a Polaroid is taken of them and the picture glued into a book where guests jot down regards for the betrothed. The table at the entrance to the huge backyard is covered in stuffed bunnies.
  The preacher beside me wears a polyester pale-blue suit. He is tall, bald and looks like he just stepped out of the Ozarks. He tells those gathered he has been asked to interpret the ceremony using American Sign Language. I see my sister-in-law, Shelli, raise her hands and twist them -- American Sign Language for applause. My best-person, my sister Dawn, is beside me. She has prepared a speech. Dawn has Down syndrome.
  The smell of the lawn, the ocean and plumerias waft past us. Down the grassy aisle march the five cutest little brown girls ever. Each looks like she was drawn for Hallmark. They wear the cutest pink dresses ever. Each carries a large stuffed bunny. Now my bride Amy exits the house wearing a *haku* lei made by a law school classmate. Amy's long black hair cascades down the front of her bridal gown. I fight tears. She is a gift from God. The guests stand and smile. In lieu of a bouquet of flowers, Amy carries a pink stuffed bunny. It is the year of the rabbit.
  I wear new black cowboy boots. Actually the boots are entirely made from petroleum products, which makes them synthetic-boy boots. These are complemented by black trousers, a white shirt with Superman cufflinks and a black and blue paisley tuxedo vest. My father has just removed my *tres*-cool tortoiseshell sunglasses. My red hair shines from under the Chinese *bob* hat I wear. The hat is a black silk cross between a yarmulke and a Muslim's hat. My momentarily to-be wife has placed a red circle with the Chinese *kanji* for happiness on the center of the hat's

band. I'm sure I look like Hop Sing, the Chinese cook from *Bonanza*, but friends tell me I look like the emperor. The only possible thing that can take away from this idyllic picture is the wheelchair under my ass.

February 2, 1983

"Mr. Shaughnessy?"
"Mr. Shaughnessy."
"Why are you waking me?" I ask. It feels as if it has only been moments since the anesthetic took effect and I drifted to sleep. Ninety-nine, 98, 97...

But that was a long time ago in a reality far, far away.

"The surgery is over, Mr. Shaughnessy. Can you tell me your name?" There is a hint in there.

"Brian Shaughnessy."

"Do you know where you are?"

"I'm at the University of Minnesota Hospital," I say as I taste... what is that taste? ... Lysol.

"Okay, very good. Can you tell me the date?"

"Feb. 2nd, 1983. Can I have a blanket?"

I am freezing. I am certain that they performed the surgery in a meat locker and that I was covered only with frost.

The individual asking questions is moving about wearing standard blue hospital scrubs. These are different than the operating room green scrubs. I know this because I once worked at this hospital ... in the kitchen. May God forgive me.

He is checking my eyes with the flashlight and then dons his stethoscope. First, he listens to my chest and heart; then, as the stethoscope slides below my nipples, the sensation nearly vanishes. I start to look down but immediately feel pain.

"You're lucky you're inside today; there was a nasty blizzard."

I am not feeling particularly lucky. I am slowly becoming aware of the fact that a group of people cut open the back of my neck, broke off tiny pieces of my spine to access my spinal canal and performed some surgical voodoo in there. Something is terribly wrong.

The Squeaky Wheel

"Breathe deep," Blue-scrubs commands. He has checked my heart rate, pulse, eyes, etc. Blue-scrubs is around six feet tall and in his mid-twenties, with brown hair, a cropped beard and Buddy Holly glasses.

"Can you squeeze my fingers?"

Oh my God! What the hell did these people do? I squeeze his fingers, becoming aware I have 10 percent of the strength I had before going to sleep. I am definitely beginning to wake up.

"Is that the best you can do?"

What the hell do you think? Wouldn't I break them right now if you gave me the opportunity? What is going on?

"Lift your right leg for me."

Okay now, THIS is big. The anesthesia clouding my thinking is hastily pushed out by the nightmare possibilities consuming every speck of gray matter. I make a Herculean effort to raise my right leg. What a simple request and what tremendous effort to accomplish ... nothing. It doesn't move. I hear my leg hit the bed. What the…?

"Very good. Now can you do that with your left leg for me?"

"Do what? It didn't move!" This can't be real, my mind shrieks, as I make the effort to lower my head and look at my feet, a move that unpleasantly reminds me that knives and other implements have been busy at work for an unknown amount of time. Why can't I feel my leg move? Jesus.

"I didn't feel my right leg move."

"That's okay. Try the left leg for me, please."

Oh, well, if you're going to be polite about it I guess I'll just do as I am asked and not bother you with *my* silly concerns. I make the effort again. I hear the thump back on the bed, but I am unaware that my leg moved.

With the calmness of a stranger asking my occupation, he asks, "Can you feel my hand on your foot?"

"Barely," I respond, trying not to lose my mind.

"Which toe am I touching?"

I start to look toward my feet but pain stops me. He continues to check for sensation; it becomes clear that it stops almost completely exactly at my nipples.

"What's going on? What happened? Can I have another blanket?"

"I'll get somebody to bring you another blanket. The doc will be in soon to answer your other questions. He's talking to your family right now."

Brian Shaughnessy

My father, brothers and grandmother have waited through the procedure. My mother and two sisters are far away in New Mexico.

What the hell is he telling them? I wonder. 'Hi, I'm the doctor that crippled your son, brother, grandson...? The surgery went just fine. You should be able to roll him out of here in a couple of days.' The only thing missing from this nightmare is the obligatory fog in old horror movies.

"Can I have another blanket?" I ask this question several times and each time they bring another blanket. The pile of blankets is now thicker than my body. A group of doctors come and perform the same tests Blue-scrubs did. This is intermittently followed by nurses doing the same. No one looks me in the eye.

Blue-scrubs says, "Your father and brother want to come in and talk to you. Is that okay?"

What will I tell them? "Yes, send them in."

"They can only have a couple minutes."

Fine, I think, since I have no idea what to tell them and what not to tell them.

My father and brother enter the room. They are smiling. They know nothing.

"Big Red! How are you feeling?" my father asks. My father is a stocky five-foot-eight inches with salt and pepper hair, a gray mustache and the charm of the Irish revealed in his dancing eyes. As is his custom, he wears a suit. My brother has a similar phenotype to mine. He is about five-foot-ten and muscular with red hair and a large neck.

"I'm freezing," I respond. "Have them give me another blanket."

Another blanket is heaped on and I continue to shiver as my dad talks about the blizzard and my brother Dan talks about a basketball game, but none of it makes any sense. I say I'm fine, tired, and sore, while my mind screams, Tell them these bastards crippled me. Tell them to make the doctor guarantee I will walk out of this hospital. Tell them I should have died on the operating table because my life is over. No one -- especially not me -- can live this way.

But I manage to keep silent and a nurse ushers them out. They tell me to get better fast; they will return the next day; and everyone's real proud and buzz buzz buzz.

"We're going to move you to the intensive care unit, Mr. Shaughnessy."

"This is going to go away, isn't it?" I ask.

"I don't know," is the three-syllable answer.

The Squeaky Wheel

"Well, who does know? Where is the doctor?" I ask while thinking, How the hell can you say you don't know? I know I'm going to walk out of here!

I look about the room as carefully as one can when he knows that the slightest movement of his neck will result in ice-pick stabs of horrific pain. There are two small beds. I am the only one in the room now although others have come and gone. There are many sets of scrubs in this room and they are all occupied by medical personnel.

Brian Shaughnessy

As We Discussed/Disgust

The Doctor walks into the room. He is tall with dark hair only beginning to reveal gray. Aside from being taller, he looks like he could be a younger version of my father. He wears glasses like my father wore for many years. He exudes the status of neurosurgeon as he moves. He sits next to the bed and says, "The surgery was more complicated than anticipated because of unrevealed scar tissue in the spinal canal." He says the paralysis is probably just "spinal shock" and should go away in a few days. But "AS WE DISCUSSED" there is a possibility I will remain paralyzed.

What the hell is he talking about? We never talked about paralysis. He said the surgery might kill me. I'm thinking, somebody better do *that* if the surgery did not because *this* is just not tolerable. The intense pain and the shock keep me from arguing with Dr. Liar.

Personnel bring a gurney alongside the small bed I am in. It takes some time to remove the blankets before they transfer me. They slide a plastic board underneath me, and as I slip from the bed to the gurney, I see a nearly pencil-wide tube in my dick. I remember one of the people in the operating room telling me he would need to do this for the surgery. I tried to talk him out of it, but he claimed it was needed, and he would do it after I was under. A nasty trick to pull on somebody sleeping. But there it is. I can't feel it. The doctor lies to me; there is a tube in my dick I can't feel... what next?

I am wheeled from the recovery room to the intensive care unit. As they move me from the gurney to the bed a realization hits. "What time is it?" I blurt out.

"11:20 p.m."

Oh my God! This was supposed to be a four-hour surgery, starting at noon, which means my love, Annie, was expecting a call around 4:00 telling her I'm okay. It's seven plus hours later. I asked my father to make that call. I know that as an attorney he has never placed a phone call in his life!

"I need you to make a phone call!"

"Okay."

"Please dial 785-8914 and ask for Annie."

7

The Squeaky Wheel

"What do you want me to tell her?"

Well, there *is* the six million dollar question. What do I want a stranger to tell one of the most important people in my life who is certain I'm dead? "Tell her... tell her... I'm fine. Let her know that the surgery took longer than they thought, and I'll see her tomorrow." I stare about the room. There are six patients, three on each side of the room. There is a glass enclosure where the nurses remain when not tending to patients. The room is dark; death, pain and profound sadness hang in the air. These blue-scrubbed nurses don't laugh.

The night is endless. A pair of nurses comes around every 15 minutes to check vital signs. I sleep but *only* because I am full of top shelf painkillers. Every slight movement of my neck triggers intense pain despite more narcotics in me than a 747 has passengers.

Periodically I am awakened by the sound of clapping. Someone is cupping his or her hands, which makes the sound hollower... and louder. I look toward the bed next to me where two people are pummeling an obese man in this manner. Why? Why? Why? Aren't I being tortured enough without this? Cut it out! Stop waking me to this! Every pore of my body cries out, but I am silent.

I pray. I tell God I can't take this. It would have been better had I died on the operating table. The pain is too great and limitations too profound for me or anyone to endure. My Catholic upbringing kicks in as I remember scripture, "Take this cup from me." I recall what that line did for Jesus and I cry.

Two nurses check vital signs and have me squeeze their hands. I do it weakly and the sensation is not "normal." One of them commands me to lift my leg. I try but it doesn't move.

"Very good."

"It didn't move!" I insist.

"Yes, it did! They both did! Try the left one again."

I try again. I don't see it moving. "See?"

"You didn't feel that?"

"I didn't feel anything!" I scream, cry. My eyes plead for assurance... a single word of hope. Instead, the two girls giggle… and walk away. I wish I could get up and kill them.

The next nurse lingers.

"Anything I can do for you?"

"This is going to go away, isn't it?"

"I don't know. They told you this might happen, right?"

"Nobody told me anything! I don't even know what 'this' is."

"When the neurosurgeon explained the surgery to you, he didn't talk about the possibility of paralysis as a result of surgery to the spine?" she asks incredulously.

"No!"

"How old are you?"

"Twenty-four."

"You didn't know that surgery in the spinal canal could result in paralysis?"

"I'm sorry; I'm a theater major. We don't know science stuff."

"No, I guess you wouldn't." Heavy sigh from her. "That should have all been explained to you, written down on the consent forms and put in your chart. What *did* the doc tell you?"

"'He said I might DIE, but that that was not likely because of my age and health."

"The surgeon should inform you of ALL risks and this is an obvious one to anyone with a medical background. Let me look at your chart, and I'll talk to you on the post-op floor, ok?"

I never see her again.

After a night in the intensive care unit I am moved to the post-operative floor. It is a regular hospital room with two beds. It looks straight down the hallway to the ward I was on before the surgery. I see the doctors and others from that side who were so friendly to me before the surgery. Now they look in and don't even acknowledge my existence. I wonder what I am going to tell my family. My friends? *My mom*? Annie. She'll be here soon...

I don't move my neck because of the profound pain. I watch TV mindlessly as doctors, nurses and med students enter, examine, and speak to and about me in a detached manner as if I am a frog in the pan of a high school lab experiment.

Annie arrives. I see her lithe, animated step and smiling face as she approaches the room – singing "Make 'em Laugh" from *Singing in the Rain*. Annie loves movie musicals. *Singing in the Rain* is her favorite. Annie's hair is almost my color. She is fair, freckled and slight of build. More than once we have been asked if we are brother and sister. I have been told the ultimate form of egotism is to copulate with someone who shares your features. She comes bearing outside food and drink -- aware of the heinous reputation of hospital food (food I once prepared — may God have mercy on my wretched soul). Her eyes meet mine and I turn away. She comes to me, setting the food on the hospital table. She sits next to me on the bed.

The Squeaky Wheel

"Hi Honey," she says with an innocence and trust for human beings that will soon disappear forever ... maybe in the next sixty seconds. My eyes meet hers -- brown to brown. Immediately, I begin to cry.

"What's wrong?" She tries to put her arms around me and becomes aware of the staples and bandages behind my neck. "Oh, can I hold you?"

"I wish you would," I struggle to say through a cracking voice.

"What's wrong?"

I explain to her that right now I can't stand up, can't go to the bathroom, can't sit up, can't hold the sandwich nor the drink she brought, and although they tell me my legs are moving, I don't know they are. I tell her there is a tube in my dick I can't feel. A single tear appears in her right eye. I tell her I have very little sensation from my nipples down and now her tears flow as quickly as mine. I tell her the doctors say this may be temporary or it may be permanent, but my mind is made up in that I will walk out or kill myself. I tell her of the nurse's nastiness. I need an ally and now I have one.

"You know," she begins -- her eyes no longer dance -- "by about six o'clock I was pretty sure you were dead. By eight o'clock I was sure. I was sort of mad at your dad for not calling and telling me that but... I mean, you're dead and who the fuck am I? I'm just some chick his son goes out with."

I try to shake my head and feel an immediate stab of pain. I struggle through sobs to speak. She puts her finger to my lips. "So, from eight until almost midnight I was going out of my mind. The phone rang and I figured one of your brothers finally got the idea to tell me. I cannot *tell* you how glad I was to hear the nurse say that you were fine and that you would see me today. These assholes don't know you. I know you're going to walk out of here," she sobs, "and I'm gonna walk out with you and tell that nurse and the rest of them to go fuck themselves. Let's eat!"

But first she helps me call my mother and two sisters in New Mexico. She dials the number and holds the phone to my ear and stares as I lie to my mother.

"I'm supposed to go home in ten days." (Pause.) "Yes, I will come down there to recover," I promise.

Annie looks sad and far away. She hangs up the phone and gives me the sandwich she carried in. She is feeding me. This is the first time. It won't be the last.

Brian Shaughnessy

Good Results

The next day I wake up very uncomfortable. I am on my side and the room smells ... fecal. Suddenly I'm aware that there is a nurse probing me in a most inappropriate manner.

"I gave you a suppository and you had good results. You're all done." She exits the room with a suspicious looking bag.

I have no idea what she is talking about, and I certainly don't want to know at this point. All too soon I will have volumes of heartbreaking information and firsthand experience. Later, I "result" in bed.

I remain on the post-operative ward for four days. Dr. Liar comes by twice with my chart and asks about progress as I choke back tears and bile. Nothing to report. I see the doctors who treated me *before* the surgery as they look through the door and leave without a word. A doctor I have not seen before enters the room introducing himself as Dr. Messenger. The new doctor tells me I am to be moved to the Rehabilitation Department of the University of Minnesota Hospital. I think, great, it's about time.

The doctor has me squeeze his fingers, lift my legs, move my neck, asks me to look away and tell him which toe he is touching etc. and cheerfully says, "We'll be moving you to Rehab tomorrow. You will be there from six weeks to six months learning the skills to accomplish your activities of daily living. The best thing to do is to plan on not getting any better -- you will, everyone does improve -- but if you don't plan on *any* improvement you won't be disappointed, ok?"

Ok? *Ok?* What are you talking about? I was supposed to leave in a few days, I'm thinking. Six weeks? Six months? That is absurd. I'm in school. I have plays to audition for. I should be starting rehearsal right now! My car is in the parking lot! I have people waiting for me, things to do. I have no *intention* of spending six months, weeks, days or minutes in this hole. How can he NOT know that I am going to walk out of here?

At this point in my life I do not have the "skills" to challenge this individual. Besides, he was out of the room before I had a chance to respond to his "ok?"

The Squeaky Wheel

The day comes. I am to be moved to the Rehabilitation Department of University Of Minnesota Hospitals -- Rehab. I picture Rehab as a place where all of this will go away, and I will be able to walk out the door. There are, of course, indications to the contrary, but I and those close to me ignore them. Never underestimate the power of denial. Although I consider the possibility that this current situation is permanent, I dismiss it immediately, with suicide as the solution.

The nurse gathers my things, preparing me for my journey. I am depressed. I will be more depressed. Then, I will experience a hell that few human beings ever endure on this earth. And it will repeat itself. And the whole time I know I'll be back on my bicycle and roller skates when the snow melts.

"You'll be fine. Come up and visit us while you're there," the nurse encourages me, as another nurse from Rehab appears to take me to my new home. The nurses slide a board underneath me. Actually, it is not a board but a plastic device similar to what children slide on in the snow in this part of the world. It works quite well for the present purpose also.

"One, two, three," the nurse counts and they slide me effortlessly onto the gurney. I am wheeled through seemingly miles of corridors. The sliding process is repeated when I get to Rehab. There are four beds and, fortunately, only one other person in the room now -- a middle-aged man on a heinous contraption of a bed. It appears to be bubbling. I see what looks like grains of sand moving through the plastic beneath the sheet. It all feels as if it were painted by Hieronymus Bosch. The nurse attempts conversation with me. She fails. She seems to take umbrage at the fact that I will not engage her in verbal discourse.

"We are here to help you with your physical needs and what you can't do on your own, but we are also here to help you overcome the emotional side of this. Is there anything you want to say?" asks the nurse who has introduced herself as Tina. She is dark and may be attractive to some but I can see an anger and contempt in her eyes directed at no one in particular and at everyone.

This invitation quashes the denial, anger, bargaining and depression that have been my life since waking up four days ago. The words, words, words flow out, out, out -- unstoppable, a Niagara of emotion.

"They told me I would leave here within the week. I was supposed to walk out with a soft collar on my neck and go back to school and everything else that I was doing. Now, I'm being told I'm going to be here six weeks to six months and that I may not walk out of here after I trusted a doctor and walked in. Nobody told me this was a possibility! I have no idea what I am dealing with!"

"... And this makes you feel angry?"

The question does not merit a response. She is suspect of my claim that I had no idea, nor was I informed that "Paralysis was a possible outcome of neck surgery."

"I just don't believe that a neurosurgeon in this hospital would do that," she says smiling with seeming glee. I decide, for now, that I will not discuss this with anyone, especially this bitch, employed by the hospital. I will walk out of the hospital, and when I do, I will tell this contemptible human being precisely what I think of her.

She goes on to notify me she will be my primary care nurse. I marvel at my continuing luck. She informs me if I want to eat I have to get in my wheelchair and go into the dining room.

It's not my wheelchair! I want to scream at her. It's not mine! Not my wheelchair! I don't belong in that thing. I'm walking out.

"If you want to watch TV you have to go into the dining room." I hope I am wrong, but there seems to be enjoyment in her telling me what I cannot do unless...and because…therefore…buzz buzz buzz.

She continues. Painfully. "I'm going to need to weigh you. I'll take that catheter out now, and we'll put a condom catheter on you. You'll be catheterized again in four hours and then every one to four hours depending on your output. This is bladder therapy so that eventually you won't need to be catheterized. Tomorrow you'll get a suppository to begin your bowel program. Every other day you'll get a suppository and then manual stimulation until you are empty. I need to mark and measure your legs to monitor swelling and make sure there are no blood clots."

An orderly brings a scale into the room. I am rolled onto a canvas that is then attached to arms on the scale, and I am cranked into the air -- 150 pounds. I can see the four beds in the room and an accordion curtain to divide the room in half. This is only pulled when my roommate wants to smoke. There is a small closet and a standard issue hospital sink for me.

I try not to watch when the pencil-sized tube is pushed into my penis – one short shove at a time. I see red, the color of pain. I writhe and clamp my eyes shut only to open them again to watch the tube fill with urine before removal. I cannot breathe while it is extracted. The manifestation of evil, Tina, moves brusquely about me, removing my clothes, measuring my legs, placing magic marker marks on them, opening and placing an odd looking condom on my Jimmy. Jimmy snaps

The Squeaky Wheel

to attention at the stimulus, which pleases and repulses me. Tina may be attractive to some, but her behavior is repugnant. She wraps a Velcro strap around James to keep the condom catheter in place, connects a short tube to the opening on the end of the condom and connects that to a clear bag strapped to my leg below the knee. She takes my blood pressure, pulse and temperature. I tell her I want to get up and she sneers and signals for another nurse to assist her in transferring me to the wheelchair.

That afternoon I am told I will be going up to physical therapy. Good, I think. The sooner I get busy working, the sooner I'm out of here.

As I wait to be moved, I listen to my roommate's thick Black Southern accent as he talks, talks, talks, and I try to decipher a word he is saying while my mind races to many other things. I wonder why I only go to physical therapy for a couple hours a day when eight hours would get me well *sooner*. I wonder what the hell I did to piss God off enough to have him put me through this. I think about the guys I picked on in grade school. I think about disobeying my parents. I think about peeing on the cat. I wonder what I must do to make things right with God so I can leave this awful smelling place. I have the faith of the mountain that I will walk out, but a mustard seed of doubt lingers.

The transporter arrives early to show me the kitchen and refrigerator, should I want to keep beverages or food in there. He wheels me past the front desk where I am introduced to the unit clerk, Tracy. Tracy is a bubbly, shorthaired, ample breasted sylph with an innocent smile. The transporter leers at her. I do too. In the kitchen, he advises I bring in outside food as the meals served are notoriously bad. Thank God he does not know my awful truth. Maybe that's why I have to go through this now....

As he pushes me to the elevator a huge recollection hits me. This is the entrance I came through to get to my locker and uniform to work in the kitchen. I would walk through that door and look at "persons" in wheelchairs, on gurneys and villainous looking contraptions with metal coming up from the chest and back -- four posts coming straight up holding a metal band about the head. I soon find out this device -- which appears to be made by Lucifer himself -- is called a halo.

I looked at these poor unfortunates in their wheelchairs, implements and disabilities and shuddered. I learned to run in the door, press the down button on the elevator and pray that it came quickly before one of these "people" wanted to strike up a conversation with me. Welcome back! You're one of us. The line from *Freaks* taunts me.

Brian Shaughnessy

I am wheeled into the community room/dining hall where I see a dark-haired man with a beard. He, like most others, sits in a wheelchair. But he, unlike most others, is flanked by women. It is not the women that draw attention to him, but the fact that his mouth hangs open and a long stream of drool extends to his dampened sweatpants. His eyes seem to hang open in the same manner as his mouth... unblinking. As I am rolled into the room his head moves slightly and slowly toward me.

"Wipe your mouth, John," one of the women commands him. Clearly he is unable to do this, and I wonder if he comprehends this statement. I am struck by the fact that if he were sitting on the couch instead of in the wheelchair; if his mouth did not hang to mid-chest; if there was not a thick, solid, viscous stream of drool hanging from mouth to lap; and if his eyes did not betray him -- then he would appear... normal.

Tina is prattling about the do's and don'ts of the community room as I am terrified by John. My mind screams, Get me out of here! I don't belong here! Jesus, what is it going to take? The hairs are actually standing up on the back of my neck. Every muscle (that works) is tense and contracted, and the ones that don't work are *struggling* to contract. The muscles of my face involuntarily contort into that pitying look most able-bodied humans manifest at the sight of a cripple... or the smell of excrement. It all happens in seconds.

I am taken from this area, go up three floors, cross a skyway, turn left and proceed approximately 50 feet, turn right, proceed approximately another hundred feet and take another elevator up to the sixth floor. The various therapy sessions are held here.

First, I have physical therapy. This is exactly what it sounds like. One works hard to regain strength and, I tell myself, return to the condition before physical therapy was required.

In the physical therapy "gym," I am introduced to Carol. She is a tall, attractive, athletic-looking woman with medium length curly, dark hair and strong brown eyes that dance like Annie's and have the intensity of Picasso's. Her face is soft and kind. She smiles and enthusiastically informs me she will be working with me twice a day. Carol is chipper, while I remain quiet and terrified. She asks a few questions and clearly senses my terror. She apologizes with a look and informs me she will transfer me onto the mat to perform some muscle testing so she can evaluate me before planning my therapy sessions. Before transferring me to the mat she tests my arm strength in different positions. Some movement is every bit as strong as before the surgery, and other

15

The Squeaky Wheel

positions are impossible. For instance, with my elbow raised and my hand on my shoulder it is impossible for me to raise either hand straight up over my head.

Carol transfers me to the mat and retains her incredibly positive attitude. She asks what I am studying in school. When I tell her theater, she becomes genuinely and enthusiastically interested.

"Are you an actor?"

"I was rehearsing for a play when I had to come into the hospital for tests," I tell her.

"What play?" she asks.

"*See How They Run,*" I answer.

She looks at me as if I had told an unseemly joke. I had.

She has me try leg lifts, move my feet up and down, try to roll over (unsuccessfully), sit up (no way) and numerous other tests. She then does what will become a twice-daily routine for me. She performs range of motion -- the stretching of the muscles of the body to prevent atrophy -- or becoming tight and useless. She stretches my toes, my feet, my legs, my hips, my arms, my shoulders, and tries to get me to lie on my belly to reach muscles I don't even know I have. When Carol -- later others -- perform this, I feel at once relaxed, invigorated and ready for a walk and/or a nap.

"Tomorrow we'll try standing at the parallel bars, ok?" she asks.

"Great. I'll be here," I respond, but I'm thinking, why can't we do it now? I want to get out of this place. You are a very nice woman, but I do not belong here, I'm thinking as I am wheeled to the occupational therapy room.

Brian Shaughnessy

THE RUBBER STAMP ROOM

Occupational therapy is a form of therapy where patients engage in vocational or other activities in a social setting, or so says the dictionary. Here I meet Jackie who will be my occupational therapist for the duration. Jackie is medium height and Caucasian, approximately 24 years old, with blonde short-cropped hair. She strikes me as more green then Carol -- likely someone who grew up in the suburbs. Jackie administers some fine-motor tests of my hands with varying amounts of weight attached to them. I am whisked into the next room where another occupational therapist -- I believe his name is Heinrich -- asks me to go about sorting mail, stuffing envelopes and rubber stamping papers. I may be audibly growling. Clearly he senses my ire and asks if I was in school, "before your injury." This is a recurring phrase that I will encounter far too often and it makes me nauseous.

I need not tell him how insulting I find these little tests. But it is here that for the first time I hear of vocational rehabilitation -- a subject we shall visit later.

I am wheeled back to the sixth floor elevator and descend, exit, proceed, turn left, turn right, cross a skyway, go down three floors and return to Rehab. It is not yet dinnertime. I ask to lie down

"You really need to work on increasing the amount of time you can spend up in the wheelchair," my primary nurse, Tina, barks.

"I am exhausted. This was my first day on this floor. I want to lie down."

Tina sneers, makes me wait but eventually assists in laying me down. A short time later she returns and removes my pants (my father would insist that they are trousers) and the condom catheter. She roughly removes a plastic, medical bag from a nearby cabinet. She rips open the bag and removes its contents. Opening a small packet of KY jelly, she removes another plastic bag from inside the cabinet. This one unfurls to about three feet in length and four inches wide with graduated numbers running the distance. She rips off the top and inside is a heinous-looking red tube suspiciously similar in diameter to the tube removed from my penis hours ago. She puts the KY jelly on the red tube, opens another packet with red Q-tip looking swabs and wipes Jimmy's crown. She comes at me with this ghastly device as my mind shrieks.

The Squeaky Wheel

Soon the bag fills with urine. She replaces the condom catheter and trousers. Soon, however, the catheter fails and I am soaked in urine. I hate Tina, myself and God for this. Nurses come -- long after I have pulled the call light -- and clean me, as I wonder how anyone endures such degradation.

I'm placed in the wheelchair and taken off to dinner. I am introduced to Joe, an 18-year-old with a halo who asks if I love Jesus; Doug, a near forty-year-old who broke his neck driving drunk for the 27th time and brags about it; Lois, an attractive woman about my age with LARGE mammaries who broke her back three days before her wedding. The ceremony has been postponed. Later, the engagement will be off. I also meet Ted, who stabbed himself twenty-seven times, called an ambulance, which failed to fasten the gurney in the vehicle, and was struck by a drunk driver entering the freeway late at night going in the wrong direction. I am introduced to Jan, who also has syringomyelia and assures me I will not be getting much better, but only worse; a young, rough looking quadriplegic, Grant, who broke his neck diving and Fred, who broke his neck on his motorcycle with his wife on the back. It was the first time his wife had ridden on the motorcycle, and he blames her for his current dilemma. We call Fred, "the grouch."

A strap that holds a fork is placed on my right hand and a straw placed in my milk. I take three or four bites of some foul substance on my plate and return to my room. Annie goes to the floor from whence I came and makes the circuitous, confusing trip to where I now reside. Soon, I am in bed, the curtain is pulled and Annie's pudendum is planted in my face. After, we cry. Later that evening my father finds his way to the room. He asks about the events of the day, wishes me a speedy recovery and commands me to call my mother. She tells me that he goes to his car and cries for several minutes before driving home.

I meet Sam, the regular night nurse who will come and stick that heinous red tube in my dick every one to four hours and flip me every hour. Sam is black, intelligent, bespectacled and thin, with short hair. He places me on my left side, which I already hate, places a pillow between my knees, under my knees and behind my back. I wear foam protective boots. After forty-five minutes I am going nuts and want to be flipped onto my right side. Sam says I must get used to spending three hours on one side as that is protocol and soon he will only flip me that often. I want to kill him. His sense of humor saves his life.

The next day I awaken to anal wrenching. The room smells a predictable smell and I look over my shoulder at a nurse wearing latex gloves. I am sure I'm in hell. Hell sucks. The nurse informs me I had good results.

After this ordeal she asks if I would like to take a shower. I assure her I would, as I have not had anything but a wiping with a washcloth for days now. She says she heard I had a rough day yesterday. I comment about my primary nurse. She shakes her head and confides that, until recently, Tina was a nurse's aid and once she got her degree she became intolerable. I languish in the shower pushing my semi-erect penis back and forth but feeling little. I am dressed and readied for physical therapy. On the sinkstand next to my bed there is a manual with the title, "Sexuality and Spinal Cord Injuries." I smile, thinking I must share this with Annie, while at the same time I think that we could have written it. I wonder if some voyeur spied us the night before and was trying to do a noble deed.

As a transporter wheels me, I look at my lap, which is soaked. I am humiliated. We return, I am cleaned, readied again and attempt to go to occupational therapy. The ordeal is repeated. I have missed both morning therapies.

In the afternoon I successfully reach the physical therapy gym and Carol asks, "Would you like some range of motion, or would you like to try and stand at the parallel bars?"

I think this is an absurd question.

"I want to stand."

She places a belt around my waist, removes the footrests on the wheelchair and carefully instructs me to hold the bars and attempt to stand. I do. The left leg is very strong and supports most of the weight. The right leg is less cooperative.

"Look at me," she commands as I stare down at my feet. She holds the strap to keep me from buckling and has me try to shift from one leg to another. I collapse into the seat. We try again and she gives little shoves to check my balance. I sit again. She is sweaty from the ordeal.

"I can't *tell* you how many people have come in here with *less* strength and promise and walked out..."

She is attempting to cheer me up and make me feel positive, but despite the surreal occurrences since waking up, I am certain I will walk out without catheters, suppositories, straps for forks, straws and wheelchairs or I will put an end to my life. I am wheeled to occupational therapy where I push and pull a modified loom to build up weakened muscles. I do not return to the rubberstamp room. I follow this routine for several days while friends and family visit. Annie and my father are present most. Annie is there daily and we are often naked.

There are two phones on the floor for the patients -- one at each end of the hallway. One is right outside my room. I steady myself, and one of the nurses gives me the headset for the phone as I cannot hold the handset. She takes the steps to call my mother in New Mexico. It has been agreed that I will go to New Mexico to recuperate after the surgery. The phone rings and my eight-year-old sister Dawn answers with a thick-tongued "Hello" characteristic of people with Down syndrome. She loves the telephone, running for it whenever it rings. She asks if I am still in the hospital.

"Yes," I say, fighting back tears. She hands the phone to my 19-year-old sister Teri. Teri asks how I am doing, and I hear my mother's voice in the background asking when I will be coming. I wrestle with lying and then give my most optimistic answer.

"Six weeks," I say and Teri repeats it. I hear my mother groan and before Teri can say another word, she is on the phone.

"What?" she shrieks. "What the hell is going on?"

I haven't revealed to my siblings, my father or my mother the hellish fears that fill most every waking moment.

"I can't walk."

"What the hell are you talking about? What did they do to you in that surgery?"

I give her the sketchiest of details (even more sketchy than I have) while she wails.

"I'm coming up there," she announces. I point out that she doesn't have the money nor will it accomplish anything. She says she is sorry and neither of us can continue.

That night my mother sleeps fitfully. When she sleeps, she dreams that she is paralyzed and unable to move. When she wakes from these nightmares she knows I cannot move... and she cannot move. Psychologists would have a phrase for this. Others would call it motherhood. There is no greater pain than watching your own child suffer.

At dinner Fred comments that he saw me standing at the parallel bars. I acknowledge this, nonplussed. Some other persons with similar conditions ask what happened to me. They usually lament the commonness of the tragedy while noting variations. Diving accidents, automobile and motorcycle mishaps, surfing, gymnastics, horses and heights are common elements that run through the stories. Most (80%)

are male, 16 to 30 years old and active people. I know from personal experience and observation that males between 16 and 30 are far more likely to be engaged in STUPID (or if not STUPID, dangerous) activities.

"When you walk out of here, moon them for me, will you?" Fred asks.

I assure him that I am going to piss down Tina's throat. He asks what happened to me. I tell him:

I was 14 years old and riding on a road after dark. That's the last thing I remember. The next thing I remember is waking up in a bed. It felt right and natural to be in a bed, and then I remembered that I'd been on my bike. I started to open my eyes and attempted to speak and saw a doctor stitching up my face. "Go to sleep Brian. Everything is fine." So I went back to sleep.

When I woke up my mother was in the room. She informed me that someone hit me with their car and left me to die in a ditch. A nurse hugged my parents when they got to the hospital. This nurse, it turns out, is the person who hit me and left me to die in the ditch. My father discovers this by going to her house the next day to get a statement. He sees a car in the driveway with a damaged bumper, broken light, snapped off antenna, broken windshield and yellow paint (same color as my bicycle) on the bumper.

"What happened to your car?" my father asks, as her husband stares, hems and haws, refusing to acknowledge my father's existence.

I have a couple hundred stitches scattered over my body from my forehead to my heels -- with two on the tip of my right eyelid. The nurse who hit me and left me to die finally admits to this deed, in the presence of my father and the sheriff. She is fined $100 and her license is suspended for one year.

I spend a couple weeks in bed, learn to walk again and go home with a neck brace, a weak arm and scars. The brace comes off within a couple weeks and I slowly mend physically and emotionally as only a teenager can.

Fast forward ten years. It is my 24th birthday on July 24. There is a *raging* party in my apartment. I did not sleep the previous night, and I fear I will not sleep this night, but I am grateful for this bash. I take a moment alone and pray to God. I thank Him for my wonderful life to this point. I thank Him for my family, my friends, never starving and all the blessings he has sent. I tell Him if my life is to end now that it's okay and that it's been a full, wonderful life.

The Squeaky Wheel

Syringomyelia. It sounds like the name of a new Calypso band. It's not.

In September I begin my final year of school to earn my bachelor's degree. Sometime in the next month I notice numbness in my right first finger and thumb. I don't think much of it, but when I am at the Student Health Center with a cold, I mention it to the nurse, who writes it down for the doctor. The doctor comes in and examines me regarding the cold and writes me a prescription.

"As far as the numbness is concerned, I don't even want to speculate about that. I'm writing you a referral for neurology," she says without looking at me. She sets down her prescription pad and picks up her referral pad. I don't make the appointment and finish the semester.

In January, 1983, the next semester begins, and I realize the numbness has now spread up the inside of my arm. I make the appointment with neurology. I am placed in a room and a doctorly looking fellow with a dark beard and white smock comes in gazing at my chart. He is cordial and introduces himself and asks me about the numbness. I explain it began in September and has now spread up my arm. He asks about previous medical history and I tell him of being hit by the car and spending a month in the hospital. The doctor begins examining my eyes and ears and thumps me on the head and about the chest. While he is examining me he asks if I've had seizures, blackouts, have been getting lost or forgetting names and events. I assure him I have not. He then takes out a pinwheel looking device that, in fact, has tiny pins on it.

"Feel this?" he asks as he rolls the pinwheel across my right cheek. I nod. "It feels normal?" I nod again. "I'm going to use it on your arm and your finger and thumb. I want you to tell me when you can feel it and when the sensation is different, okay?"

"Sure," I respond.

He takes a step back and looks at me and says, "I'm going to give you three words to remember. They are, pollywog, smegma and infantile. (Those are not the actual three words he asked me to remember). Got it?" I nod and he steps back toward me and begins to run the pinwheel over my right thumb. "Can you feel that?"

"Yes, but only very slightly."

He moves to my right first finger. "What about here?"

"The same as the thumb."

"Okay." He takes hold of my right hand with his left hand and runs the pinwheel over the other fingers. I feel its prickle, whereas on my digits I felt only... something.

"That's all normal."

He nods and moves on to the top of my arm, looking up at me with raised eyebrows every time he wants a response.

"Normal. Normal. Normal."

He then moves to the underside of my arm. He gives a series of the same looks.

"Different. Different. Normal. Different. Normal. Different. Different. Different."

We have determined the numbness runs on the underside of my arm but not on the top. It is stronger closer to the thumb and follows that pattern up to my bicep. He goes back to my chart and maps the numbness on a diagram of a body. He then takes out a safety pin.

"I'm going to use this now." He holds it up for me and then reaches for my right arm. He pokes me with the dull side in an area where my sensation is fine. "That area's normal?" I nod and he turns the pin around. He looks me in the eye and says, "Don't worry, I'm not going to make you bleed or anything," and looks back to my arm and the pin. I feel the prick of the pin. It is slight.

"You got the difference?" he asks. I nod. "This time I want you to close your eyes and turn your head." I comply and the pinwheel exchange is repeated. My responses are the same. The doctor walks over to the chart and writes this down. "Can you tell me the three words I gave you to remember?"

"What three words?" I ask, and the doctor reels around with the chart in his hand. "Pollywog, smegma and infantile," I respond laughing. (These are not the actual three words that I repeated).

"Okay... I want you to start at 100 and subtract by seven."

"Nobody said there was going to be math!" I blurt out and then begin to subtract ... slowly.

"Okay. I'm going to go talk to them over at the hospital and see about getting you in for tests."

"Am I going to miss school, or can I do this as an outpatient?" I ask.

"We'll see," he responds. "I won't know anything until I go talk to them, but I would say you will have to be admitted. But let me go check this out before we make any plans." He leaves and closes the door.

I sit on the examination table and wonder what this means. I look about the room and focus on the closed door. I stand up, walk over and open the door. The doctor is out of sight but I can hear him speaking and things sound a bit more serious than he let on. Another young man sits outside of the room and looks at me angrily. I wonder why.

The Squeaky Wheel

"I have a 24-year-old patient with progressive numbness in his thumb and arm. Possible origin of numbness in the C-5 area but could also be MS. We need to get him in for a series of tests beginning with EMI..."

I close the door and go back to the examination table and sit. This does not sound happy. The doctor reenters. "Can you go in tomorrow?"

My heart sinks. This *is* bad. But I am certain this man has made a gross mis-diagnosis that will be quickly cleared up by the tests. "No," I begin and drag out the vowel, "I have an audition tomorrow (Friday) and I'm in school..."

He seemed ready for this response. "How about Sunday afternoon then? They will admit you Sunday and start the tests on Monday."

"What kind of tests?" I ask, more bothered than concerned.

"First," he says, looking directly at me from across the room, "they will do muscle testing, where they put a small needle into the muscle and ask you to use the muscle so they can determine how well it functions. This may be followed by various x-rays and physical exams."

"How long am I going to be out of school?" I ask. This is *my* biggest concern.

"I would think you should plan on three to five days for now. Then, if they need to do surgery you would have to withdraw."

"Surgery?" I shriek. Now I *know* this man has made a grievous error. This catches him off guard.

"Well, at this point we don't know," he says honestly. "What can I tell the hospital? Will you be going in on Sunday?"

I sigh and acquiesce, wondering how this will affect the rehearsal I am in, school, auditions and all of the "business" of daily living. Then I wonder how to tell Annie, my mother, my father, my grandmother, my siblings and friends what is going on. The doctor leaves and informs the hospital I will be there Sunday. He returns to say they will be expecting me at 5 o'clock. I ask him what he thinks is going on, and he responds in some noncommittal, vague way, at which point I rise from the examination table and gather my backpack, coat and hat to exit.

"Be sure and show up on Sunday," he admonishes. He has correctly read me as a not particularly compliant patient.

I go home to my apartment. Annie is working and I can't call her. The phone rings. I'm fairly certain it's Annie and I answer. "What happened?" Annie blurts.

I explain what happened and my pending return Sunday. "Of course he's nuts! I'm sure everything will be fine," she says with amazing certainty and sincerity. "Will I see you tonight?" she asks. "Of course," I respond.

At this point I wonder who I should inform. I call my father. My mother is in New Mexico and there's no need to alarm her. Somebody, besides Annie, needs to know I'm going into the hospital.

"Big Red!" he bellows when I am put through to his office by his secretary.

"What are you up to?" I ask.

"About $300 an hour they tell me, but I don't see it. And you?"

I tell him of the audition, school, the apartment building and other things. I don't mention why I really call. As we talk I sense that he is in a hurry. "I need to be in Pine County Court five minutes ago," he says, uncharacteristically rushing the conversation.

I tell him of the events of the afternoon and that (for no reasons stated by the doctor that day) I believe it to be a "pinched nerve." I tell him that I'll have to go to the hospital on Sunday but not to worry because the doctor has assured me that the University of Minnesota is a fine hospital. He's had many clients praise the institution.

"Just get it taken care of," Dad says.

I agree and assure him I'll be going.

"Okay, well don't worry. These pinched nerves can be a problem, but they're easily dealt with. I'll see you before you go in, and I'll see you at the hospital. Love ya. Say a prayer for your old man."

Annie and I spend the weekend together. At some point I recall calling my red-haired grandmother to tell her I am entering the hospital. She assures me she will not tell my mother. The weekend with Annie is full of uncertainty, sex, some tears, occasional forays for food, assurances and finally, on Sunday, she drives me to the hospital. This may be the first time that she says, ala Katherine Hepburn in *On Golden Pond*, "You are my knight in shining armor." It becomes a through line in our relationship

I enter, register, and am escorted to the neurology floor. A nurse shows me where to keep my belongings, asks if I have any valuables, introduces my roommate and asks a series of questions about my health history. She exits.

Within 30 minutes, a bizarre-looking woman enters my room. She is not more than five feet tall and almost as wide. She is wearing a bright red dress with faux fur around the collar and a scarf. Her makeup is garish. Black lines point from the corner of her drawn eyes toward her temple. She carries a clipboard which she places on my bed.

The Squeaky Wheel

"Hello, I'm Dr. Weinstein. I'm the neurological resident who will be following your case. How are you doing?"

"I'm doing fine -- except for the numbness."

"Well, that's why you're here. We'll find out what's going on," she says, in an attempt to reassure. She begins asking questions and administering the same exam I had on Friday.

"You're too young to have these symptoms," she says, making a face that indicates she's sad. It provokes a response in me that I would like to make her sad.

She makes notes in the chart and tells me that in the morning I'll have the procedure with the needle being poked into my muscles that the other neurologist described. I have been through this before when I was hit by the car. I recall a small pin, shorter than a thumbtack and much finer, pricking me repeatedly and hearing static from the diagnostic machine.

I meet my roommate. He has been forgetting things. Soon, his wife arrives. They have children. While he is out of the room one of the nurses tells me he has a brain tumor and that the outlook for him is bleak. She senses my horror. "That's not going to happen to you!" she says unconvincingly.

The next day I go down the hall to a room where three doctors gather around a machine. They have me lie down and ready the machine. It appears the needle has grown tremendously since my last exam of this type. It no longer looks smaller than the thumbtack but as long as a hypodermic needle and thicker -- much thicker.

Two of the doctors gather around the machine while the other one pokes this monster into my arms and legs. It hurts. They poke me forty times, each time instructing me to flex the muscle they probe, which only exacerbates the pain. The doctors ooh and aah when the machine crackles and displays numbers and prints lines that look like a lie detector test. Finally, I am dismissed.

An innumerable parade of doctors, nurses and medical students enter the room and speak -- mostly to each other -- and exit. One of them is a young Asian male who appears to be the team leader. "Doc, you know I'm in school, right? Whenever possible, I'd like to go to class if there are no tests scheduled."

"We'll see what we can do."

"I'd like to go now; my English class is in 20 minutes," I assert falsely.

"Today I would rather you stayed around, but I'm sure you'll be able to do that on other days."

Well there goes any hope of my leaving today or, most likely, the rest of the week.

Monday turns into Tuesday and Wednesday. Soon it is Friday and I am leaving for the weekend. The nurses are pleasant, as are the doctors. Friends and family visit and Annie is a frequent fixture in the room. My roommate's wife is constantly there during the day. My father shows up nightly. Someone has talked to my mother, and I am scolded for not informing her and my sisters who are in New Mexico. I leave the hospital at every opportunity and actually attend one class. On my other forays I go to Annie's where we engage in the obvious. I spend the weekend at Annie's where rampant, continuous sex is practiced to perfection.

Monday, my roommate's wife is there. She visits often, as does Annie, my father, family and friends.

The probing and testing continues for three weeks. Each weekend there is a reprieve. Then the same and different tests are administered anew. The first two weeks I am injected with dye at my tailbone which goes into my spinal canal to "enhance" the x-ray. This is called a myelogram. Toward the end of the third week they decide these injections/x-rays are unsatisfactory and inform me that I am to have yet another myelogram, but this time I will be receiving "a cervical punch."

I have no idea what this means, and no one bothers to inform me. It sounds like a fruit drink. I am wheeled to the x-ray room where I receive a tiny prick behind my ear and am injected with a local anesthetic. The medical personnel then paint my neck red with Betadine, a covering is placed over my head and neck and a giant needle is slowly plunged into my spine from directly behind my ear. I cannot feel the needle but I do feel pressure directly behind my ear, and I hear it crackle with each slow push administered.

"Don't move, Brian," someone commands.

Move? Move? I don't want to breathe or let my heart beat this is so terrifying! The crackling continues, the dye is injected and I am tilted upward and downward on the table (a slower version of a paint shaker for humans) until those in attendance deem me sufficiently stirred. I am then radiated, and when the pictures return, the doctors ooh and aah quietly over what they see. Apparently there is a large mass in the spinal canal that does not belong. This is only hinted at in the room, and I am transported back to my hospital room where I vomit from the dye and pain medication.

The Squeaky Wheel

The Asian doctor in charge informs me there is a cyst in my spinal canal requiring surgery, and the neurosurgeon will speak with me soon.

Hardly soon, a tall Caucasian man with glasses and dark hair, just beginning to gray, enters wearing the customary white smock. Underneath the outer garment is a shirt and tie. I know he is a neurosurgeon and wonder why he does not wear the surgical green scrubs. He introduces himself as Dr. Liar, informs me there is a cyst in my spinal canal and *maybe* one of the other doctors on the "team" has seen this permutation of the rare cyst before. The condition is called syringomyelia and I will need surgery, which he will perform. There is a risk I will die in the surgery, he adds, but this is unlikely as I am young and fit. Before he leaves I ask him if I will return to professional baseball. He looks at the chart muttering, "pro ball," so I tell him I am kidding but ask what to expect AFTER the surgery.

He tells me I should expect to remain three days, be sent home wearing a soft collar and possibly return for outpatient therapy. Today is Friday and I am to return the following Monday evening to have the procedure on Tuesday, commencing at noon. He leaves unceremoniously. I say goodbye to the kindly medical people and ignore the unkind ones. I wish my roommate well as he must remain for the weekend. They will keep the room for me.

I call Annie and we make plans to spend two nights at a hotel. She picks me up and we return to our respective apartments and pack. I then make calls to numerous family members informing them of the impending surgery. Everyone is very supportive and more than a few say, "You couldn't be at a better hospital." My mother is petrified. My grandmother is supportive and adamant she will be there on Tuesday, as are my father and siblings.

Annie and I share a torrid weekend alternating in a nanosecond between hysterical crying and declarations of love. I have a cold sore. Monday, I am called to lunch with my father and brother Darrin. It has been strained between Darrin and me during the three weeks of testing because on the Friday before my entering the hospital for testing and the Thursday after being told I must go into the hospital, there were auditions for *Death of a Salesman,* which we both auditioned for. He received the part of Willy and I was not even offered the part of the waiter. Our theatre experience has been competitive but not without bright, collaborative endeavors.

Annie declines to join us at lunch. The three Shaughnessy men are solemn but confident the surgery will be performed without incident.

Brian Shaughnessy

Before we order, my father's eyes widen and he leans toward me and plucks a hair from my head.

"You have a gray hair," he says, grinning and holding it aloft.

I scoff, "I think I earned it in the last three weeks." They agree.

That night I talk with my mother again, as well as with my grandmother and siblings. On Monday Annie drives me to the hospital. She will not remain, as she is distraught and must work the next day. I sleep well. The next day a central line is placed through my jugular. This form of intravenous delivery is the most efficient but goes very close to the heart. I am not informed of this until after it is in place and a kindly nurse tells me.

My grandmother and Aunt Annie arrive. I am asked to consent to a discussion of my condition, the process of diagnosing the condition and the impending surgery. I agree, and the three of us go into a large room with lots of doctors, medical students, residents and ne'er-do-wells. There are more speeches and presentations from the doctors and students than there are questions of me, and I return to my room. My father has arrived along with brothers Patrick, Darrin and Daniel. I know my mother is already whipped into the proverbial frenzy of a parent thousands of miles away from her firstborn male child about to be cut open by strangers.

I kiss my family members goodbye and am wheeled to the operating room and transferred from the gurney to the operating table. Several people clad in green scrubs gather about. One man stutters ferociously. From behind the mask I do not know if he is the surgeon, but I hope he is not. I am feeling drowsy.

"That's the sedative making your eyelids heavy," a sweet, tiny, operating room nurse informs me as a man steps forward.

"We need to put a catheter through your penis, Mr. Shaughnessy," he says directly, as if he is not to be challenged.

I'm awake. "What is that?"

"It goes through your penis and into your bladder so that you continue to void."

"I just went to the bathroom, and it's only a four-hour operation. I don't think you have to do that."

"I think we do. It is standard procedure for this type of surgery. Don't worry, we'll put it in after you're under."

I am unhappy about this, but it is clearly going to be done despite my protestations. My eyelids begin to grow heavier and Dr. Liar has not yet appeared.

The Squeaky Wheel

"Begin counting backwards from 100, Brian."
"100, 99, 98, ninety..." I tell Fred, closing the narrative of the surgery after being asked for the first time, 'What happened to you?'
"Jesus," is Fred's only comment.

That night one of the nurses enters with more plastic wrapped parcels that instill terror in me. She is to remove the bandages and staples in my neck. She removes five and Annie removes the next 32. We are giddy about it, but the sensation is awful as each piece of metal slithers quickly from my skin.

I lie in bed nights thinking, thinking about the surgery, thinking about what I did to deserve this, thinking about what my family must be going through, wondering how anybody *chooses* to live in this situation, thinking about getting up and walking out. I think about roller skating or bicycling around the lakes. I think about getting up and going to the bathroom. But I can't. I look at the clock. It is now after 3 a.m. A nurse enters and sees me wide-eyed.

"You're not sleeping?" she asks.
"No," I respond.
"Is this happening often?" I see sincere concern in her face.
"Sometimes."
"Well, it's too late to take a sleeping pill. If you're in bed for longer than forty-five minutes you can ask for one."
"I know."
"There's a lot on your mind, huh?"

I laugh because I like this nurse, because she can take it, because she likes me and because she has seen many others lying in their beds wide-eyed at 3 a.m.

"How could there not be?" I ask.
"You're right." She wrinkles her face asking tentatively, "Anything I can do for you?"
"I guess knocking me out would be out of the question."
"'Fraid so."
"Then I guess not."
"Ok, hit the call light if you need me."

She leaves and I am aware of how quiet it is. I wonder how many others are awake. My roommate is asleep. The accordion room divider is pulled closed so I don't know the status of the two people on the other side. I stare up at the ceiling in dead silence, pondering all this and more when suddenly a sound shatters the silence and I shudder. The sound was nearby. Suddenly I realize I just farted. I laugh but no sound comes out. I laugh like an eight-year-old who just did the same thing. Tears of laughter roll down my face but not a sound comes out. All of these serious issues and questions being pondered in the still of night are suddenly trifling with a little scatological humor. Laughter is a powerful weapon in the battle against absurdity.

White Coats

While I am waiting for someone to come into the room, dress me, transfer me into the wheelchair and wheel me to physical therapy, a man in a white coat enters with someone. I assume this to be a doctor and a nurse.

"Hello, Mr. Shaughnessy," he begins, with slightly muffled speech. "I'm Dr. Gordon, the resident physiatrist this month. Physiatry is the area of medicine that deals with the treatment of disabilities and with the restoration of normal functioning to the disabled."

You got the wrong man, doc, I think.

"Have you met Dr. Erickson?"

"No."

"Well, he and I will work with you and the rest of the team to get you as healthy as possible. Do you have any questions?"

"I have many questions, and I have no idea where to begin. I'll ask you what I ask everyone." I notice for the first time he has moved his gaze from me to the woman interpreting my speech for him with sign language. "Is this going to go away?"

"We don't know. That's an honest answer. Naturally, we hope so. The spinal cord is a delicate entity, and anytime you go near it there is the risk of paralysis."

I am angry at his answer, but I sense a bond with this man. I find out later that Dr. Gordon became deaf as the result of surgery. Much like my own surgery, I never get a satisfactory explanation as to why this occurred. I find out medicine is not an exact science.

Ed, my roommate, cannot leave the room. There are reports he has been quadriplegic for several years, abused and abandoned by personal care attendants. The most recent instance of neglect has resulted in a

The Squeaky Wheel

hole the size of a grapefruit on his butt. He must stay in the special bed with the bubbling beads day and night. Eventually, they consent to allow him a TV. Some nurses comment that I am lucky I can watch his TV and not have to go to the common room. I don't feel particularly lucky. Each day I understand his accent a little more and most days his brother visits. Twice a week Ed announces, "Brian, I'm fixing to have me a chicken dinner. You want some?" I finally consent and it is delicious. It comes from the heart of the ghetto and even the potatoes are amazing. It becomes a ritual for us. Annie makes the runs and saves on the delivery charge when his brother doesn't come.

I tell him of my surgery and progress I am making in therapy. With sincerity I have not heard before, Ed says, "I hope you get better."

A friendly woman in a white coat is the bearer of information possibly entitled, "The Lighter Side of Spinal Cord Injuries." She drags those who have not yet been subjected to her videos into a room and shows pornography. I see a video about the horrors of urinary tract infections that plague persons with spinal cord injuries. The video stresses the importance of sterile techniques and the perils of autonomic dysreflexia -- a life-threatening condition that can lead to death or, worse yet, stroke -- worse yet because a stroke may leave one alive but with less function than a quadriplegic.

This charming companion to the inability to walk or feel is most often caused by an overextended bladder -- too much piss -- or an overfilled bowel -- being full of shit. This can also be caused by injuries persons who can't feel are unaware of. There are horror stories of being cut, scraped, burned or harmed, and the spinal cord injured individual is unaware of it until his head starts pounding, or he experiences profuse sweating, out of control blood pressure, goose bumps like mountains, nausea or blurred vision. One might add to this list: the wish to die.

The results of an overextended bladder make the sack take on an amoeba shape as opposed to its usual nice, tight, round appearance. The film goes on to discuss the horrors of urinary tract infections and the accompanying increased spasticity. The rest of the video deals with how to properly care for one's urinary equipment, which involves endless boiling of water, Dreft detergent and the diligence of Job.

A spinal cord injury interferes with many bodily functions. One of these is the sphincter of the bladder -- the valve that regulates urine flow. It either allows urine flow or clamps down and does not allow it to flow and causes the need for catheterization, which causes urinary tract infections, which cause increased muscle spasms. The urinary tract infections are treated with antibiotics, but prolonged antibiotics treatment leads to resistance and, ultimately, "bugs" that can't be killed. Drugs are used to treat spasticity and the endless other maladies of spinal cord injury. In no time I have swallowed antibiotics, stool softeners, muscle relaxants and two to seven pills three times daily. The video suggests drinking copious amounts of water (a gallon a day), not beer, not coffee, not colas as, naturally, they all do more harm than good. Failure to drink the suggested amount can also result in kidney stones. The video is boring and frightening and dictates a boring and frightening existence. I have had several urinary tract infections already. The spasticity sometimes knocks the wind from my chest. I drink a gallon of water a day.

The next video is even more profane. It begins discussing "skin breakdown" and then moves on to describe "pressure sores" and ultimately the term that describes it best -- the decubitus ulcer. This is what keeps Ed in bed, after the necessary surgery, for months. An individual with no sensation doesn't know and often can't relieve pressure on that area of skin, so the skin dies. Then the underlying tissue dies, then the muscle and ultimately the bone. Heinous pictures of huge, black holes in individuals' buttocks, back, legs and other areas of the body accompany this tale. The smell is described as worse than the wound. The cost for hospitalization and surgery can be upwards of $50,000 (in 1983).

I watch the video, turn white and promise myself it won't happen to me.

Annie brings all 100 plus of my C-90 tapes (200 plus albums) from my apartment, along with a tape player. After several days and determination I am able to press the buttons, eject the tape, replace it and play another. She brings clothing, including my Van's sneakers with the Hawaiian print, several of my hats and other items to make me feel slightly at home. My brother Patrick and his wife bring a poster of Charlie Chaplain and my father brings a small basketball hoop with a foam ball to squeeze and try to make baskets when I am not in therapy.

On the weekend there is no therapy, which strikes me as another horrific waste of time. My brother Patrick brings me a small pipe and marijuana -- to make me feel even more at home. I am in bed, so we surreptitiously light small amounts, holding it as long as humanly possible before exhaling into a pillow. The next day about seven of my friends come. I am in bed at the time but I offer them smoke. Most partake and

The Squeaky Wheel

one comments, "I don't think I've ever smoked pot in a hospital before." I comment, "Then it must be the last place on earth on your list."

A nurse enters later and transfers me to the wheelchair. One of my smiling comrades grabs the handles of the chair and says, "Come on, Briansides." The others groan the universal groan of dark/in-poor-taste humor, but I laugh a pained laugh.

That night I learn of another therapy -- recreational therapy. A lovely East Indian woman with jet black hair and deadly beautiful eyes enters and informs me that some "people" are going to a nearby bar to listen to the local reggae band Shangoya -- my favorite band. Annie and I often go Thursday, Friday and Saturday nights, arriving at the club for the first set and dancing our asses off until closing time. I'm not sure I'm ready to face people I know and have them ask questions, and I surely will have a hard time sitting still and not being able to dance. Annie must work this night.

"I'll go," I say tentatively.

"Okay," she says and tells me she will check with others to see how many will go. She leaves my room. When she is gone I question my decision. Suddenly I feel damp and I look down at soaked sweatpants, sheets and certainly skin. I pull the string attached to the call light and 30 minutes later a nurse enters my room. I tell her of my condition and she says she will inform my nurse for the evening. The lovely East Indian woman returns, and I tell her that I am unable to participate.

"That's almost a good thing," she says and continues, "because nobody else was going, so we're not taking the van out."

It strikes me as horribly unfair that if I had wanted to go I would have been unable to go because no one else wanted to go. Horribly unfair, I learn, is synonymous with disability.

Standing at the parallel bars goes well and we progress to walking. My right foot drags and Carol puts a splint on my leg to keep my toe from pointing down. The Hawaiian print sneakers do not fit over the splint, so Annie purchases black and white checkered hightop sneakers I have coveted. Annie spoils me with almost daily gifts and flowers. She brings children's toys such as a ring toss encased in water, hippo's mouth basketball and other cool toys. The cuff I no longer need for eating is needed for brushing my teeth, but when she brings a large handled toothbrush that plays "Strangers in the Night" when engaged, I no longer need the cuff. After musicals, Annie's favorite music is Frank Sinatra. This makes *Guys and Dolls* a favorite movie.

Jim, a man with quadriplegia who also works for Rehab and has his law degree, sees the new shoes and dubs me, "Hollywood." The name sticks with some at the hospital.

Jim is amazing and a huge resource. He points me toward vocational rehabilitation, should this condition continue after I leave. I assume that he went to law school *before* his injury. I am wrong. He was injured when he was 16 and is now near 40. I can't imagine how he got through law school.

Once a week I must see the psychologist, Gayland. He is inept. I feel my time is wasted because his contempt for me is almost equal to my contempt for him. Annie sees him for her/our issues, and physical therapists and occupational therapists think he is a minor deity. Jim feels he is a fraud, so we bond immediately.

With a useless psychologist, I turn to prayer. I remember a priest from my youth who was very good to us -- Padre Pates. My father tracks him down, and one night he shows up when my Dad and Annie are there. They exit quickly. After we talk for some time, I am feeling hopeful and intact. I have a prayer taped on the wall that I recite often. He gives me a blessing and departs. Suddenly I am terrified. I feel doomed and regret that I threw away my only chance to walk by allowing him to leave. I'm sure I should have chained him to the bed and had him pray over me until I could walk out. My father calls him and he returns, but each time he departs, the doom and terror return. This is often displaced by my certainty of total recovery.

When I come to lunch in the community room, it seems that each day a new soap opera has a character with a spinal cord injury. They all miraculously recover as I hope I will. In the evening I can lie in my bed or watch television in the community room. I haven't owned a TV for six years but do know of the phenomenon of the mini-series. *The Thornbirds* has been made into such a creature at this time and Annie and I watch from 20 feet apart. It strikes me as insane that the layout of the room does not allow for an individual in a wheelchair to sit with a non-wheelchair user, but I am new here.

Alex, the young, rough-looking male with quadriplegia (a "quad" to the staff -- a term that makes my skin crawl when used in reference to myself) suggests to one of the nurses that I be transferred onto the couch next to Annie. They oblige and I begin to make jokes in reference to the show. At one point a character is killed when a wild boar attacks.

The Squeaky Wheel

"Talk about being bored to death," I say flatly, and the room erupts with laughter as one of the aides looks at me with a stare that says I am insane.

The next day I am surprised to find that the therapists have heard from others about this comment and find it equally funny. Carol is pleased and says, "Your humor is showing." I acknowledge this and she asks me, "Don't you ever get depressed?"

I am shocked by this question and look at her with an incredulous, piercing gaze and say simply, "I walked in here." Her eyes immediately fill with water and she turns away.

I travel down the hall to occupational therapy where Jackie greets me. "How is my favorite patient?" she asks. I sense that she does not say this to everyone. I assure her I am as well as anyone could expect given my present circumstances. She straps me to the modified loom and I can see John -- the man I saw in the common room drooling on my first day -- with his wife and a therapist. John fell off one of those very high power lines onto his head. He was in a coma, had a steel plate placed in his head and has only progressed to this point.

He works with the speech therapist who coaches him to make consonant sounds, vowel sounds and put the two together. This is an acting exercise I have engaged in. John only grunts sounds of frustration at the therapist, turns his head to his wife and says in a voice that sounds like a 45 rpm record being played at 33 1/3, "I love you."

A box of Kleenex is passed around the room. I take several.

I am now pushing myself in the wheelchair from the therapy floor the full circuitous route back to Rehab. As I cross the skyway connecting the two buildings, there is a woman in a power wheelchair who has come to the floor days before. She says she needs sunshine to keep warm and asks, "Are you a cold quad or a hot quad?"

I want to tell her to fuck off -- that if she uses that word in reference to me again I will kill her with my own hands and, if that is not yet possible, I will pay someone else to do it. Instead, I say nothing, glower and keep pushing.

One of the nurses puts the headset on my head, and I call Annie to tell her of this incident. We quickly move on to more pleasant topics.

There is a pen and a pad at the desk. Jackie has fabricated a splint that goes around my first two fingers and thumb and holds a pen so I can write... or at least sign my name before I become exhausted. I absently prattle and pick up the pen and suddenly look down and see that I have written Annie's name not just once, but three times. Annie is elated but then scolds me. "If you just didn't think about this shit, you would be up and walking already!" Would that it were so simple. That night, we throw away the splint in a special ceremony.

    I often wonder who will come and who will disappear from my life. Many friends come and visit and wish me a speedy and full recovery. Many do not. One person calls, and after I explain the situation to him, is never heard from again. This is what happens when one becomes "special."

The Squeaky Wheel

Thou Shalt Not Covet

    I push the manual wheelchair I use out of the room to the elevator and press the button to take me to the skyway connecting Rehab with the Mayo Building of the hospital. A large crowd awaits the six remarkably slow elevators. I proceed to the "special" elevator for the Rehab patients, their transporters, and possibly doctors and cargo. It arrives with Lorraine, the operator, who sits on a tiny stool and remains there, defying physics. She sucks snot back into her head, snorting and making other barnyard-like noises.

    The usual salutations are exchanged as I board the elevator on what is the first floor of the Mayo building, and we ascend to the fifth floor. (Talk about defying physics!) I push the wheelchair out of the elevator and proceed to the desk where the receptionist greets me. She immediately picks up the mike and announces, "Brian Shaughnessy for PT," and then returns to her other duties. I take my place in the short line of persons waiting for their therapists to greet them and bring them to the gym. Directly across from this short line of people is another short line of people waiting for transporters to take them from here to their rooms.

    "Hi, Sweetie," Carol greets me with a smile. I respond in kind as I push myself to the gym. "Breakfast quiz time, breakfast quiz time!" she says quickly, loudly and happily. It has become part of our daily exchange. Every morning some inane radio personality asks a trivia question and someone who answers the question correctly wins a prize. Carol is impressed with the frequency with which I know the answers.

    "President Johnson -- LBJ -- liked this..." she searches for the word used by the radio personality "... *substance* so much that he had it pumped into every room of the White House. What is it?"

    "Oh, God! LBJ? If it was Lyndon Johnson it had to be some awful stuff," I say as the smile leaves her face.

    "Why would you say that?"

    "Because he was an *awful* man with *awful* tastes who got us into an *awful* war and probably helped to get Kennedy killed."

    "So, you're one of those *conspiracy theory* people?" She asks with a hint of distaste.

"No," I say flatly. "I'm one of those reality people. Anyway... LBJ... '63 to '68... It had to be one of those awful pops from back then." ('Pop' is the all-encompassing word used in the Midwest for 'soda'.) "Probably something citrus and diet."

Carol shakes her head in disgust. "You're too good. I don't want to play with you anymore. Let's go to work. First me, then you. But why don't you take off the armrest?"

I flip the switch keeping the armrest attached to the wheelchair, remove it and hand it to Carol. I position myself to transfer to the mat as she assists me with the placement of the transfer board. With some effort I move my ass onto the plastic board, to the mat, and slowly lie down. She performs the daily range of motion routine. She then looks at her watch. "We have a little time left; I want to see how you might sit yourself up."

I agree and Carol grabs a yellow notepad and pen. "I wanna make note of what works so you can work on that downstairs. Why don't you just try, from lying flat, to prop yourself up on your elbows." This is accomplished but I am not yet sitting up. I look at her and raise an eyebrow.

"Okay, if you lean to your left, can you straighten your right elbow and get up?"

She writes down the various attempts and failures at getting myself to a sitting position. The actual feat is never accomplished, but she writes the list of failed attempts down, underlining the ones she wants me to work on.

"I'll see you up here this afternoon. We can work on this, or we can go to the parallel bars."

She already knows my choice. "The parallel bars," I say. "You know I like to see you sweat."

"You're a brat," she says and pushes me from a seated position backwards. I straighten myself into a sitting position. "Look what you just did! And you did it because you weren't thinking about it."

She holds the sheet of yellow paper she has torn from the notepad at shoulder level. "I'm going to put this in your backpack, okay?" I nod and she opens the backpack. "What is *this*?" she says, removing a gray sweater.

"I got it from an old girlfriend. She got it from a secondhand store." It is now out of the backpack as she holds it up admiringly. It is clearly an *old* sweater with a tight knit and a sturdy zipper up the front. It looks

The Squeaky Wheel

slightly like a Mr. Rogers brand of sweater only much cooler. One of the cuffs looks like a dog chewed on it.

"I've never seen one like it! I really like it."

"You have excellent taste," I commend her. "It's my favorite sweater, too."

"Oh, yes -- it's very nice. I want one. I may have to sneak down to your room and take it from your closet," she teases.

"I'll tell you what," I begin earnestly, "the day I walk out of here -- after I piss on Tina -- I'll give you this sweater."

She continues to fondle the sweater without looking up as she says, "You got yourself a deal." Before she puts the sweater back in the bag, she goes to a cabinet and removes a small bag. She clips a small ring to the zipper on the sweater, hands me the bag with several more inside, and bids me goodbye. These are called "quad rings" and they allow one to put a digit through the ring and not have to pinch a zipper to pull it up or down. I begin to push the wheelchair out of the gym.

"Fresca," I hear her say from behind me, although I don't quite understand. I turn with a puzzled look.

"Fresca was the substance that LBJ had pumped into every room of the White House."

I return to the floor to hear that Joe with the halo was at a party the night before where friends carried him down the stairs to the basement and fed him copious amounts of beer. When they tried to bring him back up the stairs they lost control of the wheelchair spilling Joe out -- breaking the screws that held his halo in place. He will be in the regular hospital for an undetermined length of time.

I am lying in bed, in the dark, on the weekend. There is no therapy. Sobbing, I am certain my life is over when an old girlfriend, Pam, walks into the room. Pam has waist-length, jet-black hair of ringlets, lunar white smooth skin and heart-break-blue eyes. She is gorgeous and she wears hippy clothes. (She gave me the sweater Carol covets.) She had vanished from my life without a word months ago. I can't speak through the tears. Finally, I ask what happened, and she says that she did not want to complicate my life with her two children. I ask her how she knew I was in the hospital, and she says that a mutual friend told her. She has no other information. Through tears I tell her that I can't feel below my nipples, can't walk and can't piss. The list is long. Somehow we kiss. I hate myself while I am doing it, but I do it anyway. She's sitting on the bed and we're talking when Annie enters the room. I introduce them and

Annie grunts, *picks up her backpack* and exits. The backpack does not clue me. Pam exits and says she will return that night. My father enters with my young half-brothers, Billy Bubba, 6, and Bobby Bubba, 4. There is also a stepbrother in the equation -- Bubba Bubba.

A nurse enters, places me in the wheelchair and I go to dinner. I have become somewhat celebrated because when transferred to the wheelchair ... I stand. It is unusual and startling for them. This nurse is new and almost loses her balance when she experiences my assistance. "You stand!"

Dinner is ghastly and Annie sits across from me with her head in her hand. I call her name and she looks up. I reach for the Styrofoam cup, pick it up, raise it to my lips and drink. She beams and her head returns to her hand. Billy Bubba asks our father what the big deal is.

My father's smile is wider than Annie's. "Brian couldn't do that last week." I smile and pick up the unbent fork with no cuff. My father and Annie applaud -- and her head returns to her hand. After my father leaves and I am in bed, Annie demands that I not take her for granted. I'm too obtuse to realize she saw the kiss. I assure her I won't, but I already have. My father goes to his car and cries for several minutes before driving home.

Pam returns later with my roommate who I have not seen since I have been in the hospital. They bring cocaine. This changes my mood from the afternoon but there is no more kissing – with Pam or my roommate Mark.

My father, my three brothers, my grandmother, my sister-in-law and Annie arrive at the hospital. My mom and sisters are in New Mexico. It is the day the situation will be explained as well as possible. Dr. Erickson, Dr. Gordon, Carol, my occupational therapist Jackie, primary nurse Tina and the useless psychologist are there. Notably absent is Dr. Liar who performed the operation. He has returned to speak to me and check my progress several times, but he won't face this crowd.

"We have these meetings," begins Dr. Erickson after introductions, "for the family and those close to Brian -- as well as Brian -- so that everyone can understand what is going on, make sure everyone is getting the same information and not too much misinformation. I'm going to let Dr. Gordon take over for awhile."

"What Brian is experiencing right now is an incomplete injury to the C-5 level of his spinal cord. Typically, C-5 injuries result in the loss of or limited use of one's legs, loss of bowel and bladder control, loss of

The Squeaky Wheel

sensation below the nipples, varying weakness and loss of use of the hands and arms."

The key word in this presentation is loss. Nowhere in the family meeting is there any discussion regarding the "gains" an individual experiences as a result of acquiring a C-5 spinal cord injury. There are none.

"The individual on the rehabilitation floor is not regarded as sick. The team, all of us who are going to speak to you today, are here to facilitate Brian's achieving as much independence and recovery as possible. The nurses do not wear uniforms; they wear civilian clothes to reinforce the fact that people here are not sick."

The doctor uses a large diagram from Grey's Anatomy to illustrate. "The spinal cord is the major bundle of nerves that carries impulses to and from the brain to the rest of the body. In general, the higher in the spinal cord the injury occurs, the more loss a person will experience. The eight vertebrae in the neck are called the Cervical Vertebrae. The top vertebra is called C-1. Injury here means the respiratory system is affected and a person is dependent on a respirator, with loss of all function below the neck. Thoracic Vertebrae begin where the first rib attaches. Injuries here result in loss of the use of the legs and functions below mid-stomach.

"Approximately 10,000 people survive spinal cord injury every year, 80% of whom are males between 18 and 24. There are two types of spinal cord injury -- complete and incomplete. A complete injury means that there is no function below the injury, no sensation and no voluntary movement. Brian is fortunate ..."

The singular word that has not come to my mind in the time since waking up from surgery is "fortunate." But the good doctor is right ... as I later find out.

"... in that his injury is incomplete and he has some sensation and is standing at the parallel bars, right?"

I nod my spinning head, praying that I will wake up from this endless nightmare.

"Brian is standing," Carol chimes in cheerily. "He has already shown a lot of progress and recovery. I'm very encouraged for him. We don't know if he will have full recovery, but it looks encouraging to me. I've been working with these guys for five years now and lots of them with less function than Brian have walked out."

Brian Shaughnessy

When it comes time for questions my father asks, "I don't want to sound like the dirty old man here, but how is this going to affect Brian's sex life?"

Dr. Gordon begins, after the question has been interpreted for him. "Most quadriplegic males cannot ejaculate in the regular sense. Some have retrograde ejaculation -- which means they ejaculate back into the bladder rather than out through the urethra -- but most do not experience orgasm. It is not uncommon for quadriplegics to maintain an erection anywhere from 45 minutes up to two hours."

"Is that all?" my brothers ask in unison -- echoing the joke that ran through my mind. The sign language interpreter blushes as she repeats the statement. Annie smirks.

Tina must have her say. As everyone is readying to leave -- shuffling jackets, hats, gloves, and backpacks -- she talks and no one listens. She extols her virtues as my primary care nurse, the person most intimately connected with my needs on a day-to-day basis. I want to vomit.

Annie says she was unaware of much of this information and felt like an outsider, since she is not related by blood or marriage, but she intends to stick with me for the duration and, as confident as she is that I will walk out, she will stay with me no matter what my condition.

My father wishes me well and informs me how proud he is of my progress and his certainty that I will walk out of Rehab. "Give your old man a kiss," he commands. After I kiss him on the cheek he makes his usual second demand. "Say a prayer for your old man." He turns and exits, walking to the elevator to take the even more circuitous route to the parking structure. He travels up in the elevator, walks a great distance, travels up another elevator, walks another great distance through the skyway that keeps Minnesotans out of the harsh elements and goes up in one more elevator. The elevator door opens to an icy blast -- not as icy as a door opening onto the street but nonetheless an icy blast. He steps from the elevator in the direction of his car and when he arrives at the car the keys fall to the floor from his pocket. His arm and head go down onto the roof of the car and he sheds tears for his red-haired first-born male child... and for himself. He retrieves the keys from the floor of the parking structure, unlocks the car, sits down and cries for several more minutes before driving home. . . my mother tells me.

I have been thinking about this since before I woke up from surgery. After surgery there were many other thoughts barging their way into my

The Squeaky Wheel

brain and trying to anchor the thought into obsession status. This thought is recurring and pushing aside all others.

I wonder how sincere the thought is. It may just be a knee jerk reaction to the greatest hell this human has endured. It may be sincere. The thought was there before the surgery... The thought is a question I wrestle with. I wonder how it will be perceived by its intended audience... and others. I commit.

Annie arrives and I am in bed. She brings yet another of her daily gifts and a Hallmark card (from Shoebox Greetings -- the more cynical and irreverent division of Hallmark) and we talk of how we each spent the day.

"I love you," I say.

"I know," she says with the boldness of Han Solo when he uttered the same words in response to Princess Leia's proclamation.

(Pause)

"Will you marry me?"

There is only a flash of bewilderment before she processes the question and her brown eyes sparkle. She smiles broadly and says, "Yes." There is a lump in my throat.

"But this means," she begins calmly and directly, "that I better not walk into this room and see you kissing anybody."

She saw? Suddenly I remember the backpack that she retrieved and her mood that evening. It could only have been placed there while I was in a selfish, confused kiss with Pam.

"How the hell could you do that?" she asks. Now the lump is in her throat. A valid question.

"I don't know." A stock answer. "I can't believe I did it." Straight off the shelf. "Joy had just left me and she was in the middle of the disintegration of her marriage and... Pam and I got each other through some heavy stuff."

"And what are we going through? What am I going through with you right now?"

I laugh long and hard as she grows a little angrier and then joins in the laughter. "I guess, because I'm in it right now and can't look back in hindsight I didn't realize until just this second --"

"Well, realize it and don't do that to me again."

"I promise."

"Shake on it?" she asks indicating she is ready to be done being angry. It is a bit we share.

Brian Shaughnessy

"Yup," I say and do my best to flail my arms and head from the bed as she shakes arms, legs and head. We kiss. We pull the curtain to afford us the only privacy available in this room.

The next day she brings a wedding gown she has purchased from a secondhand store. I know we'll be okay despite... the incident. All appearances to the contrary, I am a lucky man.

Each morning and evening the nurses put lotion on my body. They put extra doses on the bottoms of my feet because the calluses on the bottoms from walking are peeling away like my dignity and will to live. This is a frequent topic of conversation among the patients and nurses. One male nurse, David O'Malley, knows that I am a theater major; he can quote more speeches from Shakespeare than I have read. He is a large, bearded heavyset man who must force his turkey-sized hands into the extra large gloves. More impressive than his Shakespeare is the fact he can quote the entire speech of the cowardly lion from the Wizard of Oz, starting from, "If I were King of the Forest," to, "rhinoceros/imposserous," to, "muskrat guard his musk," to, "what have they got that I ain't got." He explains this skill is from repeatedly watching the movie on video with his young son.

One day as I lament the injustice of how I came to find myself in the Rehabilitation Department of the University of Minnesota Hospital, Dan remarks, "Yup, Brian got the chair." Not to be outdone, I bemoan the loss of the calluses on my feet saying, "There goes my sole." He gets along well with my brother Pat and says to both of us, "Pat Shaughnessy, that name sounds like a guy who sells used appliances."

Many of the other nurses are equally pleasant... save for Tina.

Carol, Gayland, Jackie and the nurses want to know when I will take my first weekend pass. A terrifying prospect. They are training Annie to stick that red tube in my dick, dig shit out of my ass, transfer me from bed to wheelchair and even into my Honda Accord. It is all very easy for the professionals, but when Carol instructs Annie on the transfer into the car, Annie is defeated. Carol breaks a sweat but still makes it look easy. She removes the armrest from the wheelchair, places a shiny plastic board halfway under my ass and guides me deftly into the passenger seat, lifting my legs and placing them on the floor of the car.

We have been out for dinner or movies with recreational therapy but not solo. When I leave the hospital and encounter the general population, the STARES I get from the upright/uptight are more of a barrier to my

The Squeaky Wheel

participation than a flight of STAIRS. The general population looks at me with revulsion, with pity and with a look that says, "How *dare* you subject us to the likes of you?" Although I don't know why, every pore of my body wants to scream out, "It's *not* my fault, It's not *my* fault, It's not my *fault*, *It's not my fault*!" God forbid that these staring individuals have to actually interact with me. When they must, I sense their discomfort and horror. Sometimes I approach these people JUST to tighten their sphincters.

Often there are STAIRS to an establishment, so those of us on the special bus must use an alternate entrance -- the CP entrance. What was once the entrance for "colored people" for much of this country's history is now the entrance for crippled people. If there is such an entrance.

When away from the confines of Rehab, strangers ask what happened. I do not yet have the "skills" to tell them to fuck off -- or some variation thereof.

Neither Annie's apartment nor mine is accessible, so she asks her mother if we may spend a weekend at her place. Mom consents and 30 hours into it Annie has an anxiety attack, Brian wants to die and her stepfather drives us back to the hospital.

The next day I see Gayland. I tell him of the horrors and he says that's normal and we should try again. I feel I would rather throw myself into the Mississippi River from the nearby Washington Avenue Bridge. Certainly, this is a more pleasant option than talking with this oaf.

My father shows up for one of his almost daily visits. His wife is with him. I'm already in bed. He gives his traditional salutation.

"Big Red!"

I give mine. "Hey, Pops!"

"How was your day?" he asks as he bends down to kiss me on the cheek.

"Fantastic! I stood at the parallel bars again, and this time Carol helped me walk the entire distance. She says she can't count the number of spinal cord injured patients that have walked out of here after doing that."

I see the tears well in his eyes. He lowers his head continuing to gaze at me and asks, "Really?"

"Yup. I'm thinking that's a good sign."

"Boy, I'll say," he says as they give congratulations, encouragement and tell me to keep up the good work. I assure them it is my intent as Annie returns to the room.

Brian Shaughnessy

"Hi, Dad. Hi," she says grinning. The, "Hi, Dad," has been a standard joke with the two of them since I have been in the hospital. They greet her.

"Were you here to see the big event today?" he asks.

"No! Wouldn't you know that he goes and shows off on a day that I have to work?"

"Yeah, he likes to pretend he's humble. I think he's just rehearsing for the big show."

"Probably. He is an actor."

"What do you want in your Easter basket?" my father asks with a typical Irish, impish grin.

In a flash of inspiration we lock brown eyes and I say, with a dryness the Sierra Desert would envy, "a little grass." The room bursts with laughter.

"Well, we'll just have to see about that," Dad says.

We converse about life in and out of the hospital -- family, news, weather, sports and whatever else a group of humans talk about when ignoring tragedy -- quietly celebrating the incredible strength of the human spirit and loving each other. My father makes his move to exit but not before he kisses me again and says he loves me. I respond in kind and he gives his customary exit instructions.

"Say a prayer for the old man."

"I will," I respond.

Tonight, because he is with his wife, my father does not cry for several minutes before driving home.

I get a postcard from my old girlfriend Joy, who traveled to Boston on vacation, started an affair, returned, dumped me as a hick and moved to Beantown. The card says merely, "Having a wonderful time." No mention of hospitals, paralysis or even a get well is made.

John, who fell off the power line and broke his head, is improving. Each day he speaks more and he is walking. I think it's a miracle but Carol tells me it is common for the type of injury. "He will never be the same. It is so damn tragic. Be grateful you didn't have a head injury." I'm not grateful.

John is childlike and tries to get out of his wheelchair despite being horribly unsteady. I believe after he told his wife that he loved her, his next statement was, "Can I have a cigarette?" I see him in the community room trying to free himself from the locked seatbelt that keeps him in the

The Squeaky Wheel

wheelchair for his own safety. He moves with his feet and approaches me every five minutes. "Got a cigarette, man?" Every five minutes I tell him I don't smoke. His wife comes often and he goes to relatives on some weekends.

One night Annie and I lie in bed, and we hear him make a phone call. "Tell Uncle Darryl I have to come to the house this weekend. I gotta go. I just have to get out of here this weekend." He restates this loudly, vehemently and repeatedly. Finally his voice cracks and he says, "Elizabeth wants a divorce."

Annie reaches for the Kleenex.

A few days later my father returns. He appears to be in a hurry.

"Annie's not here tonight? He asks.

"You just missed her."

"Oh. Well, I have your Easter basket here and a card." He shows me an envelope. His voice takes a serious, instructive tone -- not unfamiliar to his children. "I'm not going to open the card now. Just make sure that Annie or one of your brothers opens this card, NOT a nurse." He stares.

I erupt with laughter. "You mean there's weed in there?" My father's eyelids drop but do not close. His shoulders slump, and he looks at me with a look that says, moron. My son is a moron. I don't know how this happened! I'm not a moron. His mother is not a moron. He did ok in school and yet, he's a moron. If he works hard he can become an idiot. I sired a moron. This look is not unfamiliar to his children. A look some of them, myself included, have inherited.

After the look, my father shakes his head as I continue to chuckle. "I hope you got it from a Negro! Then we know it's good shit." I hear Ed chuckle from his bubbling, beaded bed.

What needs to be explained here is that my father is a very straight arrow. He doesn't like drugs, he doesn't use them and his criminal clients who like, use and sell them are his least favorite people. This means that he or someone near him -- and not one of my siblings -- had to deal with that element of society, which, for him, has least favorite status. Prior to this evening this man has only taken weed away from me. Tonight, it appears, he is giving it to me. After an uncharacteristically brief exchange he leaves. But not without a kiss and his customary exit instructions.

"I will."

Easter. The day Christ rose from the dead, I can't get out of bed.

Brian Shaughnessy

My father arrives and I am sobbing. I tell him Dr. Liar was in the room and I share with him for the first time what Dr. Liar said to me after the surgery. My father grits his teeth as he does when he is angry.

"How can he lie like that to my face?" I ask.

"How can he not?" he says, transitioning from father to purely lawyer.

We go to the nursing station and ask for my chart. In the common room we page through the document, which is thicker than the phone book. We find Dr. Liar's notes -- post surgery -- where he claims I was informed that THIS was a risk and acknowledge that I knew of this possible peril. I am weakened. We continue to look through the document finding he has written this other places. Eventually we find the consent form which reads:

> I authorize the performance of the following described medical/surgical procedures upon_____.

I recognize my printed name which I am now unable to write on the line.

> I understand that the following surgical, medical, and/or diagnostic procedures are planned for me and I voluntarily consent and authorize this procedure. I voluntarily request Dr. _____ as my physician, and such associates, technical assistants and other health care providers as they may deem necessary, to treat my condition which has been explained to me: _____.

Liar is printed after the doctor's name and syringomyelia as the condition explained. Nothing more... so far.

> I realize that common to surgical procedures is the potential for infection, allergic reactions, and even death.
> I (we) also realize that the following risks and hazards may occur in connection with this particular procedure:_____

Where there was nothing printed after the above line when I signed it, is now handwritten:

> Paralysis -- quadriparesis, weakness of legs and arms
> Incontinence -- bladder and bowel dysfunction
> Loss of function -- mobility and feeling.
> Ventilatory dependency -- inability to breathe
> Sexual dysfunction

The Squeaky Wheel

A tear hits the page. It's mine.

"Did the good doctor tell you all of these things?" my father asks with the calm of the eye of the hurricane and a face with no more emotion than flat white paint. I know his guts are being ripped out and his heart is fragmenting into smaller pieces than it already has. Catholic upbringing on the farm with stoic parents, a tour of duty as a Marine, several years as a boxer and 20 years as a criminal defense attorney give him this poker face when he should be screaming like a child on fire.

My tears stop. "Fuck no. Don't you think I would have told you the weekend before the surgery if I had known that?"

"Yes, I do. What *did* he tell you?"

"He said I might die, but that because I was 24 and in good health, that was unlikely. I asked him if I would be going back to pro ball, and he looked confused. I explained I was kidding, but... He said that I would need a soft collar for 10 days and *maybe* outpatient therapy."

He allows a little of his parent personality back and says, "You can't worry about this. You need to focus on getting better and making all of the shit written here not matter. Do you understand?"

I am crying again but I nod.

"I will make copies of all of this, look into it and we will get the top malpractice attorney in the state to go after this son of a bitch *after* you walk out of here, understood?"

I nod and he returns the chart to the nursing station. Later he exits and Annie arrives. My father goes to his car and cries for several minutes before driving home.

Annie has a Chiquita banana sticker on the back of her hand. She's been shopping. I tell her about the lies written in the chart. She was never told of these risks, and she was the one I spent nearly every hour with between signing the document and waking up from surgery. First, she is furious and then she wants vengeance -- threatening to kill the man. She utters one of her two current mantras, "I hate people." We retreat to my room, pull the curtain and engage in coitus. In the afterglow I try to return to the topic of the doctor.

Annie chants her other mantra. "There, there, Honey. Annie's here. I'll take care of everything. It's going to be all right."

Brian Shaughnessy

Surprise

One evening my grandmother Nonnie and Uncle Bruce come to visit. My red-haired grandmother comes often. She comes during the day, she comes at night and she comes on weekends. When she does not come she calls. After Annie and my father, she is there the most often. It's not a contest; it's an observation.

Annie is working. This is one of the rare evenings that she is not there. She came during the day.

I am already in bed when they arrive. I have grudgingly become accustomed to greeting guests and entertaining in the hospital this way -- Marcel Proust style. I will become adept not only at entertaining but also reading, making phone calls and ultimately writing from this position.

The three of us are in the middle of a laugh when suddenly the curtain parts and my mother walks into the room. "Mom!" I say and immediately begin to sob. "You didn't tell anyone you were coming?" Nonnie asks. My Uncle -- my mother's brother -- is immediately up and offering her his chair as he flees the room crying.

"I was tired of people telling me not to come," she responds with no ill will in the statement. "How are you doing, Brian?" She asks as she makes her way around the bed and takes hold of my hand. With a trembling voice I respond, "Ok."

"I'll say he is," Nonnie brags. "You should see him in therapy! Well, I guess you will now that you're here. He works so hard and he is standing at the parallel bars and his therapist, Carol, who *really* is a saint, helps him get from one end to the other. And he works just as hard at his other therapy *while* he is standing!"

"You can stand on your own?" Mom asks puzzled and thrilled and hopeful.

"Almost," I explain. "They put me in this contraption that holds me standing while I write, or play Boggle or do something. The nurses here all know me as the guy who stands when they transfer me."

"I hate this place already," Mom says. "You've been here four weeks. You must really hate it," she says, inviting me to respond.

"Often." I tell her. "But so far I don't see any other way to get out of here."

"My God, I hate to see you this way. You know I would take this if I could. You know that, right?"

The Squeaky Wheel

"I don't doubt it for a second," I respond. "But there's no way in hell I would wish this on anyone -- except maybe the doctor who performed the surgery. No, not even him." This is the first time I utter these words about the doctor who performed the surgery.

"I'd wish it on him," my mother responds.

"Oh, Lou," Nonnie says maternally, "I don't think you would."

"The hell I wouldn't," my mother says, uncharacteristically challenging her mother. "That son of a bitch does this to my child and claims he warned everyone about it...! He'd better pray I don't run into him in the hall or get it in my mind to go and look for him. Because if I do... *this*," she gestures to the wheelchair, me and the urine bag hanging on the side of the hospital bed, "won't be needed by the good doctor. He'll just need a good life insurance policy. And that goes for the nurse who put him in the hospital for a month and caused this."

"I wonder if she knows..." my grandmother says and realizes the woman does not. "I'd like to tell her." My uncle has returned to the room but after this tirade and tears flowing from the other three people in the room, he exits again.

"Did Teri and Dawn come with you?" my grandmother asks.

"No," she responds sadly. "Teri agreed to stay and take care of Dawn. I couldn't afford to bring them all up."

Just then mom's friend Deborah enters the room. Their husbands attended law school together. They both have six children, all roughly the same age. Both husbands left for younger women. Soon, both mothers will come to know tragedy more profound than imaginable. Deborah's daughter was a runaway, constantly in trouble with the law, a substance abuser and single parent at 17. But she has recently and certainly turned her life around. By going to school to earn her cosmetology degree, she is working, excelling, clean and sober. She often cuts my hair -- now that I can't cut it myself. Soon, she will be killed in an automobile accident that is no one's fault. Her motherless son will be adopted by one of her brothers. A short time after this, another son will be beaten into a coma -- probably by the police -- and left on a county road to die -- as I was by the nurse seventeen years ago. But he does not die and emerges from the coma with a brain injury, no longer able to live independently. My mom need only deal with a quadriplegic son and a daughter with Down syndrome... so far in her life.

"Hi Deborah," I acknowledge. "Did she tell you she was coming?"

"I picked her up at the airport and we came straight here."

My mother holds my hand through the evening and returns the next day. She follows me to therapy where Carol confides, "I never had anyone work harder or want it more." Jackie repeats the same words when I go to occupational therapy.

My dear friend Andrew shows up, as he does almost daily, in the late afternoon. He and my mother are glad to see each other. The special bus that belongs to the Rehabilitation Department is not working, so I am unable to travel to Nonnie's for dinner. Andrew offers to take us. My mother calls and tells her mother that Andrew Yee will be joining us for dinner. Nonnie is horrified. "I made a mock chow mein!" My mother giggles and tells me this when Andrew is out of earshot. We travel to St. Paul where Andrew asks for second and third helpings, amusing and delighting Nonnie.

The Squeaky Wheel

Doug

One night Annie and I are lying in my bed. One of the unit's two telephones is directly outside my door. This means we hear half the conversations on the floor. Doug's conversations are the worst. He drones on inanely. Some of this cannot be helped as Doug is borderline retarded.

Doug often tells the story of breaking his neck. His monotone drawl, his mental status, and the fact he speaks of it in a manner that conveys that the ordeal is the biggest thing that ever happened to him, makes it all very sad, tragic and insufferable.

Doug is on the phone tonight. Not only does Doug use the phone often, he stays on for a *very* long time. Again, he tells the story of how he broke his neck. It goes something like this:

"Well, see me and my brother were drinking at the Fox Trap and we decided to go to the Mule Skinner's bar. (Pause) South Dakota, we were in South Dakota where I got hurt. Anyway, we went to the Mule Skinner's because it's a titty bar. I shouldn't have been drinking because I got 26 DUI's before. We come out of there and my brother says he's too drunk to drive, we should get a motel. I ask does you have money for a motel and he says no. I say I don't have money for a motel, I'll drive. The next thing I remember is waking up in the hospital screaming at the nurses, trying to pick a fight. (Pause) I totaled the truck into a tree. (Pause) He didn't even get a scratch. And me... I can't really say that I wish this had never happened because if this had never happened I would have never met you...."

Doug's brother never visits.

Brian Shaughnessy

That's *Why You Don't Kill the Messenger*

Pat and Kate have had a son. All gush over the baby. Today the little miracle visits his second hospital. As I lie in bed, I hear commotion in the hallway. I wonder if this is the arrival of my first nephew, my parents' first grandchild and Nonnie's first great-grandchild.

"Oh!" I hear the word elongated and colored in the invariable manner of a woman seeing a baby. "How cute! Is it a boy or a girl? You're Brian's brother and sister? He looks like a Shaughnessy."

I am not sure which nurse is saying the words but I am laughing when she enters to announce -- needlessly – that my new nephew has arrived with his parents. I tell her to send them all in.

"You can come in," she says to the family in the hallway. My brother and sister-in-law enter with a large bundle of blankets, clothing and baby. It *is* March.

"Hey, brother," Pat says in his usual greeting.

"Hi, Brian," says Kate. "How are you doing?"

"As good as can be expected," I answer smiling. "I am anxious to see this little guy, if you ever get him unpeeled."

Kate laughs as she works to get him out of the baby carrier, blankets, a tiny hat, a tiny snowmobile suit, little mittens and other winter baby items.

"Sorry," she says as she unbundles him, "it's very cold out there and this is his first winter and he's our first child."

"Anything short of an oven is probably a good idea," I say as Kate winces. It won't be the last time that she winces over a comment to or about her children. Devlin coos sleepily and contentedly as I watch the unveiling. The standard reaction of human beings to these small miracles is overwhelming.

"Oh my goodness, you're just so tiny and cute," I say as his mother holds him.

"This is Devlin Lewis Shaughnessy," she says as his father beams.

"Yes it is," I say as my voice cracks, "and you are a very handsome lad. Lucky you look nothing like your father." Patrick looks over his glasses with a glare, but smiles. Kate brings the baby closer as I raise

The Squeaky Wheel

the head of the hospital bed. He makes adorable baby sounds and faces through sleepy eyes. At first he is seated on my belly as Kate holds him up and one of his little hands grasps one of my fingers. I examine the tiny digits with their tiny nails. "You are *so* little." He gurgles.

"I think he's going to fuss," Kate says with a mother's instinct. "Can I lay him on your chest?"

I am happy to grant this request, and the little miracle is placed on my chest. I feel his warmth, his softness and smell that baby smell. Wow. The top of his head is visible to me, and he makes little movements with accompanying sounds. I look at the indent of the soft spot at the top of his head. I wonder how anything so perfect can be so fragile. The smell, the smell is so wondrous! It's pure and magical and smells like... like... the goodness of life. I quietly say adult things to him and babble the obligatory baby talk. He raises his head, looks directly into my eyes and only moves to nod his disproportionately large head. He carries a message.

I hear the words in my mind as his gaze is fixed on me, inches away. "It's okay, Brian," comes his message, clearly. "I come from God, sent nine months ago -- before the surgery. The message is that you're going to be okay. Do not give up. He has a perfect plan, and just as you see my perfection you must trust His plan. I also bring love."

I hear all of this in my mind and suddenly am aware of the messenger's parents in the room. They have been talking. They have been talking to me, but I did not hear it. I apologize and tell them that their son brought a message from God for me.

"Yup," his father says. "And one for all of us."

Annie's gift to the newborn child is not frankincense and myrrh but a shiny new soft, fluffy, cuddly stuffed raccoon.

The day I have feared arrives. I am in the area of the common room where tables are set up for dining. It's lunchtime and all the patients and many of the nurses are present. The elderly, gray-haired nutritionist we see most often is wearing her blue hairnet and white coat. She is walking toward me with a mission.

"Brian," she announces loudly as all heads turn toward us, "Mrs. Schweitzer in the kitchen asked me to ask if you are the Brian Shaughnessy that used to work as a cook in the kitchen."

Eyes bulge and eyebrows rise as I stammer and she waits for an answer.

"I would like to plead the fifth, but given that we have everyone's attention, I want to confess and thank you for revealing my dirty little secret."

The others never look at me the same again.

My brother Darrin arrives later and gives me a button he demands I wear. It reads: Failure Is Impossible. I put it on gladly. The therapists upstairs approve, commenting that it is in keeping with my character. I wear it at dinner and Jan, the woman with syringomyelia, in Rehab again after her fourth surgery and ever-diminishing abilities, sees the button and asks what it says *just* as I am leaving the table. Knowing her reaction, I continue my move to exit the table and the room.

"Failure is impossible," I shout, half over my shoulder. Now I am moving out of the room.

She cackles as if it were the most ridiculous thing she has ever heard. I grit my teeth and keep moving.

"No, no," she shouts. "That's great. You keep on believing that."

I mutter Annie's mantra to myself, "I hate people."

There is a guy in physical therapy who is not a patient of the Rehabilitation Department, but has come for the week. We talk, become acquainted and Carol discovers that he is from Buffalo, Minnesota. I tell him that ten years ago a nurse from Buffalo hit me on my bicycle, left me to die in a ditch and continued on her way to work at the Buffalo hospital where I was later brought in. I say that the aforementioned incident is likely to have caused my present condition, some ten years later.

He turns a little grayer than he already was and mutters, "I remember that happening."

"Could you tell the bitch of my present situation and thank her for me?" I ask.

"I would love to," he says to my pleasure, "but I think she and her husband moved."

My Dinner with Andrew or Ding-dong the Witch Is Dead

I talk with one of the nurses, having completed the four therapy sessions of the day, when Andrew, bundled up for the winter chill, enters grandly through the door.

"Bri!" he shouts as he waves and kicks snow from his boots. "What are you doing?"

"Same-old, same-old," I respond, curious about his plans.

"I just found out I aced my midterm! Let's get out of here and go see a movie!"

"You're going to drive?" I ask, infinitely more concerned about the transfer than his driving.

"Of course. My car's right outside! Let's get you in a jacket and hat and go!"

I turn to look at the nurse I am talking to. "Any reason I can't leave?" I ask, possibly hoping for just such a reason. She shakes her head. "Anything I need to do?" She shakes her head again and Andrew already has his hands on the back of the wheelchair and is pushing me toward my room. "This is going to be great," Andrew promises. "You need to get out of here more often, and not just with Annie."

I agree as he assists me in putting on my jacket and hat. My roommate, Ed, asks if I am going out. Andrew answers with a hardy affirmative. Ed remains bed-bound in his heinous, bubbling bed. "All right then," he says through his thick black Southern accent and medicated speech, "you boys have fun."

I assure him we will and ask if there is anything that we can bring him from "outside." Ed says no, his brother is coming and everything will be all right. I say goodbye and Andrew does the same and leans alongside my ear. "I can't understand a word that man says, can you?" I point out to him I just demonstrated I understand Ed, but that it took some time, as well as being in the same room with him almost constantly. "Besides, you have to have soul," I add.

Andrew scoffs, "Yup, you're a real soul-man, Brian." I am in the hallway headed for the door when Alice, one of the nurses' aides (around 50 and strong as an ox) teases me.

"Where do you think you're going?"

"I think I am going to a movie," I snap back at her -- jokingly.

She shakes her head saying, "You just live the life of Riley, don't you?"

"Not really," I say only slightly sullenly. "Anything I need to do before I leave?"

"No, just go and have fun," she says adding, "You want help getting into the car?" She is already moving for her coat. Andrew declines, much to my chagrin, as we exit the building through the two separate sets of doors. The cold air blasts my face.

The large, two-door Oldsmobile is there so Andrew removes the sliding board from my backpack, opens the door, positions me, (I am already *really* freezing) places the board under my ass and, with less struggle than expected, I am in the car. The wheelchair is placed in the trunk and, like so many times before, the two of us are off to the movies.

We arrive at the theater and the reverse procedure is accomplished. We sit through an unremarkable film made remarkable by this being my first outing with anyone other than Annie or the recreational therapy group. Andrew returns me to the car with increasing skill but diminishing strength. As we exit the parking lot he suggests, "Let's swing by your old crib!" I'm hardly in a position to argue and agree to the continuing outing. At my apartment we find another old friend, Jack (who I have known since the fourth grade), hard at work on one of the ongoing carpentry projects the two of us would be working at were it not for my surgery.

"Brian!" he shouts, exiting the building just as Andrew has me seated in the chair. I ask Andrew if this was prearranged and he laughs and insists that it was not. Jack helps get me down the six stairs and into what will be my new apartment. The three of us talk in this apartment (as we have before), and Jack speaks of his plans for the new floor. "You have those damn faux-wood things that you got for a nickel apiece." He sees my searching look. "You know, those things 3M made and discontinued? They wiggle like rubber, but they *might* appear to be a parquet floor," he says and looks at me in a manner suggesting he questions my judgment and gullibility. I laugh.

"So, I'm the guinea pig to see if they work, how they look and if you can jump on them like a trampoline?"

The Squeaky Wheel

"Would you rather install them in a tenant's apartment and have to yank them out in a month? Or, use them up in another unit and not have any left for your apartment?" Jack is ever the pragmatist; it's his damn philosophy degree.

"Okay, okay," I concede, "I can't wait to see how they look." This all feels good.

Jack begins to point out that 3M doesn't discontinue products that make the company money when Andrew, mercifully, (I don't like to lose arguments and the point has been made) interrupts. "Jack! What are you doing for dinner? Why don't we all go someplace? Someplace with beer. Brian, you up for dinner and a beer?" I ponder this for a moment and quickly decide it's a wonderful idea. Jack adds his enthusiastic response to the suggestion. It is soon decided we will rendezvous at William's Pub after, Andrew is quick to point out, Jack helps get me into the car.

The three of us go to the aforementioned establishment (an establishment where we have eaten and enjoyed beers -- sometimes to excess -- many times in the past) and with the tag-team approach to getting me in and out of Andrew's car, the process is much simpler. Inside, seated, the three of us beam. Even the waitress seems electrified with joy as she brings the beer. I lift the bottle easily and drink from it happily. Jack comments upon my progress -- not so very long ago I could not lift a Styrofoam cup, let alone a beer bottle. We are radiant. Dinner never tasted better -- for reasons similar to when Tom Sawyer and Huckleberry Finn ran away from home, caught and prepared the most delicious fish they had ever eaten. The significance of the camaraderie, the achievement, the spontaneity and the happenstance of the three of us coming together for this meal enhance every aspect of dinner.

But all good things must end. Eventually my two friends get me back into the car and Andrew returns to the hospital. It is dark; it is cold. Andrew removes the wheelchair and footrests from the trunk and places them alongside the car. He opens the door to transfer me, not aware I have been shaking my head vehemently.

"No, no, no! We're at the hospital; they get paid for this! You've already transferred me seven times! Go inside and get my nurse to do this. Andrew ponders this for a moment, begins to object, thinks better of his initial response and grins. "You're right!" He laughs. "And you are my friend, but my back is a closer friend. No hard feelings?"

"Get your ass inside and get a nurse," I admonish him jokingly, "It's cold out here! Close the door!" I hear Andrew cackle as the door closes and he enters the hospital. A few minutes later he reappears at the first set of glass doors (still inside) looking sheepish and moving slowly. I wonder what's going on as he tentatively opens the first door and slowly, dejectedly makes his way to the second door. Before he opens this door he looks back over a drooping shoulder, turning back to me with the look of someone who just lost his ass to a ferocious chewing. I wonder what happened so quickly as to take him from such a high to such ... despair. As he pushes open the second door to the outside I see Tina -- my primary care nurse and one of the few people at this institution who I DESPISE -- walking briskly toward the first door, coming up quickly behind Andrew, overtaking him and coming alongside the car door and jerking it open.

"Where have you been?" She demands angrily.

I am definitely not in the mood.

"Out!" I snap right back at her.

"Why didn't you sign out?"

"Because I never did this before. I asked two people if there was a procedure and they both said, 'Just go and have fun.' Nobody mentioned signing out. I didn't know."

"Well you know now," is her pointless retort. "Dr. Erickson asked me where you were, and I had to tell *the Doctor* that I didn't know where my patient was." She says this while shaking her head, not realizing I could not *possibly* care less -- although it does explain her foulness being turned up a notch.

"How awful for you," I say sarcastically. "Now, you want to get me out of this car?"

She is aghast at the suggestion. "Do you mean to tell me that you left with someone who *can't* transfer you?"

"No, he's already transferred me seven times --"

"Then he can transfer you again," she says, as she moves her feet and rubs her arms in an attempt to keep warm.

Andrew steps between us and dutifully carries out her order (thus ending the fight), and when my ass hits the wheelchair she turns to go back inside. But not without muttering, "Good, now I can get back to my dinner."

"I try to do a good thing. I take my friend in the hospital out for a movie and dinner, bring him back, go get somebody whose job it is to have compassion for my friend and what happens? I get a scolding from nurse Ratchet. Fuck!"

61

The Squeaky Wheel

"Exactly!" I rail. "She's toast! I'm going to make sure that bitch never comes near me again."

Andrew wheels me into my room and assists in the unbundling. He bids his goodbye, but commands I assure him he will never have to answer to that person again. I assure him she is terminated as my primary care nurse. I can feel the skills developing.

Andrew leaves. I telephone Annie to discuss the events of the day -- starting with the most recent ones.

"Cut her loose," Annie reacts to the latest exchange with Tina. I promise her I will and go on to the positive events of the day including the fact that -- perhaps for the first time since the surgery -- I felt... normal. Almost. This is one of the rare nights Annie has not come by.

I return to my room and pull the string that is the call light for a nurse. As usual, it is several minutes before someone enters. One of the nurse's aides whom I like and is my age arrives. I tell her I want to talk to Tina. She exits to get her. Minutes later Tina enters as if the previous exchange outside is forgotten or was inconsequential. She is smiling. I'll fix that. "I'm going to the Bahamas tomorrow for 10 days, and I haven't even begun to pack," she says barely looking at me. "I won't get out of here until after eleven, so I won't get home until midnight. The flight leaves at 7 AM, so I guess I won't get more than a nap tonight."

I am tempted to cut her off in the middle of that dispersal of meaningless (to me) information, but now I am glad I heard it all. I scoff in disbelief at her self-absorption, pious pose, and absolute cluelessness in regard to what is about to happen.

"You know," I begin, "my best friend in the world came here today to do me a favor and get me out of here." I see the slight smile begin to leave her face as her eyes narrow and every muscle in her body becomes rigid as she goes into defense mode. "Nobody else has done that. Nobody else has even attempted or suggested that except Annie. So, my friend takes me from here -- something everyone has been encouraging me to do since I got here, including yourself -- transfers me into his car, takes me to a movie, transfers me in and out, takes me to dinner and back here, and you yell at him for it."

"I did not yell at him, besides --"

"No," I say calmly but directly, "you *did* yell at him, and then you came out and yelled at me. I'm sorry if your memory's selective or just plain poor but that's what happened. Now please, I would ask you to wait until I am done before you respond."

"Fine," she says like a child in a manner that says 'ha-ha I spoke.'

"So, my friend takes me out per doctor's and everybody else's orders and my wishes, comes back and asks you to do your job."

"It's not my job to transfer you out of a car!" she snaps.

"Funny, I've seen plenty of other nurses do it, but I'll check with Beverly (the head nurse) as to whether that is in your job description. You're not waiting for me to finish."

She erupts. "You didn't sign out, and I had to tell the *Doctor* I didn't know where you were."

With infinite calmness I say, "So? Do you recall me telling you I asked twice about procedure and was told to leave and have fun? Besides, I don't care if you feel you were embarrassed in front of the *Doctor* because you didn't know where I was. It's not my problem. Before we get into a fucking shouting match let me just say that you are no longer to be my primary care nurse. I'm going to ask Beverly tomorrow to keep any contact with you to an absolute minimum. I will, of course, tell her how rude you were to my friend and me and that the less we see of each other the better. You can talk now."

She simply scoffs. "Fine. I'll see if I can get somebody else to put you to bed tonight." She begins to exit.

"I hope this doesn't bum out your vacation," I call out after her -- unable to help myself and confident this exchange will be packed in her suitcase and taken to the Tropics to torment her. (Customs check: 'Oh, I see you brought along a head-trip. That's going to color your vacation.')

"No you don't," she says accurately. "But I will disappoint you and tell you that I won't think about it again," she lies. She will think about it again, and I will remind her. An acquired skill.

The nurse's aide who went for Tina returns. She asks what I did to piss Tina off. I happily tell her the entire story, beginning with Andrew's arrival at the hospital. When I get to the exchange at the car, her jaw drops. She is disgusted and says that it may not be in the job description, but everyone does it. When I tell of the final exchange she giggles and claps quietly and praises me.

"She was a nurse's aide here before," she says sullenly. "She was a *little* stuck-up then, but I gotta tell you, when she got her RN degree she became God's gift to the patients, the doctors, the other nurses and the nurses' aides became shit." This is the second time I've heard this story, but I enjoy it more now. "We all hate her. I felt sorry for you when I heard she was your primary nurse. Please, please tell Beverly this tomorrow and get somebody else."

I feel vindicated for any possible rudeness and relief that others share my opinion of this woman and are aware of her status as "bitch." As Julie puts me to bed the two of us giggle (maliciously, wrongfully, but gleefully) at the thought of the hauntings that will pass through Tina's thoughts as she lies on the beach.

Shunt #2

Days go by and I have my usual parade of regular and irregular guests. Physical therapy, occupational therapy, recreational therapy and my weekly visits to the useless therapist (Gayland) continue. There is perceived progress in all save the last. My humor emerges. My balance of irreverence and politeness earns points among staff and patients. Annie remains positive as do family and friends. Andrew and his girlfriend Patty are there almost as often as Annie. My dear friends Don and Diane are there almost as often as Andrew and Patty. My father is there every day. He often brings his wife and/or my young half-brothers. Some close friends come and some do not even call. Some not-so-close-friends make regular appearances as touching to me as any visit. Patrick, Darrin or Daniel visit daily. Sometimes one, sometimes all arrive.

One day Pat comes alone. We exchange the usual greetings, and he settles into the chair next to my bed. I begin a conversation but the conversation turns into a monologue by Pat. As Annie once said, "If you're going to call Pat, you need to make sure your afternoon is free." (The applicable adjective might be verbose.) Or, as I once said to Patrick on a walk around the lake when he stopped to talk to a stranger, and we finally began moving again after half an hour, "You could talk to dirt."

He was going on about something else, but the story shifted to Devlin and the fact that the little perfect-smelling miracle was arching his back and making LOUD sounds of pain for the past several days. Kate had brought him to a clinic that prescribed aspirin and sent the two of them home. The unusual behavior continued, and my father's wife suggested Devlin be brought to a pediatrician she recommended.

By now I am very bothered by the fact that I am probably the most captive audience anyone ever had. Shackles could not give the speaker a more enslaved listener. I am about to raise my voice to my brother when his voice trembles and he reaches the point.

"Kate took Devlin to the doctor Roxanne recommended and was immediately referred to a neurologist." My heart breaks. I am so sorry I was about to yell at my brother. "The neurosurgeon came, and immediately he was in surgery." My heart is asunder as tears flow down both cheeks. I am unable to ask questions, but Patrick continues to narrate through the tears.

"They did surgery on him and he should be okay." These are needed words. "He was hydrocephalic -- you remember Karl Kozinski's brother who we always made fun of?"

I nod and the remembrance makes me cry harder. I think children will make fun of me now.

"The surgeon -- Dr. Quaker, John Quaker's father -- you remember John Quaker?"

This question makes me cry even harder. I nod and gasp for breath. John Quaker was a kid my age in my class at my grade school that *everyone* picked on. I bullied him at *least* as much as any other bully. Maybe that's why I'm here now.

"Well, his dad is a neurosurgeon and he did the surgery. Devlin has to stay in the hospital another week."

I bawl and make a sufficient communication to get more information.

"There was water building up in his brain, which was causing him the pain that made him scream and shake his head and arch his back. The doctors went in and put in a shunt --"

There's that fucking word again! Shunt.

"The shunt goes down into his stomach and is curled there for him to grow into. When he gets to be about 12 he'll need another surgery to replace it 'cause he'll outgrow this one."

This can't be happening! I think. But now I think of it in reference to someone else, not to myself.

"The doctors say that the CAT scans all show that they got to it in time and his brain is fine. They don't want him to play baseball or take up boxing, but that will be for his brothers to do," he says, and the tears give way to a smile.

I am regaining my composure and try to express my pain and sympathy when my father enters. "There's too many shunts in this family," I say. My father quickly deciphers the meaning of this, smiles and shoots a glance at Patrick as if to say, 'I thought we weren't going to torture Brian with this yet.'

The Squeaky Wheel

"He's a tough little man," my father says fondly. "Just like his uncle."
"And his dad and grandfather," I add. "I want to go see him."

They say it's not necessary and will be very difficult, but I don't care. I take Metro Mobility to another hospital and find Kate there, constantly there, where she must crawl into the crib to breast-feed him. Devlin looks into my eyes. I communicate that ... it's okay. "The message from God is that you're going to be okay. Do not lose faith. Do not give up. I'm sorry we have to go through this. This world probably doesn't seem like a very nice place now, but it is. I bring you much love."

It has been announced that I should make arrangements to leave Rehab. Annie and I have spent weekends at my new apartment. I have a familial relationship with the owner of my six-unit apartment building and have moved from the third floor to the basement. Annie has moved in and will work as my personal care attendant despite Jim's warning against this. "You're going to blur the lines between girlfriend/fiancée and personal care attendant, and you will be single." I apply for a handicapped-parking placard and for the paratransit system, Metro Mobility, and tediously explain my predicament. Both cards enabling me to utilize such services come back and, emblazoned in black ink on the line describing the duration of the disability, is the word "PERMANENT." Annie and I are repulsed but think that the small-brained peon in the office who used that stamp is unaware of the fact that I will soon be dancing again.

Brian Shaughnessy

The First in a Long Line of Abusive Agency Workers

"By virtue of having acquired a disability you are now entitled to Social Security disability income," Jim says and smiles, checking my reaction. I sneer slightly. I don't want to hear this even from this man.

"You should call the Social Security Administration and make an appointment. You can do it by phone. The sooner you make the phone call the better off you are because they start paying from the date you apply, but they don't pay for a few months at least."

I make the call to the Social Security Administration. I explain my situation and what I am trying to accomplish. The person at the other end quickly cuts me off, informing me I have to be assigned a caseworker. I ask her how to accomplish that. She needs to check the roster, she says, and places me on hold before my next breath, blink or heartbeat. She returns to inform me that Mrs. Nasty will be my case worker and then forwards me to her phone.

"This is Mrs. Nasty," I hear a terse, unfriendly voice say. I can almost see her pointed hat and wart on her nose.

"Hello," I stutter. "I'm Brian Shaughnessy. I'm presently in the Rehabilitation Department of the University of Minnesota Hospital. I recently became disabled," the words catch in my throat, "and I have been instructed to apply for Social Security benefits."

"I can't take your application now!" she screeches.

Dear, God, I think, what manner of miserable human being is this?

"I don't believe I asked you to take the application NOW," I respond. "I guess I'm looking to make an appointment with you."

"Fine." She snaps back. (I wonder if "fine" is in the Social Security Administration's employee handbook as an appropriate response only when used in a tone usually reserved for another four-letter word beginning with the same letter.) I hear her manipulate items on her desk.

"I have Thursday at 1:00. Can you be at our office then?"

"Well, I *am* still in the hospital, and it would be difficult for me to get to your office. I was told we could do this over the phone."

"Just what is your disability?" she asks, obviously bothered.

The Squeaky Wheel

"Quadriplegia."

"I'll call you Thursday at 1:00. Give me the number you can be reached at."

"Well, I'm calling from the patient phone in the Rehabilitation Department of the University of Minnesota Hospital. It is used a lot by many of the patients, so it might be better if I called you."

"No!" She shrieks again, "I have to call you!"

"Fine," I respond, trying to use her same delivery, only turned up a notch. I give her the number. She says she will be sending a copy of the same paperwork she will be filling out and that I MUST read it before she calls so I can answer her questions.

The date is made, paperwork arrives and I open the large manila envelope to find a dearth of incomprehensible information, a multitude of both perfunctory and probing questions and several places to sign the documents. I attempt to read through it -- fearful of Mrs. Nasty's reaction if I have not -- and Annie helps fill in the questions.

Thursday at 1:00 I am perched near the phone awaiting the unpleasant voice, personality and person about to call. I direct other residents of Rehab to the phone at the other end of the hall. All comply, some with a questioning look. "I'm waiting for the Social Security worker to call me," I explain. One of the residents nods and says, "I hope you don't get Mrs. Smith. She's a major bitch. I laugh and respond, "No, I don't have Mrs. Smith, but I think bitchiness is a prerequisite for the job."

The phone rings.

"Oh, my God! She heard me," I say as I maneuver to answer the phone. "Hello, Brian Shaughnessy."

"This is Mrs. Nasty with the Social Security administration calling regarding our appointment. I assume you received the application papers and have them in front of you."

"You assume correctly," I say, knowing this woman has absolutely no sense of humor.

"Fine." There it is again! "Please begin by spelling your name for me. Is there any way you can take me off the speakerphone?"

"Well," I begin, with a sense she can hear my eyes rolling, "as I told you, I am quadriplegic, so holding the phone is exhausting. But let me get a nurse to put the headset on me." I signal a nearby nurse who quickly assists.

"How's that?" I ask, hoping there is just enough sarcasm to make her wonder if I am returning the contempt coming from her end of the line.

"Much better," she says. There is no "thank you." "Now, spell your name for me," she barks crossly, continuing with the standard questions: address, income, occupation, age, employers, duration of employment; names, addresses, and phone numbers of doctors, hospitals, clinics, and institutions that treated applicant; dates of treatment; medications, laboratory and test results, medical records from doctors, therapists, hospitals, clinics, and caseworkers; marital status, dates of prior marriages, alleged medical disability, favorite color, religious background, race, mother's maiden name, siblings, hobbies, sexual preference...

She then moves on to any "assets" the applicant may presently have: savings account, checking account, real estate, life insurance policy, trust, pension plan, railroad retirement benefits, automobile, mobile home, stocks, bonds, gold bullion...

To all of the asset questions I answer "no" and by the end of the interview/interrogation/violation of self I am physically and mentally exhausted. But not too exhausted to react to this woman's final offense.

"If you GET BETTER you won't get this money anymore."

My jaw hits the table, then it clinches, my eyes narrow and the exhaustion disappears as my voice raises and the pace of my speech quickens.

"Listen, *woman*, I don't want the damn money, but I'm going to need income to leave this hospital and survive! You think I would PRETEND this shit? WHEN I 'GET BETTER' I will gladly stop receiving this money to which I am entitled by virtue of working and acquiring a disability at the hands of a doctor! I'll pay it back. Now, since I cannot write it down, you will mail me your supervisor's name so I can dictate a letter to let them know what an abusive lackey you've been."

I could have predicted her response. "Fine. We'll make a determination in 30 to 60 days, at which point you will be informed of our decision." Click.

I tell this story to my father who reacts with a painfully pragmatic analysis. "Brian," he begins, "this is a jaded bureaucrat who *hates* her job. They *train* these people to be nasty. If they don't reach the highest level of nastiness, they aren't allowed to work in the doctor's office and have to take a government job." He mimics a fictitious but based-in-reality medical receptionist. "You want to speak to the DOCTOR!? You can't speak to the DOCTOR! No one speaks to the DOCTOR! I don't even speak to the DOCTOR. Who are you to think you can speak to the DOCTOR!?"

Later, he goes to his car and sobs before driving home.

The Squeaky Wheel

One day in therapy I see the only woman in the Theater Department of the University of Minnesota who uses a wheelchair. I recognize and remember her, and she invites me to lunch where she gives me a pep talk about returning to the Theater Department with a wheelchair.

"I should tell you," she continues in the same voice she has used through her entire monologue, "that I intend to use this in the theater piece that I am writing about disability so you will get to see this on stage."

Fodder. Some loud mouth cripple is turning me into fodder masterbafication -- if you will. The degradation is infinite. She does not ask me if she can; she simply announces she will. I feel violated. I want to pound a stake through her heart.

Brian Shaughnessy

I Have Been Dismissed

My discharge day has come. I am brought up to see the worthless therapist, Gayland, one last time. Although my mood is good, seeing him does not thrill me. The mere fact that I am on my way up there brings about feelings of anger, frustration, suicide, futility and despair.

"You're leaving today," he states simply.

"That's right." I respond tersely.

"You didn't want to leave here in a wheelchair."

"Who would?" I ask incredulously.

He lets out a small laugh. "Well, yes, that's true, but others come to Rehab with the realization that they will probably be leaving in a wheelchair. You, on the other hand, planned on walking out, had a reasonable belief shared by others that that was a possibility and it hasn't happened."

I'm sure he can see how angry I am -- mostly at him -- but also at the situation.

"How do you feel about that?" the archetypal therapist's question.

"It's out of my hands."

He seems taken aback by this statement. "Ok." He is getting up. "I wish you luck." The door is opened. "You'll be coming in for outpatient therapy, so I'll see you in the hallways. I'm here if you need me." I have been dismissed.

I am aghast. The man was unprofessional and rude. The unprofessional part I have come to expect -- he never really seemed competent. But this...?! I return to the floor.

The nurses have a small party for me. My mood is immediately uplifted. We eat cake and exchange pleasantries. My therapists come by -- my real therapists – and, although there is sadness in the air, the mood is very positive. Jim, the quadriplegic attorney who has been a fount of information and assistance, rolls through the door I once entered to get to the locker room to change into my kitchen hospital uniform. He is wearing sunglasses on this bright spring day. I tease him about the sunglasses, which his nurse's aid removes to reveal a horrific black eye. I wince and groan and ask how such a thing could happen.

The Squeaky Wheel

He pulls me aside and quietly tells me that his wheelchair became possessed and without his input went off a curve, dumping him into the street and blackening his eye. I go into my room, which has been emptied of most of my possessions, and one of the male nurses follows me into the room.

"All set to go?" he asks.

"Yup," I respond cheerfully.

"Everything set up at home?"

"Yeah. Annie's waiting for me there and Metro Mobility should be here pretty soon, which means I might be here another night."

Just then Andrew enters and greets me. He asks if I want to join him and his family on a trip to Hong Kong and Mainland China in June. I nearly cry and tell him that, of course, I would like to. "Just get better," he says and leaves. I ask the male nurse if he thinks I could make such a trip. I am, of course, asking if he thinks I will be "better" within a month.

"Yes, of course," comes his enthusiastic answer. Then he shoots me. "You'll have to bring Annie to do your cares. You don't seem too anxious about going home, so that's a good thing. This can be an awful day for some people. You're lucky." There is that fucking word again! "You have a good family, good friends, Annie. A good network. Lots of people don't have that. Doug is leaving today, but I suspect we'll be seeing him again soon."

Doug is the one who broke his neck driving drunk, his 28th DUI. He was despised by patients and staff. They had to vary his therapists who would lose their patience... and their minds.

We wait for the van to take us to our new homes. It was made clear on the floor that the party was for me, even though they included Doug.

"Brian, Doug -- your ride is here," the desk person calls out.

I am handed a grocery bag full of medication. Since coming to Rehab, I have had several urinary tract infections and experienced spasticity that begins in my left hip -- radiates up and down – and causes me to stop everything until it passes or I am medicated. At present I take four to seven pills three times a day. Fistfuls. Yesterday, they injected Phenobarbital into the muscles of my legs to keep these spasms at bay. I will need to return again in a few months for more such injections.

Doug and I head for the van and hugs are exchanged -- some of Doug's grudgingly. This is not the first time I travel on Metro Mobility, and I recognize the driver. He is a large, malodorous man, missing his front teeth, who always looks surly and generally complains about the last passenger he dropped off. He is civil to me and opens the doors to the lift. It is a beautiful spring day and I wear a short-sleeve shirt. He drops the lift and I think it will break off. He then lowers it to the asphalt. I negotiate the platform, and he engages my brakes, laying a strap across my lap (to keep me from rolling off). Next, he operates the controls to lift the platform to vehicle level. He hangs the controls on the door and wedges his large belly through the narrow doors to the vehicle, negotiates the steps and assists me as I back into position on the lift.

Inside the van, four straps are placed on my wheelchair and ratcheted tight. He places a seat belt across my lap and exits to repeat the procedure with Doug.

Annie waits for me in our home. I know my family will call. I get on the van in my manual chair with no possessions besides the cache of drugs. Doug and his new live-in attendant get on with the few possessions he has. He looks terrified. The person who is responsible for his care looks like he is lower functioning than Doug -- borderline mentally retarded.

"Glad to be out of there?" I ask out of sympathy and our common bond.

Doug looks at me, smiles and nods. Uncharacteristically, he does not speak a word for the entire journey. He and his companion exit at their new apartment. I will never see him again.

The Squeaky Wheel

Home Again, Home Again

The driver reenters the van and I begin my journey home. I am going back to the apartment *building* that I lived in before the surgery. When I checked into the hospital I lived on the third floor. Now I live in the basement. There is a separate outside entrance for the basement apartment with six steps to descend, so a lift has been installed for my access. The "lift" is an angle iron cage welded together with another angle iron cage inside that ascends and descends through the wonders of an electrical winch mounted at the top.

It is a gorgeous spring day. I am using a manual chair *sans* armrests. I have good balance, strength and can push my wheelchair throughout the several shopping malls I have visited on recreational therapy trips and with Annie. The driver steers around one of the three lakes in my neighborhood. Although I despise my situation, I am hopeful. There is no doubt I will walk by February 2, 1984 or I will commit suicide. My mind is made up. My thoughts are of spending my first official night in the apartment with Annie.

The driver helps me wheel to the lift at my apartment, which he is impressed with. As I enter the lift and reach for the switch, Annie opens the door.

"Hi Honey," she says, with a bright smile and dancing eyes. I am struck by the fact that this woman really loves me, has stuck by me, has agreed to live with me -- with all the baggage and responsibility that goes with that -- and believes I will walk again.

"Hello," I say -- very aware of the driver standing behind me -- as I descend into the apartment. I can see Don and Diane inside. They have been my friends for seven years and have lived in this building with me for three of them. I helped Diane through a difficult time a few years back, and now they do the same. This is what friends do without expectation or scorekeeping. They are friends in the best sense of the word. They visited often in the hospital and... they called. There are jokes and laughter and general good feelings.

The apartment now has the dark 3M flooring that Jack installed. The walls are white and the windows are far above my head. I can only see tree branches and people's legs as they walk past. Radiator pipes run the distance and a radiator hangs from the ceiling. A four-foot wall divides the kitchen from the other room. A small door in the middle of the room leads to the bedroom.

"We're really glad you're here, Brian," Don says. "We hated to have to see you in the hospital. I think being home, in your neighborhood, with Annie and with us upstairs is really gonna bring you around. You'll be moving back upstairs in no time." Annie and Diane agree.

"I hope so," I respond. "I can tell you right now, I feel much better just being here."

"We're going back upstairs ... don't hesitate to call us if you need anything. Put us on speed dial on that fancy phone, ok?"

'I'll have Annie do it. She's the technology guru here."

Annie and I are alone in my apartment. I have been in the apartment before, having spent some weekends here as part of my transition from the hospital to the community and home. Those weekends gave Annie and me a chance to be alone and also to see others outside of the hospital. Some of the things acquired in the hospital are now in our apartment. This makes me somewhat uncomfortable. But to be here with this woman makes me insanely happy. There is a knock at the door.

It's Mike and Annie from across the hall -- more friends who knew me... before.

"This is so cool!" Across-the-hall Annie shouts. Mike and Annie had moved in while I was in the hospital. Part of that strategy was for them to be here to lend a helping hand when they could.

"I'm going to go get the TV from Target, ok?" my Annie states.

"Oh, God! Yes, do it before I change my mind," I respond.

When I moved out of my parent's house at the age of 18, I did not own a television. For six years I refused to own one. I loved not owning a television. I loved spending the time on books, schoolwork, backgammon, roller-skating, fucking, dancing, walking. I *bragged* about not having a television. Mark, who I lived upstairs with, had brought one into the apartment for a short time. The two of us would sit transfixed, not speaking for hours while watching rubbish. One Saturday morning, as we mindlessly watched cartoons, we looked at each other and agreed this monster had to go. He put it in the dumpster. So it was not so much an intellectual choice not to have a television. Drunks don't keep alcohol in the house, and junkies don't keep junk in the house.

The Squeaky Wheel

But now that I'm not in school, I have been watching someone else's TV when I am home on the weekend and VCRs are becoming ubiquitous. Besides, shut-ins watch a lot of TV.

As I am talking with Mike and Across-the-hall Annie, my Annie's redheaded sister Janice and daughter Carry stop by. Later, siblings and my father visit. My father leaves alone, as he arrived. When he goes to the driveway and enters his car he places his key into the ignition. Then he sobs. He sobs long and hard before he can make the drive home. Tears from a man I never saw cry. He cannot even speak to my siblings about me without tears flowing. I will not know this for years to come.

But now, today, as I tell the story, any tears he sheds are tears of joy.

All clear out of the apartment and Annie and I are now in our home alone. I am alongside the bed so that Annie can transfer me into it when we discover that the condom catheter has broken. My pants, body, cushion and wheelchair are all soaked in urine. "There, there, Honey. Annie's here. She'll take care of everything. It's going to be all right."

She quickly deals with it -- rinsing the pants, spraying the cushion with the showerhead in the bathroom, wiping down the wheelchair and then washing me. As I stare at the ceiling, she soaps red pubic hairs and Willy. She calls my name coyly. I look down to see her holding Willy at FULL attention.

"We can't waste that," I say, and she grins and climbs onto the bed. Moving up my body, she kisses me. We kiss long and hard and often. I kiss her cheek, her nose, her eyes and her forehead. She kisses back. All of my supposedly paralyzed muscles labor, and our breathing is short. Little groans fill the air as we press against each other. My tongue circles her ear, and she makes little gasps as I growl a low growl. I plunge my tongue into her ear. She shrieks and pulls back. Her hair frames her serious face, and dark brown eyes pierce me with a look of fear/love/pain. She falls against my chest and works to lock her fingers with mine. We kiss and writhe against each other as she lowers herself to the place where all this began. She holds it, lingers there and takes it in her mouth. I don't feel that my sensation has been compromised. After some time there, she moves up toward me, kisses me and places her pudenda in my face. My hand strokes her legs and her behind and fingers find their way into openings. In no time a resounding shriek is heard, and she rolls onto her back sweating, exhausted and panting.

Brian Shaughnessy

She looks at me in disbelief and climbs back on me. We are face-to-face and I feel myself entering her slowly as she takes more with each small thrust. With each move she gasps and with one great movement she takes all of me. *Splish*. I am fully inside of her and she is frozen, arching her back with her mouth open. She begins to thrust harder each time, and I thrust back. Apparently, I am succeeding as she squeals, "Oh my God, I didn't know you could do *that*!" We slow and she pulls herself off me and looks at me with love and terror. We say the words at the same time, "I love you."

The next day I take Metro Mobility back to the hospital for two hours of therapy. I am pushing my manual chair all over! I can open the refrigerator and handle necessities to make myself a sandwich, not easy stuff for most quadriplegics. I have strength in my legs that assists Annie in making the transfers. She has a part-time job and starts taking a class to keep some autonomy between us. She helps with the travel to Rehab for therapy on some days. She is adroit at transferring me from the wheelchair to our Honda Accord. This ability never ceases to amaze my brothers. When Annie assists, she moves me into place, removes the armrests and simply grabs me by the buttocks while I hold her around the neck. Then she swiftly and deftly places me into the seat of the car, being careful to guide my head inside. Then she lifts the legs I cannot lift by myself into the car.

My brothers, on the other hand, trying to follow this routine, fail miserably. At family gatherings my relatives gather around to assist, but Annie politely declines and the men stare in amazement at how easily she accomplishes this feat. She is my angel.

My mother has a desk made to accommodate the wheelchair. It is taller and narrower than most desks. The apartment is white throughout with a series of windows in the kitchen and front room. When the building was purchased in 1976 this apartment was a studio. There were storage closets for each of the six units located behind a small clothing closet in the studio. Jack and I ripped these closets out and turned once dirty closets into a bedroom in anticipation of drawing a higher rent. There is one window in this new bedroom. Without this extra room, Annie and I would be camped in the backyard.

The bathroom is tiny, so some minimal work was performed by Jack to allow me to gain entrance. With a shoehorn and some grease, I can get into the bathroom and the shower. Annie and I sometimes use up most of the hot water bathing and boinking.

The Squeaky Wheel

On the Road Again

    I read in the paper of a faith healer holding a tent revival in a large empty lot on Lake Street. I have enough faith to get all quadriplegics walking. I wonder why another human must function as the go-between for miracles. I ask Annie to go, but she has gone before, and she "hates those people" and doesn't want to compromise my chances by bringing... doubt or negativity or contempt or... hate. I ask my brother Darrin who is willing to go.
    The day arrives on time but Darrin arrives late -- as is his custom. "If Dad had ever *once* been on time when we were growing up, we wouldn't be this way now," he says with more sincerity than jocularity. I see Annie roll her eyes. "Oh cut it out," I say, my voice deeper than usual. My brother grins and twitches -- knowing he's been busted. "You're twenty-two years old. It's time to take a little responsibility for yourself. Besides, 'we' are not this way. I hate being late. I hate making other people late." Darrin continues to twitch and flail his arms as he draws closer in a familiar attempt to distract and change the subject. "Besides," I continue, ignoring the antics, "Teri is not late, Pat is rarely late anymore and Mom is *never* late."
    "I'm sorry, were you talking?" he says sarcastically.
    "You guys better go," Annie says, as she opens the door to the lift. I ascend to ground level where Annie meets me and pushes me to the car. My brother has not mastered the technique of transferring into the car. "Why don't you do it and I talk you through it?" she says, and Darrin nods.
    He opens the door of the car and removes the transfer board from the back seat and places it on the hood. He moves me closer to the car and removes the left armrest and footrests from the wheelchair. He looks puzzled. "Lift his left leg high and tuck that board as far under his butt as you can." He does. "But the board's not level with the seat," he says. "It will be," she responds. "Now," she continues, "lift his knees up toward his chest and lock your knees against his calves." He does. "Now slide his

butt down into the seat but watch his head and legs. Darrin looks at Annie as if she's playing a gag on him. She shrugs her shoulders, "You don't want to bang him up, do you?" Darrin begins the process.

"You really don't have to lift. It's all technique and sliding," Annie advises.

Men always are sure that there is lifting involved, whereas women usually master the technique without compromising their backs. Darrin is a man.

Soon we are on our way to the revival. We are directed to park in the dirt lot, and Darrin transfers me out of the car with some difficulty and much dishevelment of my clothing. After some straightening I am rolled across the gravel lot to a patch of grass where a large tent is set up. The two of us enter. The preacher is already speaking. I see a man of about my age in a power wheelchair. As I wonder how I can get to him to ask for details another man approaches. "Are you here for healing?" he asks in a whisper. I nod and he quickly takes me to the right side of the house where a handful of other people are seated. I listen to the preacher.

"We haven't seen too many miracles these past three nights, but we know the Lord is here," he says. Many respond with "hallelujah" or "amen." "Rev. McCarthyist will be out in a few moments for healings and a sermon." I realize this is the "warm-up" preacher. "We want to begin tonight's service with the Lord's Prayer. Please join with me." He and most of the people recite the Lord's Prayer after which Reverend McCarthyist is introduced with music and applause. He is a white preacher in a predominantly black assembly. He recites some scripture and talks about miracles and healings and then moves to the section where I am seated. There is one man ahead of me. The preacher approaches him as the man sways from side to side and smiles.

"G'evenin', Reverend," he says happily. The preacher greets him and asks him if he wants a healing. He responds that he does, very much. The Reverend places his hand on the man's forehead and begins with, "In the name of the Lord..." and ends with, "it is already done."

"It is! It is!" he says. "There's a woman over there in a pink dress who I couldn't see before you put your hand on me. Thank you, Reverend. Thank you."

Reverend McCarthyist approaches me with a sour look. "What is your affliction, son?" He puts his hand on my forehead. I tell him I am quadriplegic and he asks how that came to happen. I explain that it was the result of surgery.

The Squeaky Wheel

"You mean to say a doctor did this to you?" he asks. I nod, beginning to choke. He removes his hand and turns to the congregation.

"We put our faith in doctors and look what happens. Place your faith in the Lord!" The congregation responds.

Reverend McCarthyist again places his hand on my forehead. He begins, "In the name of the Lord..." and we pray fervently, wishing to Jesus that I can show this group, my brothers and sisters in Rehab, the quadriplegic man in this audience and everywhere this miracle. The preacher takes his hand away, stops speaking and walks away without a word.

Initially, I am shocked. I look at Darrin who is also bleary-eyed. Reverend McCarthyist works his way through the dozen people in my section as I wonder if he looked into my soul and saw... sin? Disbelief? Doubt? Satan? Why would he...? What did I...? How can God...? As these and similar questions race through my mind -- unanswered -- the collection plate comes past and the preacher begins his sermon on the evils of communism. I suddenly realize the first man was a plant. A claque, as I learned in my theater history class. The familiar diatribe on Godless communism continues. I wonder if it is the same diatribe on Godless communism I heard delivered by an elderly Catholic priest when I was in high school. Do the denominations share sermons? The refrain begins to come around again.

"Let's go," I say, turning to my brother.

Darrin looks puzzled for a moment and then realization crosses his face, and he nods knowingly and stands. We exit without a word and go to the car where he begins the preparations for the transfer... in silence. The transfer board is put in place and Darrin lifts my knees and locks his and asks, "Ready?"

"Yup."

He begins to muscle and transfer the board under me, but the chair moves. We both forgot to put the brakes on. "Oh, shit... oh, shit... oh shit!" is the increasingly loud mantra he chants as I am slowly lowered to the dirt and gravel. Darrin stands, then stomps and kicks the ground and apologizes amidst a flurry of expletives. "I'm sorry, man. What the fuck are we going to do? What the fuck am I going to do? I can call Annie."

"No, you can't. She's got no way to get here and she'll never let me leave the house again. Either you go and get somebody to help or *we* get me into the car."

He looks toward the canopy half a block and many rows of cars away. "Let's give it a try."

Brian Shaughnessy

He sits me up from behind and moves around in front of me, keeping his hand on my shoulders. He bends my knees so that it looks like I am in a sit-up position. He surveys the car, the area and me as my face is in his crotch. He reaches down and I grab him around the neck while he attempts to raise me and I attempt to push with my legs to get into the car. It's in vain. I hear gospel singing. The sermon is over. The struggling, the cursing, the bruising and the futility finally end with me seated and belted in the passenger side of the car. Darrin gets in on the driver side and slams the door. He's not mad at me. He lights a cigarette and lowers the window. He surveys me as he starts the car and pulls out of the unpaved lot. He shakes his head.
"Jesus."

No Scarecrow Here

Annie and I are engaging in the passion of the week -- cards. The game is unimportant but the diversion is. I can only hold the cards for a short time. We both have seen the cardholders offered by Rehab, but I declined the offer since I was able to hold the cards while in Rehab. I neglected the time factor. Besides, such devices are for cripples. The two of us stack cards against various implements and hold them in place with other various implements. I try slotted implements that fail.

"I know!" shrieks Annie as she runs to the stove and opens the broiler. She removes the tray that causes the unit on the left holding the rack at one of three different heights to lean to the right. It's loose. She places her hand on it, peers inside and removes it easily. She laughs and waives it overhead as she returns to the kitchen table.

"This is going to work," she announces with certainty as she places it on the table, picks up the deck of cards and neatly begins to stack them in one of three rows. She deals with rapture and dances about.

"Wait!" she demands with another realization.

She picks up the empty box of cards and places it under the stove piece, angling it, so that I can see three long rows of cards.

"Wow!" I say smiling and kissing her for her success and ingenuity. The two of us play happily and feverishly. Disability is far away and the joy of simple problem solving has us delighted. There is a knock at the

The Squeaky Wheel

door. Because the world's most obnoxious buzzer did not buzz, we know it is someone who lives in the building. I am fairly certain that it is one or both of my neighbors, Don and Diane.

"Come in," I say happily.

The logic is flawless and Don opens the door. "Do you guys have any basil?" he asks as he enters and stares at my cardholder.

"No," I say dryly, "but I have alternative leafy substances."

"That won't achieve the same results in my spaghetti, but thank you," he says and crosses from the door to the kitchen table. Don, very tall, stands over us and looks down at my cards and the device.

"What the hell is that?" he asks as I turn and look up his nose and at his mystified eyes.

"It's from the stove -- the broiler," Annie says.

Don silently turns and looks at the stove. He walks over to it and pulls the broiler drawer out and views the missing pieces. He closes the broiler, walks back to the table and examines the cardholder.

"Wow," he says with more enthusiasm than we had. "You figured that out?" I point to Annie, but before either of us can speak, he continues, "It would *really* be awful to be *stupid* and in a wheelchair, huh?"

Brian Shaughnessy

Nope, I'm Fine Right Here

Don and Diane bring a tape of Laurie Anderson. It is her newest release, "Mr. Heartbreak," and we play it often. I like it particularly because on one of the tracks a favorite author, William Burroughs, narrates. I know Anderson's reputation; that she is more than a musician.

We see in one of the weekly free newspapers that Laurie Anderson will be coming in concert. "Hey, Annie, shall we go?"

"Yes," is her immediate and enthusiastic response.

The tickets are purchased, plans are made and the day of the performance arrives. Annie is sick. She is not just cold sick -- she is polar bear white, moving at one-quarter speed, eyes barely open, moaning as she shuffles to the bathroom ... sick. "You're going to have to find somebody else to go to the show," she says with pleading eyes. I know she is worried that I will whine about having somebody else "try" to transfer me into the car.

I laugh as her eyes still plead. "Honey, not even *Brian* could be that big a prick as to make you schlep him in and out of the car and push him around as *you* try to endure what should be a good show. It doesn't matter how good the show is; you'll be miserable. I'm sorry you're miserable. I don't wanna make you any more miserable, so I'll call Pat and see if he wants to go. Okay?"

She smiles sheepishly and nods with relief. She hugs me and immediately shuffles from the kitchen back to the bedroom. I hear her groan as she hits the bed. I giggle as I dial my brother.

"Bueno," comes his oft-uttered telephone greeting.

"Do you want to go see Laurie Anderson tonight?"

"Wow! Of course I *want* to go... The question is, *can* I go. Let me think, no work tonight... no class... Kate is... let me call Kate at the bank and see if this is going to work out. What time is the concert?"

I look at the tickets on the table in front of me. They read 7:30. "The concert starts at seven," I say taking into account the Shaughnessy penchant for tardiness.

"Seven?" my brother says taking into account my penchant for giving inaccurate and earlier times. "Why so early?"

83

The Squeaky Wheel

"Because she's a classical violinist. They need to get to bed early."

"All right. Let me call Kate and get back to you."

Soon Pat announces that he is able to attend the concert, and much later that day he arrives (too late to make a 7:00 performance) to take us to the show. He enters the apartment through the side door and asks if I'm ready to leave.

"Have been for awhile," I say dryly.

Annie enters the room. "Hi, Annie," Pat says before looking at her. "I don't --" He sees her. "Oh, no, you *are* sick. I'm sorry, I thought you were just afraid." This is an old joke but Annie is hardly in the mood.

"That's right, Pat," she says, as I do the dance to get on the lift and up to street level. "I'm afraid to get out of this apartment, go see a great show and dance. Aah!" She flexes some acting muscles, "Please, please, please don't make me go out and have fun!" Patrick laughs and scowls. "See you guys later," she says, as she turns to go back to bed. She looks quickly at the kitchen table and notices the tickets there. "You might need these," she says as she hands them to Pat. I see Pat examining the tickets.

"Seven o'clock, huh?" He looks at me with mock disgust and genuine amusement.

"If we don't leave now we won't make a 7:30 show!" I say defensively. He laughs at the truth of this as we leave and he pushes me to the car.

The transfer is accomplished with the usual grunts, groans, dishevelment, neck-stretching, minor bruises and cursing that only Annie can avoid. We park in a lot across from the concert venue. Pat removes the chair and the cushion and the transfer board from the back of the Honda Accord. He brings them to the side of the car and positions all for transfer. He has talked constantly, as is his custom, since leaving the apartment. In no time I am lying on the asphalt. He struggles futilely to get me into the wheelchair. I remain silent, sad and wondering why -- or how -- I ever left the apartment.

"Oh, shit," he says genuinely pained. "What do I do now?"

"Enlist a volunteer," I say tersely.

He looks around and asks the usual question for this situation. "How does *Annie* do it? I guess I need to smoke and be a girl."

"You are a girl!" I blast. "Now *go* get some help!"

He leaves my view and a short, stocky woman in a gas station uniform appears. "Need some help?"

Brian Shaughnessy

The first instinct is to utter the words, 'Nope, I'm fine just where I am. Thanks anyway." But it is fleeting, and I acknowledge a need for assistance and my gratefulness to the Samaritan for offering. She reaches under me and lifts me like a baby, consciously trying not to get the uniform grime on me. I tell her my brother is nearby to help, and she may hurt her back trying to lift me that way.

"Nah," she says, and I am in the wheelchair. She is attaching the footrests as Pat returns with a stranger. He is mystified. He incredulously asks if she got me into the chair by herself. She acknowledges the fact monosyllabically and nonchalantly as I nod. Pat dismisses the stranger and turns to the Samaritan, thanking her profusely. He tries to hand her a ten-dollar bill. Unsurprisingly, she refuses, asks if I am okay, says, "Goodbye -- enjoy the concert," and disappears.

He pushes me to the Orpheum Theatre and I am inside before the music begins.

The concert is great.

Patrick takes me on our first outing together since he put me on the pavement of the parking lot at the concert. We go to see a movie, *Eddie and the Cruisers* -- an anemic little tale combining the Jim Morrison story with Bruce Springsteen elements to create a tepid script with weak actors but GREAT music.

Halfway into the movie I smell... feces. It's an early movie, and Annie is working, and I still must get back in the car and home. But this in no way colors my review of the movie. After the movie Pat agrees with this review -- including the music. He also disapproves of their likening the main character to Bruce Springsteen. In one scene The Cruisers are playing in Springfield. Throughout the song we see Eddie's head right next to a sign that reads, "Spring," for the obtuse and those who have no tolerance for subtleness.

"I shit in my pants," I say to Pat before we exit the multi-mega-omni-poly-plex.

"You did?" Pat says in disbelief but clearly feeling my pain and embarrassment. "How do you know?"

"I knew during the movie, didn't you? You were sitting right next to me."

He didn't know. He didn't smell it. The two of us travel sullenly and silently to my apartment. Once inside he asks what's next. As I am instructing him to put on some latex gloves Annie comes home early from

85

The Squeaky Wheel

work. She sees tears in my eyes and immediately asks what's wrong. I tell her I defecated.

She scoffs. "Is that all?"

I point out to her that it appears to be messy and this is the first time Pat has been involved. He points out to me that he has a three-month-old at home, so he often deals in this element. The two of them transfer me to the bed where it is discovered that there is shit from below my knees to the small of my back. A new record. I always want to die during this procedure. They remove my soiled clothes, clean me and set me up for the night. Some jokes are made during all of this, and then Pat goes home to his wife and child.

"How was the movie?" Annie asks.

As I lay in bed on my back, staring at the ceiling, finding it difficult to breathe because I am pressed under so much self-pity, I respond, "Shitty."

Annie laughs. Then I do.

One day, Andrew and I go fishing. "Let's go casting," he announces in my apartment with the zeal of someone who has just announced he is taking me to Jupiter. I agree, although fishing is only above bowling as a downer pastime for me. But I have had a gun pointed at me on three separate occasions. Each time Andrew was present.

"Sorry, Andrew, I can't hang out with you any more. You're a gun magnet."

"No, its you," he insists.

Andrew transfers me to the car and we drive to Lake Minnetonka. He pushes the wheelchair and me out onto a dock where I play Huckleberry Finn to his Tom Sawyer. I can cast, but he can cast farther. I land two fish. He's not getting a nibble.

"All right, Brian, this is unacceptable," he says regarding the tally.

"I got you beat sitting down," I taunt him.

"I'm going to Hong Kong and China next week," he reminds me.

"That's right" I am happy for his sojourn but disappointed I won't be accompanying him.

"For the first time in my life, I won't be a minority," he says with glee.

Andrew's is the only Chinese family in the neighborhood. They left Hong Kong for the frozen pastures of Minnesota when Andrew was five. I've witnessed discrimination against him -- that is where one of the guns came from. I am happy that he will be with other like individuals but know that the likeness will end when he crosses from Hong Kong into third world China.

My father has done more than a week's worth of billable hours preparing documents, researching and other lawyerly duties in the case of Brian Shaughnessy v. Dr. Liar. He is trying to convince the top malpractice attorney in Minnesota to take the case. I take Metro Mobility to the malpractice attorney's office, where I meet my father. I am introduced to this shyster my father speaks highly of, but who has not yet agreed to represent me. He is a tall, narrow man with brown hair, honest eyes and an expensive wardrobe.
"What can I tell you, counselor?" I ask.
"You can tell me how I can win this case," he says.
I tell him that I was not informed of the risks -- if I had been I would have informed my father or someone -- and that the son of a bitch changed the charts afterward. We review the facts and leave the office within half an hour. I ask my father why *he* doesn't take the case.
"I can't," is his simple response, but within those words I know that emotionally it will kill him, that he is precluded by the canons of the bar and that I have a better lawyer *for this area* than he is. I understand. I tell Annie of this lawyer's uncertainty. In a few days her mother sends another attorney to our apartment to garner information. Annie's mother's lawyer friend shows up and we talk.
"So, " he says, looking not at me but beyond me, "if I were to take a cigarette and put it out on your leg -- which I would never do -- you wouldn't be able to feel it?"
"Suffice it to say I would be lucky to feel ten percent of it," I say and wonder why I use the word "lucky."
The lawyer nods painfully and thoughtfully, thinking his lawyerly thoughts.
"I think we have enough," he announces, gesturing toward the wheelchair and me. "I'm sure we can get you something for this."
It won't be enough, I think. I never hear from him again.

When I sleep, at home, on our king-size waterbed I can flip from my right side to my left side at will. This lowers me in the bed and I can use my arms to pull myself back up toward the head of the bed and the pillow.
Annie brings home an electric can opener. With this, I can remove a can of frozen juice from the freezer, open it, pour it into a pitcher, add the

The Squeaky Wheel

water and make my own juice. I can take the ingredients out of the refrigerator and make a sandwich.

Since Annie doesn't drink, she moves several bottles of liquor that Darrin and I brought back from Mexico to the top of the cupboard.

"Annie, did you put those bottles up that high so I couldn't get to them?" I ask.

She grins a sheepish grin. "Yes."

"It won't work," I announce, "because I have friends in high places."

She goes off to work and after several hours I decide to try to transfer to the couch on my own. I think it all through and place the phone on the edge of the couch in case I fall down. I then remove the armrests and footrests from the wheelchair. If I am unsuccessful I will only be lying on the floor for an hour or two. I place the transfer board under my ass, one arm on the couch and the other on a wheel of the wheelchair and begin a move I have done many times in therapy. The couch, however, is much lower than my wheelchair and the mats in the physical therapy gym. My legs get crossed underneath me and I find my face planted in one of the sofa cushions. I water the couch with my tears. I scream and scream until a neighbor comes and helps me onto the sofa.

What Happened to You?

Everyone who uses a wheelchair gets asked this question. It gets asked far too often. It is an inappropriate question that the able-bodied are fascinated with. Perfect strangers (actually, this question makes them rather imperfect) will see me and struggle to get through a crowded restaurant or grocery store or whatever to come up and ask... that question.

Brian Shaughnessy

The Unthinkable Horror

My life proceeds fairly well. I rarely think of suicide. I have my friends who remain ... true friends. My family comes often. Annie is positive and marriage is occasionally discussed. Sex is great. I move more and accomplish more at physical therapy and occupational therapy. I stand at the parallel bars and I stand in the standing frame -- a contraption that holds my feet, knees and buttocks in place to allow me to stand. I left the hospital in May, continue with small victories through June, and then in July I go deeper into hell than I thought was possible. I don't remember when, don't remember how long I denied it, but I do know I told Annie first. I am getting more numbness in my right arm.

It is a jovial evening, watching a video, playing Trivial Pursuit (it has just hit the market and it is all the rage) and I say her name.

"Annie?"

"What?"

The tears are already flowing. It is amazing that I was able to say two syllables without bawling uncontrollably. I try to speak but only gasps and squeals come out.

"Honey, what the hell is going on? It's ok."

"No, I don't think it is," I respond, and am unable to speak again.

"Calm down, baby. There, there. Annie's here. Everything is going to be just fine." It is our standard exchange for these far too frequent occurrences.

Slowly, I regain some composure. "I'm getting more numbness," I blurt out and resume sobbing.

"What do you mean?" she asks, as her face turns from supportive and caring to terrified disbelief.

I explain there is more numbness in my right arm. I show her how before it had traveled from the thumb and first finger inside of my arm, to my shoulder, and now it has spread to other fingers and to the rest of my arm.

"How long has this been going on?" she asks. A single diamond tear forms in her right eye and rolls down her face.

"I don't know," I respond. "About a week, I guess."

"You're sure?" she asks. Denial. More diamonds drop.

The Squeaky Wheel

I laugh and sob. "Yes, unfortunately this is not something I would lie about." Now she laughs and sobs.

"This is so unfair, " she rages. Anger. "I don't know *who* I am more mad at, the doctors or God. How much does one human being have to go through?"

Actually, I am thinking, it's more than one human being going through it. She comes to me and sits in my lap, puts her arms around my shoulders, places her head where my neck meets my shoulder, and we both sob.

Suddenly there are two knocks at the door (the signature knock of my brother Pat) and he enters singing a Bruce Springsteen song loudly. He sees the image.

"What happened?" His mood changes in an instant, and I can already see his eyes start to well.

As I explain the situation to him, his eyes widen and he lets out a gasp of disgust and disbelief. The tears follow. He questions it also. We're beyond saying or thinking 'everything will be fine,' or any words to that effect.

"Why the hell does this happen to you? Nobody has worked harder, and there are lots of drug addicts and shit out there who deserve *this*. Why can't this happen to one of them?" Patrick asks. Bargaining.

These are three faces of depression. There will be no acceptance.

Carol, Jackie and Dr. Brock

The next day I go in for therapy. "Are you actually getting a tan?" Carol asks.

"Maybe, but I doubt it. I don't tan; I burn." I want to ease into this issue slowly. We go through much of my routine and before we set off to the parallel bars to stand, I say, "Have you seen Dr. Brock today?"

"No, but I know he's around. You're looking for him?"

"Sort of."

"He's not in trouble is he?" she asks jokingly but her radar is on.

"No." I wonder if she heard my voice crack right there.

"What's up?"

Now, here is yet another person who I have come to love who is going to be affected by this. Annie was jealous of this woman and knew there was no reason to be (thank God). The nurses and therapists do a lot for the people at Rehab, whereas the family does not have the skills. It frustrates them. The emotions can come out twisted in a crisis. We snap at our allies and befriend the enemy. All three of us know that if Annie was not in the picture... the possibility loomed for Brian and Carol. Anyone who has worked at this place can tell stories of nurses and therapists involved with and/or marrying patients. I will live the experience... later.

I look her straight in her strong brown eyes, determined not to cry, and try to be as detached as possible from my surreal reality. She listens intently. Her profession has taught her the strength in her face. But I see her strong brown eyes flicker -- nothing more.

"Let me give him a page now." I am lying on the mat after a series of exercises. "We'll go to the parallel bars after, ok?"

I nod and watch the activities of the room -- slightly numb, in disbelief that this is happening. Experience tells me that Carol is gone longer than it takes to page Dr. Brock. She comes back and the strong brown eyes are red.

"Just what the hell did the doctor tell you when you had that surgery?" she asks. *Now* her voice is cracking.

The Squeaky Wheel

I explain it again. How many times now? I have not yet learned the skill of telling strangers it's not any of their business, and this is somebody I care about, so I explain... again.

"Surgery was supposed to take away the numbness you had, right?" She is angry.

I tell her that was my understanding, although one of the medical students looked askance when asked if that would be a result of the surgery. Carol gets called over the intercom.

"That's probably Dr. Brock," she says. "I'll go tell him to come up."

She does. The doctor appears. Dr. Brock is a resident in the physiatry field and an incredibly nice guy. The head doc in this department is a jock. I get the feeling head doc's looking for a gig with the NFL -- ever aware of my own cynicism. No jock gig for Dr. Brock. He's out to practice real medicine.

I explain the situation to him. He says, "We need to get you over to Neurology for tests. I'll set it up for tomorrow."

I go home in disbelief and confusion. The night is long.

I go back the next day. Over the next few days doctors perform the same battery of tests they did before; injecting ink into my spinal canal, CT scans, etc.

After these tests I must speak with Dr Liar. I hate this man. I tell one of the nurses that I want to deal with the head of neurosurgery, Dr. Chung. Yet another doctor, possibly a radiologist, explains that when they did the first surgery, it allowed a "pocket" to open up in my spinal cord, a "pocket" that is moving up to my brain. Unless they do surgery again... I WILL DIE.

I think, "Big, deal. What makes you think I don't want to die before I would let you chop into me again?"

I tell my family. I call my mother. She loses her mind. She will be on the next flight. My father remains immobile and feigns a hopeful outlook. I know he is broken. I don't want to tell my friends. The tests continue. We visit the doctor who performed Devlin's surgery for a second opinion that confirms the first. He is the father of a classmate I used to taunt mercilessly in grade school. Devlin is fine now and contentedly sucks his two middle fingers rather than his thumb. Other than that, he is a normal child. I feel forced to be dealing with Dr. Liar and the usual plethora of medical personnel. I try to converse only with the head neurosurgeon, Dr. Chung, who Devlin's neurosurgeon recommends for this surgery. "He taught me," comes the recommendation. Devlin's doctor won't touch me because he has no experience with my rare condition.

"I have gone over the surgery in my mind a hundred times," Dr. Liar begins. (I ponder it that many times in a day.) "Nothing went wrong procedurally in that surgery," he continues. "Do you want me to perform this surgery?"

This fucker is serious. "Actually," I begin calmly, not feeling I have the right to say this, "I don't want to be talking to you now. I want Dr. Chung to perform this surgery." Dr. Liar looks only slightly put off, nods and beats a hasty retreat. I tell my mother of this, and she goes looking for a hammer and a stake to drive through his heart. She has begged me not to have the surgery and to just come to New Mexico where I anticipated going... soon.

"If I don't have the surgery I will die." Mom points out that she doesn't believe Dr. Brock wants me to have the surgery there. "He just shook his head through the whole discussion of it ..." I tell her Dr. Liar is to be nowhere near when the operation takes place. It does not comfort her.

The day before the surgery, at home with Annie (who sleeps), and my father and brother, I say, "Look, if I come out of this surgery and can't breathe on my own or feed myself, I don't want to live. "

For the first time in my life, I see my father cry. I recall his brother's protracted death when I was very young. My mother said to stay out of their bedroom, but I entered, where my father was in bed with his eyes closed. A profound sadness hung in the air. The same dense air hung in the room when his father died soon after. Today, with the same heavy air hanging in this room, he begs me not to give up and to stop talking this way.

"You have never talked this way, even when you were first hit by the car, and you can't start now." Patrick cannot speak for the tears.

My contact with my former roommate/childhood friend has been virtually nonexistent. He came once during my stay at Rehab, but did not call. He would leave my mail in a box outside his/our apartment for Annie or my father to bring to me. My birthday passed days ago and his is in a few days. Annually, we had a party to celebrate both birthdays. He has a new roommate upstairs and has announced, "We" (he and I) will be having a birthday party this night. He is unaware that I am having surgery the next day.

The Squeaky Wheel

Constant, unending, incurable hiccups have accompanied the new numbness, and they bother Annie more than me. We have tried all of the remedies for hiccups. As I sit still in the wheelchair watching a video she grabs the chair and yanks it backward. I am frightened and then I hiccup. Friends stop by for the party (unaware of the pending second surgery), and family members arrive to wish me well the next day. Andrew is back from China where he was stared at more than I would be -- even if I levitated. The people from the province could not understand Chinese wearing American clothing, only speaking Cantonese or English, and not smelling like a day's worth of work. He does not know of the surgery tomorrow and demands that Annie and I accompany him to the festivities in the back. Before I ascend the lift, Darrin appears at the window Annie sits beneath. He moos.

Annie looks at me terrified and says to all, "Did anyone just hear mooing?" All laugh as Darrin screams through the screen, "Ah, there are cows outside! They're grazing on the lawn! Make them stop before somebody gets hurt!" We all exit with tears of laughter and spend a few minutes outside where the mosquitoes are devouring everyone. On the way back into the apartment Andrew comments about a mammoth bite on my neck. I cannot feel it and begin to sob.

Andrew looks shocked. "It's not that bad!" he says. Annie tells him my condition is deteriorating, and I must return for surgery the next day. He breaks in two.

The day comes. My mother asks me to wear a family ring. I do. I go in for the surgery. 99, 98, 97... I wake up from the surgery and they tell me that they didn't do much. They say, "We opened the back of your skull, a craniotomy, and we didn't see anything ..." Ha, ha, ha. "... At least not what was on the films. So then we opened up the back of your neck -- a laminectomy. The spinal canal looked fine, so all we did was close you up."

Surgery was eight hours -- again. I say, "So you opened the back of my skull and my neck and let me spend eight hours on the table for nothing?" And they ask..."What was our choice, Brian?"

Annie comes in, but when she hears that all was for nothing she leaves, reciting one of her mantras, "I hate people." My friend Diane is on a long-planned trip to the Soviet Union and trying to contact her husband to get information. He has been trying to call the hospital to get information. They will not yet even tell him if I am alive. My father comes in. I ask for water. He's in good spirits. I ask for water, and the nurse is a bitch. I'm still asking for water, and the nurse is not giving me water.

My father is laughing and saying, "Do you remember what you were asking for after the last surgery?" And I say, "Of course I do. I was asking for blankets because I was freezing. As cold as I was then is how thirsty I am now." My father laughs and insists they bring water now. He then goes to his car and sobs.

I am moved to Recovery. My mother is there every day. Annie is there every day, as she has been all along. Ultimately, they move me from the recovery room to post-op. The doctors tell me I can be moved to Rehab whenever I want and can then stay there until I am ready to go home. In other words, we don't know what happened, and we don't know what will happen. We're not even going to pretend anymore.

I am on Demerol for the most profound pain I have ever experienced... yet. They give it every four hours, but the pain returns every three and one half hours. Inconceivable pain shoots through my head and body. My mother performs a scene from "Terms of Endearment" for the nurses. ("It's time for his shot!") I cannot be friendly with my mother, Annie, my family or other visitors. I'm sick, in pain and doped up. One day, Andrew and Betty visit and instead of saying hello, I throw up.

The Squeaky Wheel

Demerol Dreams -- Installment 1

The Demerol shots can be administered every four hours but rarely are. I have asked the nurses to be punctual with the medication, and although I am ready to press the adapted call light at three hours 59 minutes and 59 seconds, they never respond quickly. There are many other patients. The Demerol does not *just* alleviate the pain. I vividly recall the nurses being long overdue, in intense pain and my mother in the room. She ventures out to see that there are three nurses at the station seated and eating while the lights above three rooms are blinking. Eventually an enormous black nurse with a Billy D. Williams mustache enters, grunts, rolls me on my side, jabs a needle in my ass and exits. The room quickly fades and my eyes close. I wake up -- seemingly minutes later -- and see my mother seated by the side of my bed.

"I love you, Mom," I say with a self-perceived deadly seriousness. She lowers her book and turns away in laughter.

"No, I mean it," I say with seeming earnest and infinite sincerity. She explodes with laughter and nods and says, "I know, Honey."

Through my altered perceptions I realize I must sound like a sit-com drunk. I fall back to sleep.

Andrew and Betty are on double hospital duty because one of Betty's closest friends has been diagnosed with leukemia and is in the University of Minnesota Hospital enduring the ravages of radiation and chemotherapy.

With Demerol, it is hard to decipher reality from the surreal. Betty enters one time with a sandwich, and I ask her if she was just in the room. She says she was not. I explain to her that -- by my perceptions -- she had come in the room earlier with a brother or cousin. This relative brought a banjo with him. He then proceeded to remove the banjo from the case and play some of the great banjo songs of all time. Thoughtful as this may have been, it was not what any individual who has just had the back of his skull cracked open wants to hear. But for some muddied reason I am unable to communicate this to the fellow -- or else he didn't care. After a rousing renovation of "Oh, Susannah" "Foggy Mountain Breakdown" and "Dixie," this assailant moved from the far corner of the room to alongside my head. He sat with his rump on the back of the chair and his feet in the seat. From this position the banjo was next to my ear, and the performer leaned over the banjo and the bed to sing directly into my ear. I thrashed my head and made puffing sounds in an attempt to make him go away, but he only sang and played on -- as if Earl Scruggs and Lex Luther had been united into an unwanted, evil, picking entity.

Betty laughs at this story and assures me she has no banjo playing relations. "How could you even think that was real?"

"Well, after *he* moved next to my head, *you* announced you were going to get a sandwich."

The next Demerol dream is not nearly so subject to actuality. It is in 3-D Technicolor, but as I transfer from the uncertain dividing line between waking and sleeping, the characters I recall are considerably less likely to be more actual than a banjo-playing brother.

In this saga my brother Patrick, my father and I go to look at a potential investment duplex in rural Wisconsin. It was a house my father had seen advertised and I thought was worthy. Patrick concurred. The three of us walk into the house, and my father's first comment is that the house is "a piece of shit." After this opinion is offered, my brother Darrin arrives. "Can we make this quick?" he asks, "because the starter in my car is going and I had to leave it running." As we look around the house, we find ourselves in a large kitchen. Although the sons see the potential in the house, our father only sees a dilapidated old farmhouse. Suddenly, a pudgy human-looking creature with a prehensile forehead, Flintstones garb, scraggly hair and a deer-like rack of horns protruding from his head enters through the side door, squats on his haunches and begins sniffing my brother Darrin. The creature is behind Darrin, who cannot see it.

My father immediately rushes toward the creature, but is unable to negotiate the rack of the creature to attack and defend. Just then I spot a wooden phallus (Freud, anyone?) on the stove, and hurl it at the creature. It strikes the creature in the head, and he stands and reels about. As this wooden item strikes the creature's head, a VERY tall, incredibly muscular "man" enters through another door. He has wings that protrude from the side of his head -- Mars-like. He wears only a small suede breechcloth.

"I need to know who threw this," he demands as he picks up... the implement.

"I did," my father and I say. At the same time Darrin sees these bizarre creatures for the first time.

"I see," says the Mars-like creature, as the horned creature sniffs everyone and everything in the room -- looking foolish, dangerous and prehistoric. "You know," the tall creature continues as the other squats, "I

The Squeaky Wheel

abhor liars." He then goes on to explain why and demands that the person who *actually* threw the item carve him another one and return in one week, or the horned creature will impale Darrin. He makes a final clever comment, tucks the phallus into his breechcloth, admires it and exits through the same door he entered.

The horned creature clears his throat and stands upright for the first time. He speaks in a British accent. I have no recollection of exactly what he said other than it was moral, appropriate and -- try as he might -- NOT very funny. He then exits through another door.

The four of us are left to ponder this, and my father suggests a hasty departure.

"We can't," Darrin says.

"Why not?" all ask.

"I'm out of gas."

I share this story with the people I am in contact with -- doctors, friends, family, therapists -- and most try to analyze it. (Please don't.) Those who do not know Darrin all make some sense of each aspect of this story but inevitably comment, "But that thing *sniffing* your brother..."

They don't know that Darrin moos and does not go through a day without a reference to sniffing or calling someone "Sniffy."

They start weaning me off the Demerol and replacing it with codeine, which only makes me nauseous. Annie comes nightly and has brought flowers in a pasta container for a vase. She also brings a framed photograph I took from an airplane in Mexico that is a rectangle of a rainbow floating in a cloud. She brings many handsome gifts; one nurse comments about "my nice things" but never acknowledges Annie's existence. It infuriates us. One night Annie brings cocaine in for the first time since the surgery and we make out and talk endlessly.

"You're finally back to being Brian. Up until today I would walk through that door, and you would look at me like you hated me," she says. I try to object. "I'm going to bring this every night until we're broke." She brings it many nights, but my mother talks to Jim, a lawyer not a doctor, about the nausea and the lack of progress, and he suggests I be taken off the useless codeine. This works and I am finally moved to Rehab where I will soon begin working with a new therapist. Carol is leaving for the Craig Institute in Denver.

There are new people with different wheelchairs on Rehab. I hate this place, and although I have lost much function, I soon go home. I can no longer push the manual wheelchair, so we get a lightweight wheelchair, which helps little. I return daily for outpatient therapy, and we do some of the exercises I was doing before. I have not regained my former level of function. I cannot pick up a can of soda anymore. I cannot pick up a glass. I cannot write. I need a straw. This is infuriating. In order to eat popcorn, I have to pick up the bowl and put it up to my face. I can't believe I have backslid to this. I had thrown away the writing splint Jackie had made me because it wasn't needed. Now, I can no longer flip over at night, and when I wake Annie to help me, she snaps and huffs and puffs. My hands have contracted, so I can no longer use the can opener. Sex becomes only a box checked on forms.

The Squeaky Wheel

That Sound

I am bathed, defiled, dressed, swallow a fist-full of pills, transferred to the wheelchair and fed. I am at the kitchen table engaged in my daily routine of reading the newspaper. Turning the pages has become more difficult since the second surgery. My ability to take a page between finger and thumb, and pinch it to make sure I am only turning one page, is gone. I remember back to when I figured out this practice -- not so very long ago -- and how this was a great feeling of accomplishment, and the certainty that I was healing. Now, because I am unable to extend my fingers, and they have contracted into a permanent fist, I must lick the knuckles of my first two fingers and push the lower corner of the page until I get under it, so that I can flip it to the next page.

Annie readies herself for departure -- she's going grocery shopping. She asks if I am okay and makes sure I have a large container of water. She kisses me and orders me to remember that she loves me and will return. The door slams. I read a few articles, turn a few pages and am wracked by a grand mal spasm. I fall forward in slow motion. My upper back gives up contact with the back of the wheelchair, my head moves forward and down, and soon my chest comes into contact with the table... followed by my head. It is, in fact, such a slow process that there is no pain, but I can't get back up on my own.

As soon as I realize what has happened I begin to whimper and sob. I cry out for help. I cry out for Annie. I cry out for Don and Diane. I cry out for my mom. I cry out for God. I cry out. I cry. I ask Jesus how he could let this happen to anyone. I smell the paper and the ink. Sometimes, I taste it. Finally, I resign myself to the fact that eventually Annie will return, and I will sit back up. Of course this means that she will find me in this predicament, and I hate myself for that. I have no idea how long I remain like this because I cannot see the clock -- only the water left for me, the table, a few words of the newspaper and the sink against the wall.

I hear the back door of the apartment building open. I pay close attention to see if the necessary next sound in the sequence is heard to indicate Annie's return. I hear footsteps *descend* the stairs -- the right sound -- and am at once relieved and saddened she must find me this way. I remain quiet as the door opens and someone enters. There is a moment of non-realization as one grocery bag is set down. The next one hits the floor contemporaneously with the sound a woman makes when she sees someone she cares about suffering.

"Ooohhwwha!" She says as I hear her rush toward me and then push me back up. She holds me silently for some time. I hear her tears. Her face comes away from my neck and she asks, "How long have you been this way?"

"Not long," I lie.

"I'm so sorry," she says, and as she focuses on my face begins to laugh. "You know, if I were to --" she runs out of the kitchen and reenters with something in her hand. "… hold a mirror up to your face, I could …" She holds up a hand mirror, "… read the paper."

I look at the familiar reflection and see, through the freckles, clearly printed text lifted from the paper. The two of us laugh and cry deliriously.

The Squeaky Wheel

You Haven't Been Quadriplegic Very Long, Right?

I ride Metro Mobility on one of the endless trips to Oz and back -- although I am merely attempting to return home from therapy. It is one of the new, larger vans, which carries even more individuals for longer rides, which means I am picked up and arrive at my destination even later than I do with the smaller vans. Across from me in the van is a Caucasian woman, about my age, glasses, medium length brown hair, a manual wheelchair (although she has quadriplegia) and a diaphragm-sized button, which reads, "Slow Lovers Last Longer." "Kook," is my initial and opinionated thought when I read the button. When I glance at the button the second time I think, "horny kook."

Also on the van are a skeleton-thin, Caucasian male, in his mid-30s with quadriplegia; a LARGE Caucasian man with THICK glasses, dark hair and a powerful looking electric wheelchair; a blind elderly woman and two other riders. I look around the van and know that with this many individual entities of biomass onboard, I may never get home. The sense of surrealism is as thick as fog. I maintain a stony silence, acknowledging the others only with a nod.

Button-woman talks to everyone about anything and nothing. Eventually she looks straight into my silent face and says, "You haven't been a quad very long, have you?"

My initial reaction is rage, and the flames burn in my brown eyes. I shake my head, not wishing this conversation to continue but knowing from her behavior so far that I won't get my wish.

"I can tell. I can always tell. You have the look. How long since your injury?"

Although I usually give this information freely and without reticence to other individuals with the same plight, she is the wrong person at the wrong time in the wrong place. Unfortunately, I have not yet developed the skills to tell Button-woman to piss-off.

The abacus in my mind adds up the time. "Nine months, one-week and three days," I answer with an accuracy and tone to seal her lips or send her conversation back to one of the other riders.

"Oh-ho-ho-ho," Button-woman says with compassion, pain and condescension. "You're just a *baby*." She elongates the "a" in baby, thereby convincing me (perhaps inaccurately) that the entire statement was pure condescension. She has, however, piqued my interest with one of her statements.

"Just what is 'the look?'" I ask, hoping for the briefest of explanations.

"Well, let's see," Button-woman says, striking a pose as if she were the sage of the disabled. "It's a timid look..." she searches, "a look that says, 'I don't belong here, what the hell happened, I hate this.' It's a look of fear."

She has rung the bell at the fair, and the man has handed her a cigar.

"It sucks, doesn't it?" She again hits the nail on the head. There is an unclear utterance from the large man in the back of the van. It sounds something like, "You got that right!"

"Well, now, Paul, don't," she scolds him, "he's just a baby..."

I don't belong here. I don't need this shit. I'm trapped on the endless fucking bus ride. I hate this woman already. These thoughts repeat themselves as her empty insight continues.

"It's okay to be quadriplegic," she says, and the fellow in the back scoffs, and the thin man in front nods. His fingers are curled like mine are, but his knuckles have no lines. I promise myself I will not live to see my fingers take on this appearance. "You just need to know how to deal with it. I still have a full life. I don't work; I have a roof over my head; I get out from under that roof in the winter --"

"To ride on Metro Mobility for hours?" I ask.

"You just need to be prepared," the thin man says. "Right now I'd kill for some water."

My initial impression of this man is that I like him, and that he would not talk solely for the purpose of hearing his voice.

"How long have you been a quad?" I ask, and the word 'quad' catches in my throat as I begin my challenge.

"Sixteen years," he says more than matter-of-factly -- almost proudly. Almost.

Christ. I'm thinking that there's no way I will put up with **this** for sixteen damn years. I say, "And how old are you?"

"Thirty-two," he says, with the look of a person wondering where this is going.

"Oh," I say happily, "then you've been a quad exactly half your life and were able-bodied exactly half your life." I try to say this merrily as I think of the horror of becoming quadriplegic in high school. Adolescence is hard enough and in many ways *those* children transitioning into adulthood are even more brutal toward individuals not deemed worthy, or cool or ... like... their own myopic peer group. Give an electric wheelchair to a jock, a freak, a nerd, a stoner, a stomp, a geek, a dweeb, an egghead or the homecoming king, and the coolest or the lowliest has just become a social leper.

The thin man smiles and nods. "Yes," he says laughing, "half and half."

"So, you're telling me after sixteen years that you just need to be prepared to be a quad?"

He nods.

"But you're on an endless bus-ride with no water! And nobody here's got it, and even when you get home -- which may be tomorrow -- are you able to get your own water? Do you have water?"

He sees my point. "My girlfriend will be there to give me water. She's a nurse," he says, clearly proud of her.

Button-woman cannot tolerate not speaking anymore. "I'm no different than I was before my injury. I have lovers, friends, family and -- don't get me wrong -- sometimes it sucks." She turns her head to speak to the man in the back. "Paul, you just need to be like me." I doubt her last statement and am again amazed at the unlikelihood of this far too common statement and its slight permutations. She continues. "Monday I was pissed off, feeling sorry for myself, hating everything and everybody, waiting for my *late* attendant, so I just threw myself out of my chair and onto the floor and cried. It works really good; you should do it."

What inane words. At times the thin man and I are able to have brief exchanges. The large man in the back is delivered to his destination and, *because* he is in the back, there is a dance of wheelchairs to allow him to exit. Four restraining straps on three electric wheelchairs (that would be 12 in toto) must be removed along with the three individuals' seat belts (fifteen straps) and the individuals in those wheelchairs must reposition themselves to allow for his exit. Four straps removed from the big man's chair and the seat belts from the big man's lap precede the exit. The three up-front wheelchair users position themselves to create clearance for his exit. He narrowly threads the needle between us and exits to the lift. This large vehicle leans to the lift side until he is on the ground.

Brian Shaughnessy

The lift is closed, (mercifully, as it is winter in Minnesota and every opening of the door causes any warmth to rocket out of the vehicle and up, up into the atmosphere) and the three of us are again restrained with five belts each before the driver travels back down the yellow brick road. Eventually I arrive home where the five belts are again removed, the lift is readied and I venture onto it. I descend to ground level, and the van driver accompanies me to the lift of my apartment. He opens the door, and I enter the lift that will lower me to apartment level. I grab the switch (which is very cold) and press it to my chin. The motor of the lift makes its loud sound, and the pulley turns, lowering the cable and the cage to my apartment level. The driver has already come from the lift entrance to the stair entrance, descended the stairs and knocked on the door. No one is home. He removes the key attached to the wheelchair, unlocks the door and I enter. Inside, I turn around and he replaces the key. I thank him, he wishes me well, I warn him to watch his head on the angle iron of the lift and he departs closing the door.

I am home alone in a very warm jacket in a very warm apartment. I don't throw myself on the floor, but I do cry.

Poo-Poo 2

My brother Patrick, his wife Kate and son Devlin become almost nightly visitors. Devlin always has a stuffed raccoon named Poo-Poo with him. This is the raccoon that Annie gave him at birth. He carries it by the snout while he sucks on his middle two fingers. I, invariably, have transferred to the couch by the time the three of them arrive and Devlin -- precocious in his speech, manner and vocabulary -- immediately puts down Poo-Poo, removes his fingers, and asks permission to push my wheelchair. He pushes the empty wheelchair from one end of the apartment to the other and back again for the hours they are there.

Brian Shaughnessy

Size Nine Shoes

It's Carol's last official day as a physical therapist for the Rehabilitation Department of the University of Minnesota Hospital. Soon she leaves for THE Rehabilitation Department of the United States -- Craig Institute. Craig Institute is the premier rehabilitation facility for persons with spinal cord injuries. In the strange rash of spinal cord injuries to central characters on soap operas that I watched while living at Rehab, each character went to an unnamed facility in Denver where they were miraculously cured. That unnamed facility would be Craig Institute. Craig is the best and so is Carol; they are lucky to get her.

"You guys are still coming to the party at Gayland's, right?" she asks, confident of the answer. I look at Annie who nods and assures Carol that the two of us will be present. "His apartment is small, so don't mention this to other... people, okay?"

"I understand," I say with a serious look. "You don't want any *losers* to show up at your going-away bash." She laughs and tries to convince me that such is not the case -- that she wishes "all her friends" at the hospital could join in the festivities. I mock her, and she gives me a friendly little slap. She assists in transferring to the mat -- much more difficult since the second surgery -- and positions me for range of motion. Carol takes a hemostat clamp and clamps off the tubing that runs from the condom catheter to the urine bag. This is done to prevent expelled urine from returning to my bladder, thus contaminating and causing another urinary tract infection. She begins the daily stretching routine and, as the three of us talk, others stop by to say goodbye to Carol and to wish her well. At some point, Lane, the woman who will take over Carol's responsibility for me, comes by to observe and play. No new personal or world records are attempted. My strength and ability have not reached their pre-second surgery level.

"Brian wants to give you something," Annie announces as she reaches into my backpack and removes a shoebox sized, gift-wrapped parcel.

Carol is turned slightly away as Annie says this and as she turns back around she says, "Oh," with surprise. "Aren't you a sweetie. You didn't have to do that."

The Squeaky Wheel

"I know I didn't *have* to, and I know I *shouldn't* have, but I *really* wanted to, so it's not really about you -- it's about me," I say and cackle maniacally. With a laugh Carol sits down and examines the package as others look on. "After that laugh, and knowing *you,* I'm afraid to open this now."

"Don't be," Annie says simply and with tenderness.

Carol removes the wrapping to reveal a Stacy Adams men's shoebox -- size nine. She laughs and looks around the room. "I think these are probably too small for me," she says characteristically. She often comments about her big feet. She is a tall woman.

She removes the lid to reveal its contents. It is my gray sweater, given to me by the woman I was kissing when Annie entered my room. The sweater Carol coveted. The sweater I promised to give her, "... the day I walk out of here." It is neatly folded and a quad-ring is attached to the zipper. Carol realizes what it is, and the merriment on her face vanishes and is replaced by sadness and disbelief.

"But this..." she raises her head, "I can't take this from you," she says as her strong brown eyes reach maximum saturation, and her voice weakens.

"You earned it."

She immediately begins to cry loudly and uncontrollably as she grabs the box and bolts out of the room.

I look at Annie who appears somber and does not meet my eyes. I look to the other therapists who gathered to watch the exchange. Some of them have tissue. I see Lane whispering to one of them. I know she is explaining the significance of the now fourth-hand sweater. Soon, all of them know, but it is not *soon* that Carol returns. The other therapists commend me – verbally or through looks or touch or thumbs up or hugs -- for my gift. Carol returns much later and won't meet my eyes. She gives me a long, hard, quiet hug and says, "Damn you for making me cry. But that is, without a doubt, the nicest gift I've ever gotten from a man. No, from anybody."

I can't help myself. "It's a rag!"

Now she meets my eyes. Brown to brown.

"No it's not."

Brian Shaughnessy

Made in China

My mother visits from New Mexico. She stays in my former apartment upstairs, so she has many opportunities to visit and talk. It's very complicated for me to get upstairs to that apartment. It requires two individuals (at least) to bring me up four sets of stairs. Mom visits downstairs. Annie is working part-time and going to school part-time. She is attending a different community college than we attended because she doesn't want to encounter and explain the current situation to people we both know but not well enough to have seen or called in the last several months.

Whenever mom visits *anyone* in the family she must remain busy. She sweeps or washes dishes or dusts or cooks or... Today she talks while she straightens and dusts shelves above the desk where I work. Finally she sits, briefly, so she can look at her son.

"I'm so sorry this happened, Honey," she says through pained blue eyes. I tell her I know. "And people can be so insensitive and just plain stupid." I let out a tremendous scoff of agreement and nod. "A friend of mine was telling me that someone else was talking about our family -- which I hate to even hear -- and was saying that I had two kids with disabilities and the other person responded, 'why would she have another kid if the first one had a disability?'" We look at each other and shake our heads. Then a great silence falls.

"You know," she begins tentatively, staring blankly down at nothing – and I know this is going to hurt. "I think about this," she gestures toward me but nothing moves except her one arm, "and I get so sad." My mouth and chin begin to quiver as they do before I cry. "I ask God to give it to me -- to take this away from you and give it to me." Her eyes don't move and she barely blinks. I cannot speak for my silent crying but I shake my head. She looks at me. "You know I would take this if I could." It is not a question, but it does allow me to harvest the strength to speak. "I wouldn't let you," I manage to say. She continues, "I think, 'How could this happen? Why Brian?' And... " The glazed look in her eyes clears and she turns. I know a stake is about to be driven into both of our hearts. She breathes deeply. "I thought -- why couldn't it have been Dawn? I mean, if you *had* to do this to one of my kids, God, why not the one..." she breaks down. "Am I a bad mother for thinking that?" I shake my head and we attempt to console each other. Then she goes back to dusting the shelves.

The Squeaky Wheel

We talk, but her back is to me and I am not looking at her when suddenly -- and simultaneously -- she shrieks, and there is a crash of something breaking. "Shit! Your mother is so clumsy," she admonishes herself. "I'm sorry. It was such a pretty little vase. I promise to replace it. God damn it!"

I look at the broken blue and white shards on the floor, and although I am outwardly laughing and honestly telling my mother not to worry about it, inside I am saddened, because my dear friend Andrew Yee brought this tiny blue and white vase back from China along with three other gifts. Weeks before, he entered my apartment and proudly unveiled the tiny vase and its tiny wooden stand, a Coca-Cola bottle with Chinese characters on one side (a newly introduced product to these Communists -- Diane brings a Pepsi bottle with Russian script back from the Soviet Union), a small stone that was a piece of the Great Wall of China (I scolded him for that gift) and many small vials of "royal bee gel," which are opened with an included small, round stone used to scribe the neck of the vial.

"I went into what would be the equivalent of a pharmacy/hippie healthfood store and told the guy, 'See, I got this friend back home...' He said that this should fix you right up," Andrew had said as he demonstrated how to open the vial and then place a small straw into it so I could suck out the brown viscous contents. The Coke bottle and vase were displayed on the top shelf. The Great Wall rock was placed in the blue vase for safekeeping.

But the place of safekeeping was not so safe. My mother has dustpan and broom already in position. "Wait a second," I say calmly -- trying not to alert her. "You see that little brown rock in there? Can you pick that out and put it in the..." I look above for the appropriate place, "...in the Chinese tea box?"

My mother looks at me as if she's worried about my mental health. "Can I ask *why* you're keeping that rock?"

"Emotional significance," I say laughing to myself and to keep her from discerning any significance to the now broken clay. She laughs and dismisses it as young madness and places the small rock into the nearby Chinese tea box.

She prepares dinner and Annie arrives and the three of us eat. Then she and Annie wash the dishes. I keep looking for an opportunity to tell Annie not to let my mother know that the vase came from Andrew by way of China, should my mother bring up the fact that she broke it, which I know she will. That opportunity never presents itself, but after some time my mother announces that she is going upstairs for the night. She bids us goodnight and kisses us both. I feel relieved that she won't know.

As she exits she says, "I'm sorry about the vase." She turns, *at the doorway*, and says to Annie, "I broke his blue vase." A realization hits my mother. "It wasn't yours, was it, Annie?"

I am desperately trying to communicate nonverbals to Annie who is not receiving them.

"Blue vase?" Annie asks puzzled. She is five feet in front of me and five feet behind my mother who has the door open and is about to ascend the stairs.

"Yes," my mother says disgustedly. "It was small and on the shelf over there, and I knocked it down when I was dusting. So stupid," she says, shaking her head as the door is about to swing shut.

Annie ponders this information not looking at me and says, "The one Andrew brought back from China?"

I hear her groan/wail as the door closes.

Months go by. Annie begins to resent me and I begin to resent Annie. We feel trapped but we don't share our feelings. I feel guilty for resenting her, and I am hurt and angry that there is no intimacy. We watch videos and occasionally venture out, but the apartment becomes more cluttered and the paralysis spreads from me to her. This whole time I return to Rehab and I talk about going over and looking at the parallel bars...but that is all I do. I finally go over one day, but I know I can't stand. And that was the last time. And that was sad. Carol's replacement physical therapist orders me an electric wheelchair. It is big and ugly and makes a heinous high-pitched, taunting, electrical sound when you press the joystick.

We make plans to go to Hawaii. Eight months go by between the first call and receipt of a check from Mrs. Nasty, the Social Security bureaucrat who asked 987 questions. Even after monthly calls, she gives some lame bureaucratic excuse from the manual for delaying the benefits to which I am entitled. "I don't have your Z-28 form or proof that you're from this planet," and variations thereof. In reality it is punishment for my outburst during the initial interview. Ultimately, my father calls Mrs. Nasty and informs her that he is a lawyer and if she does not send a check within ten working days he will be forced to take action. The check arrives within a week. The delay means I receive payment for the months accrued. This is fortuitous because the check is remarkably close to what it will cost us to spend a month in the tropics.

Our apartment and our lives have become very dark. The shades are pulled, and we watch videos. We do agree to go visit my mom. Across-the-hall Annie will join us. We arrive at the airport early, and I am transferred from my wheelchair to a dolly with a plank nailed to it for my ass, and then tossed into a seat like an out-of-style suitcase. On my first flight with wheelchair I am seated in the front of the plane with my Annie and Across-the-hall-Annie. I am probably mid-flight when one of the flight attendants who *had* been particularly helpful looks at me with a smile and says, "So, how did you do yourself in?"

""Do myself in? Do myself in?? It's none of your fucking business you ignorant.... Do myself in...? If I told you how I was 'done in' you would sit down in a fucking seat and cry. Then you would cry some more. Then you would apologize to me for asking. Then you would cry again. The implication of your statement was that I made a conscious choice to *cripple* myself. If you knew how far that was from the facts you would hand your paycheck over to me. I have the fucking nerve to get on an airplane and humiliate myself in THIS manner and not just stay home and you have the unmitigated audacity to ask THAT question. How fucking dare you? Now... get the fuck away from me or I will have your pathetic excuse for a job -- which you are inept at I hasten to add. I'm serious. I'm not just saying that because I'm offended. I will sue this fucking airline and own this fucking airplane. Jesus."

At the moment she asks the question, that response burns into my brain in a nanosecond. Unfortunately, it remained unspoken... at the time.

I vividly feel a dagger plunged into my heart, while my brain is compressed and my body goes limp. I see both Annies (along with myself) dropping jaws at this question. Three people in a row catching flies. Flight-bitch grins when she asks and continues to grin at our open mouths. Her grin says, "Aren't I clever?" No, honey, as a matter of fact, you're not. The tears usually gush from my tear ducts as if a hose was turned on, but at that point in my life I guess I was all cried out. My throat tightens and my vocal cords tense as I start to explain, when a sentence or two into it I realize I do not owe this prying, rude, ignorant, smiling bitch an explanation -- especially when she phrases this over-asked question in such an insensitive manner. I say that I am not going to explain it to her.

She later asks Across-the-hall-Annie as she is exiting the bathroom. Annie ignores her.

One would think that this could be an all-time winner for the most ignorant phrasing of this omnipresent question. But it's not.

My mother meets us at the airport. She is elated and apologetic for not bringing Dawn.

"There was just no room with the three of you, and the wheelchair and your stuff."

"Don't worry about it, Mom," I advise," she'll see us soon enough."

When I talk to Dawn on the phone she is bubbly and excited and tells me of her adventures in school, in the yard and at-large. She explains this with a very thick tongue. But she always asks, "Are you still in a wheelchair?"

I choke. "Yes, baby, I am still in a wheelchair." She is now 7 in years but not nearly that in her mind. It is something of a blessing.

"Brian's here, Brian's here. Annie's here, Annie's here," she chants as she runs from the house to the car where I am being extracted. She kisses me.

"You know what, Brian?" she asks not even suspecting that I know the answer to her question.

"No, what?" I ask her innocently.

"I love you," she says with an asymmetrical smile and dancing eyes.

"I know that," I say sternly.

The smile vanishes and she becomes serious. "No you don't."

"You're right," I say and I hear the Annies laughing.

My Annie and Across-the-hall Annie go on a brief sojourn of their own. It is to be three days, but they come back after one day. My mother had tried to transfer me and I wound up on the floor. She clearly feels worse about it than I do. She gets her gigantic neighbor to lift me. Dawn is a delight to be around, as is my mom. But I'm in hell. My mother sees and asks me to hang on until the following Christmas. I agree to do so but I am lying.

Annie and I travel to Sanctuario, known locally as "Little Lourdes and the site of miracles." It is said that if you take the dirt you can be healed. We take a jar of the dirt back to Minneapolis. We put it on my body at night and I sleep with the dirt on my body. The next morning I awaken muddy but quadriplegic.

The Squeaky Wheel

1984

Annie and I go to Hawaii. We spend a month on Maui. Rainbows, infinite shades of blue beaches, palm trees, flora and beautiful women greet us. Within three days while doing my morning cares she begins to cry. I say, "What's the matter?" She says, "This is not a vacation."
The dagger is in my heart and I am broken again. I know it's true. "I'll call a nursing agency and get somebody to come in." Annie declines this offer and together we enjoy Hawaii for an eye-opening month. Every morning Annie transfers me to a beach chair where we lounge oceanside. Somewhere during this time I make the decision to return to school. I had promised myself I would commit suicide before I would return to school in this condition but I rationalize the choice as the bargain I must make with God to get rid of this awful wheelchair. I hate myself for "agreeing" to go back to school in a wheelchair and not killing myself and I hate God for making me go back to school in a wheelchair. But he forgives me. I feel he wants me to return to school and then I will be able to walk again.
The "vacation" ends and we return to Minneapolis. Patrick, Kate and Devlin arrive, and I am on the couch. Devlin looks at the new electric wheelchair and then at Uncle Brian and Aunt Annie with a confused/hurt/betrayed look. The four adults want to cry.

I will return to the University of Minnesota in the fall and I contact the appropriate offices. A very nice DVR counselor assesses me, encourages me and tells me to go into computers. I decline. I will continue to seek an English and Theatre degree. The Office of Students with Disabilities is surprisingly unhelpful, but it is 1984. Their best piece of advice is to go to the bookstore and buy some carbonless notepaper, so I can ask people in my classes to place a sheet of this miracle parchment under their ordinary paper and leave with a copy of their notes. I ask if the classrooms are all accessible. I am told if the classroom is not accessible they must move rooms. I am advised to scout ahead. I ask about testing facilities and liaisons and am told I should talk to the Professor.

Brian Shaughnessy

Although vocational rehabilitation will be paying for my schooling I look into student loans. I have learned that my previous student loans have been waived because I have "acquired a disability." This is much too polite a term for what I and others have endured. I apply for a student loan and am told that because I defaulted on a previous student loan I am no longer eligible. I explain to the individual at the bank that I did not default but acquired a disability. He investigates and finds that the "coding" is the same for a default as it is for crippling. He begins processing my application for a new loan. Just as we are finishing the process, many days later, this very nice person is acting a little sheepish and says, "My boss insists that I tell you that you won't be able to waive this loan because of your disability." I feel sorry for this person and a bit enraged at his boss. "Tell your boss that won't be a problem," I begin and deliberately pause. "Tell your boss that I'm planning to get out of these new student loans by dying!"

The Squeaky Wheel

Stay off the Sidewalks

My DVR counselor, Joe, refers me to Courage Center for driver's training to reacquire my driver's license. We have ordered a van and DVR has paid for the modifications. The paperwork dance and calls are complete and Tony -- a nicely dressed guy a few years my junior, with thin, dark hair and a friendly manner -- Caucasian, 5' 8", married with children -- shows up at my door for instruction. I begin by attempting to unlock the panel at the back of the van that will gain me access to the switches that will open the side doors of the van and lower the lift. This is accomplished with much toil and sweat, but Tony assures me it can be made simpler on my own van. I enter the lift, ascend, board and position myself (with Tony's assistance) behind the steering wheel. Tony tests me with various controls and appropriate devices for the vehicle and for my hands. My right hand has a splint that runs from my palm to the middle of my forearm with a pin protruding from it that slips into a hole on the steering wheel. This device allows me to control the direction of the vehicle. The splint on my left hand runs the same distance and has an opening on the palm that slips over a lever to control the acceleration and brakes.

I wonder why I am bothering with all this shit when I know that eventually I won't need it and can get back in my Honda and drive.

With implements in place I back out of the driveway and point the van, Tony and myself in the direction of the street. I begin the next portion of the lesson in a large parking lot nearby. I then proceed to the fairly safe one-way 25 mph parkway around Lake of the Isles, followed by an equally safe two-way road around Lake Calhoun. Tony smokes a butt, ogles women and tells me about his wonderful life and job. I am happy for him. The two hours go by quickly, and Annie is relieved to see us return safe and sound. Tony informs me he will return for the next four days.

Each day driving becomes both easier and more challenging. Each day I circle at least two of the four lakes near my house. On Thursday Tony says, "My wife has been wondering why I've been coming home horny every night until I told her you lived by the lakes. This is great!" he says, pointing out a handful of young women in bathing suits. I agree.

And now we're off to the freeway. My heart races, but this area of instruction is without incident. The next day he tests me on all areas that will be included in the driving exam and takes me for another spin on the highway. Perfect. Still, I'm not sure I am comfortable with the contraptions and splints and modified key holders required to get me on the road. My road test is the following Tuesday.

Tony shows up, and I drive to the licensing department. A few minutes into the test my hand comes away from the steering wheel. The pin comes out of the hole, and I look at the Examiner who stares straight ahead -- uncomfortably. I apply the brakes and stop to replace the pin, but I have crossed the centerline and failed the test. The Examiner is quite kind and clearly disappointed for me.

"When you come back to take the test again, if something like that happens, just put on the brakes and put that back in place," he says, motioning toward the pin on my hand, "and resume driving. If you had done that today you would have your license. Good luck."

Tony returns to the vehicle with a wide-eyed look that asks, "Did you pass?" I explain what happened.

"Oh," he says dejectedly, "that's my fault. You needed a few more hours before you were ready. I'll check my schedule, and I'll be over next week. We'll get it right next time."

His kindness overwhelms me. I want to quit. I know it's not his fault at all, and when he shows up the next week, I am most grateful. One day I am driving, and it is after 5:00. "Do you usually work this late?"

"Never," he says shaking his head. "As a matter of fact, I'm not billing for this. You're just *such* a nice guy and Annie... I want you to have this. I had another quad who failed this week, and he wanted to come back the next day and take the test. I told him to talk to his counselor and then to call me to arrange a time when the vehicle was available. He said it would be almost two weeks. He's an asshole."

"You should bill for this," I say, trying to keep my eyes from misting and feeling I have nothing more to give him.

"That's okay."

That week I return to take the test. The administrator of the test is taking me through the steps and telling me to signal at various intersections. The turn signals are mounted on the door at my left elbow and as he tells me to "turn right" or "turn left" I bump the appropriate button with my elbow. After a half dozen turns the administrator timidly asks, "How are you signaling?"

The Squeaky Wheel

I desperately want to say, "mind control," but do not. Later when I share this story with my dear friends Don and Diane, Don comments, "Yeah, on my home planet where I'm a trapeze performer..."

I pass the test and get my driver's license but remain terrified of driving.

What Happened To You...

"You're so lucky! You get to ride around in your little chair while the rest of us HAVE TO walk." This one from an elderly woman at a department store.

Brian Shaughnessy

Besides That, How Did You Enjoy the Show, Mr. Shaughnessy?

The van arrives, DVR adapts it, and I am trained and licensed to drive it. Dear, sweet Miranda has reappeared in my life. A beautiful blond woman with deadly, loving brown eyes and self-esteem lower than the Mariana Trench. She heard from a mutual friend about my... situation. She wants to come by. I discuss it with Annie, and Miranda has dinner with the two of us that week. She brings beer. After dinner Annie immediately retreats to the bedroom. It is clear she is not threatened by this woman -- she may be somewhat relieved that I have other female company.

I am relieved that Miranda's self-worth seems to be climbing, and she is pursuing a degree in Greek, which she is passionate about. The two of us talk long into the night and agree to see a play the next weekend. I have not yet driven without my instructor. Annie continues to drive, which is fine with both of us.

The day for the play arrives and Annie's sister and sister's daughter spend the day with us. Janet has brought beer, but I decline because I know I will be driving that night and am terrified. Evening approaches and Miranda arrives with dinner. We eat and get ready to leave for the performance. I open the door to the outside by hooking my arm through the rope on my doorknob and pulling the door. I back onto the lift and pull the door closed with the rope on the *outside* doorknob. I pull the bulb with the up-and-down switch to my chin and send the lift up by pressing it against my chin. Since the second surgery I can no longer hold the buttons down on the controls. I ascend and back off the lift and roll to the driveway. I fumble with the device that holds my keys in a manner that almost allows me to use them. I unlock the small box on the back of the van that hides the switches to the door and lift. I press the switch that opens one door. I press the switch that opens the second door. I press the switch that lowers the platform from vertical to horizontal. I press the switch that lowers the lift to the ground. I then back onto the lift and press the switch that raises me to the level of the floor of the van. I enter the

The Squeaky Wheel

van and operate the switches to reverse this process. I then position myself behind the steering wheel and engage the hydraulic device locking the wheelchair in place. I again struggle with my key device to get it into the ignition and start the van. I wrestle to place the large cuff on my arm that extends from my hand to the middle of my forearm and to my left hand that will allow me to operate the lever for the gas and brake. I then wrestle to put on the similar cuff with the pin that goes into the hole on the steering wheel that will allow me to guide the van. I pull the straps of the cuff tight with my teeth and Velcro it closed with my chin. I tell Miranda to put her seat belt on. I then put the van in reverse and inch out of the driveway. I pull on the lever for the brake with all of my might and shift the car into drive. I fumble to have the pin find the opening of the hole on the steering wheel that will allow me to steer. It slips in. Coitus. I calmly drive to the University of Minnesota and, because of my intimate knowledge of this facility, know there is handicapped parking behind the student union.

There are several parking places along a curb, and I choose the one that is farthest back so that no one can park behind me. We celebrate this first outing under my captaincy and go to a very talky, feminist, possibly whiny play. She talks to one of the women she knows in the play -- who sneers at me -- and the two of us depart.

I am devastated to see that some selfish prick has ignored the yellow paint forbidding parking on the curb immediately behind my rear tire, and has left me very little room to back out. Worse yet, there is a vehicle with a handicapped permit equally close to my front bumper. Coeds walk along unaware of my plight as Miranda and I re-enter the van with all of the previous rituals. "Please put the seat belt on. I would never recover from seeing your pretty face go through the windshield." Miranda complies and I begin to inch forward and backward in an attempt to free myself from the constraints of the fore and aft cars. I am clear of the front car when I push the accelerator all the way forward and all eight cylinders of my new Ford van respond appropriately and propel the vehicle across the narrow street and into contact with a four foot high brick wall. The vehicle stops immediately and a large section of the brick wall lies on the grass. There is several thousand dollars of damage to the van and several thousand more to the wall. But Miranda is okay, and I have a small cut on my forehead.

Paramedics, police and a tow truck arrive. My only choice for going home is to have the paramedics put me on the gurney, lift my heavy electric wheelchair into the ambulance and drive me home ... but not before I see my van being towed away. In my driveway the paramedics turn on their huge floodlights to let all my neighbors know I have done something stupid. Annie is outside in an old lady robe looking concerned and sad. Some words are exchanged, and Miranda goes home to have a well-deserved beer.   Annie and I enter the apartment in abject depression.

"So," she begins, with a mischievous twinkle in her eye, as she places her hands on my knees and leans in almost touching her nose to mine, "besides that, how did you enjoy the play, Mr. Shaughnessy?"

Armed with carbonless notepaper, I return to college. Always fearful of running into someone I knew – before – I don't want to have to explain *this* to them. I avoid theatre classes for this reason.

The Squeaky Wheel

My Cover Nearly Blown

I am attending three classes on Monday, Wednesday and Friday, which allow me four days of not having to make the journey to campus via Metro Mobility and the often-accompanying horrors of that mode of travel. I drive the electric wheelchair with my left hand and despite falling forward and being unable to right myself, I still refuse the addition of a chest strap to the wheelchair that will prevent this from happening. In my mind such a device is for cripples.

Each trip to campus instills the fear of seeing a former friend or acquaintance and having to explain my current situation. I pray that this won't happen. I know that between my mode of travel and my red hair I am hardly anonymous. One day I travel toward the English building from the campus bookstore (perhaps procuring carbonless notepaper) when I see Daniel, one of my former teaching assistants from a physics class. Despite his time and effort -- he came to my house and spent *hours* trying to teach/beat/impart an understanding of this totally foreign language -- I received the only D of my college career. Even so, we remained friends, and he lived briefly with Andrew.

Daniel exits the large doors of the stately English building. Before he descends the forty-plus stairs, he stops frozen. It is at this moment I become aware of his presence, glance to the top of the stairs and think, "That looks like Daniel with a beard." Without looking back I am aware of this person's open mouth and disbelieving eyes. As I turn away from the building and Daniel, I look one more time -- for a millisecond -- to the top of the stairs. "Yup, its Daniel," I think and go to the untraveled grassy area behind the building, where I sob.

Another beautiful, fall day (perhaps on another carbonless notepaper quest) I am traveling past the tables of the various proselytizing student organizations set up on the main mall. I see a fellow student, Stacy, from the Theater Department. She is a woman I dated twice but never boinked. From the top of the stairs she throws the same look my way that Daniel had. I see the look and turn to flee. I sense movement from her but the quantity of organisms, tables, distance between us allows me to hastily beat an exit to the same untraveled grassy area behind the English building, where I sob.

Fall turns to a merciless Minnesota Winter -- made even more merciless by the addition of an electric wheelchair to the equation. One day (no doubt procuring yet more carbonless notepaper) I arrange to be picked up at the Spanish building -- right next to the bookstore with their secret stash of magic sheets of vegetable fiber -- rather than my usual locus. I must travel some distance across campus, and rather than make the trek back in the freezing cold, I have arranged for Metro Mobility to pick me up there.

As I wait (a virtual guarantee when relying on paratransit) in the warm hallway with several layers of protective clothing I am unable to remove by myself, I hear a voice from my past. I turn and see another woman I dated, Cheryl, from a Spanish class. This relationship *was* consummated. Initially she has the same look that Daniel and Stacy had. She continues to speak with someone as she glowers at me. Her words slow. Then a look of contempt followed by satisfaction crosses her face. I fear this is because almost immediately after the relationship was consummated I was not heard from again. I am unable to push open the doors that will send me into the freezing cold and allow me to avoid potential dialogue. Cheryl finishes her conversation and disappears into a room. This time I giggle at the possibility that she did not acknowledge my existence because I never called, and then I sob.

Two others from "before" see me, recognize me and confront me on two different occasions during the school year. I explain with the fewest words possible the need for the item under my ass. Both of them have become born-again Christians and invite me to their church. I thank them and decline explaining, "My spirituality is my own; it is surprisingly intact and inexplicable."

In my first quarter I take three English classes. I am determined to raise my GPA from an annoying 2.9. Annie buys a typewriter and types my papers while I dictate. An interesting albeit annoying change has come about in my academic aptitude. Whereas "before" I did well on paper and sucked at test taking, I am now experiencing the flip side of that pancake. My papers come back with C's and one hitherto never experienced D, while I set the curve for the tests. This translates to an A,

The Squeaky Wheel

a B, and a C in my first quarter, which raises my GPA to 2.91. The next quarter I experience the same grades, which leaves my GPA unchanged. My final quarter at the University of Minnesota sees the same sequential grades.

I lament to Annie and Andrew (back from his first year of law school) my inability to raise that which really doesn't matter. "I thought people in wheelchairs were supposed to be smart," I say and see an opportunity, "like the Chinese!"

Andrew scoffs, "Never worked for me."

I usually travel by paratransit to and from the University. I must bundle up in warm shoes, heavy coat, pants, scarf and hat but cannot wear mittens or gloves as I will not be able to operate the joystick. All of this clothing remains on me while I sit through three classes.

One day I wait at Rehab for a ride – on the Metro Mobility that keeps all riders waiting... and waiting... and waiting. Jim, the great quadriplegic lawyer/resource is on his way out. I ask him for a ride. "How long until your bus comes?"

"Half an hour," I say and try to explain delays, other pick-ups drop-offs and information of which he is well aware.

"Half an hour," he says, shaking his head and rolling his eyes, "that's nothing in the life of a quad."

Before he leaves he tells me that Doug -- my Rehab mate with the 25-plus DUI's -- has died. He went into a nursing home where his bedsores became so acute they killed him. Muscle spasms wrack my body.

I am tortured. I ask my friend Don to refer me to a shrink as he works with many therapists. I see a woman two times who always appears to be terrified. She has me fill out the MMPI -- the Minnesota Multiphasic Personality Inventory. This is a shrink tool wherein individuals answer true-false questions like, "My stools are dark and tarry," and are diagnosed through their filled-in dots to statements about states such as anxiety, depression, masculinity-femininity, paranoia, craziness and a propensity for killing puppies.

On my first visit after taking the MMPI I enter her office and she asks me how I am.

"Tortured," is my one word response.

She replies by telling me, "I can't help you."

I'm sure I am going to kill puppies. I wonder what on the test made her decide she was dealing with a helpless sociopath. She says she does not have the skills to treat someone with my level of loss. She is referring me to someone from the Veterans Administration who treats individuals with disabilities. She says I may need medication. She manages to say something profound and incomprehensible.

"Your level of loss? You take a man who has been divorced by a wife cheating on him with his best friend, a man who has lost his parents and children, been fired from his job, abandoned by his friends, and has no financial resources, car or worldly possessions -- that man cannot begin to know the level of loss you are experiencing." I ask her what, in the test, indicates to her that she cannot help me. I ask this in a stammering voice.

She says, "You scored high in this area which indicates a personality disorder." I'm sure this translates to puppy killer. Then she says flippantly, "Some people score high in this area who are very creative."

Quack, I think. Doesn't she know she is sitting in front of someone very creative? Can't she see that Picasso has no strokes on me? I travel downstairs to wait for my special bus. I am broken and wanting to cry but I see another individual in a wheelchair waiting near the door. It is the woman with the button that said, "Slow lovers last longer." She tells me she is just coming from the doctor who could not help someone with my level of loss. She does tell me something very important -- that there is a medical transportation service I can use when I have medical appointments. I do not need to rely on the Metro Mobility system. The medical transportation service will take me directly from my home to the doctor and back home and will appear at the appropriate time. I can't believe no one has informed me of this. This is my first discovery that the "gimpvine" is my best resource.

I see the person whom the previous therapist refers me to. He brings in his psychiatrist who immediately decides I am not in need of medication. I see the new psychologist for five visits; during the fifth visit he says, "Not everybody needs to see a shrink every week." I agree. He has helped me infinitely more than Gayland ever did.

The bitter cold in Minnesota is heinous. My mother implores me to come to New Mexico where my brother is also living and attending school. One cold winter day, while again waiting beyond my pick-up time for Metro Mobility, the decision is made. I will go to New Mexico. Annie agrees to accompany me, but she will not remain.

The Squeaky Wheel

I complete my English degree requirements at the University of Minnesota and plan to complete my theatre degree requirements in New Mexico.

The Royal Scam

As I ready for my move to New Mexico I ponder the infinite agencies I deal with now and the fact that they will ALL have to be contacted, as their services may have to be terminated while I reapply for the same services through the same but different agencies (with the same but different bureaucratic Nazis) in New Mexico. Just pondering it is exhausting and daunting -- the actual doing will be uncomfortable/tedious/degrading AND exhausting and daunting. I wonder if it's all necessary. I begin with a call to my vocational rehabilitation counselor, Joe, who is a very, very nice/friendly/supportive/reasonable human being – a rare creature among the petty bureaucrats. My experience is that the previously listed adjectives never describe bureaucrats. Actually, the term "human being" sometimes does not apply. Soulless automaton is a prerequisite for these positions.

Joe is happy that I am leaving for warmer climes. Minnesota Vocational Rehabilitation will continue services in New Mexico -- it is not the first time the program has paid for someone to go to school out-of-state. He says it will be "too complicated and unnecessary" for me to terminate my services from Minnesota and reapply for them in New Mexico. He also warns that although the Vocational Rehabilitation program is federal, it is run by each individual state. Some states have very poor service and virtually no funding. "I've heard horror stories from people who move here from other states. Besides, I know you're going to do well, which means you, me and our program look good. I wish you luck, and I know you will work hard down there. Call me when you're settled so we can cover tuition and books. If you need anything else, be sure to ask. We may not be able to cover it but ask for it anyway, and I'll do my best."

Brian Shaughnessy

    This sort of support and simplicity makes my heart sing, my eyes mist and gives me hope for myself and others -- maybe even petty bureaucrats. Maybe.

    Confused Bob, the latest in a long line of personal care attendants who have assisted me mornings and/or evenings, has agreed to accompany me to New Mexico and work as my live-in attendant. Confused Bob is approximately six feet tall, thin, moves and speaks as if he is gay and is now wearing his hair in dreadlocks. Confused Bob is Caucasian. He doesn't understand why a black man at a bar got angry with him for sporting that style. I explain to him that it is part of the religion of the Rastafarians. "The who?" he asks. I send him to the library.
    Confused Bob is the latest of many personal care attendants (PCA). The first was a Puerto Rican woman who spoke almost no English. She was followed by an angry lesbian woman who was certain I was trying to exploit her and not appreciating her abilities... or mustache. She was replaced by Howard Halitosis who listened to Three Dog Night and other marginal bands of the early 60s. Howard would tuck a coffee bean between his lower lip and gum which made his breath all the more rancid. He was replaced by someone Annie had to follow around the house to make sure he didn't steal anything. Next was a sweet, beautiful, capable woman who grew up not far from Annie and knew some of her siblings who left for more hours with another client. Spasms wrack my body.
    Mom calls. Since she has a degree in counseling and has worked for various service organizations, she has been asking about the services in New Mexico. "By ALL reports there are NO services for you in this state, and I'm not surprised. What I'm hearing is that the best thing for you to do is keep Minnesota Medicaid and have them pay Confused Bob, provide supplies and whatever other medical expenses you have. I mean, you just keep that address and have Annie forward everything, and if we run into difficulties we deal with it. But there won't *be* any difficulties," she says, trying to convince us both.
    "Okay, Mom," I say as the wheels turn, and I think about the implications of this arrangement. This will involve several areas of my ongoing needs. Annie will have to pick up medications and mail them to me; doctors (which I will certainly need in New Mexico) will bitch about the 20 percent not covered by Medicare and will bitch about having to bill Minnesota Medicaid for their services; wheelchair repair may have to come out of my pocket; leg bags and other supplies will have to be

The Squeaky Wheel

shipped monthly; fascist bureaucrats may need to believe I am physically in Minneapolis at my apartment; my monthly Social Security check, Medicaid card and other mail will have to be forwarded (some of the correspondences say "DO NOT FORWARD" in no uncertain terms); Confused Bob will have to mail his timesheet to someone -- likely Annie -- in Minneapolis for her to drop in a Minneapolis mailbox so the envelope has a Minneapolis postmark; we will have to get the annual paperwork for continuing services forwarded and returned; and on, and on...

But if this is what it takes to enable me to join my mother, sister and brother, flee winter, test my relationship and finish school... I'll do it. The next call is to Minnesota Medicaid. A question answerer informs me that absence from the state for six continuous months will terminate my eligibility for Minnesota Medicaid -- unless I'm in school. I call the woman who is the social worker for the agency that provides the hours and payment for my housekeeping services and visits or checks up on me every six months. Before I can ask a question she informs me that she will be visiting next week and will only return annually now. I call the sister agency, which provides hours and payment for my personal care services, and the question answerer begins asking too many questions, so I abort this call. Annie agrees to forward all mail appropriately (she will collect all mail and place it in a large envelope which my father will provide with sufficient postage) and always tell callers that Confused Bob and I reside there and "just stepped out."

The medical supply company is only too happy to send my supplies to New Mexico. The wheelchair repair company will make every effort to meet my needs within the limitations of a 2000-mile relationship. We begin packing.

I want to leave the stereo behind, so Annie generously buys me a boom box and packs up my hundred-plus audiocassettes, which hold an entire album on each side. As we move onto the clothing and other sundries, the phone rings. It is the woman from the handicapped student office at New Mexico State University. She tells me that despite her promise of a two-bedroom house, I must either accept a tiny dormitory room or find my own housing. I explode.

"You're telling me this 10 days before I'm getting there! You want me to stay in a fifteen-foot room with another person when you're aware that all of my equipment and supplies take up tremendous amounts of room? I'm 26, quadriplegic and moving. I can't stay in a dorm room!"

"So you'll be finding your own housing then?" she asks vapidly.

The Office of Students with Disabilities in New Mexico is even more anemic than the one in Minnesota. I try to point out to a person who works with persons with disabilities that finding an accessible house, close to campus, in a town of 50,000 in New Mexico, is only slightly more difficult than walking out into the nearby desert with a metal detector to find the lost treasures of the Incas. She blames the housing people for stringing her along and blah, blah, blah. I have no choice but to take the dorm. I will move into the box with my attendant. She promises I will be moved into a house within two months. I doubt it.

I call Confused Bob and give him the unfortunate news. He is disappointed but still willing to make the move. Annie, naturally, is angrier than I and rails for some time. This leads to sobbing and holding and saying I don't deserve this shit.

"I know."

She continues her tirade in my arms, and I diffuse it with the words that always disarm this bomb. "There, there, Honey, Brian's here." I already feel her head on my shoulder begin to shift from sobbing to laughter. "He'll take care of everything."

The Squeaky Wheel

Part II: PEACE AND WAR

The Squeaky Wheel

Searching for the Land of Enchantment

    A percentage of my worldly possessions are packed into my modified van and Confused Bob, Annie and I are off to New Mexico. Annie flashes me her breast from the floor of the van in what has become the extent of our sex life.

    My big brown van pulls into the driveway of my mother's house. Dawn, amazingly and characteristically, is waiting outside in the desert sun. "Brian's here, Annie's here," she announces. When Dawn knows her siblings (or any visitors) are coming she immediately starts asking when they will arrive and counts the days. She is invariably looking out the window on the day of arrival and shouting, "Hurry up (insert name of visitor here)," which understandably infuriates my mother. Mom comes out the door; Dawn has already climbed into the van and is raining kisses on Annie and me.

    "Who are you?" she asks the driver in dreadlocks.

    "I'm Confused Bob," Confused Bob responds.

    "Where's Patrick?" she asks and Annie, Mom and I grit our teeth.

    "Why do you always ask for someone you know isn't coming?"

    "I don't know."

    "Should we drive back to Minnesota?"

    An adamant, "No."

    My mother feeds us Southwestern fare and depletes her milk supply.

    "Is the store close?" I ask and my mother informs me that it is three blocks away.

    I have an idea. "Dawn, do you want to go to the store with me?"

    She looks up from the pawnshop guitar her brother Darrin gave her. She stops strumming tunelessly. Dawn, like all children, loves music and sings and dances unhampered by inhibition. If one were to look for the "blessing" in Dawn's condition it would be her freeness. She has yet to experience the constraints of discrimination. Sadly, she will.

    "Yeah," she says with dancing eyes that imply she would rather do few other things. She is slightly puzzled. Annie is not puzzled and senses my plan. My mother looks concerned.

    "How..., no..., I'll go in the car," she says concernedly.

Dawn and I exit the house with the others following. Dawn climbs onto the battery pack on the back of my wheelchair and holds the push handles.

"Are you ready?"

"Yes," she says as if it was a silly question.

"That is so cute," my mother says smiling as her eyes reveal the pain of looking at her two children with disabilities and the thrill of the realization that they will help each other.

Dawn directs me to the store giggling all the way. She sings and shouts orders as if she were the captain of an ancient ship. "I love my big brother Brian," she cries. She is the functioning hands in this equation as we pick up *la leche* (Spanish is the main language here) and travel home.

Darrin has arrived. "Hey, brother," he begins in a standard greeting as he hugs me. "Gladjer here."

"So am I."

The prevalent color in Las Cruces, New Mexico is brown. The earth is brown, the adobe houses are brown and the landscape is brown. It is the merciless brown of the desert that is at the same time the powerful brown that gives rise to the cactus. The cactus is the "bad-ass" of the plant world. Cacti are rodeo clowns and all other flora are mimes. Cacti scoff at 100-degree heat and a blistering sun. They pierce the impenetrable earth and go deep, deep to drink. Then, they cover their leathery skin in an armor of needles and dare any of the scarce fauna that can endure their environment to have a bite. After a rain, just to prove they can, cacti flower in magnificent beauty unseen in any northern garden. When the sun goes down you can here cacti whimper their gratitude for the respite.

This brown gives rise to mountains. The grand Organ Mountains can be seen from everywhere in Las Cruces. At sunset they run a kaleidoscope of colors from red, to orange to purple mountains majesty. But this majesty is second to a desert thunderstorm. Lightning bolts as wide as the road stretch from earth to heaven with a crack to let one know this is God's work.

Annie is checking in with me at the dormitories while some 18-year-old child behind the desk asks Annie for MY Social Security number, the spelling of my last name, and whether I spell Brian with an I or a Y. I am seething but Annie misses it. It's one of the jokes we always make that wheelchair users cannot answer their own questions. We unpack a percentage of my worldly possessions and I discover that my complete

The Squeaky Wheel

stereo -- not the boom box -- is in the van. I look to Annie who grins like a naughty child. We make love one night in New Mexico. When I pursue her the next night I am rejected.

Confused Bob, Annie and I drive 60 miles to El Paso so that Annie can take her flight back to Minneapolis. I am terrified and very aware that my heart, as an organ, controls my destiny. We hug -- each of us in tears -- as she waves and walks onto the jetway. As I exit the airport I say to Confused Bob, "That's the most painful thing I will ever do." But I am wrong.

My brother Daniel has also relocated. He has traveled to England for a year of schooling. I go to my mother's every weekend -- not yet ready for theatre parties.

My dormitory room – also Confused Bob's room -- is a fifteen-by-fifteen-foot cell. I cannot get to the mirror. It is an odd sensation to not see yourself in the mirror for days -- for weeks. Along with the disability, it contributes to an overwhelming feeling that one does not exist.

I set up my just-larger-than-a-twin-bed waterbed and Confused Bob uses his wafer thin futon. I befriend our neighbor Miguel, a Hispanic paraplegic soulmate, with whom we share a bathroom. He uses a brace on one leg and every morning we walk to the cafeteria. He uses his manual wheelchair as a walker. It is an odd sight to see someone pushing an empty wheelchair.

Darrin and I take a directing class together. I direct *Lone Star*, which takes place in back of a Texas bar where Roy is with brother Ray. Roy, former high school hero, is back from Viet Nam and tormented. Roy cherishes three things in life: Lone Star beer, his wife Elizabeth, and his classic pink Thunderbird car -- not necessarily in that order. In rehearsal, I look for opportunities to create more humor. At one point in the play the stage directions dictate that Roy and Ray sing a verse from, "Your Cheatin' Heart." I direct the actors to finish the first verse, look to each other, step away and begin to sing a second verse. It gets big laughs with an audience. I try to find an opportunity like that daily which endears me to the actors. They want to be funny -- without asking to be funny.

Darrin directs *Lone Star's* companion piece, *Laundry and Bourbon*, in which Roy's wife Elizabeth and her friend Hattie are folding laundry, watching TV, sipping bourbon and gossiping about events in the town.

They are joined by the self-righteous Amy Lee. The directing class is taught by Tim -- a man who has not had a millisecond of schooling beyond high school. He has, however, enough success as a theater individual to be hired by Mark Medoff -- Tony award winning author of *Children of a Lesser God,* the first acknowledged disability play. Medoff is a New Mexico State University theater deity and big supporter of me. Tim is also acting in many of the school productions and should not be teaching… or should be learning to teach and not acting. He swaggers and believes he has more talent than the entire department. He is a sociopath. He befriends me and begins buying Valium from me. I learn not to listen to his promises.

He does, however make me a regular visitor to his home, tries his best to share some of his knowledge and is aghast at my daily horrors. We keep each other at arms length.

"You challenge people to be your friend," he accuses… accurately.

"Cut it out."

Working in the theatre at the New Mexico State University is beyond enriching. I become fast friends with Mark Medoff. The connection we share amazes him. He quotes from Joseph Heller's *Catch-22*, and I recognize it. He is comparing the loyalty of Macbeth's troops to Nixon's secretary who erased the eighteen minutes on the tape. He calls her Evelyn Woods. I correct him -- humbly, comically and at the correct moment. "Rosemary Wood was President Nixon's secretary; Evelyn Woods was the speed reading instructor. You have the wrong sister." The twenty people in the room become slightly tense, as I have challenged our leader. But Mark laughs and says, "I need to hang out with you more." I know of the Baal Shem Tov and more Yiddish than the rest of the *goyim* in the state of New Mexico. He laughs at all of this and says, "You're like a red-headed Jew." He directs me; I direct him. He helps me write a play and I have the privilege to work on one of his plays. He likes what I write and direct, and his offer to write a play about me is joyous.

Producing more than a few plays empowers me. Writing plays makes me feel confident I can. The support from peers and faculty makes me cry. My family is damn glad I am nearby. I meet various spiritual healers who perform cool non-traditional therapies. They compliment my aura.

The Squeaky Wheel

Autonomic Dysreflexia In the Real World

Because Mark Medoff keeps a journal, anyone taking a theater class is required to keep a journal to be reviewed by the instructors. I can write anything, and if I don't want it read, I can indicate so. Confused Bob puts me to bed one night. I sleep. I dream.

I dream I have an appointment with Dr. Liar at the University of Minnesota Hospital. After leaving the lobby and entering the exam room, hospital personnel transfer me to a table that assists me to sit up. The nurse enters, checks my vital signs and exits as she says, "The doctor will see you soon."

The doctor enters and I glower at him. He greets me perfunctorily and begins an exam. Suddenly, my brothers burst into the room. Quickly and efficiently they barricade the door, subdue Dr. Liar, affix him to a chair, use the medical tape in the room to silence him and remove guns from a backpack. As I look on, puzzled at these rapid actions, Darrin shouts, "We got him!"

My brothers have Dr. Liar taped to the chair, and a handgun is first waved in his face and then brought to neck level. Pat looks at the drawing of the spine on the wall. "Let's, see... Brian, your injury *started* at C-5..." He looks at the chart on the wall and moves the gun to the appropriate level on the doctor's neck. "That would mean a shot approximately here -- to equal your injury *before* the second surgery. *Now*, however, you underwent a second surgery and don't have the abilities you had after the first surgery... which were significantly less than before you went to sleep and let this FUCK touch you." As he says the operative word "fuck" he shoves the pistol into Dr. Liar's neck, who lets out an appropriately muffled squeal of pain.

I stare in shock but say nothing as Darrin takes the gun from Pat and continues. "But the injury moved up," he looks at the chart and back at the doctor and the gun, "to approximately," he slides the gun up to a higher level as Pat points to the corresponding level on the diagram ... "here. My vote is that you pull the trigger here." Pat nods. "But if you want to have a little mercy I can move the gun down to T-12 and then this fuck," he does what Pat did to emphasize this word and nets the same result, "can push his own wheelchair, clean his own *shit* and maybe -- after much rehabilitation -- be a doctor again... although he still won't be much of a human being."

"Or you can spare him your daily hell and just put one... here." He raises the gun to the doctor's temple as Dr. Liar squeals, and I hear the sounds of people trying to get into the room. "What's your druthers?"

I am squeamish. "Cover his eyes," I say in a prayer-like trance. Darrin and Pat look at each other and laugh as they tape over Dr. Liar's glasses and tape the glasses to his head. In the misty dream world the gun points at the doctor's white coat, at his lower back, and my brothers assist me to get my finger on the trigger. My finger is on the trigger, the gun is pointed at his back, people are trying to break down the door and my brothers are screaming, "Do it!"

My finger comes off the trigger, and my hand falls away from the gun.

"I can't," I say and wake up. I wake in a bed soaked in sweat. My body is clammy and wet, my head is pounding, my mouth is dry and has an awful taste in it, and my head throbs in a pain that resonates throughout my body. I can hear and feel my heart beating in my ears. It is beating much too fast. This is the medical condition known as autonomic dysreflexia. I saw it in those pornographic movies while in Rehab. It is brought on by the clamping down of the sphincter in my penis, which causes my bladder to overfill, and results in the previously described condition. It leads to stroke. I promised myself it would not happened to me. Another promise broken.

Confused Bob removes me from the bed and places me in the shower chair. I look at the broad, WET outline where my entire body just lay as I get light-headed and the room begins to go gray. Confused Bob also keeps a journal, so when I ask him to take mine out -- before any morning routine has been performed -- he does not flinch. I dictate the dream to him with the conclusion that I could not pull the trigger. Then I describe today's condition and add, "Today, I could."

Confused Bob writes this and gets up, awkwardly hugs me, strokes my hair and inappropriately kisses my head and rushes out of the room. Some of Confused Bob's confusion arises from his uncertainties about his sexual orientation.

Miguel gets a roommate who has CP and can walk but his speech is very compromised. His story is that he was just dropped off there to go to

The Squeaky Wheel

school. Our hearts bleed for the poor soul, but he turns out to be a behavior problem and runs up and down the hallways all night, rents a VCR and lots of porno movies, asks where he can score a prostitute and generally and totally demolishes Miguel's life for two weeks. His parents show up and drag him back home to Godawful New Mexico. His presence at the University and in Miguel's dormitory room was arranged by the woman in charge of the handicapped student office. You remember, the one who promised me a house and stuck me in a cell.

Frequent calls from Annie become less and less so. What were weekly calls from her in August and September have diminished to less than one per full moon by October. Somewhere along the way I realize that when I say, "I love you," she does not respond in kind. I question her on this, and she says that of course she loves me but does not want to mislead me as far as the relationship goes. This leads to the inevitable question asked by every male presented with this information in whatever permutation the object of their love presents it.

"Who are you fucking?"

She adamantly insists she is not "fucking" anyone. Somewhere between these lines I know that if she isn't, she will be soon. Now, while I attend classes and rehearse for plays, this pain eats at my liver. I think that's it; that no one will ever love me again. *I'm* fucked. It's the tape that plays in everyone's head after being rejected. It's just turned up louder with fewer quiet times when there is a wheelchair under your ass.

The phone call that makes my rejection abundantly clear -- Annie says she would rather not visit for Christmas -- sends me into the heartache from which there is no distraction. Confused Bob returns to the cell that is our dormitory room where I sit at my desk, and my eyes go over the words, words, words in the textbook, but no meaning is gleaned from them. I might as well be running my contracted, insensate fingers over Braille. I pray that the lack of sensation in my fingers will move to my heart. It doesn't.

After 20 minutes in hell, I ask Confused Bob to drive me to my mother's. He looks up from his colored pencil drawings, sees the pain and immediately agrees to this unprecedented weeknight trip. I spend weekends at Mom's but have never gone there during the week. Confused Bob pulls into the driveway, and as I descend from the lift, Dawn looks out the window. My mother looks more than concerned by this visit, and when I am settled in the house, I state the information just received. She says that she is sorry. She, too, has received painful information that very night.

"Ah, well, then you're no help," I say but when I hear my mother's painful information I am no longer concerned about Annie or myself.

"Danny called from England," she begins trembling. "He was talking crazy, just crazy. He says that he is quitting school because some people asked him if he was born-again. They took him to what sounds like a commune. Did I screw up?" She looks at me pleadingly. "He asked to come back here for Christmas. I told him if he wanted to, yes, of course, but that since he was in Europe he should travel and see Europe. When you talked to him you told him the same thing. He got robbed in Rome -- he is lucky to be alive -- he felt foolish for that and some cult has him now."

"What?" I scream through my shock.

"He's crazy, Brian, I told you that. None of it makes any sense. He says that he's born again and that your father, his wife, Walter Cronkite and my friend Barbara are devil worshipers in their spare time."

I look up at her and stare the incongruity straight in the face.

"Walter Cronkite?" I ask.

"I told you he was crazy. He said he wasn't coming back to the colonies, is not going to school, that we all are heathens and are going to burn in hell if we don't believe what he believes."

"Then he asked for money."

I write my first play. It is an expanded version of the surreal dream I had in the hospital replete with a guy with wings on his head, a guy with horns and a father and three sons in the kitchen of a house they are thinking of buying.

Amazingly there is a woman in my playwriting class who wishes to transport me to the class party. I have informed Dr. Brad -- the 60 plus-year-old instructor with the personality of Playdoh, a small chip on his shoulder for not being Mark Medoff, and a possibly insane wife who talks to her shoulder when she is addressing someone (still a wonderful human being) -- that my brother will take me to the party. But up jumps Lester -- not her real name but one that was used as a variation on her name -- offering to take me in her van. I am flattered because: 1) she is interested at all and 2) when we were discussing the three student plays chosen for production this school year, one of which Darrin penned, the manner in which she discussed his play indicated to me that she had amorous interests in my brother.

The Squeaky Wheel

The party is tolerable and as Lester comes from Nebraska we are able to correct the pronunciation of the local folk when discussing wolves. The regionalism is that they leave out the "L" in the word "wolf" -- making this beautiful but feared animal sound like the bark of a very small dog – "woof." We are speaking with one of the women in the class who refers to the canine in this manner. I see a midwestern reaction from Lester. I tell the woman that there is an "L" in the word. Lester laughs uproariously as the woman insists that the L is silent. Dr. Brad settles the dispute.

Lester is about five foot nothing and skinny as a sixth grader. She has short brown hair and the fullest lips a Caucasian woman ever possessed. Her smallness, cynicism and intelligence -- as well as the glasses she sometimes wears -- remind me of my friend Diane. Lester goes home to Nebraska over the break. Confused Bob and I decide to terminate our relationship and a new quadriplegic woman, who everyone tells me is gorgeous, moves in on gimp row.

Rochele is dark Italian and her caregiver, Sharon Strange, is a trollop. After I hire Sharon Strange to replace Confused Bob I learn from Rochele that Sharon boinked more men on their three week sojourn from Rhode Island to New Mexico -- including a couple of coeds in adjoining dorm rooms -- than Rochele has in her 27 years on the planet. Rochele has been a quadriplegic one year longer than I. She tries to give the impression of sweet sugar in the chair and most of the men who come in contact with her believe it. I suspect otherwise, but we find ourselves intimate.... and frustrated. Rochele is average height -- sitting down -- and dark-eyed with dark medium length hair and slight of build. Strangers on campus approach me and tell me that she is gorgeous. I find her attractive but can't use the adjective that is being stated to me. We do share the bond of paralysis. We share variations on the same stories from hell. We are lamenting the need for PCAs (Personal Care Assistants) -- and at the same time being grateful that someone will perform our cares -- and the fact that no matter how you treat them there are always problems.

"Confucius say," she begins with these words that demand listening to the rest of the statement, "when you treat the employees who live in your house as employees they resent it, but when you treat them as friends they take advantage of it."

"I never knew Confucius was quadriplegic."

Annie calls looking for pills. She sobs like a woman who has lost her family and village. She wants to take enough Valium to end her life. For an instant I would like to help her. Then I chastise myself for even thinking it. I assure her she is not a bad person and that she should get help and reconsider this thought. "There, there, Honey. Brian is here. He will take care of you."

Christmas with the family in New Mexico is grand. I receive four copies of Garrison Keeler's *Lake Woebegone Days* from folks back home. Tim -- the actor who should be taking teaching lessons or the teacher who should not be acting -- invites me to assistant-direct a play that is set in a concentration camp and in which the cast is thirty women. I agree and I am a more frequent visitor to his house. The housing office has granted me a two-bedroom house that I move into with Sharon Strange who begins fornicating with Confused Bob. I thought I was rid of him.

Besides That How Did You Enjoy the Play, Mrs. Lincoln?

I meet Rochele at her dormitory, and we proceed to the theater. She is using her manual wheelchair, so traveling is slow but rewarding. I am happy that she is able to push the chair herself and negotiate the campus. At the front of the theater, forty-plus steps rise up to greet us, but we travel another half a block where the grade is slight. This circuitous route brings us back to the front doors of the theater with minimum effort. We enter and procure tickets and go off to one of the two areas where a wheelchair user can park and watch the play. Naturally, these two sections are in the back of the theater. Invariably, in any theater, they are either in the very back or the very front.
Rochele enters first and delicately maneuvers to allow me maximum room for the larger electric wheelchair. We manage to situate ourselves so that we can both see the stage, and only one wheel of my wheelchair extends into the aisle. But, sure enough, the house manager tries to tell me that because of this "wheel in the aisle," we must sit in separate areas of the audience. I inform her that this is unacceptable; one of the faculty members attending the performance instructs her to lighten up. She does so grudgingly, and we watch the play unpestered.

The Squeaky Wheel

At intermission I see my brother and his girlfriend. We decide to rendezvous at my house after the performance. After the play Rochele and I exit the front doors of the theater. There is a large patio area in front of these doors prior to the numerous steps.

We go left to take the longer circuitous route down to the street. Rochele sees that there is a very steep, perhaps twenty-foot long sidewalk that leads directly to the street. She eyeballs this trail, and I implore her to forget this option, as I rarely attempt it even in a much more controllable electric wheelchair. "I can do this," she insists, as she struggles to get her uncooperative fingers into the bicycling gloves that she believes will slow her descent. I plead with her to just follow, saying that I cannot stand the thought of her missing the curb cut and going off the curb into the street while I watch, unable to change the outcome or assist in the recovery.

For whatever reason, Rochele pushes the wheels on her wheelchair and immediately tries to apply the appropriate pressure to each of the rims to guide her through the narrow opening that is the curb cut and out into the street. She fails. This is one of those incidents that takes only seconds but seems like it lasts for days. I watch her and the wheelchair slowly go to the left, off the sidewalk and then off the curb. The front wheels of the wheelchair immediately dive toward the asphalt, and Rochele is pitched into the street with the wheelchair landing on top of her. Splat. I watch in horror. When she hits the pavement I am already on the way down this luge trail.

"Are you okay?" I ask with frustration, sympathy, anger and love. She sheepishly indicates that she is and asks me to back up the perilous sidewalk and bang on the closed doors of the theater for assistance. Amazingly, my brother appears at the door.

"Rochele just did about the stupidest thing imaginable, and her wheelchair went off the curb. She's lying in the street."

Darrin rushes out the door and down the ramp. Two passersby in a car are already following bloodied Rochele's instructions to get her back into the wheelchair. Darrin takes over and the volunteers flee. He pushes Rochele back to her dormitory room and bandages the scrapes on her knee and elbow. She claims to be all right. We decide to cancel the rendezvous. Darrin scolds her, and she reacts coyly and sheepishly. He shoots me a look that asks, "Is this person insane?" I raise an eyebrow and tilt my head in the universal gesture for, "At this point, we don't know." Once assured that Rochele 's personal care attendant is on her way to put her to bed, Darrin exits. While we wait for the attendant, I turn to Rochele and ask the obvious question:

"So, besides that, how did you enjoy the play, Mrs. Lincoln?"

She bids me "Sweet dreams" as I exit. I am suspect of this oft-repeated phrase of hers.

Other people with spinal cord injuries ask THE question, but they usually wait until we have shared war stories. It can occur at an initial meeting. My brother doesn't understand why it is okay for fellow wheelers to ask the question, but it is a gross affront for a biped to ask it. The answer is: it just is.

Medical people -- doctors, nurses, therapists, phlebotomists, etc. -- will ask but with less frequency than the general population. And they almost invariably ask one of the many variations of the question. They ask, "How did you get your injury?" More often than the general public they will preface it with, "May I ask?" I usually -- but not always -- answer these professionals' questions, although it often has nothing to do with the medical matter at hand. The medical variation to the basic question is not limited to medical personnel.

I have a cache of "lie answers" that I make use of.

Version 1: I am doing oceanographic research on the spotted dolphin in the Bahamas. I was scuba diving with some other zoologists and the dolphins when a shark came by and spooked them. One of the dolphins crashed into my neck and broke my spine.

Version 2: I was a journalist for National Public Radio in El Salvador when Somoza's days were numbered. I was taking pictures of a military parade when one of the soldiers came over and put the butt of his rifle to the back of my neck. Ping! I went down like a rock. My neck was broken. Luckily... pssst, luckily is maybe not the right word -- anyway, the soldier walked away and some other journalists got me to a hospital, stabilized and into Mexico and then home. It was in the news. 1983, you remember that? Most people say they don't. Most.

In my infamous Version 3 response to the question that makes my upper lip curl as if Elvis was sniffing a dead guy in Jeffrey Dahmer's refrigerator, I tell the uninitiated: I'm not really from this planet. Back home -- where I was a trapeze performer -- there are only redheads and blondes. And there are two suns, so NOBODY leaves the house without SPF 70. Anyway, the blondes and the redheads have been at war for centuries, and I was forced to flee. But gravity is less there, so here I'm confined to this wheelchair...

With my assistant directing tasks complete, I turn to my own project. I cast Darrin in the lead role of *Sexual Perversity in Chicago*, which is about two young men, Bernie (played by Darrin) and Danny, and two young women, trying to sort out their lives while making the singles bar scene. It is a hilarious play by David Mamet. The rehearsals range from fun and productive to tedious and pointless. Lester has been helping me with the costumes and other designer aspects while I suck face and give hickeys to Rochele. Ultimately a relationship with Rochele appears futile given our limitations and I have kisses and coitus with Lester. Rochele 's statement that, "There is no hell in Rochele," turns out to be inaccurate. She becomes malicious and sends me a letter that begins with words borrowed from Bruce Springsteen's least known song. "You are not man enough for me to hate." I read no further and burn the missive. Unrelated to any of this, Rochele has plummeted off another curb.

The dress rehearsal for *Sexual Perversity in Chicago* is abysmal. The wrong people are walking out at the wrong time; people don't know their lines and it looks like the thing will stink. The theater and our rehearsal space are up a long flight of stairs. A clever fellow who is the stage designer has made a ramp that is placed over the stairs, opens, and allows me to get to the first landing. The ramp is then placed on the next set of stairs and I complete the journey with someone in front of me and someone behind me to keep me from falling over backwards. I am in a brave new world.

I have the actors write down the scenes they are in, number them and hang it backstage. I instruct them to cross out each scene so they know which scene they are up to for their entrance. The play is short so we are able to perform two shows each night. I fear both shows will stink.

The show opens, the audience fills and I sit in the hallway. I hear uproarious laughter. The show is clearly performed without any confusion that the audience can discern. Rochele views the first performance; Lester attends the second, after which we travel to a party where I get drunk and tell Darrin that he "saved the show." The other actors ignore my drunken rantings and thank me for the opportunity to work with me. Lester and I go home.

Tim's wife, who is not a sociopath but a very kind woman, mother and artist, had painted a wonderful rendition of the cover of the play, *Sexual*

Brian Shaughnessy

Perversity in Chicago on a 3 x 5 foot flat (theater talk for canvass stretched over boards to give the appearance of walls etc.). She took time and apologized for what she felt was a poor hand painted on the sign. I was going to bring it home and hang it on my wall but Darrin, our friend B.G. and I decide it should hang outside the door to the upstairs theater that they had schlepped me up the stairs to so many times. But the theater is full of fragile little egos at all levels. There is another play to be performed in that space *in five weeks.* Before we have a chance to say otherwise, some sorry excuse for a human being (the director) paints over the artist's work with black paint and puts the name of the upcoming play in block letters. From comedy to tragedy with a coat of paint.

You Think That's Funny?

Gomar and I are in a Shakespearean literature class together. Gomar is lithe, Caucasian and slight of build with light brown hair and gorgeous blue eyes. Her freckles and body type remind me of Annie. She is the only person I know in the class, and I am the only person she knows. Everyone else is from the English department or is a science major begrudgingly filling an art requirement. Gomar and I sit in the back of the class. I can get no farther into the room, and Gomar sits with me. Although Gomar is my brother's girlfriend, and we are becoming closer, there is an awkwardness that remains.

The instructor is thrilled that the Theater department is staging *Macbeth* this semester and demands that all of her students attend. She is even more thrilled that we are in the production (I am playing Hecate, the main witch, and Gomar is playing one of the three witches present throughout the play) and directs a disproportionate number of questions at us.

One day I arrive in class feeling fine. Gomar enters a few minutes after the class begins, as she does every class meeting. Fifteen minutes later a switch flips in my body, and suddenly my nose begins to run like a waterfall -- like twin waterfalls from both nostrils. The door is closed, and there is no way I can exit. I have no tissue. I have no handkerchief. I have no rag. I can't reach my socks. I'm not wearing a long sleeve shirt. I begin to wipe the snot on my palm, and then my wrist, and then the back

The Squeaky Wheel

of my hand and arm. Soon I am engulfed in an unending cascade of mucous. Sinewy threads of snot run from my nose to my hand to my arm to my lap to my face.

I am wiping the snot on the Complete Works of William Shakespeare when Gomar's sphincter either tightens more or loosens some, and she cautiously asks, "Can I get you a tissue?" I nod quickly -- doubly enveloped in my situation -- and Gomar runs out of the room returning with a roll (or role since we both fancy ourselves actors) of toilet paper. Between my instruction and Gomar's professional taking of directions I am soon cleaned up, and a ball of tissue is placed in my contracted fingers.

At the end of class we exit, and I thank her for her assistance. Then, affecting a challenging tone, I sneer and say, "I bet you thought that was pretty funny, didn't you?" Gomar's mouth opens in shock, and she shakes her head and begins to protest, when I interrupt – "Yeah, yeah, there's Brian the invalid with snot from his eyebrows to his lap. Hardy fuckin har-har-har. Pretty funny, huh?"

She shakes her head violently and protests, when I decide to end it. "Yup: go to class: watch the handicapped guy's nose run like a faucet and giggle like hell." She senses something. "*You* may think its funny, but (pause) it's snot, it's snot, it's snot."

Both our heads go back in laughter and the awkwardness is gone forever.

The production (very cool, very much fun) is directed by Mark Medoff -- with Tim playing Macbeth and Darrin playing a Lord. We use futuristic cool costumes and sets. The theater purchases all of my costumes, which I am then able to purchase for 25 cents on the dollar.

I tell Lester from the beginning that she reminds me of a song by Marshal Crenshaw -- "Cynical Girl". She shares the same amusement/contempt of human beings as I do, as Annie does, as my dear friend Diane does. It is clearly a trait I am drawn to. One day she shows up at my house unannounced. Marshal Crenshaw is singing, "I'm going out looking for a cynical girl... I hate TV."

"Your timing is perfect," I say.

She shakes her head looking down. "I heard the song playing when I walked up and I thought: Do I wait three minutes for this thing to end? But given that the gods played it and I showed up on cue... I always thought I was kind of Pollyannaish," she lies as she plants a big wet kiss with her full lips on my mouth. This is followed by her raising her blouse to reveal small, perfect breasts... without a bra!

"I commend you on your fashion sense," I say as I focus hot breath on her eraser shaped nipple. She squeaks and convulses slightly. And then...

So, Are You Guys Still a Couple?

The van is packed, the goodbyes are said and Sharon Strange and I point the van north to Minnesota. I'll miss my mother, sister and brother, but I'm excited that I will be seeing the other members of my family. Arturo, who will be my personal care attendant for the summer and possibly the next year upon my return to New Mexico, takes the first shift driving. Arturo is his usual sedate self, while Sharon talks endlessly, constantly and pointlessly. Arturo looks like a real life version of Slow Poke Rodriguez from the Speedy Gonzales cartoons. He is thin and moves at three-quarters speed.

"I can't wait for you to introduce me to your friends," Sharon says, as I look at her through disinterested eyes.

"Why?"

"Well, I just want to meet your friends, you know, and see what they're like... like Jim."

Now I understand. Sharon is a second-rate opportunist as transparent as air. Jim is a friend from Africa. Sharon likes black men and fucks anyone that will have her. But lately Arturo has had that responsibility/opportunity, and the woman is only going to be in Minneapolis five days, or so she says. Arturo displays his usual poker face in response to her request to meet Jim.

We pass Albuquerque, and I say to Arturo, "You're now farther north than you've ever been in your life." He laughs at this, agrees and looks at me with a grateful gleam in his eye for this job and voyage. Sharon immediately begins speaking again. After six hours I am surprised that the two of them have not yet smoked pot. After nine, I am in shock. Although Sharon smokes often, Arturo smokes like the proverbial choo-choo. This fact, coupled with a muscular condition, causes him to do everything at three-quarters speed.

The Squeaky Wheel

We arrive in Denver and select an appropriate hotel. Sharon immediately announces that she has a friend here who she will be contacting, so Arturo will be putting me to bed. She looks at the information on the phone, picks it up and announces, "It doesn't cost anything to call from the room." She has an uncharacteristically short conversation with the person, and it is clear he will be there in 30 minutes. I ask her to assist me with a phone call. Her head snaps back, and she sneers at me.

"I'm going out with a friend. Have Arturo do it," she barks, and she goes into the bathroom and slams the door. I wonder why in the name of God I allowed this person to come. Arturo assists my call to Carol -- my ex-physical therapist from the Rehab Hospital in Minnesota. She is thrilled to hear from me and says she will be there soon with pizza. I tell her to take her time. I tell her this because I would prefer that the Amazon bitch -- a.k.a. Sharon Strange -- be gone. Sharon's friend shows up and she is. Arturo makes sure he is in the bathroom at this time.

Arturo turns on the TV and vacantly watches the news. He exits to smoke a cigarette and returns muttering. Arturo is not much of a talker, but he is a mutterer. "What the fuck are you mumbling about now?" I ask with mock anger and genuine concern. He mutters, hesitates and says, "Why am I putting you to bed? What if I had someone to see here?"

"Arturo," I whine," don't make *me* feel like I'm in the way. I'm sorry she's in the van. I'm sorry I hired her. I'm glad you are now working for me. Don't fuck it up." He realizes the situation and nods.

Carol arrives and we exchange teary-eyed greetings. She remains the handsome, dark, gleeful woman I knew who helped me at the lowest point in my life before moving here to work at the Craig Institute. "You have a breakfast quiz for me?" I tease her.

She laughs. "No, I was expecting you to have one for me." The two of us explain this reference to Arturo and indulge in the pizza. As Arturo and I drink beer she drinks cola. We talk of her job and my life in New Mexico. Carol began on the spinal cord injury unit at Craig but has switched to the brain injury unit. She laments how tragic her patients' recovery and future lives are. She points out a fact of which I am now well aware. "You became a quad in the worst way I've ever known. I've been doing this a long time now, and I've heard every variation on the story. Even at Craig, you win the prize. But you are *still* so much better off than *any* of my patients with head injuries...."

"I know," I say through the same eyes that greeted her, blurry now for other reasons.

It is mentioned that Arturo was also in a rehabilitation hospital. Carol asks why and Arturo responds, "Scleroderma."

"Oh! Really? And you work as a personal care attendant?" She looks back, her eyes wide with concern.

"Not to worry, Arturo is the best. I'm lucky to have him... and to be rid of the last woman who worked for me in New Mexico for five months," I add under my breath.

"Good," she proclaims. "I've known a lot of quads, and I know that finding and keeping good attendants is their biggest nightmare." It has remained unspoken but obvious that Annie is out of the picture. Carol scolds me for not letting her know that I am in New Mexico doing theater.

"Las Cruces is not *that* far from Denver. Next year when you're directing your plays, I expect invitations. You know I would love to see your work, you brat." She says this with the deliberateness of one attesting her faith. The look in her strong brown eyes and her tone suggest she is very interested.

I promise to write and to invite her to the plays next year, but I don't. I later hear that she is married. A few years later I hear she is divorced. Several years later a friend from Hawaii moves to Denver, and I ask her to check if Carol is still working at the Craig Institute. She writes back to me that she checked, and that no one has heard of her. But this is from a source not noted for truth.

Carol leaves and Arturo puts me to bed. He follows and soon Sharon returns. The next day the morning routine is performed by one of them, and the van is again pointed north. This time northeast. There is tension in the van from the moment the ignition turns. Arturo began the driving on this trek. So far Sharon has not driven a meter. She wants to play the tape she received the night before from her friend. She wants to play the same tape over and over again. It was settled yesterday -- each individual picks a tape in rotation (starting with me), and any tape can be vetoed by the other two. This is again explained to Sharon.

"Why do you get to pick first?" she asks.

"Because it's my van," I say, not even wanting to point out the obvious or have an argument.

"But this tape is so eclectic and East Coast. It reminds me of Rhode Island and New York. You'll be home sometime tomorrow, and you can listen to your midwestern music all you want then."

The Squeaky Wheel

"Or," I pause, while I decide whether to deal with her East Coast arrogance or not, "you can take your too cool ass to the back of the van, put on your Walkperson (a dig at her professed feminism) and shut up." She laughs her obnoxious, phony laugh and shows me one of my three cases of music. It is the smallest one. It is -- clearly -- all my tapes that she likes placed into a single case. I realize it in a nanosecond.

"Show me the black case."

Sharon looks up with surprise and disappointment. She shakes her head and slams the case closed, making it clear that I am unreasonable in her mind. She is small-minded.

The rotation of tapes begins, and when Sharon tries to play her tape for a second time, she is vetoed. It becomes a joke with Arturo and me. She complains she's being ganged up on. I point out to her that she is not, and that she brought it on herself. Arturo says barely five sentences during the daylight hours as he journeys into hitherto uncharted territory for him. Meal stops and bathroom stops are made, the sun goes down and he continues to drive. Sharon offers to relieve him, but he declines.

Well into darkness Arturo relinquishes the wheel. He does so at a convenience store where Sharon makes her adjustments and preparations as if she were Mario Andretti and his entire pit crew. Arturo emerges from the convenience store with a small bag. He opens the passenger side of the van and begins to make his preparations. He places a Chicano tape into the player. He then does something I have not seen before. He reaches beneath the passenger seat and turns it around so the seat faces the back of the van rather than the front. He then reclines the back of the seat so that it touches the dashboard, climbs in, and removes a Slim-Jim and a quart of beer from the bag. He opens the bottle and leans back and closes his eyes -- rapture.

Sharon and I look at each other, impressed by this picture -- save for the open bottle in my vehicle. She begins to drive and Arturo enjoys his music, beer and another Slim-Jim. His window is cranked wide open, and it is a beautiful, starry spring night. We travel for nearly an hour before Arturo launches the glass bottle out the open window, and we hear it crash on the side of the road.

"Arturo! Don't be doing that," I shriek from the back seat. "That's not cool." Sharon is muttering assent. Arturo remains in his very relaxed pose.

"I hate to litter and there's no need. We could have dropped it in the trash at the next stop! Now it's just more broken shit on the side of the road!"

"Yeah, stupid," Sharon feels compelled to add.

Crack! Arturo has straightened up, pivoted and punched Sharon in the jaw while she drives. Amazingly, she barely flinches. I am in shock, but I realize that this is not the first time she's been smacked.

"Stupid? Stupid? Stupid! Who's stupid now?" I try to speak but it's pointless. "Don't *ever* call me stupid again, or I'll break your face. You understand that, woman? You call me stupid, you piece of shit? Are you going to call me stupid again? Are you going to call me stupid again? You better answer the question."

"Arturo, leave it alone," I say quietly.

He resumes his position in the chair with his arms crossed. "Nobody calls me stupid."

Sharon continues to drive silently.

"That was uncool, Arturo," I say.

Fifteen minutes into the darkness Sharon pulls over. "I'm not driving anymore," she announces and climbs out of the drivers seat, over me, and onto the couch in the back of the vehicle. Arturo slowly rises from the passenger seat, begins to return it to its original orientation, thinks better of it and leaves it as it is. He takes his place in the driver's seat and continues toward Minnesota. A short time later he stops at another gas station/convenience store.

"Que quieres, Bro?" He asks what I want from the store -- in Spanish. This is quite possibly the first time that Arturo has spoken Spanish to me although he knows that I know enough to have traveled in Mexico. It is the *only* time he has addressed me with the slang, *Bro*, common among Chicanos in New Mexico for other Chicanos and rarely used when addressing *gringos*. I understand the strategy.

"Nada," I respond. I want to tell him, 'and I ain't your Bro -- I ain't nobody's Bro who punches women.' Sharon is busy scribbling in her journal.

Arturo returns with a cup of coffee and resumes the drive. He drives for two hours and the two of us rotate tapes. He pulls into a motel parking lot and puts the van in park. He turns and looks at me. It is after midnight. *"Que piensas?"*

"Well," I begin -- wondering how to deal with all of this, "I think we are now four hours from my house. We can continue to move toward that destination, but you have to drive because I don't think Sharon is going to drive another inch." She remains silent, lying on the couch in the back. "Or, we can take our happy little family and put the three of us in a very

The Squeaky Wheel

small room for several hours and then have to look at each other during the day for the last four hours of the drive."

Arturo is clearly not thrilled with the options. He looks at his watch, at the motel, at me and out the front window.

"It's your call. You made this situation."

Arturo puts the van in drive, and I watch his eyes in the rearview mirror for four hours to make sure that he stays awake. We pull into my driveway in Minneapolis and it is still pitch dark. The two of them begin removing things from the van, and we proceed to the side door where I roll onto my lift -- still up from when I left ten months ago. I take the bulb switch in my hand and place it to my chin to engage the switch to lower the lift. It descends to entry-level and I enter. The apartment is sparse but not entirely empty.

"Where are the phone and the phone book?" Sharon begins barking again.

Even with Arturo's inappropriate actions I have no sympathy or tolerance for this woman anymore. I am about to snap at her that I just got in the door, when I see the phone and phone book in the corner of my eye and indicate them to her. She busies herself calling the airline to change her reservation. Suddenly I hear something in the bedroom. I quickly realize that it is Annie speaking. I know I was not supposed to be here for some hours, but I can't believe she is still in the apartment.

"Annie?" I call out with only slight disgust. After several minutes she emerges sheepishly and sleepily.

"Hi, Annie," I say with only a slightly acerbic tone. She is muttering incoherently, looking at the floor and grinning slightly.

"Give me a hug," I say with only a hint of sarcasm. She complies. As she does, I can see into the bedroom. I can see my bed. I can see a pair of legs in my bed. I can see that they are male legs. I know they belong to the loser (Annie's sister Janice's term, not mine) who answered my fucking phone the other day. I know they belong to the person who has been on the scene for some time, perhaps before I left for New Mexico. My emotions rage, but I say nothing. I don't bother to make introductions, but Sharon introduces herself and I introduce Arturo. I ponder taking Arturo to breakfast so that the various players can deal with their exits. But for some perverse reason I decide to stay and see how this plays out.

I wonder if the legs will emerge and face me or exit through the window. They walk into the living room and introduce themselves.

"Hello, Brian, I'm Goober," he says with a southern drawl.

He extends his arm to shake my hand. I do not reciprocate but look at him for some time without saying a word. I want him to squirm. He does. But I am kicked in the guts.

"Charmed," I respond. He leaves within the minute. Arturo maintains the same expression as the wall.

Annie does not acknowledge this but tells me that she is not working today and that she will be back to take the last of her things. Sharon asks Annie for a ride to the airport. I cannot believe the arrogant assumption of privilege and the flagrant disregard for other human beings by this woman. Annie is looking at me, and I am shaking my head vehemently telling her not to go, but she agrees anyway. I begin to move toward the bedroom and see on the floor in the corner Annie's wedding dress she brought to Rehab and the chili pepper Christmas lights I had sent as a gift. Kicked again.

So, Sharon is putting me in bed. She asks if she can sleep in my room so she doesn't have to see Arturo. I grudgingly agree. As she changes she says, "I wanted to bust out laughing when that guy came out of the room and introduced himself to you."

"Yeah," I say in disbelief, "that sure was funny."

I close my eyes and pray that I won't dream of any of this.

I graduate. My Minnesota family celebrates with me and makes regular visits. My red haired maternal grandmother has Arturo and me over for dinner. She tells Arturo that I named her Nonnie and generally gushes over me. Arturo leaves to bring the van to the front door and Nonnie tells me she is losing her bridge club. She says that two of the members have passed away in the last few weeks. "Despite my heart condition I have had a very full, uncomplicated 79-year life," she says celebrating. She follows me out to the van, watches me load up and remains outside of her apartment waving and watching as we head back over the Mississippi River into Minneapolis.

My friend Andrew is back from San Jose where he has just completed another year of law school. He dismisses his accomplishment as nothing and claims he parties more than he studies. Andrew, Arturo and I travel to the same establishment he brought me to on a first outing from the hospital. As we are about to enter the bar I pull onto the grass and ask Andrew if he will drain the urine bag which hangs from my leg underneath my trousers, as he has done before. "Isn't that what Arturo's for?" he asks but then sees that Arturo is parking the van. Andrew pats me on the back and squats down to do what I cannot do on my own.

The Squeaky Wheel

I called Sandy, the woman who worked for me just before I left for New Mexico. Through the unspoken dance of pheromones and glances she let me know I should call her when I return from New Mexico. We date several times, but in a few weeks Arturo and I are off to Rhode Island for a "postsecondary rehabilitation program. The title is "Shake a Leg."

Rochele and Sharon Strange are there. Sharon is wearing a purple tank top that was given to me by Annie's mother. "You stole my shirt!" I accuse.

"But it was old and ratty and I really like it."

"Okay, I guess then it's okay that you ripped me off. Anything else missing that I should know about?" She shakes her head and acts indignant. "Good. That shirt was a gift. You can give it back to me tomorrow."

But there are also many fun, friendly persons with disabilities who share the horrors and the triumphs that I am living. In the five weeks that we are there we travel to Cape Cod where I visit my old girlfriend Joy. Joy sent the "wish you were here" postcard when I was in the hospital. She visited Annie and me once and informed me that if she had been with me when the injury occurred she would have remained. I told her, "I don't think you would." And I added, "I know I wouldn't." She agrees to see me anyway.

"Shake a Leg" consists of many therapies. Rolfing, Feldenkrais, massage psychological -- group and individual, water, traditional physical therapy and recreational therapy. We have lots of outings. I become intimate with one of the physical therapists -- Janice. Rochele tries to sabotage this relationship from both sides -- all sides -- but the shrink tells Janice that there is hell in Rochele. Janice says she will visit me in New Mexico.

My dear redheaded maternal grandmother is ill. I send several postcards from Rhode Island, as is my custom to her when traveling. I am informed of her illness three weeks into "Shake a Leg" and at the end of five we beat a hasty retreat back to Minneapolis. We leave on July 4th weekend; finding a motel is impossible. We drive and drive and drive. As we cross into the St. Paul city limits I know she has died. I return home and call my brother Patrick who says he will be right over. He enters with my sister and my mother. I should know what's coming. I am lying on the couch and my mother kneels next to me and places her hand on my chest. My siblings stand at the foot of the couch.

"Nonnie passed away, Honey."

"I know," I say without a tear. "I know she went to a better place and its okay."

Darrin arrives that night and the funeral is the next day. At the service, no less than six and probably ten kindly old ladies walk past me at the back of the church, place their hand on my shoulder and say, "She loved you so much." Now the tears flow.

Mom remains another week. One day while we sit in the apartment she asks, "How did you feel when you got home and found Annie here with another man?"

I begin to answer this question and realize I have told no one of this. "How did you know?" I ask.

"Annie told me while you were on your way back," she says.

I never answer the question but am amazed at Catholics' -- and nondenominationals' -- need to feel guilty.

That Sound -- Installment 2

Arturo has gone off to New Mexico for a week in an attempt to score reefer, return with it and make us both some money. Through the state service I find a woman who will do my cares but cannot remain at night. Proletarian Peggy is an attractive, dark haired woman. She is tall with small breasts, wears no bra and rarely makes eye contact with me. She is performing the bulk of Arturo's duties, and my brother Pat makes sure I get dinner and fills in as needed.

One night I am having dinner with Darrin and Gomar -- visiting from New Mexico -- when Proletarian Peggy calls to say she will be over soon to take me to First Avenue Nightclub per an earlier discussion. I am holding the phone, and I look at Darrin and Gomar. I explain that I am having dinner and spending the evening with them, so I tell Proletarian Peggy to go on over to the club and to give me a call at closing time.

"If I get too tired while Darrin and Gomar are here, I'll have him put me to bed," I say as I raise my eyebrows and look at Darrin who nods with an "of course" look of assurance.

The Squeaky Wheel

"Are you sure?" Proletarian Peggy asks. "We can just come by and make sure."

"No, no. Just give me a call and make sure you let it ring 20 times because I'm really, really slow."

She is grateful and thankful and asks if I've eaten and other personal care attendant-type questions.

"Fear not," I say. "I'm in good hands."

The three of us at the table finish dinner, converse, drink beer and play backgammon. Darrin asks Gomar if she is lucky to be his girlfriend; she grins and agrees fatuously. She sits in his lap and he smokes constantly. Periodically he will light the lighter and bring it toward Gomar who blows it out delightedly. Soon it is after 10:00. My brother asks if I want to go to bed as they will be leaving soon.

"I think I'll wait for Peggy," I say, and *he* asks if I am sure. I assure him I am. They leave and I go into the other room and turn on the TV. I watch some of the Tonight Show when I am wracked by a grand mal seizure. My back arches, my knees come up, my minuscule balance disappears to nothing and my head once again slowly descends to my knees. "No, no, no," I say as I realize what is happening and then begin to whimper and sob. I cry out for help. I cry out for Darrin. I cry out for Proletarian Peggy. I cry out for my mom. I cry out for God. I cry out. I cry. I ask Jesus how he could let this happen to anyone. I smell my pants. Sometimes I taste them. I have no idea how long I will remain like this, but there is a dreadful certainty that I will be setting a new record. I scream fire. I scream rape. I scream. I sob. I cry and wail. I curse God, myself, Arturo, Peggy, Dr. Liar and myself some more.

The phone rings. I cry harder. Each ring -- all 20 of them -- makes me sob all the more. Then the pain and cramping set in. Prayers, pleading, screaming, tears, apologies, promises -- accomplish nothing. The TV -- which I cannot see -- plays the Star Spangled Banner and then taunts me with the single note that all television stations play when they broadcast nothing. This continues for hours. During this time I continue my pleading/screaming/crying/apologizing/praying/yelling/promising/begging until I hear the alarm clock sound in the apartment upstairs. I know from experience that this means it is now 6 AM. In a few moments I hear the footsteps of the nurse who lives upstairs walking out of her bedroom.

"Annie!" (Interesting that she too has this name) I scream with more force and decibels than I have been able to muster in the last seven hours. The footsteps stop for a moment, and then I hear them in rapid succession. I hear her apartment door open, and she must *leap* down the stairs, as she is opening my apartment door and calling my name almost before the apartment door upstairs closes. She runs to me and makes the same sound the other Annie did a year ago.

"Ooohhwwha!" she says, as she struggles to sit me upright. I see she is wearing a light blue robe, and as soon as I am straightened she puts her arms around me -- exposing lovely breasts. I feel better already. She asks how this happened and I quickly explain the Arturo to Peggy to Darrin to spasm to Peggy's taunting phone call. She asks what she can do, reminding me that she's a nurse. I quickly direct her on the transfer and undressing. She covers me with a sheet and kisses me gently. I thank her profusely and assure her that I will call her later.... much later. Within minutes I am asleep.

I don't know when, but I am awakened suddenly. Proletarian Peggy stands over my bed. I explain to her the mishap of the previous evening and how it became a problem until 6 AM when rescued. I tell her that I will spend the day in bed and that, no, I do not want to eat anything at this point.

"But Peggy," I say, as she turns and looks at me, "please call the wheelchair guy and have him put a chest strap on my chair today."

As I alternate between sleep and consciousness I hear Proletarian Peggy cleaning the apartment, telling the story to unknowns on the phone, assuring upstairs-Annie that I am fine and asleep, and ultimately entering my room with a large dinner and a beer. The next day there is a chest strap on the wheelchair, and the apartment is spotless. I call Sandy and tell her of my fate. She comes over, massages me and spends each night until Arturo's return.

Darrin and Gomar are painting the apartment building. I have Proletarian Peggy come at set times during the day. Today I am starting to experience autonomic dysreflexia. I explain what's going on to Darrin and the risk that I may have a stroke. "So?" He asks open eyed. "So, either you have to shove a tube up my dick or I gotta call an ambulance.'

He winces, crosses his legs, asks where Proletarian Peggy is, transfers me to the bed and does what needs to be done.

Arturo got ripped off. He wants me to share in the losses. I point out to him that I made abundantly clear that if that was going to happen it was his responsibility. Carlos, the maniac quadriplegic Arturo once worked for, calls me and asks me if he can live with me in my house -- his old house -- in Las Cruces, New Mexico. I do not want to turn down a

The Squeaky Wheel

follow quadriplegic so I foolishly agree. Arturo and I repack the van and return to New Mexico. Allowing Carlos to live with us turns out to be a poor decision and severs any relationship between Arturo and myself -- as Arturo said it would.

Mickaylee

I return to Minneapolis in October to have a medical procedure performed that is not available in New Mexico. This procedure involves sticking a syringe through my urethra and injecting a substance into my sphincter to keep it relaxed and keep me from experiencing autonomic dysreflexia. Short of this procedure, they would cut the sphincter. I want no more knives cutting me anywhere -- especially there.

I fly from El Paso to Dallas where I have just missed my friends' wedding. They meet me at the airport anyway. They meet me for all of seven minutes as I travel from one plane to another. This is my first flight alone and I feel like SuperQuad. I also bash my head against the seat in front of me on landings. This makes me feel like no one should have to live in my condition.

Annie's sister Janice and Janice's child occupy my apartment as I arranged. Although my brother Patrick and his wife Kate have just had their third child, Aidan, they insist I stay with them. My brother builds ramps to get up their front stairs, and the couch is readied. I make all the necessary arrangements for Pat to be reimbursed for doing my cares. I do make arrangements to stay in a nursing home, but when I go with Pat to view the place, and we hear someone in her room moaning, "Help me," but no one makes a move to assist, Patrick insists I stay with him.

Their daughter Mickaylee is initially pleased and enthralled with her new brother. She is two years old. Mickaylee is a beautiful blonde, heartbreak blue-eyed girl who looks like she posed for one of those paintings of the disproportionately large-eyed girls. When Aidan is on the couch (and I'm not) she often runs from across the room and up to her brother shouting, "Baby guy, baby guy, baby guy." She then abruptly stops and leans over the infant and peers at him. She then says, "Baby guy," points, nods and walks away.

Brian Shaughnessy

Whenever Mickaylee takes a drink of sparkling water (a very popular beverage in Minnesota) her eyes and mouth clamp shut and she shakes her head, as a somewhat pained look crosses her face. When her eyes and mouth reopen she lets out a pleased "aah" and reaches for the bottle again.

The novelty of the new baby wears off for her soon when she realizes that he demands a lot of her parents' time. Within a year she is sometimes (albeit rarely) mean to her younger sibling. One day we are in the park behind my apartment with Pat and his family. Mickaylee only acknowledges Aidan's existence when he agrees to be her dog, Cutesy. (An interesting side bar -- when Patrick and I were children I made him play Lassie to my Timmy. He was 3 and lost and crying and a policeman asked him his name and he responded, "Lassie.") Seemingly unprovoked, unsolicited and unrelated to anything that has occurred in recent moments, Mickaylee will announce -- out of the proverbial blue of her eyes -- "Aidan's a dog." This almost always elicits a bark from Aidan who does not speak until he is four years old.

Kate tells me that Mickaylee hit Aidan because he refused to be her dog.

"Mickaylee, you can't hit Aidan if he won't be Cutesy," I say with the voice of experience. Mickaylee looks at me sullenly. "You need to thwack him on the nose with a rolled up newspaper." Mickaylee's sullen look has turned to one of questioning. Clearly, she wonders if her Uncle Brian is serious or exercising the little-understood-by-a-child-of-four art of sarcasm. Kate only winces.

While staying with Pat and his family I have a manual chair. Although limiting, it does make air travel easier, and the airlines do not lose, break or mistreat this needed item as brazenly as they will a power chair. We all are outside on a beautiful crisp fall day. I am tired, and Pat reclines me on a slight grassy hill. I awaken with Styrofoam blocks piled on my chest and face. Mickaylee has been playing with her uncle.

I travel to the University of Minnesota hospital where I am to have the procedure. I meet my doctor, David D. Delaware -- or 3D, M.D., Ph.D. as I refer to him. He is a tall muscular man with caring blue eyes and little time for extraneous bullshit. "How's my favorite patient?" he asks as he enters the room and greets me with the Vulcan sign for live along and prosper. I respond with my usual greeting and ask if he is adding any more letters after his name. He laughs. "Yes, I'm working on my masters in business now because medicine has become such a business…" I have shit my pants and am being cleaned up. "Smells like my eighteen-month-old in here."

The procedure is completed and I'm given a complementary pair of green surgical hospital scrubs and a bag with my soiled britches inside. "Have a good life," 3D, M.D., Ph.D. says as he rushes off to his next duties as doctor, teacher and mensch.

Devlin continues to suck his middle two fingers. The stuffed raccoon given by Annie, which Devlin named Poo-Poo, has become crusty and dirty. "What happened to Poo-Poo?" I ask and Devlin looks somewhat puzzled as his dad explains that Poo-Poo's condition is the fate of all stuffed animals that become a child's favorite.

"Damn!" I exclaim, "I think Poo-Poo should have a new name."

The fingers are removed from his mouth, and Devlin looks up wide-eyed and somewhat puzzled. "What?" he asks.

"Oh," I begin ponderously. "How about... Snotrag?!"

Devlin looks with the wonderment and amusement I recall looking at my uncle with when he would tease me. His bright blue eyes dance as his dad scoffs and looks downward shaking his head. Later, his mother winces at the new name.

Poo-Poo Born Again

My father's sister -- my Aunt Phyllis -- is visiting from Phoenix. She is staying with another aunt. My father and his wife have a summer barbecue, which brings together my own large family along with cousins, my father's sisters and my niece and nephew. My father's house is an homage to kitsch. When one enters the driveway they park behind a car with the vanity plate "LOVE ME" which is parked next to perhaps the sounder advice of the vanity plate which reads, "DENY IT." In the yard are a painted Virgin Mary, birdbath and other plaster-of-Paris icons. When you open the door you are greeted by plastic flowers, fuchsia carpeting, neon green covered French provincial furniture and more painted and fired lamps of circus scenes, a gold painted three foot Venus de Milo (not the real one) with hanging rhinestones, gilt frame pictures, ceramic light switches and infinite cherubs. Plastic crystals hang from everything as the sunshine beams through white gauze curtains with dingle balls onto the white painted fireplace. A faux crystal chandelier hangs in the dining room of more white French provincial furniture.

In the pink kitchen is a pink oven and matching microwave, a wrought iron patio furniture table and chairs and an African gray parrot. It talks. It also makes the beeps of the answering machine, announces, "Bubba, telephone," and can whistle the Marine Corps Hymn from inside of his hyper-ornamental French provincial cage. He is something of a metaphor.

The bathroom has numerous bars of soap and every bathroom product in the universe. The reading material includes word searches and monosyllabic crossword puzzles.

There is a bedroom filled with products purchased and never again revisited.

After dinner everyone is gathered in a circle on the screened porch. Devlin periodically removes his two middle fingers from his mouth and speaks haltingly but like a tiny adult. Poo-Poo's snout is clung to with his non-pacifier hand. I am seated directly opposite him in the circle, and he is getting most of the attention from the roomful of adults.

"Devlin, what is your raccoon's name?" Phyllis asks, unaware of its rechristening.

Devlin is looking at her with his left middle fingers in his mouth and his right hand on the raccoon. His eyes immediately dart directly toward me after the question is asked. The fingers remain in his mouth as I tighten my lips and shake my head in tiny nearly imperceptible movements. His bright blue eyes increase one million lumens, as he pulls his fingers slowly from his mouth, looks directly at me, grins ear to ear, wrinkles his nose and blasts in a voice at a decibel level hitherto unreached by a two-year-old: "Snotrag!"

Everyone in the room laughs. Then my Aunt Phyllis cries, "Brian," chastising me for the new moniker.

"What makes you think *I'm* responsible for that name?" I ask, thinking I know the answer.

"Because Darrin's out of town," comes Phyllis' response.

I return to New Mexico to work with Mark Medoff. I direct him. He directs me. We work together on a play that I am writing. We work on a play that he's writing. I continue to make regular visits to my mother's house. Lester is dating the set designer, and the airline that the physical therapist was to visit me in New Mexico on folds. Mark asks me where

The Squeaky Wheel

I'm going to graduate school. I say "Hawaii," even though I haven't applied.

I direct *Steambath*, the story of a man who wakes up in a steambath that is actually a waiting room for the afterlife. He's joined by a stockbroker, a sexpot, a hoodlum, two homosexuals and others--who listen to a Puerto Rican janitor who does card tricks and is God. Darrin wants to play God but I point out to him that he is neither Puerto Rican nor Hispanic. I cast him as Tandy, the man who chokes to death on Chinese food. One cast member -- there's always one -- has absolutely no talent, will not listen to direction and is a huge concern to the rest of the cast. I should replace him after the first rehearsal but I do not. The sexpot walks onstage, takes a shower, grabs a towel and continues walking to which Tandy responds, "Does she come here often?' We give the audience her backside through cheesecloth. We close but could have run for several more weeks in that seventy-seat theater. Everyone loved the show, although one adolescent (perhaps not chronologically) expressed disappointment at not seeing more of the naked woman who appears briefly onstage.

We have the cast party at my house and one moment I sing Frank Sinatra's, "Summer Breeze," with Raymond and the next moment I am kissing Bethany -- a young, blonde, buxom, tie-dyed Marilyn Monroe/ Janice Joplin hybrid. We like it and continue.

Darrin, B. G. and I are also taking a theater of the absurd class. Darrin and B. G. begin to tout the absurdist writer Zeduh. I have not heard of this person, the instructor has not heard of this person and, mercifully, the rest of the faculty has not heard of this writer. But many of the students in the class and the program have heard of Zeduh. One woman claims that at her old school they had a Zeduh festival. Another student loses respect for our instructor because she has not heard of Zeduh. All of this is very interesting because the pieces that Darrin and B. G. bring in written by said Zeduh are actually penned by Darrin and B. G. It's the emperor's new clothes, Darrin tells me seven years later.

I apply to the University of Hawaii. My mother helps fill out the paperwork and promptly deposits it in her desk. Weeks go by, and I ask about a response. Now she mails it. Years later, she confesses to this maternal act. I get my reply. The University of Hawaii Theatre Department makes a very generous offer. Mark Medoff says they want him to teach there next semester, "so we can write a play about you while we're there!"

I return to Minneapolis after Christmas. I need another shot in the dick and I'm visiting family and friends. This time I am able to stay at the Courage Center -- a secondary rehabilitation facility. The nurses' aides, nurses and therapists are young sympathetic creatures, so it is no surprise that many of them take home a quad or a para. I am given a cup holder and mouthstick and a mouthstick holder. I refuse to use these items. Proletarian Peggy visits as do Sandy and other friends. One of the nurses enters my room and asks what is going on. I look at her questioningly.

"Since you arrived there has been a parade of beautiful women coming into this room," she says and I laugh. "And your timing is great. They miss each other by only a minute. What's your secret?"

"Stick around after your shift and find out," I tell her.

She laughs. "Okay, I'll just call home and tell my husband that."

I travel to one of my favorite stores in Minneapolis and find a very cool sweater. It is black and white and buttons up the front. Printed in black on the white sweater are rows of polar bears. Underneath the polar bears it says, "How to dress sensibly." When I purchase it the clerk compliments me on my choice.

The next day the nurse's aide is performing my daily cares and dresses me and transfers me into the wheelchair. I point to the bag containing the sweater I purchased the day before and ask her to help me put it on. She removes it from the bag and examines it with a slightly disappointed look.

"Can I be honest?" she asks pointlessly.

"I don't know you well enough to know," I respond.

"I don't like it."

"That's okay. I will get four compliments on this sweater before I leave this building today. When I am away from here I will get at least another four and I will continue to get compliments on this sweater... (pause) and you're wearing polka-dots."

Just then another nurse enters the room to give the polka-dotted one a message. She turns to me and says, "Nice sweater -- where did you get it?"

"One," I say, looking at the fashion dot.

We all exit the room and approach the front desk. The unit clerk stands up from behind her seat and leans over the counter. "What a great sweater! Where did you find it?"

The Squeaky Wheel

"Two..."

That evening, after eight different people have complimented me on my sweater, one of the other residents asks me, "Have you always had a disability?" I tell him that I have not, that I acquired it three years ago. He says, "Forgive me for saying so, but I wouldn't trade places with you for anything."

"Why?" I ask, believing I know the answer.

"Because I don't know any different so I really haven't lost anything."

I knew the answer.

"I'm so proud of you, Brian," my mother begins. "When you came down here with Annie the first time, I knew you didn't want to be alive. But I know that when somebody is going through that you need to give him a target date, so I did. When I made you make that promise I knew that you would make that day and if you didn't want to live by the next Christmas, that we would take your Valium, some alcohol and drive to a cold, deserted place in northern Minnesota and we would both take the Valium." I begin to sob. "There is just no way I could continue living if one of my kids did not want to live." She is also worried about my brother Daniel who remains in a cold place in England and only communicates to tell us we are sinners and that he is better than that and to ask for money.

Dr. Brad asks me to play God in his play, *A Merry Medieval Christmas*. I cannot refuse this man. He certainly cannot direct, but he allows me to improvise and add my own lines. We do the show two nights and I get rave reviews from everyone except my ingrate roommate Carlos. He does not even bother to attend the show. "Playing God is no stretch for Brian. I see him do that every day here," is his reason.

He is filling the house with pot smokers and low lifes. Disgusted, I am going to relocate to my mother's when she calls me and tells me not to allow the freak to force me out of my house. I give him the pink slip. Arturo has already been replaced by Pablo, a thin, gay Hispanic male, at a time when thin, gay males are frightening. AIDS hysteria is the norm.

Dr. Brad has the cast party at his house. This is my second visit to his house. He and his wife have about 13 cats. Everywhere there are little cat dolls. There must be five dozen cats in the visible areas of the house. There are paintings of cats hanging on the wall. There is a chandelier of cats. "When my surreal play opens on Broadway, THIS is going to be the set when the curtain rises," I tell Dr. Brad who laughs slightly and then tacitly acknowledges the appropriateness of my statement.

The Road to Outer Space Is Paved with... Black Humor

The short piece I wrote for my Theatre of the Absurd class is a favorite. I finish my second week of the three-week run of *Working*. Friends and strangers tell me -- directly and indirectly -- that my performance was great and that, "you made me forget you're in a wheelchair." I take this as high praise.

Darrin and B. G. -- who never tire of discussing, analyzing and planning the craft -- arrive with me at my home. As I must often, I wait for my current personal care attendant to appear to put me to bed. Darrin makes the offer but I decide to wait for Pablo. The three of us talk of recent plays and of Mark Medoff's writing class in which we are all enrolled. We are all talking of plays we have written, directed or acted in and the conversation hits a lull.

"What about your spaceship play?" B. G. asks. B. G. has been living in a classroom to which he has had keys for almost a year now. When he appears at my mother's house, he often takes a shower. People in town ask if we are brothers, so apparently he looks like a dark haired version of myself. He smokes as often as Darrin and is tightly strung.

"What about it?" I say with a sneer.

"What if we all work on that," B. G. suggests. "I bet Mark would let us work on it in his class. How good can any of those other plays be?" he says with a look of contempt. None of our plays were selected for the class.

What I am feeling and what B. G. is saying is the contradiction *everyone and anyone* involved in theatre either resolves and succeeds in overcoming (to some level) or submits to and goes off to sell shoes or aluminum siding. B. G. -- and Darrin and I -- believe that each is more talented than ANYONE in the department. And that includes the guy with the fancy award. I can love other thespians but am certain that my own talent far outweighs anyone else's. Each of us looks forward to proving it

The Squeaky Wheel

and palling around with other Pulitzer Prize, Academy Award, Antoinette Peary, Grammy and Nobel prizewinners. But concurrent with the cockiness is the fear you'll be discovered as a fraud with no talent whatsoever.

"You guys don't want to work on that piece of shit; and I don't want to work on that piece of shit," I say, certain that I suck, and that I will be discovered for what I am-- a fraud or, worse yet, without talent in the face of recent success acting, directing and writing.

"Well," Darrin begins, calmly removing his shoes. "It might remain a piece of shit if we don't work on it." We are just talking.

"They've already *picked* the plays that are going to be workshopped in that class... and mine ain't one of 'em," I say pragmatically.

"Yes, but Brian, they are doing Garland's goofy-assed play," Darrin says. "Mark likes you -- for reasons that are beyond most of us." I laugh at this truth. "I want to stick a sock in his throat when he calls you a red-headed Jew," he says, as he removes his second sock and delicately lifts it to face level with a smug look of satisfaction as he carries it to his nose and sniffs happily.

"Don't do that in my house," I joke.

"You can have a sniff," he responds curtly. "We could do your play in the booth," he says in an epiphany. "The booth looks like a spaceship..."

"And if we put the audience in the attic theatre we can have twelve to twenty people watch it..." B. G. adds.

Darrin picks up. "And we pump the sound out to the audience." These guys are getting excited.

"They're never going to let us do a show in the booth," I interject, and Darrin rolls his eyes.

"They might not let *us*," he indicates B. G. and himself, "but they would let *you*. Besides you were supposed to stage the fucking thing last semester for an independent study, weren't you?"

"Yes, but that has been forgiven and forgotten!"

"But you don't want it *forgotten*. You want to *do* it. You are *entitled* to do it. We are here to *help* you do it. Brian, you can make this happen."

I think about the amount of work involved and how far this is from what usually goes on in the theatre. It's attractive *and* crazy.

"How long does the show run right now?" B. G. asks.

"About half an hour."

"If we do it in the booth we don't need any set pieces. That means we don't bother the staff or faculty. They like that. We can get a couple of other people to help with tech."

"We pull three costumes – there are three characters, right? -- pull them from the *Macbeth* production from last year. We find futuristic, funky costumes and do the show four times a night -- on the hour."

"Just like Disneyland," B. G. adds sarcastically and joyously.

"No way," I say. This all seems insurmountable with such a short time left in the semester.

Darrin has been ferociously scratching his feet -- between his toes, up top, underneath and the nails. He hits himself three times in the forehead with the ball of his hand and then sternly says, "We wouldn't be on the *moon* if people said 'no' as much as you have tonight!"

He has a point. The possibility of this all happening unfolds before me. I am flattered that they want to work with me.

"Okay. I'm in."

They are glad to hear this. "Do you have three copies? We'll read it now."

"I don't have three copies, but I have one, and we can share it for a read through." B. G. looks at the title. "Why *Sarah's Last Waltz*?"

I grin, "You'll see."

We read through it; it runs about 35 minutes. "Great title," B. G. says. "This is going to be awesome."

"If Brian's done saying, 'no,'" Darrin adds. He lifts the same fingers that have been digging at his feet for over an hour to his nose with a pleased look, breathes deeply and lets out a satisfied moan.

"Who do we get to play the girl?" B. G. asks.

"Leslie was very patient with me and had such a tiny part in *Steambath* that I'd like to throw her this bone," I say.

The collaborators concur. "Give her a call tomorrow and see if she'll do it," B. G. says.

"Let Pablo know that we're going to be working late hours, and we'll be in the house, so his snippy, faggot-ass doesn't get stupid on us," one of them says.

"He'll be glad," I say. "He writes and encourages me to write more. He even reads to me some nights."

They both turn toward me with a moderate look of disgust. "Cut it out," they say.

The next day is Mark Medoff's writing class. We bring three copies and ask Mark if we can read it. He checks with the other class members

The Squeaky Wheel

and, since nothing is being offered up, the play is read. I had adapted (stole?) a short story to serve as this one-act play. The basis of the material is a science fiction short story entitled, "The Cold Equation." In the story an eighteen-year-old girl stows away on an emergency transportation ship that the reader would do well to picture as the shuttle on the original Star Trek. There is a single pilot who must take the ship and cargo to a planet in crisis. The girl hears that the ship is being dispatched, and her brother is based on this distant planet. It is her only chance to see her brother for many years. She stows away, is discovered and informed of the implications. With her aboard the ship it is too heavy to make the flight on the allotted fuel. The rest of the story discusses the inevitability of her death, and she is zapped into space after last words with her brother.

Dramatically, I need three characters. I cast them as a doctor, the pilot and Sarah. I explain the title, as Sarah "just waltzes" onto the ship without realizing the consequences. I also name it for the film, *The Last Waltz*, a documentary of The Band's final performance. Little is changed from the story other than three characters and the fact that sending Sarah to see her mother instead of her brother raises the stakes. It is painfully similar to the short story. I add an exchange between the doctor and the pilot about the arguably most beautiful women in the universe. I borrow the name of one planet from Kurt Vonnegut and a race of people from Tom Robbins. The crewmen lament the plight of the men of the planet who breed once with these women -- who also have an intoxicating aroma -- at which point their copulating organs are ripped from them, and they die, introducing a premise I saw on a PBS special about insects. Possibly the only original idea in my play is the pilot's response to this story:

"Talk about coming and going..."

Mark listens to the play and, in addition to recognizing and approving of the Kurt Vonnegut reference, hears the once deadly serious drama as funny. Others in the class agree.

"So it wants to be comedy," Darrin observes, only slightly surprised.

"Hell, yes," Mark says. "And you three are just the ones to do it. (A tribute to his teaching/encouraging skills.) "You guys need to write and perform this with the same seriousness you just read it. You need to commit to it and make it like *Batman* -- you remember *Batman*? Commit to the absurdity of the situation -- don't treat it as absurd but... do what you're doing: passionately argue that which deserves no *discussion*. Understand?"

The three of us nod, as does most of the class. Some are clearly lying, and Mark sees this. "Okay, here we have a situation where the hero has to die. Because she's a young woman going to see her mother, we care about her -- work hard to make us care about her even *more*. Sarah stows away on the ship as a result of her uninformed actions and must die. If she doesn't die, then the three of them die, and it sounds like the planet they're going to will die, as will Sarah's mother. So, from the time we discover her on the ship until the time we zap her into space, there really is no decision to make then, is there? Now, if I take this serious issue -- her life versus everyone else's life -- and argue about it for thirty to forty minutes, it can only be comedy!"

The collaborators share looks of glee at the prospect of making this a comedy. We are also relieved because the three of us are probably much better situated to comedy than tragedy. After class, we agree on what has already been tacitly suggested -- the three of us share equal credit as writers, directors and producers of this baby. I go to Sherry's office. "You remember I was going to do my play for an independent study?"

She nods and looks sympathetic. "Yeah, I know, with your health problems last semester... it's okay."

I feign a puzzled look and explain that I'd like to do the play in the booth. Her interest is piqued as I explain. She shares an office with Eileen, the grand dame of the theater department, who loves everything *not* traditional in the theater but directs only the most overdone, tedious plays in the history of the art form. She taught our theater of the absurd class. Eileen's interest is also piqued, as she listens attentively and enthusiastically encourages the endeavor. Darrin and B. G. are busy enlisting friends to assist with the technical needs of the production. The Guardians of the Booth can no longer stop this -- nor would they.

Because I have not yet learned to use the computer DVR has provided, we begin working on the play that night with B. G. at a typewriter. I am in my bed and Darrin sits at the foot of it picking his feet. B. G. is typing as we settle a word, line or exchange. The bedroom is not large but the three of us work contentedly. We work through it piece by piece. So far Sarah says little more than "I only wanted to see my mother" repeatedly. I keep offering this line up again. "She just said that," Darrin says and rolls his eyes each time. But progress is made. Each time the play is read in class, it becomes better. The three of us spark off of each other wonderfully. One night Darrin asks B. G. (Darrin is

The Squeaky Wheel

the pilot and B. G. is the doctor), "If I ask you, 'how *did* you know it's a she?' when she's hiding... what is the *only* response you can have?"

I have no idea how to respond to this question. B. G. looks blank for half a minute and then grins ear to ear as he says, "For God sakes, I'm a doctor!"

I point out that if this is said, the pilot needs to be a captain and his name needs to be Jim so that later in the script when the doctor is insisting that there must be a way to eliminate 100 pounds of excess weight -- other than Sarah – and the doctor asks the captain, "How do you know?" the only possible response from Jim will be "For Gods sake, doctor, I'm the Captain."

One day at class Mark asks if I've heard from the University of Hawaii regarding graduate school. I tell him I have not. He announces a break in the class, and the two us go to his office and place a call to paradise.

"Hello, this is Mark Medoff here at New Mexico State University, and I'm sitting with my student Brian Shaughnessy who applied to graduate school there. Can I talk to the director of the graduate program?" I listen while he reintroduces himself to the director and asks about my status regarding admission to the Theatre Department of the University of Hawaii at Manoa. I listen while Mark's intense brown eyes drill holes into me, and he mutters "uh-huh" about seventeen times. He then thanks the person he is speaking to, says he will see them in December, and hangs up.

"Well, they want you," he says, looking at his desk. "They're offering you a tuition waiver." He says this as if there is going to be a list. I extend my arm and pull it horizontally toward me. "An additional Asian Pacific scholarship of $6000 a year." My arm does that motion again. "Work as a teaching assistant for another six grand." I pull the imaginary prize lever a third time. "And they want you to direct a play."

"Wow," I shout. "All that, and I get to live in paradise?"

Mark scoffs. "They're getting you cheap! They're lucky to get you, and *you are* doing them the favor -- not the other way around. Don't ever forget that and don't act any other way. You have talent. Universities are not always places to learn and grow... unfortunately. But congratulations, and I look forward to writing a play about you in December. Let's get back to class."

The class resumes working on another student's play. I want to announce to them my pending trip to the tropics and all of its perks. But I don't. I do interrupt Darrin for a moment and tell him I've been admitted to graduate school in Hawaii. He congratulates me. I then give him the laundry list (one at a time) of the perks. I deliver the information in the same manner to B. G. By the next day everyone in the department is congratulating me.

Long nights are spent writing and rewriting. Darin and B. G. never sleep anyway, but this is taxing for me. Humor and bits of drama sometimes come from what we do at the time. I am in bed one night as B. G. types at my desk, and Darrin feverishly claws at his feet. We have decided to create another unseen character. The Captain attempts to make contact with the planet that Sarah's mother is from and goes through the outer-space version of what the guy Radar O'Reilly on *Mash* had to do to place a phone call. The character receives the moniker, Scooter. If you want something, you must make a deal with Scooter to get it. As Darrin digs at his feet I suggest that Scooter ask the Captain to get him some Monrovian foot powder, at which point the Captain asks, "Still got them stinky feet?"

Darin has been more attentive to his feet than to what I just said and responds, "They don't stink, they just itch!" and vigorously resumes picking between his toes. B. G. has understood, and we laugh. I finally say, "And that would be *Scooter's* response?" The exchange is explained to Darin and B. G. types the dialog. This occurrence of life becoming art repeats itself and creeps into the script several times. The three of us continue to work in my room – for weeks -- with me in bed, Darrin scratching and B. G. typing late into the night. Sometimes Darrin must put me to bed. We make time to rehearse with Leslie during the day. Leslie is a fairly attractive 18-year-old Caucasian with brown hair and no clue as to what subtext means. As is my pattern, when someone raises his or her voice to me I say, "Sorry I blew up." She has heard this many times and as B. G. tries to explain subtext to her he says, "When Brian says, 'Sorry I blow up...'" She has no clue.

The daytime rehearsals are a working/creative period. We all attempt to make sure the various components are "working." We occasionally invite a handful of friends to come and give input. I am sleep deprived. The other two musketeers sleep less, but tempers *never* flare even with endless changing of lines -- even after I think they are "set." This is hell for B.G. on a typewriter.

The Disneyland production is set to "go up" in two days. Now we work with adrenaline-induced creativity. Darrin and B.G.'s first two fingers

The Squeaky Wheel

of each of their right hands are a sickly yellowish-brown from the constant presence of lighted cigarettes.

Rewrites, rewrites, rewrites and more rewrites take us until about noon the day of the performance. At this point copies are made and given to our friends who are assisting on sound and lighting. Then some *final* changes occur to the script and are penciled in by the nervous technicians. The technical director of the theatre -- and the main guardian of the booth -- informs me that the recording for the off-stage characters of the Commander and Scooter will prove too difficult and tenuous for practical use. He suggests that my two technicians play the characters. They are terrified by this development but quickly pick up yellow highlighters.

The first show is to begin at 6:00. At 5:45 Darrin, Brian, B. G., the technicians and Leslie are shuffling pages and panicking in the attic theatre. Pillows have been placed in front of the four-by-six-foot window that allows the technicians to view the smaller student production stage and make appropriate lighting and sound changes during a production. To the left of this window (inside the booth) is a massive dark window that allows the technicians to view the main stage production. Looking through the tiny window -- with nothing added -- it looks like a space ship. The actors and technicians add a row of five chairs behind the pillows. Behind the chairs is a platform slightly higher than the seats -- thus creating room for five more onlookers. Four more chairs are placed on the platform for the final row of audience members.

At 6:05 I see people coming up the stairs and banish them back down until they are called. I look nervously at Darrin who simply looks up and says, "Don't start freaking. *We* still have to perform this fucker." The 6:00 show begins at 6:25, and goes perfectly in front of a full house. Three or four people must come back for the 7:00 show (which will, of necessity, begin late). The 7:00 show is nearly full. Technicians, Scooter and Commander are adding their own pre-show bits. Only my mother shows up for the 8:00 show, which is somewhat worrisome, but I ask her -- after offering a private viewing -- to come at nine or ten, as we can use this time to fix things and relax.

The 9:00 show has about 10 people, and my mother returns at 9:45. Again she is the only one, and the actors are far too exhausted to perform a private show. She laughs good-naturedly and agrees to return the next day at 6:00.

We have a full house for the 6:00 show on Sunday, and my mother is not yet there. I have saved her a seat. The person downstairs does not know this -- nor does he know that this woman is my mother -- and tells her to come back. "This is the third time I've been sent away!" she blurts out. The girl comes upstairs, after finding out that this is the mother of two of the three playwrights (and sometime mother to B. G.), and is relieved that I have saved her a seat. The four shows are performed roughly on the hour, and those involved are sad to let it go.

"I'll be hanging this uniform up with a lump in my throat," B. G. says.

I suggest that everyone return early Monday, set up a video recorder and perform *Sarah's Last Waltz* one more time for posterity -- without an audience. Everyone is excited and agrees to this, but when I arrive at the theatre late Monday morning, I am the only member of the production there. One of the guardians of the booth has already removed the necessaries for taping. But the production didn't suck. In fact, not a bad word was said about it. The audience laughed throughout, and the women in the costume shop are amazed that I have directed two productions and acted in another in the course of a 15-week semester.

The Squeaky Wheel

Oh, What a Tangled Web...

I am in the office of the New Mexico State University Theater Department saying good-byes and making whatever arrangements are necessary when moving on to graduate school. Goldie is in her office pouring over a grade book. She sees me and smiles pleasantly as I chat with the office personnel.

"So, what's going to happen when you get to graduate school in Hawaii, and they see an F on your transcript for stage management?" she asks with a modicum of concern and a wheelbarrow full of an attempt to dig at me. In order to direct plays I was forced to take Goldie's stage management class. I did so grudgingly, knowing that I would never function as a stage manager. I test her.

"Don't give me an F," I say. Goldie cocks her head and raises one corner of her mouth to communicate that that is not going to happen.

"Actually," I begin tentatively, feeling slightly guilty, "you agreed that I could audit the class. So, I never registered for it..."

The slight smile on Goldie's face evaporates -- but not entirely. She tries to look disappointed, but I can see she is impressed by this calculated maneuver to avoid taking a compulsory (and universally regarded as boring and useless) class. And, she is absolved of having to give me an F. She looks away from me and down at her desk, feigning disappointment.

"You scammed me," she says, struggling to look betrayed and unimpressed.

"Yeah," I say, feigning shame and embarrassment, "I know. I feel *really* bad about it, too. But it'll pass."

I call the office for handicapped students at the University of Hawaii at Manoa -- the KOKUA office. I am quickly put through to the director, Ann. I know immediately that she has a disability, only because I sense it over the phone. She tells me the KOKUA program will provide me with note takers, (no carbonless notepaper here), library assistance, a large office with study cubicles and rooms, transportation and test taking facilities. They also function as the liaison between professors and students. Hawaii is sounding more like paradise every day.

Brian Shaughnessy

Pablo asks to accompany me to Minneapolis, where I'm spending the summer before starting graduate school. I decline. One night when I had people working on a project he found it necessary to slam doors and act like a child -- or a prissy gay man. I don't want to drag that back to Minneapolis. Proletarian Peggy and my mother will be driving back in the van with me. My significant other, Bethany, wears hippie clothing and likes to drop acid and go to amusement parks. I do not share this hobby. I understand that she is 18 and has just transferred to New Mexico State University from her high school. One day we are walking across campus when she mentions something about her birthday in July and, "turning eighteen."

"Wait, wait, wait" I begin trying to decipher what I just heard and its implications. "You're not 18?"

She is grinning ear to ear and about to double over with laughter. "No," she says as she is convulsing.

"You know I'm 28," I say.

"Yes," she says barely able to speak. "I'm sorry, I thought you knew you are going out with jail bait."

"Just promise to bake a cake with a file in it when they build the special cell for me."

"You don't have to worry about that," she says almost gaining composure. "When my daddy is done with you you'll need a box, not a cell."

Proletarian Peggy has to keep delaying my departure. She is delayed in flying from Minneapolis to El Paso. This buys me more time with Bethany, but one day as we have make plans to drop acid and go to the amusement park (or something else) Proletarian Peggy walks through the door. Bethany and I continue to kiss as Proletarian Peggy carries items out to the van. I arrange to buy two pounds of marijuana from Carlos, we pack the van and leave for Minneapolis. My mom arrives at my house and we all get in the van. Before pulling out of the driveway I send my mother back into my house to get the seat for the shower chair which I have forgotten. She returns from the house rolling her eyes and carrying a piece of paper. It is a letter from Pablo saying that since he hasn't been paid his final paycheck -- issued by the state of Minnesota and consistent as rush-hour traffic -- he is going to hang onto, in essence a toilet seat, until he is paid. Odd extortion.

We arrive back in Minneapolis without anyone punching anyone in the face while driving. I am disappointed to discover that I will pay a price

175

The Squeaky Wheel

for working so hard in New Mexico. I experience my first decubitis ulcer on my butt -- another of the horrors of the Rehab films I saw and promised would never happened to me. Proletarian Peggy and I travel to see Dr. David D. Davenport or 3D, M.D., Ph.D. He says to stay in bed until the wound is closed. Before we return home Proletarian Peggy takes me to happy hour where we get very drunk on half price liquor and eat free food.

I spend a few days in bed and Proletarian Peggy feels the wound is not healing fast enough -- she wants me to see a specialist. We travel back to see 3D, M.D., Ph.D. who says the wound is not that bad and that I can put any type of medicine or dressing onto it. "If you want to see Dr. Dayton I will refer you." Proletarian Peggy approves as Dr. Dayton saved the foot of a diabetic friend of hers with his platelet derived healing formula. Diabetic's have their extremities lopped off regularly.

That night I sleep on Proletarian Peggy's bed -- she sleeps on mine. We try to position me so that the wound on my butt is getting air. I wind up with a wound the size of a dime on my penis.

"Our first penis wound," Dr. Dayton comments when he enters the room after Proletarian Peggy and I joke with his nurses. Dr. Dayton is a big, heavyset man with a white doctor coat with buttons exploding. He will be rich soon from his miracle medicine. "C-5 quadriplegic with a penile implant, yes?" he asks me as he looks at my erect penis pointing at my chin.

"No, but thank you for asking," I say as he is moving to examine the other wound. They draw blood and create the frozen popsicles that are to be used over the course of the summer to close the wound on my butt. Proletarian Peggy and I travel to another happy hour before returning home. Back home I meet Peggy's friend Alexis who is a gorgeous, well-proportioned, sultry Hispanic/Caucasian woman with my sense of humor. We are kindred souls. She is also an actress. Peggy disappears. I know from Alexis' reaction that this was not planned and eventually she transfers me to bed and undresses me and covers me with a blanket. She lies next to me on the bed, strokes my hair, kisses my cheek and tells me she will help anytime that this other idiot fails me.

The next morning I scream at Proletarian Peggy, "Either do the job or get the fuck out of my house."

She is already annoying Across-the-hall Annie and Mike by just walking into their unlocked apartment. Proletarian Peggy believes that all property is communal except hers. She wears my clothes, takes the van without asking and one day I see her boyfriend in a shirt of mine.

Brian Shaughnessy

Whenever anyone enters the apartment -- her friend or mine -- and I am not in bed in the backroom -- they ask, "Should I leave? Is something going on?" It's not me putting out these unspoken messages that suggest an interrupted lover's spat or that we were just about to have sex. Proletarian Peggy is tall, thin and blue-eyed, with dark ringlets framing a face and complexion that says 'Irish' almost as loudly as my own. She is attractive and sits in my lap whenever we go to parties or happy hour. It's a damn shame she's insane. She also exhibits this lap-sitting behavior when guests come to the house -- unless it is her boyfriend.

I do not stay out of bed as often as I stay in bed and it becomes a lost, drunken summer. Proletarian Peggy sells most of the marijuana. I give a quarter pound to a friend of mine and never hear from him for the rest of the summer. Later, when he enters treatment, all participants must confess the heinous deeds they perpetrated when they were using cocaine. This friend, John, who I have known since high school, wins the prize from the other junkies for committing the lowest act -- stealing from a crippled friend.

Darrin returns for the summer. My father and his second clan, my siblings and my Aunt and cousins are to gather for dinner and festivities. My old roommate, Mark, joins us. Everyone is horribly delayed by the annual Minneapolis Aquatennial parade occurring blocks away. "Whoever said, 'I love a parade,' never got stuck in the traffic," I say.

The last thing I remember from that evening was a woman knocking over my drink. She drunkenly and emptily asks if there is anything she can do. I foolishly say, "You can buy me another drink. She grudgingly brings another Long Island ice tea to the table.

The next day I awake in my bed -- unsure of how I got there or who put me to bed. I ask Proletarian Peggy where my wheelchair is. She looks at me as if I were an idiot and responds, "Darrin and Mark brought you in here at about 2 AM in a broken wheelchair. They said you went off a curb and the wheelchair broke. Today is Sunday so I can't even get anybody out to fix it until tomorrow."

Although variations on this drunken distracted theme repeat themselves over the summer I do spend much time in bed and I lose the ability to feed myself with the universal cuff and the Uri Geller Fork. Each time I try to spear a morsel of food my wrist flips over and flings the food onto the wall or another person.

The Squeaky Wheel

Proletarian Peggy is not without her tricks. Given that I am to be trapped in bed and have sold my TV, she brings me to Target where I purchase a TV and VCR (to be returned before I leave for Hawaii). Target is a lending library for electronic appliances. My Target charge card is my library card. One night she leaves and she puts in Blue Velvet. There is a scene that is so terrifying I want to turn it off but cannot. I do not have a set-up for a telephone or the remote. Suddenly I realize it's Dennis Hopper, relax, and 30 seconds later am terrified again. The movie ends, the TV kicks on and the Amazing Randy -- a man who debunks the paranormal -- is explaining that faith healers avoid people in power wheelchairs. Sweet dreams.

The next day Proletarian Peggy enters the room and suddenly is jumping back and looking out the floor. She looks over toward the bed and announces, "Your night bag leaked and there's urine all over the carpet."

"Use chucks (blue pads that go underneath me to deal with any incontinence) to soak up as much of it as you can, then use some of the old towels underneath the sink and then spray it with Lysol. We'll get somebody to clean the carpet later." I know the routine.

I spend the next day in bed. In the late afternoon I hear Proletarian Peggy talking for some time on the phone. She enters my room with a self-satisfied smirk and two glasses of wine. She gives me a sip.

"Mark Medoff just called," she begins. I told him that I had heard a lot about him and was going with you to Hawaii. He said that he just got a letter from Professor Fragilego who's in charge of the theater department and he says they are not going to let Mark write a play about you when he teaches the class. This dude is telling Mark he wants a 'nuts and bolts' playwriting class from your buddy who's won a Tony. Mark says he won't be teaching the class there. He says you should look into other graduate schools because Hawaii is not interested in your best interests. (Pause) I knew it wouldn't work out and that we wouldn't be going to Hawaii." She says this with the authority of a person who was afraid to move to Hawaii.

I am depressed but I cannot imagine that this will not happen. I call my former roommate Mark and instruct him to procure us some cocaine -- to commiserate. The next day I talk to Mark and he again encourages me to look into other graduate schools or to come back to New Mexico where together we will work on the play. I then call Darryl Cannis, who is in charge of the theater department at the University of Hawaii at Manoa. He is apologetic and explains that professor Fragilego has been very sick, just had surgery, and has just only now returned home from the hospital. Darryl is confident that everything can be worked out. I explain this to Proletarian Peggy who remains pessimistic.

The next day Proletarian Peggy and I travel to a party at Don and Diane's. Proletarian Peggy sits on my lap and pouts. I wear the black and white checkered sneakers that Annie brought me while I was in Rehab.

"So," Diane begins with a beaming grin, "you guys looking forward to your trip to the land of rainbows, poi and plumerias?" She asks with unchecked elation for me. Proletarian Peggy goes into her rant about yesterday's information and how she knew Hawaii was hell. Diane looks at me as if she wants to cry.

"I'm not so sure it's as awful as that," I say rolling my eyes. Proletarian Peggy begins her rant afresh but Diane shares my optimism.

I take time to see a play at the Tyrone Guthrie theater with Don and Diane. We begin what becomes a regular outing for when I am in town. We have dinner at the theater and enjoy each other's company. We watch a great production of *Volpone* with cross-gender casting and codpieces sticking out from most costumes. At intermission a beautiful, blue-eyed blonde greets me. I dated her while in the theater department at the University of Minnesota. She beams, tells me how glad she is to see me and is writing down her number and asking me to call her. She does not even mention that I am sitting in an electric wheelchair. I tell Don and Diane how much that aspect of the exchange pleases me.

I look at the phone number and turn to Don and Diane and say, "She's such a lucky girl to be getting a call from me." Don concurs and says, "You still got it -- even with a wheelchair under your ass."

"Yeah," Diane begins with a smile and a slight sneer, "but you're still a cad."

Two weeks before I am to depart for Hawaii, Proletarian Peggy announces that she will not be going to Hawaii and that I shouldn't either. I tell her to bring me the phone. I tell the state agency that refers potential live-in attendants of my situation and to have interested applicants call me. Proletarian Peggy pouts and exits. I wonder what the fuck she is pouting about -- I'm the one that must travel 5000 miles, isolated from family and friends, find a suitable companion and hope that the bastard does not smother me in my sleep. The wound on my ass is still not healed. I scramble to find a new attendant. I choose Poorly, who was working at a very respectable post-Rehabilitation facility called Courage Center. Poorly is a short blonde with waist-length hair, Raquel Welch breasts and tattoos on her left-hand. One says, "hi," and the other is a smiley face :-). She tries to wrap a scarf around the two to hide them -- unsuccessfully. Her aura suggests trailer park. She will be leaving behind her five-year-old son. This gives Proletarian Peggy, Annie -- who has been hinting at a tryst all summer, her sister Janice and everyone with a modicum of common sense including me concern. But I leave in two weeks...

My dear love Annie without whom I would have never survived to tell this tale is easing back into our passion -- theater. She auditions for a Tennessee Williams play and gets the lead. I find this out from a kindred soul, Alex, who has only just met Annie and does not yet know Annie's importance in my life, and has also been cast in the play. I instruct Alex that at their next meeting she must approach Annie, tell her she has a message for her and then grit her teeth and with increasing rage say, "Little pearl buttons!"

This was an oft-repeated line from the play that I would say to Annie as she dressed me. It always caused doubled over laughter and was heard with the same regularity as, "I hate people," or, "There, there, Annie's here..." or any of the other handful of through lines in our relationship.

"You would have been so proud of me," Alex begins when next I see her. "I told Annie I had a message for her. She said okay, and I got right up in her face and said, "Little pearl buttons." Alex grits her teeth appropriately and explains that Annie laughed and asked, "How do you know Brian?"

"What did you tell her?" I ask.

"I told her I was your main squeeze and your lover."

I will never understand women. I revel in the image though.

Proletarian Peggy announces there will be an aloha party for my going away. Kegs of beer, food and tropical accoutrements are purchased for the festivities and many of my friends but more of Proletarian Peggy's friends attend the bash. I give myself alcohol, someone else gives me marijuana, someone else gives me cocaine and one of my dear brothers makes the supreme sacrifice and offers me psilocybin mushrooms.

I said while I was in Rehab that if I ever again ingested psychedelic mushrooms I would lose my mind. Tonight I prove that statement. I am in bed terrified and Across-the-hall Annie -- who tonight is a drunken nurse -- is trying to assess and help me. Darrin and another altered friend offer altered assistance. Across-the-hall Annie calls the emergency room of the University of Minnesota hospital for their opinion. Naturally, they say to bring me in.

This sounds like a trip to hell -- or more hell than I am already in. "I can't go to an emergency room where they will stick the cripple on drugs over to the side until he fully loses his mind and then, when its time, put him in the psych ward."

Just then Proletarian Peggy enters the room. "What are you doing in bed? I thought you were... "

Those present explain that I'm having an overdose. Across-the-hall Annie asks, "Do you have your doctor's home phone?"

I tell her that I do as I look at the clock, which says 2:18 AM.

"Let's wake the asshole up," comes her caustic statement.

Proletarian Peggy jumps to 3D. M.D., Ph.D.'s defense. "Dr. Delaware is no asshole."

Across-the-hall Annie begins to explain but Proletarian Peggy is not one to listen. She would rather talk.

"He is so cool and he loves Brian."

Across-the-hall Annie will have her say. "When I am working at the hospital, where most of the doctors ARE assholes, and one of the patients is having a crisis at night we love to say, talking about the doctor, "Let's wake the asshole up."

"I'll bet Dr. Delaware has snorted a line or two," Proletarian Peggy finishes.

The two exit the room and return minutes later. "Wow," Across-the-hall Annie begins, "your doc really does love you. I said, 'Is this Dr. Delaware?' and he said yes, and I said, 'this is Across-the-hall Annie. I am a nurse at an unnamed hospital and I have your patient Brian Shaughnessy here,' and you would have thought that he was shot out of a cannon."

"'What's wrong with Brian?' he said, totally awake and with more concern than any doctor I have ever talked to in the middle of the night." The party is winding down and there are very few people left in the backyard park or apartment. "I told him that your pulse is up and your blood pressure is down and that you are on alcohol, marijuana, cocaine and mushrooms..."

I scream a stifled scream.

"He said to bring you in."

I tell Annie and Darrin that I will remain in the bed and if things get worse I will have Proletarian Peggy -- looking drunken, concerned and

The Squeaky Wheel

pained sitting on the corner of the bed -- deliver me to the emergency room. Proletarian Peggy begins to scold me for choosing Poorly to go with me to Hawaii. She says she is not to be trusted. She says that when Poorly fails me she will come to Hawaii and take care of me. "Just call me and I'll be there." She says, "I love you. I have loved you a long time and I am going to continue to love you."

I cannot believe I am hearing this and stuck in bed and overdosing. I am surely in hell. I feel awful that someone is telling me she loves me and I only want her out of my room. I fall into a comatose sleep.

The next day I am up and answer the phone.
"You didn't come in," says 3D, M.D., Ph.D.
"The thought of lying on a gurney until sunrise kinda sobered me up," I sheepishly respond.
Heavy sigh from 3D, M.D., Ph.D. "You've got to be more careful who you get your shit from, Brian."
Maybe Proletarian Peggy was right. He wishes me well in my travels to the tropics and recommends a classmate of his to be my physiatrist in Hawaii. I tell him I will see him next summer and instruct him to take a trip to the middle of the Pacific. He says that that will never happen given his responsibilities.

I have dinner with my family at a restaurant for my bon voyage. It is the first time I am able to keep the food on my fork since being forced to bed. The therapists at Rehab have come through for me again -- they stretched my arms and got me working so that I can feed myself. It is the most delicious salad I have ever eaten. My 4-year-old nephew feeds me large French fries with his little fingers.
"Ouch," shouts a calm little person's voice. I look down and see half a French fry and a short finger protruding beyond that with teeth marks. Devlin looks at me as if I have no sense at all. He seems to be saying, Even I, at four years old, know better than to bite the hand that feeds me... What's your excuse? I apologize through my teary laughter.

I arrive in Honolulu. The Airlines has lost my batteries for the wheelchair. Poorly rents a moped, gets a job as a stripper and makes ready to abandon me. Nonetheless I attend school. I am the teaching assistant for Introduction to Theatre. When I first enter the Theatre Department I am immediately handed my first paycheck -- having done nothing.

Brian Shaughnessy

The women of Hawaii are the most beautiful women on the planet. Each of the varied races has its own beauty and when mixed results in the best features of each race. The mostly beautiful, petite Asian girls wear black shorts and red shirts -- usually tank tops. Their skin is magical and their long, black hair can be braided into ropes thicker than the ones I once shimmied up in junior high.

Some of these goddesses work at KOKUA -- the office serving handicapped students. KOKUA means 'help' in Hawaiian. The theater department also has its share of magical, multi-racial beauties. When tropical temperatures and plumeria waft through your nostrils it is surprising that any task is accomplished. The "KOKUA girls," as I come to refer to them, assist me in most of the endeavors of school. Cold is pronounced 'code' and gold is pronounced 'gode' and other aspects add to the charm. Paradise squared.

I share my new campus apartment with a fellow quadriplegic and a fascist Hawaiian who orders me around and threatens me. Poorly unpacks my suitcases and out drops a prepackaged syringe wrapped in more packaging that says Fortaz. She asks me what it is.

"Heroin," I say grinning at my new roommate because it couldn't possibly be.

"You better not bring that shit in here," he says yelling at me. "I'm not going to stand for that in my apartment."

Silence. Poorly and I exit to our room and both indicate that the man is an asshole. This fascist roommate tells me I cannot bring people into the apartment.

I begin my search for a new attendant. I call home to discover that Proletarian Peggy was clearly drunk and out of her mind when she made her declaration of love and her promise to come to Hawaii. I also discover she has been driving my van, which I told her to leave in the driveway. I instruct my brother to take it away. One day I return from class and Poorly is half asleep on her bed.

"I tried to hock the engagement ring I was given," she begins. "The ring is a fake and its not worth anything. Can you believe that shit? I was going to marry that guy."

Not only do I believe it, but I am pleased by the information. Trailer park traitors attract trailer park traitors

As Poorly is devoting more time to her other livelihood, she finds a neighbor of mine with muscular dystrophy whose brother is his caregiver.

The Squeaky Wheel

She subcontracts to this thin, 18 year old Caucasian felon to perform the bulk of my evening cares. One day my wallet is missing.

"Somebody who works for you took it," Poorly self-evidently explains.

I suspect her over the kid.

The Entrée of Stench

Poorly has made it clear that she would rather be anywhere else than in this apartment, and that I am a sap for hiring her. She has found her calling -- to shake her ass naked on a "stage" for a dollar a squat. I was her ticket to the tropics and no more. Fine. I beat myself up for choosing Poorly and for my poor selection process. I curse Proletarian Peggy for agreeing to go with me to Hawaii and then reneging on the deal with only weeks until the scheduled departure, leaving precious little time to interview and select my traveling companion/roommate/personal care attendant.

After sufficient self-flagellation, I inventory my resources and call Ann at KOKUA. (I was right. Ann has a disability. She is blind and has been running the KOKUA office flawlessly for ages. She is in profound pain right now having just lost her sixteen-year-old daughter in an automobile accident.)

Ann is, naturally, sorry to hear of this turn of events. Actually, she's angry and tells me she feels *she* has been duped by Poorly. I tell her that I feel *at least* equally duped, foolish, angry and now desperate. We discuss options, and she agrees to put in a request that I be admitted to the Rehabilitation Hospital of the Pacific until I can get matters resolved. The Rehabilitation Hospital of the Pacific says that because my situation is not a "medical emergency" they cannot get reimbursement from Minnesota Medicaid. Therefore, there is no room at their inn. Ann clearly has some clout and tells me she will continue to press for my admittance. I call the appropriate agency to send out applicants to fill Poorly's position. I'm trying to make arrangements in less than the two weeks notice I have.

I place a call to the Hawaii Center for Independent Living and speak with Busywork Juan, to whom I explain my dilemma.

"Well," he begins with exuberance and confidence, "you happen to be in the right place at the right time. I have a really good guy -- lots of experience, very professional -- who is not too happy where he is now. They don't pay him much, and he can never get time off to see his girlfriend. But in Hawaii that's pretty standard. What kind of arrangements can you give him?"

I explain to him that I am still a resident of Minnesota and that therefore Minnesota Medicaid pays a personal care attendant eleven hours a day at a rate of over eight dollars an hour. I practically hear the phone hit his desk. *"What?"*

I repeat the rate to him, and he laughs. "Brian, that is *so* much more than Hawaii pays that I would advise you to *never* give up that residence. How is it that they pay while you're here?"

I give him a vague answer, and he tries to press for more details. I shift the conversation back to the specifics of the potential employee he is recommending. "Has he ever worked for you?" I ask, knowing that Busywork Juan is also quadriplegic. He has not. He explains his living arrangements boastfully as I shake my head and roll my eyes at the other end of the receiver.

"I need to know that this guy will do the job! I need to know that he won't kill me in my sleep! I need to know that I can *stand* this human being in the same room -- not just apartment. I'm trying to go to school and have a life. I'm new in Hawaii, Juan," I say with calm urgency. "If I am going to stay in Hawaii, I need to be in school, and I need to have an attendant. What's this guy's name?"

"His name's Stench Colt."

I laugh. "Could he have a more macho name than that?"

"I didn't really think about that," Busywork Juan responds. I wonder what he thinks about while he is at work. I'm sure it is not work.

I get a brief bio and glowing testimonial from Juan regarding Stench and arrange to meet with him the next day. Juan and I also set up a time that I can go to the Hawaii Center for Independent Living and fill out the obligatory paperwork. "Is this guy the *only* one I have available on such short notice?" I ask, wanting things perfectly clear.

"This is the *only* guy... period," he says with an urgency I don't doubt. Ann has made it painfully clear that the attendant situation in Hawaii is "abysmal." She attributes it to several factors, including a dominant Asian culture that tends to take care of its own family members -- sometimes to the detriment of the family -- as well as a less progressive state than Minnesota regarding persons with disabilities.

The Squeaky Wheel

Juan says that he will contact Stench to check on availability and a time the two of us can meet. He calls back shortly and offers the next day at 10 AM. I agree. Within a few hours Poorly returns. The contempt we share for each other is thicker than the walls. "Did you find somebody to take the job?" she asks. In the question I hear hate, contempt, and definite glee at her control over me.

"Someone's coming tomorrow at ten to interview," I respond flatly.

"Really?" she asks, sounding startled. "Are you going to hire him?"

I can't understand why there seems to be concern in her voice.

"Probably."

She follows up with a battery of questions about the new person -- gender, experience, age, living arrangements, etc. -- most of which I cannot answer. Although it is the middle of the afternoon I decide to go to bed because of the sore on my butt. Besides, if I don't go now Poorly may not be able to subcontract the little felon brother of the kid with CP to do the job. She positions my chair and then removes my shirt, seatbelt and armrest. She leans into me as if she was carrying a bag of rice on her shoulder, and I am quickly transferred to the bed. She removes my clothing, connects the night bag and performs range of motion while she talks.

"I was telling one of my girlfriends from the restaurant about my job." Right now she's pretending she's a waitress instead of saying she's a stripper. I have wanted to burst her bubble, but passed several times. "I told her that I used to work at Courage Center and everything I did there, and that now I'm working for you doing your cares."

Working for me? Doing my cares? What the fuck are you talking about, I think. You're never here! You hire the little thief to come in and do my cares so you can go squat for a dollar! She continues. "She said that she could never do this kind of work, and she thought I was really cool and special for doing it." Where the hell is this coming from, I wonder. You want me to stroke you or ask you back? You want me to concur that *you're* special? Forget it. "She said that there aren't many people who would do it." This self-promotion continues for 20-plus minutes while she spends longer than usual doing my range of motion.

The next day, as is done on alternate days, Poorly again performs range of motion, sticks a suppository up my ass, transfers me to the shower chair and goes back to sleep while I shit. I read at my desk and every fifteen minutes she rises and puts her finger up my ass to dig/stimulate the shit out. About an hour of this and I am off to the shower, clean and transferred back into bed, dried and dressed. She brings in the electric wheelchair, positions it and transfers me into it. I turn on the power, and the meter only goes halfway up.

"Why're the batteries only halfway charged?" I ask, in a tone that is puzzled and pissed.

"You didn't *tell me* to plug it in, Brian," comes the answer from the living room. "You know you're responsible for your own cares. You would have never made it at Courage Center," she says with a scoff, as she comes back into the bedroom with her arms folded.

Oh, beautiful, I think, we are going to be petty for the duration of this sentence. "So... suddenly you're telling me that I need to tell you every night to push the wheelchair into the living room and plug it into the charger?" I ask.

"That's right," she says with a gleeful smirk. I will not dignify her with rage.

"Fine," I say, as I turn around and exit past her and into the kitchen. "Bring the charger over to the table and plug me in while I have some cereal. And bring the book on my desk in here." Because I know the way this simple-minded little Hitler wants to play this out, I pause before adding, "Please."

She complies and prepares a bowl of cereal and straps the spoon and the universal-cuff to my hand. I eat and read as I await the arrival of Stench. The breakfast is finished, the utensils are cleaned, and my universal cuff placed back into the backpack. For some reason Poorly is not asking (rather, announcing) that she's leaving for an indeterminate amount of time. She sleeps on her bed in the room and eventually, a few minutes before 10 AM, there is a knock at my door. I notice the wheelchair meter is almost at zero (indicating a full charge) and turn toward the door. I see a tall, overweight, sweaty man -- about my age -- with dated black glasses, a short haircut and prematurely gray hair. He's wearing shredded cut-off shorts and a white rag of a paint-splattered T-shirt from which his large hairy gut protrudes. I call to him to come in as I seriously consider, for the first time, going back to Minneapolis and throwing Poorly out of my apartment.

"Hi, I'm Stench. I guess we both spoke to Juan," he says, as he tentatively comes into the apartment and surveys it. He stinks. By this I mean that he is actually malodorous.

I begin stoically, barely hiding my disappointment. "Let's give you my first test," I say, grinning as Poorly exits the bedroom and breezes past the two of us and out the door. "Why don't you unplug this charger from my chair and wrap the cord around the charger."

The Squeaky Wheel

He does this quickly, and I invite him to sit so that I can ask him about his experience. He tells me that he worked for a quadriplegic in California for over a year, and he has been in Hawaii for nine months. Before that, he says proudly, he was in the Air Force for four years. I wonder what he gained in the Air Force other than a three-minute haircut. He stinks -- literally. Apparently he did not learn grooming habits or how to take care of one's uniform. I explain my daily routine: range of motion, suppository and bowel program on alternating days, shower, condom catheter, getting dressed, transferred to wheelchair, breakfast and off to school. This is not uncharted territory, Stench tells me, as he worked for a quad and is currently working for an elderly man with Alzheimer's. Stench tells me his client's wife is too controlling, and she demands his presence virtually 24 hours a day. He finds this especially unsatisfactory as he has a girlfriend, and these demands virtually eliminate their "sack time." Stench likes to use military lingo.

I tell Stench that he must share a room with me. Also, because he will be living on campus, the powers-that-be would like him enrolled in a class. He tells me -- again proudly -- that he has his Ph.D. in Military Science, but that he could register for a class. Stench claims that he has an IQ of 160 (or some ridiculously high number for someone who doesn't bathe). I tell him that it is my experience that people who state their IQ numbers are usually lying. He flinches at this and asks me about chow -- seemingly a rather dear subject to him. I explain to him that I have just been offered a free "meal ticket" which entitles me to breakfast and dinner at the student dining hall. He looks somewhat puzzled. I explain this translates into him *not* having to prepare meals for me. He asks how he is to eat. Slightly miffed and sure he lied about the number, I explain to him that he can purchase a meal card, or that he can purchase his own food and prepare it. He complains that he was fed at his last job. I tell him that is not part of the bargain here. He says with a grin that I could buy him a meal card. I decline, and the grin immediately leaves his face -- replaced by a look of surprise. (What did the moron expect?) I ask what he makes at his current job. He does not answer. I tell him to do the math and decide if the pay and freedom differential might offset his having to buy his own food and pay his portion of the rent.

He has already done the math. He continues in his beneficent tone saying, "I know how badly you need me," and, "I'm good, I'm very good," ... at what he does and other like statements. But, he would like food included. I decline flatly and tell him he is welcome to stay where he is, and I will continue to look for a suitable applicant if the terms are not suitable. I know from Busy-Work Juan that the pay rate offered is much better than Stench can get elsewhere -- chow included or not. Stench says that he will accept the job. I inform him of one more thing. I tell him that I smoke dope, and that he must occasionally assist in this practice. He says that he does not smoke dope (nor approve -- funny, I don't remember asking). "If you want to fuck up your life, that's your business," he says, but given that I am in *graduate school* while he is in rags, begging for a job, it means nothing.

I ask how soon he can begin. He says that he will need to give his current employer two weeks notice. I am clearly disappointed by this and wonder how I will maintain myself short of entering The Rehabilitation Hospital of the Pacific in the meantime. Stench says that he will try to make arrangements with his employer and Busy-Work Juan to begin sooner. As we conclude, he moves toward the door. "I'm in demand because I'm good -- very good," he says, nodding and turning the corners of his mouth down for pointless emphasis. He exits.

I shake my head at the thought of living with this person. Then I shudder. As I turn to call Ann at KOKUA, Poorly reenters. "Are you going to hire him?" she asks. I know I am being taunted.

"It would seem I don't have much of a choice," I say in a Pledge of Allegiance tone.

"He's fat," she says and giggles.

I roll my eyes at her, her statement, her own pudgy belly and my predicament. "Yup, and he smells bad," I say in an attempt to let her know that I chose this fat, stinky individual to be in my home over her. The attempt fails.

"When can this guy start?" she asks with concern.

"Two weeks."

"That long? Do you want *me* to keep the job?" she asks, looking forlorn.

I'm not sure what she's asking. "Do I want you to keep the job for two weeks?"

"*No*," she says girlishly and in a tone usually reserved for one's lover, "do you want me to stay here like we planned and be your attendant?"

Now... I can't believe *this* question. My mind lashes out in a tirade. Are you nuts? Do you think I'm simpleminded? The urge to utter these statements and others races through my mind as Poorly begins to list the contingencies of her remaining to torment me further. Mainly, what I hear is, buzz, buzz, buzz, but occasionally I hear one of the demands. "I have

The Squeaky Wheel

to be able to keep the other job. I have to...." You have not fulfilled your end of the bargain since we arrived, I think. The demands continue, as I calm down. Ultimately she asks, "Well, how about it?"

I look at her. She's smiling with her head tilted and a saintly expression -- as if she has just offered me Betty Crocker, Hazel the maid, a soul mate and sex kitten, all in one package.

"No," I say, realizing she has priced Honolulu apartments and has not negotiated another place to stay yet. The solicitous smile has left her face and daggers are blasted at me as if from a gun in a Star Wars movie. "I think it's best if you leave when he moves in."

"Fine," she says angrily, "I can stay with one of my girlfriends from work. I make $100 a night! I don't need to stay here."

No, I think, mercifully you *don't* have to stay here.

As my butt has not healed, the doctor and the Rehabilitation Hospital of the Pacific (not half the man or doctor 3D, M.D., Ph.D. is) demands that I spend three weeks in bed. I have already befriended classmates and my professors are willing to accommodate. I have no TV. I do not even have a radio. I cannot read a book while I am in bed. I stare at the four walls for three weeks only interrupted by Stench who brings my meals from the cafeteria, bathes me etc. The KOKUA program has given me a "meal ticket" which entitles me to eat at the student cafeteria for free. I have him position me and I strain to get a look in the hand mirror everyday so I can keep a watchful eye on the shrinking wound on my *okole* which I learn to be the Hawaiian word for hind end.

When Stench is not in the apartment he is with his girlfriend of the same weight class. He returns one night and asks me how I am. I tell him the obvious, bored. He says that this is about to change as he is present for stimulating conversation and entertainment. He does what appears to be a 23 skidoo move.

"Did I ever tell you about my family trip to the Grand Canyon?"

I shudder at the thought.

One night he brings my meal.

"Can I have your fat?"

After three days he asks me to compare him to other attendants. I begin to explain that it is too soon to draw comparisons.

"So I'm the best?"

160 IQ.

Brian Shaughnessy

Ann has arranged for a community nurse to monitor my healing. She comes one day with a social worker who provides me with a small, long bag which attaches to the side of the wheelchair. I can keep my wallet -- and other items I would prefer not to have stolen -- in this bag and monitor them better than from the backpack behind my head.

Stench does not bathe. This is very disconcerting. He tries to wash my face with a washcloth he has used on himself and has not yet been washed. I order him to bathe himself and threaten him -- put sheets on your bed and do not use my linen -- or leave. Although he has been ordered not to eat my food, one day his girlfriend, who could not fit into Stench's clothing, sits in the kitchen eating a box of my crackers to its completion. As they are about to leave and out of her earshot I say, "Pick up a box of Ritz crackers while you're out."

Three weeks have ended and concurrent with that the wound on my *okole* has ended. I resume schooling. The easiest article of clothing to place on me is sweatpants. Every morning Stench reaches for a pair of sweat pants. When he does this I instruct him to put jeans on me -- because they are the most difficult to put on. Getting up at the correct time is a problem also. I need enough time for the routine and to get to the cafeteria for breakfast before my first class at 9 AM. One morning it appears very light outside compared to our usual rising time.

"What time is it?" I ask. Stench keeps my clock next to his bed. It is a small travel alarm clock. He walks over to the clock, turns back to me and says, "7:08."

He performs some range of motion and I realize this cannot possibly be the time.

"Let me see the clock."

Stench gets a surprised look, sets my leg on the bed, walks over to his side of the room and returns with my alarm clock. It reads 7:28.

"So did 20 minutes just pass or did you lie to me?" He says nothing. "Do it to me again, even about the time, and you will leave the next day." Ph.D. in military science.

The bureaucratic hurdles are over and Stench receives his first check. He goes out with his fiancée, Peggee, (honestly, that's how she spells her name) to purchase clothing to replace his shredded white shorts and the single other shirt he owns. He brings home bright colored striped shirts that do not quite cover his enormous gut. The few other articles of clothing he brings home, if worn by a seven-year-old, that seven-year-old would be made fun of on the playground. 160 IQ. He

The Squeaky Wheel

also brings in the latest copy of *Soldier of Fortune*. He likes to pretend he knows what the military is up to by watching Pearl Harbor. He says a nuclear war is at hand and he packs a mesh bag with flippers, snorkel and a can of Sterno. I ask what the parcel is for and he says, "In here is everything I need to survive a nuclear war. I wrote my doctoral thesis for my Ph.D. in military science on the survivability of nuclear war."

This person, who lied to me about the time, expects me to believe this installment.

One day I receive a letter from Elizabeth, the woman I dated from the University of Minnesota who I met at the Tyrone Guthrie Theatre. I read it at my desk and after Stench reads it, without permission, he asks me who the letter is from. I explain it is from a friend from home. He asks if she is pretty. I say that she is drop dead gorgeous and Stench puffs up his chest, sticks out his face and says, "Not as pretty as Peggee," about the woman he has just become betrothed to. I look at him with a 'get serious' look but say nothing.

"I've seen pictures of Peggee when she weighed 150 pounds. She was beautiful. She's going to get down to that weight after we get married."

150 pounds would equal 1 1/2 Elizabeths I think... but I say nothing.

My clothes go into the laundry and they come back seemingly unchanged. It would appear that Stench stuffs as many articles of clothing into a machine as is humanly possible and does not bother to add soap.

"Do you not use the laundry detergent I buy?" I ask in total seriousness.

"What sense would that make?" he asks.

Since I can't make sense of anything this man does I choose not to respond.

The apartment continually smells of urine. I ask him why this is.

"Because you wear a condom catheter," he says with the tone of someone who believes they have 160 IQ and they are talking to a moron.

"I also lived in three other houses or apartments and none of them smelled this way. (pause) But you didn't live there."

The conversation ends.

Brian Shaughnessy

  The Minnesota Twins enter the playoffs and ultimately win the World Series. When they win the American League championship my father sends me a sweatshirt, a hat, a Homer Hankey and a pendant. Stench, who knows nothing about baseball, hygiene, fashion, attractive women, time, caloric intake, laundry, housekeeping or war, cheers for the Twins' opponents. Since we do not have a TV I go to the common room of the student apartments to watch the game. I am on my way out and he says, "Don't forget your hat, the banner, your sweater and Hankey. Your dad told you to wave them when you watch the game."
  I turn my wheelchair around and travel back into the bedroom almost rolling over Stench's toes.
  "And I told you not to read my fucking mail, you selfish piece of shit."
  I begin interviewing for new live-in attendants. Stench informs me that he is marrying his fashion consultant girlfriend and will be leaving my employ in December. I just pray it won't take that long to find a replacement. His fashion consultant girlfriend lives with her grandparents. He gives me this number in case he's ever away and I need to get hold of him. I call once.
  "Peggee's grandparents said, 'I hope that Brian does call again, he's such a pest,'" Stench tells me with a grin.
  "Give me the phone; I want to call them."
  Now he is terrified. I demand the phone, I find the number and I start dialing. I know what's coming.
  "They didn't *really* say that," Stench shouts. "I just said that because when you called we got busted having sack time."
  "I know. I'm going to tell them you're a habitual liar. Hello, Mrs. Dumberthandirt? This is Brian -- we spoke last week. Stench works for me. Stench tells me that..." and I relate the story to her... seemingly. I ask if the, "pest" story is true. I then tell her about being told it was 7:08 when the actual time was 7:28, that Stench reads my mail and "kinda stinks." Stench stands in the hallway -- pouting and staring at his infantile shoes. I continue with these comments and finally tell him, "Your future mother-in-law wants to talk to you."
  He looks up from the floor, his face white as rice and steps into the room. He takes the telephone handset from the holder, places it to his face and says hello. He hears a dial tone. Do I need to say that I never made the call?

The Squeaky Wheel

Along with myself, some of the other directing candidates in the Master of Fine Arts program are anxious to direct. Since there is no way that all eight of us interested can find the space, time, and actors to each perform even a one-act play, we decide to divide up the several monologues from a single play.

Most of the aspiring directors choose to direct one monologue. I choose to direct two but I will defer if someone else wants to direct one of the monologues I am coveting. We begin auditioning women at various hours and after two days I am sure I will not be able to direct even one of the monologues. We decide that there will be a lottery for the directors and each will cast in that order. I choose last. On the third day of auditions, Jacqueline -- a gorgeous, brown-haired, silken divinity -- reads for the part. She seems to totally get it. Most classmates agree that she is the right person for the role. Her eyes are a dark turquoise, her voice soft and sultry as jazz on a hot summer night. I call her and cast her.

On the fourth day of auditions we get another crowd of eight attractive, aspiring actresses. One of them speaks almost no English. Another one is the most perfect island girl I have yet to see. Her soft, highlighted jet-black hair reaches the middle of her back. Her tresses hang straight, becoming ringlets at mid-length. The brown skin of her face gives power to her dark loving eyes. She has a western nose but it is her perfect, full, calling lips that win the beauty prize on her face. Her name is Ec'Lane.

She is tall for a local girl -- and thinner than most. Her long thin neck leads directly to soft, petite shoulders that reveal time in the sun. Her arms are defined and elegant – like a dancer's. Her breasts fill a C-cup tightly; her brown belly and deep naval call to me. She claims the snap on her jeans has malfunctioned leaving her unbuttoned and tugging her trousers on alternating sides as they try to fall off her hips. She has the right amount of bubbliness for the character and the right amount of indifference as to whether or not she is cast. I want her... to play the part. I am certain that one of the other directors with a higher draft number will snap her up. They don't.

I do. One of my classmates comments that I "cast the prettiest girls who auditioned." I ask the others if these two women were not also the most appropriate for each role. Most agree. Stan, one of my new friends who also hails from Minnesota and will never leave the tropics, says, "You did the right thing, Brian. For the pieces and for yourself. Daniel is just jealous cuz his wife would kill him if he cast them."

Brian Shaughnessy

I find out from the feminist professor I teach with that the local girl earned a scholarship out of high school for her acting ability -- perhaps also for her loose-fitting Levi's.

I tell my friend Diane back in Minnesota that Ec'Lane and Jacqueline are as beautiful as poems. We decide all beautiful women should be referred to as poems rather than as babes or....

We try to rehearse daily as we all live on campus. I convince Jacqueline that rather than the scene taking place in a bar with her in a black evening gown – as suggested by the author -- it should take place in a seedy dressing room. She should wear tight black lingerie as this will show more of her character's tattoos and suggest something more.

Jacqueline loves the idea. I tell her we must look at tattoo books and travel to a strip club or two... on research. She agrees. I borrow music from Lou Reed's "Street Hassle" for the intro and exit to her monologue. Ec'Lane gets her sparkly cheerleader unitard. Both of these gorgeous women are willing to rehearse at my apartment, but because of the smelly, sub-human I live with, we rehearse at the theater.

Both of these nubile visions come to me with personal issues and look long into my eyes with quivering lips, but I choose to be paralyzed. Even though I miss these seeming opportunities at interpersonal relationship, audience members tell me that the monologues I directed were their favorites.

My quadriplegic, Nazi, Hawaiian roommate shares his room with a Chinese national who can barely speak English. The quadriplegic Nazi will not allow the curtains opened, so the Chinese national removes them from the curtain rod. This results in the Hawaiian Nazi trying to hit the Chinese national with the armrest of his wheelchair. The Chinese national moves to another apartment but not without informing me that he does not believe that Stench has a Ph.D. in military science. I now tell the Chinese national that Stench has said very few true things since I have met him.

I am to meet Sheila – an attractive East Indian woman who verbally tackled me in the library. Sheila's friend -- seemingly lesbian -- seemed very bothered by Sheila's dialogue with me. This woman got in between the two of us, usurped the conversation, insisted they were late (staring at me every time she made this statement) and stopped just short of peeing on Sheila to mark her territory. I am to meet Sheila outside of Manoa Gardens for lunch. I arrive a few minutes early and sit outside the glass

The Squeaky Wheel

wall that separates me from the inside patrons. I am content to listen to the music, view the outside patrons and smell the scent of plumeria wafting through the lanai. I am midway between the designated entrance door and the designated exit door. Today has gone well, and I am content to meet someone new -- and female -- for lunch. She is already ten minutes late. I am unconcerned because this is Hawaii (Hawaiian time runs later than *manana* time or CP time), and she is a woman -- which to me means I must allow for "reasonable" tardy-time. Plus, even the slightest potential for sex lessens the sting of waiting.

Another ten minutes pass and my companion has yet to arrive. People exit through the door to my left with their lunch, and I smile at them as they pass. Some of them greet me, and some of them look away. One tall, thin Caucasian collegian exits, scowling and carrying his lunch. He is overdressed for any college campus -- especially the University of Hawaii at Manoa where not even the University President wears a long-sleeved, collared shirt, pressed slacks and expensive shoes and belt. But the scowler does. He turns toward me and sees me in his path. I meet his eyes, smile and nod acknowledgment. The overdressed stranger walks directly up to me, leans over his food and into me and says, "I've suffered more than you, pig," straightens and walks on.

First, I am in shock. Then, I am terrified. Why would a sane person say such a thing? I tremble slightly and nausea has eclipsed any hunger I may have been experiencing. I see this "person" sitting on a stoop -- alone -- eating his lunch and glowering at me. I feel... paralyzed. I don't know whether to respond or ignore this cretin. I know he wants me to be afraid of him. I don't want to be, but I am. I think, I didn't know it was a contest! I wonder what I could say to him. Minutes pass and I look up again from my lap and see him still on the stoop. As I wrestle with my emotions, a thought comes to me. Would Carlos tolerate this? Knowing the answer, my hand automatically reaches for the joystick on the wheelchair. I am moving toward this person before I look up and see that he has gone.

It is now thirty minutes past Sheila time and, shaken, I decide to go home. I never see the antagonist again.

I have dinner and too many beers with my friends and classmates Stacy, fellow transplanted Minnesotan, and Gale, good-natured artistic director of a theater company in Maine. I tell them of the afternoon incident. They want to hunt the man down and hurt him. They follow me unsteadily back to my apartment, and with Stench not yet back, the two of them lift me into bed and cover me with a sheet.

"I love you," says Stacy, stone-faced through his wire-rimmed glasses. I look beyond him to Gale who, in a look, conveys yes, Stacy is drunk and speaking emotionally and uninhibitedly but I feel the same way.

The next day my quadriplegic, Nazi Hawaiian roommate threatens me and tells me not to bring my "fucked up drunk friends" into *his* apartment.

"Why, are you jealous I have friends?"

He makes a threatening move and takes the armrest off of his chair as if he is going to swing it at me. He never brings people into the apartment. He never *talks* to anyone.

"Kiss my ass you fucking jerk!" This is not just *your* apartment, *your* island, or your world. I can bring guests in here, and I just *might* smoke or drink too." The fascist is making a fist and approaching me. He keeps telling me he will kick my ass. "So, hit me, call the cops if you want, but if you threaten me again I will have your dumb ass arrested. Okay, buddy? ... brother?" He doesn't speak to me again. He sits in his room and only leaves for class.

There are, however, other students with disabilities that I get along with. I meet many at the KOKUA office. There is an attractive blind woman (slightly sighted), Jennie, who takes the stage at one of the local radio station's bikini contests. She is also in the theater department. She is a poem.

One weekend Poorly calls to say she is tired of taking her clothes off. She will travel back to the mainland to visit her mother. She says she will pay for the airline ticket I purchased to get her to and from Hawaii. Our agreement had been that if she did not last the full nine months she had to pay her own fare. She wants to come by and pay her own fare. Stench will be out and I must remain in bed. I instruct him to stash the ticket in one of my few books but to leave the receipt out in the open.

Poorly arrives and sees the receipt on my desk.

"This isn't an airline ticket, Brian. You're trying to rip me off."

I start to explain that it is a receipt and that the ticket is elsewhere but Poorly begins to rifle my drawers and then proceeds to the shelves. I am screaming fire, rape, help, you fucking bitch and many other phrases but she finds the ticket, examines it and exits. I've been taken again.

The Squeaky Wheel

Black *Skin*

One day I return home from morning classes when I realize that the condom catheter has failed and that I am now soaked with urine. I enter the apartment and discover that Stench is not about. He, like all the other attendants before him, is free to come and go as he pleases, so long as the basics of getting me to school on time, getting me fed, bathed, put to bed at night, laundry, shopping, etc. are met. I curse Stench for not being there, and then recall that he was beginning his part-time job -- as a Kirby salesman -- today. I curse him *again* for subjecting anyone to the horrors of a Kirby salesman. His absence means that I will not be able to get undressed, cleaned and into non-urinated clothing before the next class meets. I will miss class. I look at the books strategically placed at my desk for just such occurrences and resign myself to the fact that I must stay here and peruse the books while continuing to urinate on myself. This is not a pleasant option, but certainly one exercised before.

I wonder if there is another way to get someone to change me. Student Health is not an option. Even if they could transfer me and clean me, I would need to bring new clothes -- unworkable. KOKUA? No, no one there has the skills, and it's not their job. Suddenly it occurs to me that my neighbor, Dan (the kid with muscular dystrophy and a drive for drugs instead of academics) has a roommate/attendant, Derek, who works in the field. I move away from the desk and toward the door, struggle with the doorknob, and roll down to his apartment. The stereo blasts -- a sign of life. Whether it is intelligent or helpful remains to be seen. The stereo blasts Grateful Dead music -- a sign that it could be Derek. I knock on the door and, mercifully, Derek is home alone.

"Hey, man," I begin -- aware that Derek generally DESPISES all of Dan's friends -- "look, I know you don't like to work as an attendant and that's why you're leaving but..." I gesture toward my soaked pants, "I'm soaked, Stench is not home and I would like to get changed so I can make it back to class. I'll give you ten bucks to help me out."

Derek wears his superior attitude more conspicuously than his glasses. I believe he has a reason to wear the glasses. He looks down at me (perhaps figuratively and literally) and nods slowly as he realizes the situation. "Sure, I'll help you. Let me turn off some things here, and I'll be right out." He shuts down the obvious electrical appliances, and we return to my apartment. We talk and walk, and I think that perhaps Derek has not placed me on his "to be despised" list. Back in the apartment he transfers me deftly and begins to remove my clothing. We make small-talk appropriate to such an exchange -- whatever that may be. He looks about and positions the work area and asks for a basin, washcloth, towels and soap. I direct him to the appropriate materials and select alternate clothing. With my clothing off, he begins to clean me. Suddenly a horrified sound comes from him.

"Dude!" he exclaims, "did you know you got an area of black skin back here?" His eyes flip from my backside to my face.

"No," I respond quickly, puzzled and concerned. "What do you mean, black?"

"Just what I said. The skin is black. I had an accident on my motorcycle, and the skin on my leg looked like this after awhile ... but not this BIG an area."

Now I am becoming alarmed. "Just where is this and how big an area are we talking about?" I ask.

"Well," he says, looking and assessing, "it's right above your ass, and it's about..." He holds up two hands, each with his first finger and thumb extended, and indicates something the size of a coffee-can lid. I shriek. "There's a hand mirror over on the desk -- bring it here." Derek nods and retrieves the mirror and positions me (very tricky) so I can see it. I shriek again. It *is* the size of a coffee-can lid... and *it is black*.

"Yeah, this can't be good. What do you want to do?"

My mind quickly processes the current situation and decisions are made. "I want to know why the dumb shit I have working for me didn't tell me this! But for now I'll get cleaned up and dressed and go to class." Derek nods and goes about his duties as we speak of other things. Just as I am cleaned and dressed Stench enters.

"I thought you were starting your new job," I say.

"I did. I quit. It sucked."

I shake my head in mild disbelief at the brief exchange with this 160 IQ moron. In a prior conversation Stench was extolling the virtues of Kirby vacuum cleaners, Kirby salesmen and the fact that this was his ticket to big money.

"Of course it sucked! You're selling Kirby's! I told you it would suck. Anyway..."

I explain to Stench that he should hand ten dollars to Derek since Derek did his job. Stench begins to whine but quickly removes his wallet

The Squeaky Wheel

and hands Derek a ten-spot. Derek thanks him and eyes Stench's collection of military hats. He walks over to them and begins trying them on. As he removes one, he puts on the black beret. "This one's cool." He says this as if the rest are a joke. They are.

Stench mutters something I don't hear, and Derek looks at me with a 'What the fuck is his problem?' look.

"What did you say?" I ask.

Stench looks concerned that he has incurred my wrath. "I just told him to ask next time he puts on my clothes." He sees me rolling my eyes. "You wouldn't like it if he came in here and tried on your clothes," he whines defensively.

"Nobody would put *on* your clothes," I snap at him. "They're big, they stink and six-year-olds wouldn't wear them because other six-year-olds would say that their mother dresses them funny!" Derek giggles and signals that he is leaving from behind this sad excuse for a human. I say to Stench, "*You* can put me back in the chair, but Derek tells me that there is black skin on my back!"

I can see him shifting nervously. He responds with his stock answer -- a lie. "No there isn't!"

"Really?" I respond staring at him. "So, Derek is lying, it's 7:28, I'm a pest, and I'm seeing things, right?" Derek is now crossing his arms and leaning against the wall.

Stench stares blankly for a moment. "I wouldn't call it *black*," he says, as if he is the doctor, and we are dolts.

"Really?" I challenge further, as I see Derek shaking his head. "What would *you* call it?"

"Darkened."

"Well, you certainly didn't call it *anything* to let me know it was fucking there!" I yell.

"I *did* tell you," he insists. Derek interrupts this domestic scene.

"If you don't need me, I'm going to take off," he says, moving in the direction of the door. I assure him he can leave. He stops and gives a serious look. "Are you sure?" he asks. He shakes his head and sneers in the direction of Stench. Again, I let him know he can leave. Before he is out of the room he demands I call him. I assure him I will and instruct Stench to put me in the chair as the interrogation continues.

"Really, you told me? You told me that there was a black -- no, excuse me – a 'darkened,' area the size of a coffee-can lid on my tailbone?"

"Yes!" he insists.

Brian Shaughnessy

"Funny," I say, as I am placed in the wheelchair, cowering at the man's smell, sweat and touch, and wondering why I didn't have odorless Derek perform this task, "after spending three fucking weeks in bed trying to get a wound on my ass closed you would think I would remember something like that." I call out to him. "I'm going to class. We'll discuss this when I get back."

I go to afternoon classes and then to work at KOKUA. I ask one of the workers if she would like to go to a play with me that night. She agrees. I am relieved that I won't have to face the vulgar person in my apartment -- and my life -- for several hours. When I return home he is playing solitaire. I quickly instruct him to put me to bed. In bed I ponder how to quickly dismiss Stench and hire one of the other recent applicants for the job. Miraculously, as I ponder this, the door opens and Lance, one of the applicants, enters with a paper plate covered with foil – leftovers from a barbecue. I tell him what transpired that day and ask if he can begin immediately. He laughs and says that he can be back tomorrow, but that this very night he cannot because he has his sons with him. I arrange a time for him to meet me, as he feeds me the items from a family picnic. Lance exits, and I fume at Stench... quietly... in my mind. I chastise myself for hiring, keeping and having to smell this incompetent.

The next day I begin the inquisition again through the morning routine. I tell Stench he never spoke of the condition. He insists he did. Variations on this continue through the shower and dressing and a realization hits me. "Bring in my box of ice cream bars," I say to him. He looks slightly dejected but plods to the kitchen and returns with an open box of ice cream bars. One remains. I have not touched them.

"You ate my food... again! Go get the box of crackers."

He returns with a third of a box of crackers -- crackers I have not touched.

"Are you going to lie to me about eating the food or tell me I'm imagining it's gone?"

He stares and does not respond. "Did you eat my food?"
"Yes."
"Okay, that's better. Did I ask you not to eat my food?"
"Yes."
"Is it an arrangement of your employment that you eat my food?"
"No."
"Would you agree with me that I should be reimbursed for you eating my food?"
"Yes."

201

The Squeaky Wheel

"What would that amount be?"

He seems ready for the question. "Ten bucks."

"Okay," I say, thinking that amount seems too high. But I am not about to argue given the fact that this pig has not even bothered to inform me of a very serious condition -- a condition infinitely worse than the one I just spent three weeks in bed trying to heal while this person supervised that progress. I ready myself for the pink-slip statement. "Give me ten bucks." As he did previously, he reaches into his back pocket, takes out his wallet and removes $10. He hands it to me, fully aware that I cannot take it. I quietly look at the money until he removes my wallet from my backpack and places it inside.

"Now go pack," I say calmly. He barely looks surprised at this request and slowly moves past me and into the bedroom as I turn the wheelchair to speak further. "I'll be back at 1:00, and you will be gone. I'm going up to ask them at the desk to make sure you don't *steal* any more of my *food*. Leave your keys at the front desk. If you're not gone by 1:00, I'll call the cops -- not just those sissy campus security either -- real cops. Understood?"

He looks back at me from the bedroom pathetically. He looks fatter, sweatier and more clueless than usual. I honestly feel sorry for him. He attempts to maintain a dignity he lacks. "Of course I understand," he says and shakes his head as if I were the moron. This was the wrong thing for him to do.

"Do you? Do you? Do you, really?" I ask, bringing the wheelchair as close as possible to his toes. He takes a small step back. "You understand that I brought you into my home, paid you better than any other person is paying someone for the same services, saved you from another job where you were a *slave* for food and a roof, asked you *not* to eat my food or use my linens, and you couldn't even respect those wishes! You watched me spend three weeks in bed trying to heal a much smaller sore. Your primary job is to alert me to the early stages of a condition like this, and you failed! You lied to me daily. You ... you lied to me about what fucking time it is! You *fucking* asshole! You are not *fit* to be around people! I fucking trust you with my life and my body, and you fuck me! Shame on you. Shame on me for being so fucking stupid as to let you in this house in the first place, let alone allow you to stay almost four months. Shame on me for not firing you when I caught you in the first lie. How could I...? If this thing on my tailbone is serious I will see you in jail. Shit, I will have you killed. Now get the fuck out!"

I storm toward the door and out. Stench has no idea what his neglect will cost me. Neither do I... yet.

Dark Days in Paradise

Stench has been banished from my home and told if he is seen again, he will be arrested for attempted murder. This likely means I will not be the best man at his upcoming wedding. Lance has taken over as my new live-in attendant. He is local and had interviewed for the job before the discovery of the black skin. The discovery of Stench's neglect results in Lance's immediate employment despite the fact that he is ingratiating, already considers us "buds" and laughs at everything I say. This, coupled with the fact that when we run into Lance's sister on campus and I ask her -- in Lance's presence -- if she would recommend Lance for the job, she gives an odd look but does not comment, makes me uncertain of my choice. Clearly, however, this person is an improvement over Stench.

During the second day of Lance's employment he fills out the paperwork for payment and forwards it to Minneapolis. He has a pickup truck into which he transfers me and enlists a volunteer to lift the electric wheelchair into the bed of the truck. Today Lance accompanies me to the Rehabilitation Hospital of the Pacific where the doctor and his nurse immediately refer me to a plastic surgeon. The plastic surgeon views the damage done to my tailbone, acquires a surgical scissors and removes the LARGE offending areas. He then shows Lance how the resulting wound needs to be dressed. I explain to the doctor the wondrous platelet-derived formula I brought from home. He is nonplussed and informs me that I will be in the hospital, that he will perform surgery and I must then remain three to four weeks to recover. This surgery cannot take place until the first week of January -- after the five-week Christmas break -- during which I have nothing scheduled before the beginning of the next semester.

Lance tells lies. Like Stench, it appears to be one of his favorite pastimes. Participatory delusions are what I believe the psychiatrists would call it. One night, while eating at the cafeteria, he returns with several desserts and claims someone just asked him how the team was. I call him on this, and his claim is that someone mistook him for a college football player. Lance is five feet tall and five feet wide. I point out to him

The Squeaky Wheel

the absurdity of his claim; once again he is "disappointed" that I think he would lie.

It is not yet Thanksgiving and I begin to research the possibility of returning to the mainland for the surgery to 1) get the task accomplished sooner; 2) not miss any class time during the next semester and 3) be around my family for Christmas. My brother Dan remains in the judgmental, accusatory, money-grubbing cult. I speak to my mother in New Mexico. Rochelle, who actually proved that there is hell in Rochelle, has invited herself to my mother's for Christmas. I wonder how my mother can consistently be such a kind soul to people who really do not deserve such treatment. Darrin will remain in New Mexico and Dawn, who now lives in a group home with other Down syndrome girls, will be at my mother's for Christmas... along with Rochelle.

I want to tell my mother to tell the bitch Rochelle that she cannot visit. Instead, I tell her I'm fine and already have plans for Christmas... in Hawaii.

I am shocked by the amount of time for recovery. When I ask why, if the procedure *must* be done, it cannot be done sooner, the doctor informs me the operating rooms are booked for elective surgery. The doctor says that everyone wants their face-lifts, eye jobs and hair transplants so they look good for New Year's Eve. I ask why, if this condition will eventually kill me, this does not take some kind of precedence over a face-lift or an eye job. The doctor informs me that this is not yet a life-threatening condition. We leave this doctor's office and proceed to a handful of other plastic surgeons, looking for one who will perform the surgery sooner. They all tell the same story.

That night, Lance invites over a handful of my acquaintances on campus plus the kid with CP and his drug addict, thief brother, one of the football players and some other neighbors. They are all in line to taste a substance I am unfamiliar with -- crystal methamphetamine -- ice, in the parlance of the street. I pass on trying it, although Lance says "I got it for us." They all take their turns taking a hit of this crack-like substance, until I order them all away. My redneck roommate smells nothing and makes no comment.

The next day is without scheduled classes so I call the Rehabilitation Department of University of Minnesota Hospital to see if there is a run on plastic surgery during the holidays in Minneapolis. Dr. Dykstra informs me that there is not. He will begin to make inquiries and arrangements. Lance and I exhaust the list of plastic surgeons in Honolulu. Each specialist tells the same story, until I find one who thinks he can get the wound to close. My new partner/roommate/personal care attendant/confidant and I believe this last specialist, and I plan to spend the entire Christmas break in bed in the student apartment. Lance celebrates by getting more crystal methamphetamine. This time, I try it.

Crystal methamphetamine has none of the charms of cocaine. There is nothing euphoric, pleasant or mellow about the experience. The substance immediately makes one hyper, paranoid, sweaty, nauseous, self-loathing and wanting more of it. Somewhere in the course of the endless night I realize I must teach a class the next morning. I ponder canceling the class. Lance expresses his "disappointment." I ask what the fuck he is talking about. Lance believes I should have "tricks" designed just for such occasions.

"I don't usually take such vile shit, and I ain't never gonna do it again," I say. He says he is still *disappointed*. I think the appropriate question here is who the fuck asked. Once again, I wonder at my predicament.

Lance definitely has a Jones. I try to point this out to him but he comes back with a million excuses and rationalizations ... or, in the parlance of the treatment community, bullshit. He smokes almost daily and is awake far into the night, rubbing the glass pipe with his favored rag, examining the implement and then placing the lighter to it. This is terrifying to watch from my bed on the other side of the room -- paralyzed. More terrifying is when he puts me to bed, puts up the side-rails and begins one of his glassy-eyed, incoherent rants about an uncertain topic, which, even if I knew the subject matter, would not interest me. And this man is a vast improvement over the last.

Lance is, over all, good to me. Despite the drug problem and its accompanying baggage, he keeps the house fairly clean (the apartment no longer smells of urine). The bedroom is neat, the kitchen and living room are tidy, the bathroom shines and laundry returns smelling laundered, *appearing* clean and neatly folded (as opposed to inside out and stuffed into laundry baskets and then drawers a la Stench).

My tuition is paid for, I am receiving a check from the Theatre department for my work as a teacher's aid, my monthly Social Security checks arrive in a timely manner forwarded by Proletarian Peggy in Minnesota. Tim, the instructor/actor from New Mexico who promises to bring me back to teach and direct a play (I think we both know this is an empty promise), makes regular purchases of my Valium. I am financially comfortable.

The Squeaky Wheel

One of my classes in the first semester is a Theatre of Japan study. For a final project we can elect to 1) write a paper; 2) write a short play, perform a short scene from a Noh, Kyogen, bunraku puppet Theatre or a Kabuki play we have studied. I elect to write a kyogen play. Kyogen are short, comedic pieces performed before the long, tedious, nearly motionless, stately but horrifically BORING Noh plays. I meet with Professor James R. Brandon -- one of few western experts in Kabuki -- a fine instructor, scholar and artist who also was born in St. Paul, Minnesota. I give him the first draft of my short kyogen play. I borrowed a Bob Dylan song, "Man Gave Names to All the Animals," made some changes, kept the rhymes (not a part of kyogen but allowed me to mimic the kyogen style on a faster tract). Dr. Brandon enjoys the piece but he encourages/demands that I make it more kyogen.

I tell my friend and classmate Stan that I am in the midst of writing a short kyogen play. He says that he and two other classmates were planning to perform a kyogen play for their final project. He volunteers to perform the one I am writing. He loves and embraces the rhymes, which we begin to turn into puns. The other actors love it and on the last day of class we adjourn to a performance space. On a chalkboard Stan has Japanese-ized our names. He gives a brief intro and turns the chalkboard around revealing where Anna, a classmate and kyogen actor, has drawn the stately pine tree, which is the backdrop for all Noh and kyogen plays. The giggling begins before the play does and Dr. James R. Brandon looks like a five-year-old with a front row seat at Disney On Ice. We're a hit.

On Thanksgiving Day Lance transfers me into the truck, loads the power chair and the shower chair into the bed of the truck and we drive to the most famous beach on the planet, Waikiki. He gets me into the water, and I float about behind the wave-breaking wall where the children swim safely. Once out of the ocean I am submitted to the freezing shower. On the way home we stop at *Zippy's* to enjoy a turkey-flavored shake on occasion of the holiday. At home I speak to my mother and tell her that I have been in the ocean for the first time and lie to her that I had turkey dinner with friends. Despite a hot shower and piles of blankets it takes hours to stop my shivering.

The semester ends, good-byes and "talk-to-you-soons" are exchanged and I go back to the student apartment. The Nazi/Hawaiian/quadriplegic roommate has gone home to the Big Island for the break. Lance and I share the apartment alone for a few days and then his two sons come to stay for most of the remaining five weeks. I spend most of that time in bed. Lance changes the awful smelling bandages on the *worst* looking wound three times daily. Once a week I return to the plastic surgeon who is amazed by the "accelerated healing" resulting from the use of platelet-derived formula. I experience my first Hawaiian Christmas alone in student housing. Friends invite me to Christmas festivities, but I do a shuffle, declining Peter's invitation by explaining I accepted Paul's and permutations on this theme. Lance brings a plate of Christmas cheer and I, again, lie to my mother that I spent this day with friends, as I stare out the window from bed. I spend my first Hawaiian New Year's Eve -- December 31, 1987 -- listening to the endless rat-a-tat-tat of firecrackers.

    As the day for classes draws nigh, the wound on my coccyx explodes. The weeks spent in bed, in Paradise, on vacation would have been better spent flying to Minnesota and having the surgery there because I would now be healed and ready for the first minute of class. The doctor who claimed he could close this wound cannot even perform the surgery now. He refers me to a colleague, as I make phone calls to Minneapolis to inquire about surgery there. I purchase a nontransferable airline ticket from Lance's football player friend. Then, with the input of my family, the decision is made to have the surgery performed in Hawaii and to convalesce there. The Theatre department and the KOKUA program will make sure I get my assignments. I take back my bankcard from Lance and destroy it. His football player friend has already spent the money I paid him for the ticket and is busily trying to resell it as I pack for the one-month hospital stay. The pretense is they will pay me back. I have doubts.

    When I phone my mother with this information, she loses her mind. She quickly makes arrangements for her first trip to Hawaii. I check into the hospital, and the nurses and attending physicians are all very pleasant. The plastic surgeon is particularly sympathetic to my needs and impressed that I am determined to remain in Hawaii and complete graduate school. The football player apologizes for not having the money to pay me back. He has no tolerance for hospitals and promises he will pay me back. Now I'm sure I will never see the money. The nurses occasionally snap at me, but mostly I am surprised by the question, "Why are you so nice?" I say I was raised that way. Despite three horrific attendants (one of whom remains), months in bed, and now another month in the hospital (out of school), I sing *and* believe the words to a popular song of the day: "My Future's so Bright, I Gotta Wear Shades."

During my first full day in the hospital Lance asks if he can borrow money. So far the Minnesota State program has not paid Lance, but I *have* -- from my own funds and *in advance* of every pending check so he can pay for his crystal methamphetamine habit. I decline to lend him a dime. Within a few days Mom arrives from New Mexico with B.G.'s mother. Within hours Mom has Lance pegged as a substance abuser. She wonders what the hell it is he's abusing. I know better than to say that it's amphetamines, but it slips.

If Mom lost her mind upon being informed her eldest son would be entering the hospital yet again for yet another month, for yet further surgery... this would be the occasion for her to be slipped comfortably into a straitjacket and medicated for a decade. She knows drug addicts, because she is a counselor. Even her friend can recognize the behavior of someone with a habit. Lance is trying to tour them about and get them to the hospital, but he stops at every other phone booth. This type of behavior does not require Colombo or Scotland Yard.

The surgery is performed, the $100,000 bed that my roommate Ed was on at a rehab hospital in Minneapolis is placed under me, a stand to hold a book open in front of me is mounted to the bed and I am given a mouthstick to turn the pages of the book. Friends visit, and although the fragile egos of the University of Hawaii at Manoa Theatre department have nixed Mark Medoff's plans to write a play about me, I will still be directing him in *Greater Tuna*, a very funny play in which two men play about seventeen different characters each.

"What can I bring you? he asks.

"Gummybears and beer."

He laughs at this request but brings them both when he visits. I will be out of the hospital in time for the rehearsals and he instructs me to continue taping select incidents from my life since acquiring a disability. I have been dictating and sending him tapes which are then transcribed by his secretary in anticipation of a dramatic work. Lance opens one of the latest installments, asks what it is and begins reading. I tell him to put the pages away. Now, he asks if he may read it. I tell him he can read this latest transcribed tape but no more. He sits in the room and reads all 15 pages -- this, from a drug addict who does not even read the numbers on the front door. Lance laughs often, loudly and will turn to me and ask if a passage is true. I assure him every word is true. He demands to read the rest. I consent, unlock the words, words, words and tell him to be very careful as they are my only copies. For the next two days, he reads, laughs and occasionally gives me his unsolicited opinion.

One night a *lovely* Filipina nurse enters my room. I have not seen her before. She introduces herself and I grin, thinking that's not the name you were born with. We'll call her Helen. She offers me range of motion -- something the other nurses have not offered and possibly are unfamiliar with – and it is very pleasant. Although the condom catheter comes loose at least three times, she does not lose her patience. We talk through most of the evening. At one point she enters the room and asks if I have ever heard a local band called The Hat Makes The Man. I look at her in shock and ask her if she knows the name of the band we are listening to on the cassette player. She does not. It is Men Without Hats. We both enjoy this little coincidence or borderline irony. I appear to be getting all the signals to ask for her number.

Some clod is mopping my room and asks, "What happened to you?"
"When?"
"Why are you in a wheelchair?"
"Because I can't walk."
"But why can't you walk?"
"I forget."
"What happened to you?"
"Fuck off."

Helen is my nurse again the next night. Lance brings marijuana and a small pipe. I take tiny hits and exhale into a pillow to minimize telltale odors. Helen appears in the doorway with a shocked look.
"You guys are smoking," she says from the doorway. "I don't know anything," she says and closes the door as she shakes her head and exits. My level of respect for this woman has risen. Mom comes by and Lance exits. He exits because he knows that she knows that he is a drug addict. Helen is more attentive than any nurse has been. She is a float nurse which means she may not be back to this floor in my remaining days/weeks. When I know that it is time for her to go home I ask her for her number.
"I'll come back," she says simply. I don't know whether this is a blow-off or sincerity. "I know you're not leaving for a while. Good luck. See you later."

The Squeaky Wheel

I realize that the date is January 31, my red-haired grandmother's birthday. I wonder what Nonnie had to do with our meeting. My mother is visiting again just before she must return to New Mexico.

"I really hate to leave you," she says and sobs.

"I know, Mamma."

As she regains control and gets ready to leave, Helen walks into the room and sits at the foot of my bed.

"Mom, this is Helen..." I say. Mom exits after the introductions.

Before my attempt to get Helen's number we had disagreed about the author/performer of the 1960s song, "War." She has made a trip to the record store and their giant volume of recording records and she is the winner. Green light. I am to call her when liberated from the hospital. I call my mother and thank her for her hasty retreat. I tell her of the pending date with Helen. I tell her that I believe Nonnie had something to do with our meeting.

"Everything is going to be okay; I'm not going to have any more problems like this," I assure her.

"Oh, really," she says with the suspicion of a woman who has six impish children. "What makes you so sure?"

"I'm going to marry Helen," I say uncharacteristically.

That night I dream I am a 17th century sailor with rank. I look awesome in my uniform. The dream is a version of *Mutiny on the Bounty*, and I travel to tropical islands with a Bligh-like captain who hates me because I am Irish. I am ordered to remain on the ship while the rest of the crew is able to travel to the islands to indulge in pleasures 17th century sailors indulged in when traveling to the tropical islands never before seen by white Europeans.

The other sailors travel to the islands in boats and the Islanders bring canoes out to the boats, but the captain does not want the locals to see my red mane. Through some dream dissemination of information we discover that I will be held in a higher rank, which he would not be able to tolerate. Each day a gorgeous island girl -- who looks surprisingly similar to Helen -- travels to the beach and her eyes stay fixed on the ship. I can view her up close with my "spyglass" but she cannot see me. She arrives at the exact same moment every day. She spends more than thirty minutes brushing her waist-length hair. She is, naturally, topless. She applies different oils to her hair, face, torso, legs and feet. She then spends time preparing meals, cloth or baskets for the day. Other villagers try to have her leave the beach but she refuses.

Brian Shaughnessy

One day she arrives with a straw mat, drops it on the sand, sits and begins to slowly stroke and caress her hair and body. She gently fondles her firm, ample breasts while one hand plunges beneath her scant *tapa* cloth. She falls on her back with her knees up, her legs tense, and her back arching until it appears through the spyglass as if she will snap in half. Her breathing shifts from long deep breaths to short little gasps as her hand movement beneath the *tapa* cloth quickens until a piercing scream reaches the ship. She lies motionless and panting for quite some time. She tosses the *tapa* cloth aside, rolls unto her belly and repeats the performance.

Through the magic that the heart brings, the red haired minor deity winds up with the brown goddess. The union brings love; ultimately they are killed either by manipulations/misinformation of the captain or a jealous island male. I awaken to a teenage discharge on my belly. The nurse makes no comment.

The day before I am to leave the hospital after my three-week stay many nurses and hospital personnel come by to wish me well. The sweet young night nurse -- who I believed through the first three weeks was a nurses aid -- comes in to say goodbye. She is very kind and complementary. I ask her if I can call her. She takes a piece of paper out of her pocket with her name and number already written on it. I have her put it in one of my folders while I thank her.

She grins coyly as I stare back.

"Kiss me," I say with uncharacteristic sureness.

Her eyes widen as she steps toward me, places a hand on my chest, leans in and runs her fingers through my hair. Her lips lightly touch mine, back off and then press long and hard against mine. Our mouths open and our tongues dance for space in each other's mouth. She keeps looking toward the open door.

"Go close it."

I cannot believe my good fortune. She comes back from the closed door and I tell her to lift her top. She complies and sweet, scented brown breasts with delicate, dark bullets for nipples are mashed into my face. After not nearly enough of this I ask her to remove her lower covering. She says she cannot and must get back to work as it is nearly time for the next shift and for her to give report.

"I will definitely call you," I tell her as she giggles and straightens herself. She kisses me on the cheek and exits.

I call the number I have been given but do not reach this wondrous night nurse, so I leave my name and number. I call a second time and

211

another message is taken from me. I call a third time and the same voice tells me, "She lives with her boyfriend, you know."

Back in school I am taking the most ethereal, difficult class of my graduate career. All my peers are taking the same class but appear far less puzzled by it than I am. I am trying to get my brain around Brecht's concept of justice and am sure that the three weeks I spent on a very expensive bed would not have helped me decipher these concepts any easier. The instructor, a thin, middle-aged Aussie, who is without doubt the most intelligent member of the faculty, tries to explain different theories to us mere mortals. He talks of an exercise in which actors portray different characters of different ages, genders, socioeconomic background and religion. He stops and looks at me.

"Very much like what you are doing with Mark Medoff in *Greater Tuna*," he says.

I see the foppish pain of the department turn his head toward me and then in the other direction to ask a classmate a question. He then looks back to me. This man is pretentious, self important, effete, arrogant and -- the characteristic which both explains the proceeding adjectives and makes them even more intolerable – without talent.

"So, who do you know to get yourself selected to work with a Tony Award-winning playwright?" he queries in his swishy manner.

I start to explain that I know him from New Mexico and this was all arranged before I traveled to Hawaii. I just can't do it.

"Mark Medoff had Manoa Valley Theatre call here and ask for the best, brightest, and most talented directing student in the department to direct him in this play. Rehearsals begin Saturday. Ta-ta," I say as I see an opportunity to escape through the side door has presented itself.

A 17-year-old kid, Cliff, has been cast to play numerous roles with Mark. I missed the audition process, as I was flat on my back -- flirting with nurses. Mark and Cliff show up at my apartment on Saturday. We have our first read through. I take some notes and point out some aspects of the characters and script to my actors before we begin our nightly three-hour rehearsals. We work through scenes in small pieces slowly and then string them together to work larger portions of the script.

"You guys ready for notes?" I ask them. I can see Cliff shoot a glance at Mark -- checking his reaction. Cliff has scored big. Many people auditioned for this part and he is the luckiest kid in his elite high school to be working with this man. I am just some dude nibbling on *his* glory. We go through the notes and Cliff exits while Mark and I share a beer.

"You saw him checking you out when you asked about notes?" he asks. I grin and nod in mid swallow. "Thank God your notes were good -- thank you for them -- otherwise we would have problems, but I think we are going to have a great production."

We do. There is much media coverage; my flight attendant friends are able to travel to Hawaii to see the play; I receive rave reviews from sincere friends; and I am deemed lucky to work with a big shot. I am able to offer complementary tickets to the classmates who are in my directing class for which this will be my class project. Professor Fragilego -- the man who sabotaged Mark's writing the play about me this semester -- is teaching my directing class. He comes in late and leaves at intermission. I am told he always leaves at intermission. The day arrives when we are all to critique each other's work. There is a woman in the class who came up to me after she saw the play and said it was fantastic. "I'm sure Professor Fragilego will give you an A." The effete fop is also in my class.

"Okay," Professor Fragilego begins, "I guess we're up to Brian's play."

Before he can say another word the Fop pipes up, "I heard you didn't like it. I didn't like it either. I saw a much better production of it in San Francisco."

I look to Gale and Stacy, my only comrades in this war zone. We are all rolling our eyes.

"I'm sure you heard that I left at intermission," Professor Fragilego begins.

"I hear you *always* leave at intermission," I say honestly and calmly.

"You missed all of that great stuff in the second half?" Gale says with mock disbelief. Professor Fragilego sneers at him.

"I don't *always* leave at intermission," he says. The only plays he does not leave at intermission are the plays he directs... then *others* leave at intermission. I am slightly bashed by less talented, jealous specks. Stacy and Gale praise the project and give me some honest, constructive criticism. Then it is the turn of the woman to speak who said, "I'm sure you'll get an A.".

"I really didn't like it," she begins. I place my jaw back in the socket and lean as far forward as a human being can lean with a strap around their chest. She gives a review and then it is my opportunity to speak.

"What disappoints me most about the endeavor those of us in this room have chosen is the rampant, needless hypocrisy. For instance, this

The Squeaky Wheel

Bull-Dyke sister of Satan (not her real name nor how I actually referred to her at that moment) came up to me at the end of the play and gushed and exclaimed she was sure I would get an A from that man," I say pointing to Professor Fragilego. "The man who is *teaching* and *grading* this class.. That's okay, Mark Medoff is down the hall about to give a presentation to the interested students. A presentation that will not be compensated by this university -- where he should now be teaching as a visiting Professor I hasten to add. I am going to listen to what he has to say which I am confident will be honest. Anything else?"

I finally find the time and work up the nerve to call Helen. We talk on the phone for well over an hour. Somewhere in the conversation she makes a statement about a daughter of hers who is taking a Humanities course at a community college. My mind immediately translates this into a roommate who is taking such a class at a community college. I invite Helen to see the show. She agrees. On the night of the show she asks if she can bring two friends. I find this odd -- and quite costly if I cannot get complementary tickets -- but God smiles and it happens.

Helen meets me at the theatre. She is a poem. She has shoulder length brown hair, bronze/brown skin, three freckles next to her left eye and a sweet, tentative smile. She wears a white muumuu, different than the traditional in that the material around her breasts is like a tube top. I have not seen this before and do not know what message it conveys. She certainly looks cute. A sullen Caucasian woman and a well-dressed Japanese poem flank her.

They all enjoy the play and we have drinks afterward. I have just purchased a van, but I am at the mercy of paratransit, which ends at 9:30, or to traveling strictly by electric wheelchair. I am not sure what to make of the evening. The Caucasian woman is moving to Ohio, but Helen's lovely, bubbly, sophisticated, (hard to pull off bubbly and sophisticated) Japanese friend asks many questions, praises the play and insists that I invite her to all of my projects. I wonder if I am being set up. Helen remains quiet. I travel home uncertain of my status with Helen.

I receive an overdraft notice from the bank. This makes no sense and I travel to the bank to investigate. There have been many, many withdrawals in the last few weeks with my ATM card. At the bank, I am surprised that I do not have my ATM card. One of the bank employees tells me that while I was in the hospital Lance had come in demanding my ATM card. He didn't give the card to him. I travel home and ask where my

ATM card is. Lance says he has it. Many of his belongings are already packed. I have already filed a complaint with the police and they are outside. He dares to get angry with me that there are cops outside.

"I could have fucked you in the ass, stuffed dirty stocks in your mouth and shit -- but I didn't," he says in his defense.

I stare unblinking for half a minute. "Is this the part where I'm supposed to thank you for only stealing my money? I can have them take you to jail right now. Get the fuck out of my house," I say.

He starts spewing more nonsense, which could only make sense to someone whose brain has been perforated with crystal methamphetamine.

"Can I go to dinner with you to the cafeteria to talk about this?" he asks, already wondering where his next meal will come from.

I scoff. "Leave now or your dinner will be on a metal plate."

"This just proves that your opinion of me hasn't changed since I walked in here to help you."

"You proved to me today that you're a thief. If I had that opinion of you, 'when you walked in here to help yourself to my cash card,' you would not have spent the night. (pause) Officer."

I hire Raymond to work for me for the next few weeks before I leave for Minneapolis. He is a large, Hispanic, gay man who loves to do the laundry and talks incessantly. Sadly, he has no driver's license and cannot drive my new van.

The Squeaky Wheel

Third World Dilemma

I make a date with Helen -- our second -- to go see the reggae band, Third World, at the Waikiki Shell. The Shell is similar in layout to the Hollywood Bowl. Handi-Van will not make reservations to pick anyone up after 10 p.m. They will, however, almost invariably pick me up and return me home much later than 10 p.m. There are no accessible buses. I have the tickets and discuss the situation with Helen. I have recently purchased a van with an ingenious collapsible ramp built by a new friend, David. Given that I have no insurance and Helen has not yet driven the van, we decide that taking the van would be unwise. So we decide to travel in her vehicle, take the manual wheelchair, and ask my new attendant Raymond to transfer me into and out of her car at home, while Helen will enlist a volunteer at the concert to assist her in getting me in and out of the vehicle.

Helen arrives -- only slightly later than our arranged time – and I am swiftly transferred to the passenger seat of her vehicle. It has been a long time since I sat in the passenger seat of a car. It feels good, and natural and familiar to be sitting here. She remembers to grab the handicapped parking permit from the van.

We travel to the Waikiki Shell cheerily and without incident, and park in a handicapped-parking stall where Helen removes the collapsible wheelchair. She opens the passenger side door and positions the chair for transfer. She puts the large cushion in place, and as we look about to enlist a volunteer, a tall Caucasian man asks, "Need a hand?" His arm is already coming from around the waist of the Asian woman he is with, as he walks toward us.

I thank him and instruct him on how best to assist Helen. "You come under my arms, and she will come under my legs, and when she counts to three you both lift. Cool?" He nods and utters the familiar "yeah, yeah, yeah" commonly encountered in the Hawaiian parlance known locally as Pidgin. It is always said with a rapidity that suggests to the uninitiated visitor that the speaker is put out or one is giving them useless information. That is not the intent.

216

I am quickly placed in the wheelchair, utter the appropriate thank yous, and the big man pats me on the shoulder. "Have a good time at the concert."

Helen begins to push me toward the gates where the ticket-takers take tickets. The two of us are waved away from the turnstile toward a large gate that must be opened. Again, it strikes me that these "barriers" remain only to reinforce in persons with disabilities the not-so-subtle notion that they are at least an inconvenience, if not a bother or a burden. Again, I say nothing. I am here to have fun.

Helen looks fantastic. This woman is graced with full, dazzling lips begging to be kissed. She has spent much time on her hair tonight, but her face is adorned only with eye liner. Her short, short black dress reveals gorgeous gams. She had kicked off her high heels to do the transfer and slipped back into them when the volunteer accomplished this feat.

As we make our way to the chained-off area of grass designated for wheelchair users and their companions, I hear a female voice happily call my name. A young Asian co-ed runs over and gives me a hug. She gushes that she got an "A" in her theater class, of which I am the teaching assistant. I *know* I am uncomfortable and sense that Helen is. "He helped me get an A," she squeals with a broad grin. Helen nods.

The comely young woman bids us to enjoy the concert. We assure her we will and part in the direction of our "seats." Another employee removes the chain that permits us to enter the grassy area designated for wheelchair users. Helen positions me for optimal viewing of the stage. This is my first time at this venue, and I see there is a large paved area in front, where unaware, able-bodied, vertical people will have the opportunity to stand and block the view of the stage. I point this out to the employee before he goes to get Helen a folding chair.

"No worry, cuz. I no let anybody stand there." And he doesn't.

While he goes to get her chair, Helen goes to get us a beer.

The band comes out and performs. Although Helen has not heard of the band, she clearly enjoys it. I am pleased she enjoys it. Listening to the music reminds me of life before my surgery when I often went to a local bar, Duffy's, to listen to my favorite Minneapolis band, Shangoya. They would play reggae and Calypso, and I would often show up for the opening note of their first set on Thursday, Friday and Saturday to dance my narrow, white ass off. I am known to friends and acquaintances by this behavior and to strangers who encounter me regularly as "the guy who never wears jeans."

The Squeaky Wheel

These memories and being on a date with a lovely Filipina create a feeling of euphoria. Accompanying this is the profound sense of loss and tragedy over the events of and since February 2, 1983, and my inability to dance as I once did. To be Irish is to embrace and revel in this mixture of opposite emotions. Pain and joy, beauty and ugliness, defeat and victory *in combination at the same moment* send me -- and all Irish I am told -- into the highest level of transcendental states. I once told my friend Diane, a very intelligent, artistic soul, of being drawn to the music of *Everything but the Girl* because "it is so beautiful and still creates such a feeling of melancholy that I call it, 'music to slit your wrists by.'" She laughed a long time and replied, "Oh, Brian..." more laughter, "that's so Irish!"

About five songs into the concert Helen turns to me from the folding chair and takes my hand for an instant. With a look that says, "I'm really sorry that you can't get up and dance but THIS MUSIC dictates that my body get up and shake my buns," she releases my hand and does. I am pleased that she enjoys the music that much and feels "free" enough to dance in my presence.

Able-bodied louts make their way past me and try to stand in front of me and to step over the chain to feign friendship, ergo acquiring a better vantage point to view the concert than back in the cheap seats. Neither the employee nor I allow them to interfere with my enjoyment of the concert.

"That was such a great concert!" Helen says at the close. "Thank you so much for asking me to go! Now I want to buy their albums."

Naturally I am pleased by her enjoyment of the concert and the evening. We wait for some of the crowd to go out.

"Hey, man! I'm Bongo -- remember me?" shouts a guy I met a few days before, who is going into the Peace Corps soon. I nod. "Was that a great concert or what?"

I agree with him and introduce him to Helen. Somehow the two of them wind up several feet BEHIND MY BACK. I hear him asking her if she likes reggae music. I hear him asking her if she has been to a certain local bar that features reggae music. I hear him ask her if she would like to join him there sometime.

I am using the manual chair on grass and am unable to wheel about and somehow convey displeasure to him. Helen gives him a "some other time" brush-off and comes to the side of the chair. As she is releasing the brakes on the wheelchair, he stands on the other side of me. I'm pissed -- but only mildly.

"You wanna give us a hand getting me into her car?" I ask, burning a hole into his head with my stare.

"Sure," comes his enthusiastic, intoxicated, clueless response.

I am wheeled to the car and the procedure performed upon arrival is repeated in reverse with Bongo. Seated in the car with the door open he continues talking. "I love you, man," he says, as he puts a green fluorescent item common at concerts around my neck. I shoot Helen a quick, uncertain glance. "Take it easy," he commands and with my head turned toward him he kisses me on the left cheek. This historical repeat is not lost on us. He closes the door and departs.

"What a weirdo," I say flatly. "The guy hits on my date, LITERALLY behind my back, kisses me on the *left cheek* and tells me he loves me."

"You're jealous," says Helen, and before I can respond that I am actually aghast at such inappropriate behavior -- especially toward a man with quadriplegia -- she continues. "That gets you points."

Unaware that there was any tallying going on, I *am* aware enough not to correct this misunderstanding. Maybe I am jealous. We return home and Helen wakes up Raymond who sleepily emerges, removes me from the car and wheels me to my bedroom. Helen announces that she is going to sit in the chair in the bedroom while he puts me in bed, given that she has seen me naked before. I don't argue.

Raymond and Helen both lived in San Francisco (yes, Raymond is gay) and swap Bay Area stories. Raymond continues to talk... and talk... and talk. Hours go by before Helen announces she must go. She comes to me and quickly kisses me on the left cheek and begins to head for her car. Raymond says he will walk her to the car. He takes more time than is necessary for simply walking another human being to the parking lot and saying goodbye.

"Boy, can that girl talk," he says, actually referring to himself. "Are you okay? You have everything you need?"

"All I need now is sleep."

"Good night," he says and exits.

I close my eyes with a contented smile, knowing it was a wonderful evening, and that I will see this woman again.

The semester ends in May but I remain through June to play in Hawaii. I can roll from my apartment at the University to Waikiki Beach and on to Ala Moana Beach Park and get back to my crib as the power indicator on the wheelchair begins to blink dangerously low. I am loving the tropics.

The Squeaky Wheel

Raymond packs my bags and another friend, Julie, insists on accompanying me to the airport. I have known Julie since before I met Helen. Julie is tall, half Caucasian and half black. She is attractive but she wears her low opinion of herself like loose fitting clothes. Her long curly hair and cadence suggest she is Hispanic. Since our first encounters I have tried to lead her down the road to coitus. She steadfastly maintains she would but for her boyfriend. We exchange creative writings for each other's feedback.

I have made the arrangements for an accessible cab to take me on an expensive ride to the airport. Continental Airlines does not want to honor my ticket. I decide to save this battle for another day and purchase another ticket and get the lackey's name to torment him later. He then informs me that Continental Airlines will not remove the batteries from my wheelchair. I explain that they have removed the batteries from my wheelchair previously but again his worldview is no bigger than his interpretation of the employee manual.

Mr. Limited Worldview gives Julie a sundry collection of tools and she begins to try to extract the two twelve-volt batteries from the container in which they reside. They must then be placed in a special box to avoid the acid spilling and damaging other luggage, the contents and the airplane. Julie is cursing the airline, the tools, the batteries and Mr. Limited Worldview.

"How are we doing?" the drone asks Julie.

"What are you talking about, ' we?'" she barks with an attitude I have not yet seen from her. Julie's hands are filthy, her jeans will disintegrate from the battery acid, tools are strewn about the terminus and I must now rush to the gate to catch my flight. She wears the "Hawaiian Tropics" model Vans sneakers I surrendered to her as they no longer fit my swollen feet. She follows while an airline lackey pushes the battery-less wheelchair to the terminus. At the jetway, as I am about to be schlepped from my wheelchair to the dolly with the plank nailed to it for my ass which allows them to stow me on the airplane while my wheelchair disappears from my sight for several hours so they can torment it further, Julie removes a pungent, beautiful white ginger lei and places it around my neck. She attempts to give the traditional peck on the cheek that accompanies such a gift. I turn and catch her on her under-adored lips with a big, wet, long kiss. There is no resistance.

"Huh," she responds with a look I choose to interpret as the look of someone who wishes they had allowed such behavior long ago.

Brian Shaughnessy

"Now you got to wait until August to see if you want more of that." She is clearly pondering this as I disappear down the jetway.

En route I find myself freezing despite several blankets. During each landing I fall forward and crack my hand against the seat in front of me. When I am removed from the plane and taken to baggage I am informed that they have misplaced my batteries, but they will be delivered to my home within 24 hours. I tell them that this is unacceptable, but the paratransit vehicle is waiting to take me to my apartment. I have a live-in attendant I have not yet met who is waiting for me there.

The paratransit driver wears a ridiculous wide striped shirt of alternating circus colors. He wears Robin Williams ala Mork suspenders with NRA, Republican Party and other borderline fascist pins affixed. His gut is larger than Stench's and it would appear that the same person dresses them. This oaf fails at a swagger and then tries to state that I am the coolest thing since the Corvette. He nods his head toward me as if we are compadres. We're not.

"Hawaii, huh," he begins unsolicited. "Never been there but I'm going to go someday."

If your mom will let you, I think.

This gem comes from a paratransit driver who deals with individuals with disabilities all day and gets paid almost minimum wage.

"So," he says, with a grin that says he's trying to be clever but just winds up looking oafish, "I'm going to guess that you broke your neck driving drunk. Maybe on a motorcycle?"

An explosion of expletives nearly erupts from my gut ignited by lava-hot bile. But another Irish blessing reveals itself.

"Really?" I begin. I am the picture of the calm before the storm. "Do you work at the fair guessing weights and ages and shit?" He looks in the rearview mirror. The smirk is gone, replaced by a look of puzzlement. He is uncertain if he has just been insulted. "Is this part of the hustle now, you clueless troglodyte? Don't they give you even a minute of, oh, I don't know, what would I call it? Sensitivity training? What to say and what not to say to someone you are *serving*? Even if you are right …" he now has a look that says, see, there, I knew I was right. "… which you are not, fuck face!" His eyes narrow in the rearview mirror. "Good! I want you pissed. I want you to be offended. I want you to be a tiny percentage of how pissed and offended I am. You should not treat *any* human being that way. I will be sending a letter to your boss "

He scoffs. "Go ahead. They're not going to fire me."

"Don't be so sure. And do not say another word to me for the duration of this trip."

He complies.

I arrive home and my brother Patrick and his three children are there. Patrick has readied the apartment and replaced the dark 3M faux wood flooring with black and white checkered tile -- this pattern matches the sneakers I acquired and wore in rehab that Annie brought me. I approve. But I look about the apartment and immediately notice that the five-foot by five-foot painting my mother had given me is gone. This was a treasure of my mother's that she wanted me to have. I had often answered "yes" to people who sincerely asked me, "Is that a real Picasso?"

My books are gone. The clothing I left in the closet is gone. A leather fringe jacket I purchased with my own money in 1972 is gone. All 20 plus of my varied hats are gone. I open empty closets. I look in the storage closet -- empty.

"You let Proletarian Peggy steal all of my stuff when you threw her out," I rage. Pat immediately looks puzzled and hurt. He confesses that he did not perform even a cursory inventory when the incarnation of evil and insanity left the apartment and another "friend" moved into my stylish apartment for a few short months. The last time I talked with Proletarian Peggy she had called me in Hawaii because she took umbrage at the fact that I was having Pat take the van from her. Pat was in the apartment at the time for the farewell conversation.

"You don't trust me?" Peggy asks.

"No. I told you not to use the van and to leave it in the driveway. Instead, you took it to Wisconsin."

"Pat, shut up. How am I supposed to work around the apartment if I don't have a vehicle?"

"The same way everybody else did. Janice worked last year and did not demand my van to live in the apartment and vacuum the halls. The van was never part of the deal. I had him take my albums because you don't respect my things. You promised me twice you would go to Hawaii with me and it never happened."

"So you think you can get somebody to live here for a few months while you're gone and not give them anything. (Pause.) Pat, shut up, I do not have psychological problems. You do."

"You don't want to live there, leave. We'll get somebody else."

"Oh, after all I've done for you, now you're going to throw me out of your apartment?"

"What you did for me you were compensated for. You even got money on the weed."

"You're a fuckin' ingrate, Pat. I am not psychotic." Click.

The Macintosh computer that Vocational Rehabilitation purchased for me and a sculpture I purchased in New Mexico are all that remain in my apartment.

"Art and technology... you're covered," Diane quips when she is not ranting about someone (who proclaimed their love to me) stealing from me.

When I tell my father what happened, he is infinitely more pragmatic.

"Thieves don't like to work very hard. That's why they choose the elderly and persons with disabilities. They like easy targets. Before the Nazis came for the Jews, they killed people with disabilities. File a police report and make a claim to your insurance company." But then he exits to the driveway and cries. He cries for what should have been; he cries for what could have been; and he cries for what is.

"Well," I say to Pat as his children play about the empty apartment. "I always said I wanted the apartment furnished like this." Pat looks puzzled. "I always wanted an apartment with only the shelves, a table and no chairs or couches. That way when somebody came into my apartment I could ask, 'Would you like to sit down? Tough, 'cause I'd like to stand up but I don't get that choice so you don't get to sit down.'" Pat laughs a pained laugh.

Patrick, his children and I jump a startled jump. The doorbell for my apartment is the most annoying buzzer in the world. It has a deep, electrocuting sound and bowel-triggering rattle. I have wanted to replace it since I purchased the building in 1976. It is now 1988. I see the self-help tapes at the bookstore. They're about how to quit smoking, how to enjoy sex more, self hypnosis and overcoming procrastination. I keep meaning to buy that last one...

Pat travels upstairs and I can hear him explaining to the buzzers that they should use the other entrance on the north side of the building as I cannot ascend the stairs from where they buzzed. Patrick enters with two individuals.

The Squeaky Wheel

"Hi, I'm Steve. I'm your supervising nurse from Badland nursing agency. The state has made some changes now and the nursing agencies oversee the nurses aides, etc. So you'll be seeing a lot of me and even more of this guy here," he says, motioning to the tall, frightened-looking fellow with him. "This is Gary. He'll be living with you until you go back in... August?"

I shake hands with Gary and confirm that I will be returning to Hawaii in August. Pat announces that since things are under control he will return at another time. He clandestinely indicates he will bring marijuana. I tell Gary if he works out he has the option of accompanying me to Hawaii. Gary looks mildly interested but not adventuresome enough to make the trip. He asks if there is anything he can do for me now. I tell him to start unpacking the suitcases. He asks about the furniture. I tell him I was ripped off. Both are shocked.

Steve is a slight, fair-skinned Scandinavian, hippy looking soul with wire-rimmed glasses. He has a larger, more varied music collection than I -- a difficult feat. As we talk I discover that he has just relocated to Minneapolis after a painful divorce. He previously lived in Grand Forks, North Dakota. This is the godforsaken area of the world of Pam -- the beautiful, Moon-skinned, long-haired goddess with heartbreak blue eyes I was kissing when Annie entered the room. Steve tells me that they were friends when she was separating from her husband -- I was part of the equation to that nastiness and I feel myself shrinking.

"I will come out tomorrow to do my nursing assessment and fill out the other paperwork. Will they have your batteries back here soon?"

"Anybody's guess," I say as the phone rings.

Continental Airlines is on the phone and announces that someone will deliver the batteries within the next hour. Steve departs, Gary and I unpack, I call the police and the insurance company, the batteries are delivered and installed and Gary and I fire up the brown van that has been stored for the winter. I explain to Gary the importance of accelerating slowly and turning slowly as I will lose my balance and the wheelchair and its contents (me) will fall to the floor. Gary rides a sports motorcycle.

We grocery shop and travel to the Target store where I purchase my seasonal television with built-in VCR. A lumberyard that was located by my apartment has become a strip mall. It has the obligatory Chinese restaurant, national chain of mediocre food restaurant, drugstore, liquor store, photo store, bookstore and other sundry capitalist endeavors. It also has a video store – a video store with porn. I pick up some egg fu young, beer, film, copy of *Catcher in the Rye*, and some porn. Gary cheers.

"Do you smoke dope?" he asks wishfully. You don't ask this question unless you're fairly sure of the answer.

"Hell no, do you?" I ask with contempt and disgust.

Gary disappointedly examines his shoes pondering his answer when I add, "Only losers who watch porn would smoke dope."

We return home to eat the Chinese food, drink beer, look at porn and go to bed. Gary says he thinks this job will be okay. I am mourning even more loss in my life. Although I have lost the ability to... the list is long, I'm doing the mental inventory of what is no longer in my apartment. It's only stuff, but it's stuff that was *mine* and that I had an emotional attachment to. And some selfish prick *took it* from me.

I call a friend of Proletarian Peggy to track her down. I reach her and she is bubbly and friendly. She tells me she has big news.

"Eric and I are pregnant."

I feign interest and ask if I might ask a question. She permits this.

"Do you know where my stuff is?" I ask through clenched teeth.

"N-no," she stutters seeming to be honestly surprised by the question. She says it was there when she left and asks if I am accusing her of taking it.

"I'm just asking if you know where it is," is my response as I want this conversation to end as soon as possible.

I follow up on my call to the police and encourage them to check her home. They tell me to give them a list that they never follow up on. The insurance company is unsympathetic.

"I don't see how we can honor a policy in which your roommate takes your belongings," the adjuster says snottily. She later arrives through the side door where she sees me, in my wheelchair, through the window before she must duck her head to avoid the lift that brings me up from basement level. Her shoulders slump and her face and eyes give that, oh, that poor pathetic invalid, look. We go over the massive list of stolen personal belongings and I must tell her what year I procured these items as they are all subject to a yearly depreciation. Several months later I receive a check.

I visit my family and we have regular outings. I also hook up with old friends. I make my friend, Tim, (Tim won the prize for being the biggest scumbag of all of the drug addicts he was in treatment with for stealing from his quadriplegic friend) paint my apartment in retribution. I call him,

The Squeaky Wheel

reach the voice mail and say, "Tim -- this is Brian. Do the right thing." He does.

I send Helen a card and ask her to respond. Please. It works and she sends me a lovely card with her incredible handwriting and a stamp she has saved for several years.

I have several outings with my friends Don and Diane who rendezvous with me at their home, at my home, at the Tyrone Guthrie Theatre and at venues where Diane periodically plays.

Dr. Yank

Because I am confident things will progress with Helen, and that soon I will not want to wear a condom catheter all of the time, and because several other quadriplegic males have informed me that a suprapubic tube frees Willie for more important functions than urinating, I decide to have the procedure.

A suprapubic catheter enters the bladder through an opening created surgically above the waist. This allows for the urine to drain out of the bladder through the tube and into an awaiting bag. With this I no longer need to wear a condom catheter, worn on Willie with adhesive to hold it in place. Unfortunately, it does not always stay in place. With Willie's frequent change of status from attention to at ease, and the limitations of adhesive applied to an area on a man where one would *never* ponder applying adhesive, the condom is sometimes "blown." This results in my being soaked in urine. If I don't wear the right color trousers *everyone* knows I am soaked in urine. And even if I do wear an appropriately dark pair of trousers, it is only a short time until the characteristic nitrous smell sends out the message.

So I decide to have the "procedure" that will put the tube through my belly just a few inches below my naval. Some of my fellow quadriplegic males call this "a second bellybutton." I announce this decision to my physiatrist who is not delighted. He tells me to call the urologist and make the necessary arrangements. I do, and soon I am in the good doctor's office.

"As your urologist," he says with a thick Eastern European accent, "I can't recommend the procedure. It is no different than keeping an indwelling catheter through your penis -- that tube is expressway for infection. I would much rather you have a sphincterotomy."

It is that last word that causes my eyes to narrow and bulge a bit as my testes retreat. In my mind's eye, I cross my legs. That last word is the "procedure" wherein the doctor goes up through my urethra ("piss hole," to use the parlance of the street) and cuts the sphincter (the muscle I once used to keep from peeing before the first... "procedure"). "You'll piss Hawaiian Punch for three days and then you're done," a member of the brotherhood of quadriplegics told me in an attempt to convince me to get this... "procedure." I didn't need another nail to decide against it, but if I did, that would have been the one.

I rise to the occasion. "I've met a half dozen other quads who have a suprapubic tube, and they swear by it. All of them claim no infections. Right now, every time I'm through with one dose of antibiotic, I have to start another one to treat another infection."

"You won't have fewer infections this way," he says with empty authority.

I sigh heavily. "If I get the sphincterotomy, it's irreversible. Let's assume that one day they find a cure for paralysis. On that day I'm walking, but I'm still wearing a leg bag and a condom catheter all the time," I point out to the good doctor.

"No," he responds, "there are surgical sphincters that could be implanted."

"I'd like to free Willie now, doc."

"Okay," he says without blinking or changing expression. "We do the procedure now then."

He walks to the phone and asks for assistance to get me onto the table where the surgery will be performed. Another call and a nurse enters and quickly readies the instruments. In a short time I am on the table and a shroud splits me in half and separates my torso from the doctor and his crew. A local anesthetic is used, and I watch them all move quickly as if they have done this a hundred times. In less than half an hour I hear the snap of gloves being removed.

"How are you feeling, Brian?" he asks.

"Fine," I answer honestly.

"Do you want to be admitted for the night, or would you rather go home?"

The Squeaky Wheel

This is a good question, and I ponder it for a long time. Gary has begun his employment as a live-in attendant with another quadriplegic, and no one is staying with me in the apartment. But I am feeling independent and empowered and stubborn and have few fond memories of nights in this institution.
"I'll go home."
He nods. "I'm going to give you something for pain," he says, as he huddles over his prescription pad. "If there is any problem you should come back immediately. All right?"
I assure him I will, and soon I am back in the wheelchair. The call has been made for my ride home, and I have pain medication. I get home and take the pain medication but in a few hours feel nauseous and light-headed. It is only a few days before I am to travel back to Hawaii for my second year of graduate school. I roll from the desk and lean over to the mirror, where I see a blanched Brian. Even the freckles have begun to disappear. There is a knock at the door. The nurse's aide for the evening has arrived.
"Hello, Brian. I'm Jody, and I'm actually a nurse. You don't know me, but I certainly know you. I've heard lots of good things about you from Steve and Rhoda. You live in Hawaii, huh?" She says in one breath.
"I'm glad to hear that you're a nurse; I'm not feeling real good," I say sluggishly and apologetically.
Her nurse mode kicks in. "Oh? And what does 'not feeling real good' mean?"
"Well, I had a suprapubic tube put in today. I'm pale, nauseous and feeling kind of faint."
She opens her bag and removes the blood pressure cuff. "So, you had surgery today?"
"Yeah, I guess I did."
"You guess?" she says wide-eyed, pumping up the sphygmomanometer. "They cut into your belly and bladder and put a tube in there. I'd call that surgery. Your blood pressure is pretty low. We'd better get a look at that site."
She lifts the sweater I am wearing and there is a drop of blood on the shirt. She lifts the shirt to reveal a Tampax-sized dressing drenched with blood. "Wow," she says, with no emotion attached to the word. I am quietly freaking out.
"Where is your live-in attendant?" she asks, as if she's asking where the bathroom is.

"He moved in with another quad a couple of days ago. I'm leaving for Hawaii in three days."

"So who is here at night?"

"Just me."

"I'm thinking we should call an ambulance."

"I'm not going to argue with the nurse."

"Okay, so who is your doctor, and what hospital are you going to?" she asks, as she picks up the telephone and dials an ambulance service without calling 911.

I give her the information. "Who did that surgery?" She asks.

I give her the doctor's name, and she smiles. "I know him," she says, and no more.

The ambulance arrives. I have already gone up on the lift and outside. The EMTs take me from the wheelchair and place me on the gurney as the nurse instructs me to call the agency and let them know if someone needs to come in the morning or if they are going to keep me in the hospital. I feel that she knows that they are going to keep me in the hospital.

At the hospital they diagnose me with internal bleeding. When the good doctor did the procedure he obviously cut something that shouldn't have been cut, and the blood spilled into my gut and out the new opening. "Let's get him a transfusion type "O" stat."

I am scared but soon breathing oxygen and asleep. The next morning the good doctor returns with three other dudes in white lab coats. I am not introduced, but two of the three have their names embroidered on their coats. I assume this means that two of them are residents, and one of them is a medical student.

"Brian, what the hell happened?" the good doctor asks me, feigning jocularity while his eyes show concern. I am not feeling jocular.

"I think that's for you to tell me, since you're the doctor," I say with controlled rage and a laser glare. "But if I had to diagnose it, I'd say you fucked up."

The good doctor lets this one go, as do two of his three cronies. But one of the two doctors with his name on his lapel -- a Doctor Friendly (who was not) -- glowers at me and looks to the others for their reaction.

"Let's get an x-ray -- abdominal. We need to see if we have to do surgery, okay, Brian?"

"I really have nothing to say," I say, although I have very much to say, starting with how dare you even fucking suggest surgery to me again.

The Squeaky Wheel

The x-ray is taken. The good doctor and his cronies look at the x-ray and tell me there's clotted blood that has to be removed.

"They're preparing the OR now," he says, as I pray there will be no surgery.

"Can I call somebody in my family and let them know what's happening, or are you just going to rush me up there?"

The doctor takes out a pad and pen. "Who do you want us to call?"

"I'd like to make the call."

He puts the pad and pen away, and I wonder if he will ever apologize for this.

"We'll get you a phone," he says, as he turns to leave. "I'll see you upstairs in the OR."

Now I am presented with another six-million-dollar question: whom do I call? My mother will lose her mind, so it is better that she be told afterward. Although my father maintains a granite exterior, this will stick an ice-pick in his heart. I call my brother Patrick and explain the entire situation to him. He is devastated, but it was the right decision. "I'll be there when you get out of surgery," he assures me, after many expletives and cursing out the doctor and the hospital.

In the OR the anesthesiologist says, "We can do this with a local anesthetic, which would be better, or we can put you under. Which do you want?"

Without hesitation I say, "Put me out," not wanting any part of *more* surgery. The anesthesiologist looks surprised and begins to speak, but then closes his mouth, nods, and soon I am out. 99, 98, 97...

When I awaken from the surgery I find they have placed a tube down my nose and into my stomach. The pain is insufferable/inhuman. It is equal to the pain I endured after they opened the back of my skull.

"Your brother is here, and we'll be moving you up to the floor soon," a nurse in the recovery room tells me.

"What is this tube for?" I ask, coming out of the haze of anesthesia. I turn my head ever so slightly, and I am pierced with a thousand of those ice-picks that would have gone into my father's heart... or -- infinitely worse -- my mother's.

"That's sucking all the nasty snuff out of your stomach -- the anesthesia, gastric secretions, and acids. We need to make sure it doesn't go where it doesn't belong. If it doesn't come out through that tube, you'll get distended and throw up," she says. "You see that brown guck in that jar next to you?" She motions toward it with her head, and I move only my eyes in the direction that she pointed for fear of jarring the tube and feeling a thousand more ice-picks. I can see what looks like a gallon size glass jar with a tube running into it, and about an inch of thick, vile looking poison collecting inside. "You don't want that in you right now."

"Can I have some water?" I ask innocently enough.

The nurse turns away from what she is doing. Her sparkling blue eyes glaze over with sadness and her jaw drops, leaving her mouth agape. "I'm sorry, no food or water for three days."

"Three days?" I move ever so slightly and the holders of the ice-picks catch the movement and plunge their weapons. The pain returns two-fold. "I'm supposed to be on a plane in three days. Are you telling me that this thing is gonna be shoved in my nose for three days?"

"Very likely," she says, and I know that she is hurting for me and angry that she is the one who has to give me this information.

"Am I going to be in here longer than three days?" I ask, pleading that the answer is no, of course not, but...

"That will be up to your doc -- who should have been in here by now -- but I think you can count on it." Another nurse enters, and this one exits quickly.

I begin to ponder the equations that this information creates. I must now change my flight back to Hawaii to an as yet undetermined date. This will require a ridiculously complicated phone call to the airline. I will have to call the person accompanying me to Hawaii to work as my aid this year. I will have to call Ann at the KOKUA office. I will have to contact the Theatre Department and let them know. I will have to call Helen. I will have to call my mother, and I will have to call her before a sibling does. I will have to call the nursing agency. And on, and on, and on... This doctor really fucked me up.

The good doctor soon enters without his lackeys and gives me the same information the nurse just did, only with a thick Eastern European accent. He says my brother will be in, and I will be moved up to the floor. Still, there is no apology. My brother Patrick enters with his characteristic swagger -- grinning.

"Hey, man. How are you doing?" Before I can answer he is upon me. He places his hand on my chest and sees the tube shoved in my nose. "Oh, my God! What the fuck did they do to you?" He leans in closer to look at the tube. "Please tell me that thing only goes into your nostril."

"Nope. It's shoved all the way down to my stomach. And if it looks like it hurts, it does."

The Squeaky Wheel

"I can imagine."

"You think so? Multiply what you're thinking of by a thousand."

He nods. "Does Mom know you're here?"

"Not unless you told her." He shakes his head. "Did you tell anyone?"

"Just Kate. I was hoping that that would be your job. I mean, I'll do it, I'll tell everyone. Just don't make me have to tell Mom. Besides, you were always the snitch in the house," he adds grinning.

"Fuck you!" I say playing this sibling game. "As I recall, it was you and Darrin always running off to snitch on me. Besides, you're adopted. I told you, I saw the papers in the lockbox that Dad kept in their closet. Your name was Tyrell Jones, and your real daddy is black and in prison. It's time you found out."

Pat stamps his foot, doubled over with laughter. It's a new variation on an old game. Two men enter the room.

"Mr. Shaughnessy?" I nod. "Hi, we're here to take you up to the fourth floor."

"Sure," I say, anticipating a rain of ice-picks. "Just, please, please, please be very careful of this tube in my nose. It's very painful."

"I can imagine," the shorter of the two men says. I look at my brother and then back at the transporter.

"No, you can't. Listen, get the nurse and see if I can have a pain shot." The taller of the two nods and exits. He is back in a moment shaking his head. "She says you get orders upstairs." I marvel at my good fortune.

I am transferred from the bed to the gurney, rolled to the fourth floor and transferred from the gurney to the bed with possibly the minimal amount of pain that can be inflicted upon a quadriplegic under such circumstances. It is still excruciating, but once I am laying flat and not moving, the pain decreases exponentially. But every slight movement of my head creates a new depth of hell. I beg for water, but the nurses can only swab out my mouth with a damp, rancid-flavored sponge on a stick. My brother sits next to the bed, and we talk, as the TV drones on pointlessly. I concentrate on not moving any muscles other than my jaw and tongue, and these I keep to an absolute minimum. An emaciated white male nurse enters and introduces himself.

"Hello, Mr. Shaughnessy. My name is Larry the Tormentor, and I'm your nurse for the evening. I'm going to have to change the dressings and bathe you."

"Okay, but just please be very careful with the tube in my nose, because the pain is incredible."

"Not a problem," is his response, but he seems to make every attempt to prove otherwise. My brother stays in the room as I exhibit behavior unknown to the two of us. With every movement of me by the Tormentor there is blackout pain. I shriek, I threaten, I curse, I scream, I plead, I cry. He remains silent.

"*Scream.* God, fucking damn it! *Scream.* Could you fucking be careful? *Shriek.* You are fucking killing me! *Scream.* I told you this tube down my nose was put in by fucking Satan!"

And then there is a brief moment where the pain diminishes to manageable, and I apologize to the Tormentor.

"I'm sorry, but you have no idea how much this hurts," I say with relief -- thinking that the horror is over, and I can go back to concentrating on lying still as a rock. But it begins again.

"Are you out of your fucking mind? *Scream.* Are you deaf? Are you fucking stupid? *Shriek.* Or do you just not give a fucking shit about the pain you are causing me? Please, please, please just stop it!"

And then there is a brief moment where the pain diminishes to manageable, and I apologize to the Tormentor.

"I'm sorry, but this is insane. Human beings should not be subjected to this. Annie, sweet Mother of Jesus!"

And it begins again.

"Ouch! Fuck! Ouch!! Fucking...!! Are you a fucking moron? *Scream.* You cocksucking pussy, I'm going to fucking kill you if you don't listen to me and stop this torture immediately. Ouch! Fucking stop! Jesus, Jesus, Jesus kill me! *Scream. Shriek. Plead.*"

And then there is a brief moment where the pain diminishes to manageable, and I apologize to the Tormentor.

"I'm sorry. I'm not usually like this, but I'm sure I have NEVER experienced pain like this."

The Tormentor has not said a word. He exits the room. My brother -- who I have seen grinding his teeth and tensing every muscle while he watches this man without blinking -- asks, "Would you like me to kill him? Because it would give me great pleasure to punch his stupid face in."

"No, man," I say exhausted and breathless. "I want to believe that that was not deliberate."

I see out of the corner of my right eye my Tormentor enter again. He is carrying bandages, and I am sure I am going to die a slow miserable death. The process and exchange are repeated for the same length of time as before he exited the room. It feels like days. I sob.

"Please, stop it! Please, stop it! Please fucking stop it this fucking instant! Have you no soul? Where the fuck is 'do no harm?' You ignorant piece of shit. Just kill me! Just kill me! Please, just fucking kill me because this can't go on, you stupid fuck!"

"I'm all done," he says simply.

"Me, too," I say and apologize again. My brother again tenders the offer to kill the Tormentor, with the Tormentor in the room. He hastily exits. I lie still, and my brother talks with me briefly and then announces he must leave. He sheds a few tears and commands me to call my mother and father. He'll take care of the siblings.

"*My* dad. He's *my* dad, not yours. Your daddy is Tyrell the jailbird." He laughs honestly, shakes his head and exits with a lengthy goodbye as he backs out of the room.

I lie in the bed as motionless as a two-by-four. In fifteen minutes there is a single spasm that the ice-picks pounce on. Then the Tormentor returns.

He looks pained. Not nearly as pained as I, but pained. "I'm going to have to move you again," he says softly and apologetically. "But," he says, looking left and looking right, as if we were going down at a busy, seedy intersection ... "I have a shot of morphine for you if you want it."

Want it? I think, I don't *want* it... I *need* it. This is such joyous news I don't even wonder why I did not get the offer before all of this insanity began. Of course I fucking want it. "Bring it," I say with the authority of the commanding General of the armed forces talking to a peon. The Tormentor -- who has just become my Saviour -- nods (something I would not dare do) and exits. In a moment he is back pumping a hypo full of salvation into the IV port. Immediately the pain begins to diminish. I feel slightly altered but not nearly as altered as when I was given Demerol. I want a full vacation, not just a day off. Although I know that I could make the request to change the medication for the duration, and that it would readily be granted, and that I would then be *flying* instead of merely floating in the pool, I don't. I have not yet learned the "skills" of "self advocacy" or whatever the fuck the term of the day is for getting what I want when I have a disability.

The nurse returns and does whatever he needs to do, moving me about with only the occasional pain of a single blunted ice-pick. I sleep. Perchance I dream. Perchance I dream of walking, of flying, of walking into that neurosurgeon's office and pissing on his face. When I awaken a new nurse enters and introduces herself. I tell her I need an adapted call light and her assistance with making some phone calls. She exits briefly and returns to tell me the call-light has been ordered.

"Who would you like to call?" she asks pleasantly.

"Let's start with my father," I say. I give her the number, and she dials the phone. Amazingly, my father answers. I explain the occurrences of the last 24 hours -- highlighting the tube in my nose.

"Jesus," he says in disbelief. "I'll be down in a couple hours -- can I bring you anything?"

"Maybe a gun for that nurse."

"I'll see what I can do," he says through the laughter. "Did you call your mother?"

"I'm about to."

"Okay," he sighs. "I'll see you soon. Love ya."

I call those siblings I can reach and then my friend Tim.

"Are you out of your mind? Jeez. Brian, aren't these the same son of a bitches who *did this* to you? Why would you go near that *building,* let alone let them touch you?"

His logic is solid. I like my physiatrist and decide I will see no other doctors at this establishment. They will not be allowed to treat me in any manner before garnering two more opinions, and then I will have other doctors treat me.

The moment I have put off has arrived. "Anybody else?" the nurse asks. "Yeah, my mommy."

The nurse looks at me with a mother's pain. Not the pain I have experienced today and not the pain my mother is about to endure... again.

My calling card is removed from my wallet, and the dance is performed, and then my mother's number entered.

"Hello," she says unsuspectingly.

"Hi, Momma," I say, trying to choke back the tears. My attempt fails. "What's wrong?"

My chest heaves, my throat tightens, my chin pushes my lower lip into my upper lip, which pushes my upper lip to my nose, which begins to run. My eyebrows come down, and my eyebrows move toward my eyes, as my eyelids nearly meet and tears flow into my ears.

My mother begins to cry. "Honey, what's going on?"

The nurse wordlessly asks me if I am able to hold the phone. I nod -- slightly. She then indicates she is leaving and raises her eyebrows to

The Squeaky Wheel

ask if this is okay. I repeat the same motion using even less effort, and the nurse runs out.

I get a handle on the tears and explain -- voice cracking -- the occurrences of the last 24 hours, omitting the tube in my nose and the accompanying incidents.

"Oh, my God! What are these people doing to you?" she says and berates the hospital, doctors, God, Hawaii and... the list is long. "I'm getting on a plane," she says -- meaning it. I laugh and tell her that won't be necessary. She says she wants to, and that she knows there is nothing she can do. I point out to her that as soon as I leave the hospital, I will pack and leave for Hawaii. "Then I'll come to Hawaii." I laugh again and tell her she probably cannot stay in the dormitory. This exchange continues and soon we are both laughing. "I'm so sorry, honey," she says with the truth and manner only spoken by a mother with a suffering child.

"I know."

For three days I cannot drink a drop of water nor eat a morsel of food. Apparently I am hydrated and "fed" through the various bags that hang from the IV pole. I watch the clock, and every four hours I call the nurse and have them give me another dose of morphine. It eases the pain but little more. I miss the interplanetary flights and Theater of the Surreal dreams of Demerol.

I get the usual hospital visitors: my father ("Give Me a Kiss." Done. "Say a prayer for your old man." "I will."), my siblings, my dear friends Don and Dianne, Janice and Carrie, a few other friends, 3D, M.D., Ph.D. (*He* has no reason to pay me a visit, but *he* comes by to tell me that *he* is sorry this happened.) Pat and I sit and he eyes someone he knows.

For three days the tube remains in my nose sucking viscous, black bile from my innards. With each hour the harvest diminishes. The pain diminishes with each day, but it still hurts like hell. The nurses come to check my vital signs, give me dope, feed me, wash me, stick a suppository up my ass, violate me anally as they dig shit from my bowels (some complain about this duty, not thinking about how it is from my side), whine about their lives, befriend me, hold the phone when I make and receive phone calls and listen to my stomach for "bowel sounds," which -- when they reach the appropriate frequency, volume and pitch -- will be the green light for the tube to be removed from my nose. The good doctor with the thick Eastern European accent comes by once or twice a day. Sometimes he is with his underlings, and sometimes he comes alone. The underlings rarely speak, and the good doctor with the thick Eastern European accent does not grill them with questions in the dreaded "Socratic Method" of teaching utilized in both medical and law school.

With each visit I ask him, "Can we take this damn thing out of my nose yet?" "Not yet," is his answer until deep into the fourth day. On the fourth day he and the underlings appear. I ask the question. He looks at my chart and then listens to my stomach with his stethoscope. "Okay, we can take it out."

Granted, my senses may be fuzzy from the morphine and the time in bed, but I believe that as soon as Dr. Friendly (who was not) hears "okay," he drops his clipboard and leaps from the farthest corner of the room to the side of my bed. With feet barely planted he yanks the tape from my cheek -- placed there to stabilize the tube and minimize the ice-picks. As I involuntarily suck in air with accompanying indescribable sound, he yanks the tube from my nose and holds it over me like a trophy fish. It all happens in a nanosecond. One giant ice-pick impales me through the nostril.

"Fuck!" I scream, lengthening the vowel to a not previously reached distance or pitch. "Are you out of your fucking mind? You stupid piece of shit! Is that the way they teach you to take that damn thing out, or were you sick that day, Doctor -- or are you just a fucking moron? God damn it! What happened to 'do no harm?'" This is all said in a millisecond. I turn to speak to the good doctor and see him and the other lackeys hanging their heads. "He," I say, indicating Dr. Friendly (who was not), "is never to come near me again." I turn to Dr. Friendly (who was not), no longer encumbered with the tether of a nasogastric tube, who looks down at me (literally and figuratively) with Elvis' sneer and the stance of a man in a dick-sizing contest.

"I understand," says the good doctor. "Brian, you and I will talk later. Dr. Friendly (who was not) and I will talk now," he says, as he and the boys exit with Dr. Friendly (who was not) following with his tail between his legs. Again, no apology comes from either doctor.

My brother calls to see how I am recovering. His three children have kept him busy, and he apologizes for not making an appearance in the last 24 hours. "When are you getting out?"

"Nobody has said yet! But some prick *yanked* the tube out of my nose."

"What?" he asks, and I can almost see his furrowed brow over the telephone. I explain what transpired that afternoon. "What can you do about that?" he responds appropriately.

The Squeaky Wheel

"Besides kill him? I asked that question of the nurse after he left, and she said she would call Patient Advocacy. Some woman came up a couple hours later. The nurse was cool. She said that you take that thing out quickly, but you sure don't yank it out, and the dope who did it was getting yelled at by... Professor Doctor. I told the Patient Advocacy woman I didn't want the prick near me again except to apologize, and then I wanted him thrown out of medical school, his license revoked, and then I wanted to stick a rake up his ass -- rake-end first. She said I wouldn't get all that, but that there are 'disciplinary procedures' that he would be subjected to. Which means... I don't know, probably that he doesn't get to look at any naked women for a week. Then, Professor Doctor came back and apologized for Dr. Shit-Head -- but not for screwing up on his surgery and keeping me here another week."

"Speaking of being here another week," my brother interrupts, "Whining Wayne called today and asked when you guys are leaving."

"I wish I knew. Is *that* why you're calling? For *him*? I told him yesterday on the phone '*I don't know.*' Why didn't he call me?"

"Well, he said he didn't want to bother you since you're in the hospital, but you know he's not getting paid right now."

"Of course I know he's not getting paid!" I blurt out. "He works for a quad. He knows if his client gets sick and goes into the hospital he has to take it on the chin -- or the wallet in this situation. Hey, if I could -- I'll call him." I say tersely, realizing what transpired.

"He's moving to Hawaii!" my brother says in his defense, "You, of all people, know how expensive everything is in Hawaii."

"I'm the guy who told Whining Wayne. Did he call and whine?"

"Kind of."

"Okay. At least I know where I stand. I'm a commodity to him and a ticket to Hawaii." My brother begins to interrupt. "No, no. I'm not complaining. I don't care if he *hates* me as long as he does the job and doesn't torture me with nonsense or kill me in my sleep. Christ, he can bugger little boys as long as I get fed and bathed and to school on time."

This is my third indication that there may be problems with Whining Wayne. I had tendered my modified Personal Care Attendant offer to Gary to join me in Hawaii. He could work for me in Hawaii, but he would have to share in the rent (a condition not even enforceable in Minnesota). I explain to Gary that in Hawaii I live in student housing. I am returning to the same two-bedroom apartment I occupied last year. The two-bedroom apartments are occupied by four students. Each student pays a less than market value fee for his share of the apartment. Student housing does not accept Section Eight subsidy from the government, which is irrelevant since I am still on the many-year waiting list for Section Eight entitlement services. But I did present a compelling argument to the Director of Student Housing who considers allowing my attendant and me to occupy one of the bedrooms for the price of just me. Gary declined the offer but Whining Wayne -- Gary's long-term friend and the individual responsible for Gary's entrée into the Personal Care Attendant field -- accepted.

Before I agree to the arrangement with Whining Wayne -- who was working for another quadriplegic as a live-in attendant -- I ask Gary if this would be a wise decision.

"He's a hell of a guy," he begins. "We've been friends since grade school and have worked together. Since he works for Barry, you know he can do the job..."

"I hear a 'but' coming," I sing.

"Well...," he struggles to say it. "He's a whiner."

"What does he whine about?"

"EVERYTHING!" he says, with a vein sticking out of his neck. "He whines about his girlfriend, his mom, his sister, smoking, drinking beer, Barry -- don't misunderstand, I love him. If it wasn't for him I would have never gone into this work, and I wouldn't know you. We've known each other for years, but..." he shrugs his shoulders and tilts his head. "There it is."

The second indication that there may be problems with Whining Wayne came when I went on a road trip with him, Barry and Gary. We were having beers at an establishment. "I'm not ripping off your attendant from you, am I?" I ask Barry with some concern.

"Hell, no," he responds. "Glad to get rid of him," he says jokingly, but with an element of truth sticking it in like a knife. "Now you can try and wake his ass up."

My head immediately jerks 180 degrees to where Whining Wayne is seated. His face wears the look of guilt. "Please don't make me late for school, 'cause if you do, you will be one out of work, living on the beach with no ticket home, personal care attendant," I admonish him.

He nods silently, looking straight ahead, and turns toward me, "And that would be a bad thing?"

And now this from my brother...

I instruct Pat, "Tell him not to whine to you and to call me. You can't do anything that he can't... or whatever I'm trying to say," I tell him, and then the conversation becomes friendlier.

"I'll see you tomorrow then," my brother concludes. "Love ya."

The Squeaky Wheel

Three more days go by, and I am released. No apology comes forth from the good doctor for his mistake, nor does Dr. Friendly (who was not) make an appearance to apologize or yank on anything else. I did see him lurking in the hall one day when the others were in my room. I desperately want to question him as to when I can expect an apology, but I still lack the skills.

I return to my apartment via my van with Patrick at the helm. His children ride along, also. In the driveway of my apartment Patrick exits the van, unlocks the controls for the doors and lift, presses the switch that opens the right door, then the switch that opens the lift door, then the switch that lowers the platform. At this point I maneuver myself and the wheelchair onto the lift. Now I press the switch on the arm of the lift and am lowered to the pavement. I roll off the lift. Patrick presses each of the four switches at the back of the van to reverse this process and closes up the vehicle. He locks the control panel, and we proceed to the lift on the side of my apartment that I roll onto (with the children) and Devlin holds the switch that lowers the lift to the level of my apartment. It's his turn.

Inside the apartment Whining Wayne sits in the only remaining chair. All the furniture, kitchenware, art and sundries have been packed away save my dresser and bed. Someone will occupy my apartment in my absence. I see my open suitcases on the bed in my room. Mike grins as he smokes a cigarette. "What's up, man?" He asks.

"I'm trying to get to Hawaii!"

My bags are packed, the television is returned to the Target electrical appliance lending library, we travel to the airport, my batteries are removed, we arrive in Honolulu, my batteries are lost and I am delivered home. I no longer have the quadriplegic, Hawaiian, Nazi roommate, but a mellow local kid and a Jewish Caucasian kid wound tighter than a medieval catapult. Schooling begins, dating continues with Helen, and Wayne begins to complain about everything from the cost of food to the inability to drive to another state.

Wayne sets two alarm clocks -- one of them is over my head -- and every morning one goes off, he hits the snooze button and goes back to bed. Then the other alarm clock goes off and he rises, crosses the room, hits the snooze button and goes back to bed. This sequence continues until I'm screaming that he is a cock-sucking selfish asshole. Each morning we arrive moments before the cafeteria is about to close and then I must rush to class. Some mornings we miss breakfast.

The giant yellow van I purchased before leaving for Minnesota acquires insurance, proper licensing and whining Wayne to drive it. He is invited to drive it even when I am not in the vehicle but... he whines about the cost of gas. I tell him to go to church or someplace other than a bar where he will actually meet people. He declines.

One night Helen, whining Wayne and I travel to a bar. Whining Wayne maintains that if we can just do this once a week he will have no problems in Hawaii. He wants me to take time out of my compromised life to "pal around" with him. He has already whined to friends and family back home that he "hates Hawaii." When asked why, he tells them "It's boring." When asked why it is boring his laundry list is: "No place to drive," "no place to shoot pool," and if he could get away with it he would add, "I can't snowmobile here." He tells me he will be returning to Minnesota before Halloween. It is only because his mother tells him he has yet to keep a commitment in his entire life that he agrees to stay until after Christmas.

At this establishment we meet a co-worker of Helen's who is with a Hispanic, biker dude who hails from... Minnesota. He keeps Wayne from whining some because he has cocaine and will show Wayne where to shoot pool. We travel to another concert that is outside and sold out. We are outside the gates fraternizing with the other procrastinators and misers who have time and money to buy alcohol and drugs.

"Helen," one of the cheap, late, future Betty Ford Clinic patrons continues in a loud, slurred screech, "is this your boyfriend?" Helen sits on my lap as I sit in the wheelchair. The speaker's eyelids hang and her head movement is slow and erratic.

"Yes," she answers.

I am impressed by her directness. Later when I ask her why she responded so quickly she asks me, almost challenging me, "Did I say the wrong thing? I figured if I said, 'no,' that she would try to take you from me."

I'm very surprised by this as I always figure that questions from these people are always freak-show or wondering how the fuck some beautiful babe finds herself stuck with a liability in a wheelchair.

"I could lose you in a second," she says seriously.

I find this an unbelievable statement and choose not to continue this line of questioning but instead kiss her and move toward the bed. Helen and I become closer and I'm glad that I have freed Willie.

The Squeaky Wheel

We like to give whining Wayne a buck to go buy himself ice cream. He prefers to pout and sit in the living room and watch our roommate's black and white TV while he smokes cigarettes and lofts the butts out the open front door. Meanwhile Helen and I light candles, smoke marijuana, play music and lick each other. My creative energy is devoted to theater and lovemaking. Helen sits in my lap parked next to my twin bed. Two self-standing closets divide the room in half with Wayne's bed against the other wall.

Helen sniffs the books that I will use for the semester. Her olfactory sense is insatiable. Helen moves with a natural grace of one that "consents" to the alleged rules of gravity. She glides. She exudes a sexuality that pulls on an ancient naval officer's soul like the moon on the ocean. I kiss her about the forehead quickly, squeakily and kindly and linger with the kisses as I reach the three freckles next to her left eye. I focus my hot breath here as I bring my tongue toward her ear and plant kisses along the way. The tip of my tongue traces the ridges of her ear as I wait and breathe... pondering whether to slip my tongue gently into her ear or jab my tongue into her ear.

She presses her head against my mouth and I plunge my tongue into her ear. She fights not to pull away and I slip my articulator in and out of her ear. As our breathing quickens, small involuntary moans eek out and juices flow. Helen brings her shoulder to her head in that desperate/wondrous place wherein we find ourselves drawn to and discomforted by the pleasure.

Helen "presents" her hand to me, which I kiss, bite and lick as I work my way up her shoulders. I bite just where the back and arm separate and she pulls away only to present the inside of her arm for kisses to the inside of her elbow and back down to her fingers. She is holding my head and we're kissing. She grinds on my knee staring into my eyes and biting her lip. She deftly drops to her knees and begins to remove the footrests of the wheelchair while also working my zipper. In a flurry of flesh, fabric and wheelchair accoutrements we are in bed and she is naked on top of me.

I slowly pay homage to her shoulders, neck, chest, biceps, breasts, belly, nipples, ribs, waist, buttocks (left & right), thighs, calves, knees, ankles, arches and toes. Her damp, downy pudendum tickles my chest, chin, lips, nose and forehead before my nose becomes planted in her naval -- in honor of the dream. My chin coaxes her down until I am looking at her black, sex-goddess labial lips. Helen screams when Mr.

Tongue meets Lady C. She repositions and the same conclusion is reached.

After we begin to recover I ask if she will consent to being employed as my supervising nurse for Badland Nursing Company back home. She comatosely accepts.

I am directing *End of the World with Symposium to Follow* at Manoa Valley Theatre.

I leave a message for Joe, the hardest working set designer on seven continents. The message says, "Brian is planning end of the world -- wants your help."

Joe agrees to allow me to take an independent study so that I can design the set for the aforementioned play. It is a comedy about nuclear proliferation. It is to be my Master's Thesis production. My faculty has approved it. I am going to get paid at a community theater to direct it; I will be graded and people with some talent from the community will come to audition instead of doing a college production wherein one is often begging for people to be in your play. Rehearsals won't begin until next year but this project, for me, must begin now.

I am taking Shakespearean acting from Professor Noel Cowardly. He is another aging big fish in a small pond. Because he was once the stand-in for Lord Lawrence Olivier, he keeps a magazine picture of the great actor framed in his office and feigns an intimate relationship with the man. I procrastinate the early class assignments and finally present Professor Cowardly a scene, monologue actually, which he suggested. I perform the scene the first time and he says, "What I saw was a traditional, fairly stodgy interpretation of this." He challenges me. I return with the piece entirely redone and watch the eyes of my audience/classmates lock with mine from the first spoken syllable. My classmates smile delighted smiles, laugh genuine and unexpected laughs. Professor Cowardly is called Noel by all students and faculty. This is most appropriate as he, like Professor Fragilego and Tim in New Mexico, has no advanced degree. Professor Cowardly laughs loudest, most sincerely and most pleased. My classmates, who are miserly with their applause, clap ferociously.

Professor Cowardly wants me to perform the piece one more time and then to rehearse regularly with Maile. He heard about the Jocasta production and has not found a way to deal appropriately with Maile because of her disability -- blindness. I promise I will help Maile.

The Squeaky Wheel

Maile probably should have won the bikini contest. She and I have become much more conversant. I watch her one day as she walks up the long, narrower ramp that has been placed over the stairs at the back of the theater. Maile wears white shorts and burgundy thongs. This is a time when thongs are not worn by most coeds. I wonder if it's Maile sending a message of clearly seen sexy underwear or if it is an "oversight" on her part.

We decide we shall do a scene from *The Tempest*. We travel together to the KOKUA office. I am smitten with her beauty. She is tall, ample bosomed, muscular and has hair that changes from black to red to nearly blonde with semi regularity and professional results. Maile has magical lips, a great complexion, and an athletic body with a playmate's breasts. Her eyes are of green jade.

We arrive at the KOKUA office and I am brought with Maile into the room with the enlarger. The device will turn a twelve-point letter into a very large icon. Tammy begins reading, "If, by your art my father..." in the scene she pleads with me, Prospero -- her father, to stop whipping up my black magic. We are able to read through it a few times and she understands and we agree to rehearse at my apartment that night. Whining Wayne hides in the other room -- afraid he might actually meet someone. Maile and I work on the scene and she sits with her feet up and one heel at all times against her clitoris. I wonder how much of my leering she can see.

In the scene I ask her and she remembers her mother and then I tell her, "Thy mother was a piece of virtue..." She always misses the cue at the end of this exchange and I swear I'm seeing her panties dampening as she makes the little squeak women make when they hear just the right thing said just the right way. One heel replaces the other at her pudendum.

When we work the scene in class Professor Noel Cowardly spends the entire time working with Maile. He then tells the other class members if they were real students of the craft they would have learned at least as much as Maile did. I learned plenty.

Brian Shaughnessy

The Revenge of Dr. Friendly (Who Was Not)

Helen calls me to say she wants to take me to dinner. She is sounding very sweet and coy about the invitation that is both endearing and suspicious to my romantic and cynical nature. Soon she is at my apartment wearing a sexy black dress and looking in the yellow pages for a suitable dining establishment within rolling/walking area. She chooses a Japanese restaurant and we set out for our meal -- and whatever else she has planned. She clearly has plans.

The two of us order. (Actually she orders, as I have the same level of familiarity with Japanese menus as with nuclear reactors.) The appetizers arrive and I ask her to remove my Uri Geller fork, which is bent at a 90-degree angle. "Nope." She grins as she picks up the ornamental chopsticks. "Tonight, I'm going to feed you." As a one time rehabilitation nurse she realizes the numerous issues involved in her statement (or so I think) -- independence, control, appearance, etc. "Is that okay?" she asks coquettishly and with concern.

I look into her loving dark eyes and take in her medium length black highlighted hair, her brown skin and face with the three freckles next to her right eye, her full, smiling lips, her white teeth, the soft shoulders and the sexy black dress.

"Hell, yes!" I respond to this sensual offer. She lifts the first morsel to my mouth and it is more than the quality of the food that delights my taste buds. Right now they are doing the wave on my tongue as if Balanchine choreographed it in costumes by Armani. Each bite, each sip of wine, each kernel of rice, each giggle from this woman is an ancient Greek celebration for my senses. I have no idea why my senses appear to be turned up to 12 on a dial that goes to 10 but I don't care. The two of us have a wonderful meal.

"I want to know where you see our relationship going," she says with a grin as she rocks slightly in her chair with a glass of wine held to mouth height but half a foot away. Her eyes dance. The heel of one foot is pressed against her pudenda. She sniffs each morsel of food as she lifts it to her mouth or to mine.

"Going?" I ask, seeking clarification. My suspicions were not misplaced.

"Yeah," she says, as only a girl from California says 'yeah' -- making it sound both darling and doltish in the same moment.

"You mean like... what... marriage?" thinking she couldn't possibly mean that. My disbelief must come out in my words.

She sighs, her shoulders droop and the glass of wine is placed on the table. "Well, yes, eventually. I haven't thought about getting married again for almost twenty years, and I didn't think I would ever think about it again. But the way you *talk* makes me feel like *you're* thinking about it."

"The way *I* talk?" I say growing even more puzzled. "My Midwestern accent?"

"No," she says becoming more stern and less amused. "It's the words that you say."

"Like what?" I ask sincerely, wondering how I so misled this woman. At this moment I am also flattered that she would even entertain such a serious commitment with someone many, many women would see as an asexual liability.

"Don't make me have to repeat *your* words."

"No, please -- I need to know how I may have misled you. What exactly have I said?"

She pauses and looks away and around the restaurant and then launches into it. "You say things like, 'You're the one for me,' ' We belong together,' 'I'm the man for you,' and that you had a dream that you know me from another life!"

Not exactly an engagement ring, I think, but I see her point and apologize.

"So, what do you want?"

"I," I begin, "I would like to see us continue in this relationship and see where it goes. But I know I'm here for another year or two and then will probably have to go to the mainland to get work. Your daughter is here, you have a place here, and you're dug in, but I want to do theater. Unless I can land a job here -- which is a possibility -- I'm going to have to go to the mainland."

Silence. I ask her how she feels about what was just said. "Disappointed," is her one word response. The word stabs my heart like a knife. No sex tonight, I think. Apologies are proffered and disappointment expressed and she accompanies me back to my apartment... and leaves.

The next day I vomit in the early morning. The meal of the previous evening has considerably less charm. I forego classes and remain in my room. I am at my desk trying to study through the nausea and the profound sadness I feel from the night before when Helen enters and puts her arms around me from behind. I am relieved and confused.

"I didn't expect to see you again," I say.

"Why not?" she asks genuinely.

I laugh. "Because you were disappointed! You don't hate me?"

She scoffs and responds to each question in reverse order. "I don't hate you; I don't think anyone could hate you. Besides, my disappointment doesn't mean I don't want to see you; I just wanted to know where we're at."

Soon I am nauseous and vomiting again while Helen holds my head and a bucket. She tries to give me juice and crackers but they come right back up. The two of us return to bed where we make love, vomit, brush my teeth and make love again. This pattern continues into the next day when I forego all food. On day three I feel like my "flu" has passed and I can go to school. I drink some apple juice and within minutes it comes back up. Helen, Whining Wayne and I decide that it is time to go to the hospital. Helen forbids me from going to her hospital (as she does not want this relationship known to her co-workers), so I am driven to Queen's Hospital.

I arrive at the hospital and Helen tells me to call her when I know what's going on. She does not want to be around as she is fearful that it will reflect on her nursing abilities.

"I don't know your number," I have to tell her as she is climbing back into her car.

She looks at me as if I just kicked her in the teeth. "You don't know my number?" she says with profound sadness and disbelief.

"I can only call you from the phone on my desk; I have you on speed dial."

This makes perfect sense and pleases her. She smiles and walks toward me and digs in her purse. She writes her number on my arm.

"Now you won't forget it." With that, she gets into her car, gives an apologetic look, waves and drives off.

Whining Wayne and I enter the hospital and report to the emergency room. I am quickly moved from the lobby to triage and into one of the cubicles for further assessment. Whining Wayne is already on his way home. A nurse examines me by taking the usual vital signs and surprisingly quickly a doctor examines me and asks questions. I give him my history as well as the events of the last 72 hours. He appears puzzled but not startled and leaves the area, returning a few minutes later to ask

The Squeaky Wheel

more questions. With these questions answered he nods and leaves again.

"Mr. Shaughnessy, have you had any abdominal surgery within the last year?" he asks, returning with cocked head and squinting eyes.

My nauseated stomach drops lower than a bastard crack addict's morals. This can't be good, I think.

"Yes," I say tentatively, anticipating the next question, "in August."

A Sherlock Holmes solving the mystery satisfied look paints his face and he nods with certainty.

"You probably have an adhesion from scar tissue from that surgery and its causing a blockage in your intestines that allows whatever you eat to only get to the blockage and then has to come back up, yeah?" Only the 'yeah' is a question. This is a very common tag at the end of sentences for the local Hawaiian English speaker. "We're going to get an x-ray. You're not in pain?" he asks incredulously.

I ponder this, "Some, not much more than the nausea though."

The doctor grins. "You're lucky." There are those words again. "If you weren't quadriplegic you would be in unendurable pain."

Soon they are trying to radiate my gonads again. "Can you cover my balls?" Tired of *always* having to ask this question and tired of asking it in a more technical/testicle manner, I address the radiological technician using the parlance of the street. He does so grudgingly. (Why would a simple request -- a request that is actually common sense and part of their job -- *anger* someone?) Afterward I find myself in another exam room off the emergency room with five other nurses, aids and a doctor.

"Have you had an NG tube before, Mr. Shaughnessy?"

I thought my stomach had bottomed out moments ago. Wrong, very wrong. And now I am surrounded.

"Yes," I say, as I feel my skin become even whiter and wetter thinking of waking up with this implement of pain in my nose and Dr. Friendly's (who wasn't) subsequent unprofessional/insensitive removal.

"We're going to have to put one in now," the third doctor I've seen today says apologetically. I nod and he opens the heinous rubber tube and moves slowly toward my nose. I vaguely recall the others in the room holding me (perhaps down) as this pinky-wide implement is shoved through a nostril. The initial pain is like an ice-pick in my face and there is another two feet of tubing. Each push of the tube is certainly more painful than a twist of the rack. I groan with each push. Every muscle of my body that still can contract is contracted. The people around say,

"Swallow, Brian, it will go easier." How the fuck do you know? I think, as I attempt to swallow between my restrained screams.

Ultimately, the process ends and I apologize for my ranting. All nod and say that it's OK; then someone speaks the unbelievable.

"It's curled, doctor." I don't like the sound of this. The doctor looks at the person who said this as if they insulted his mother. He looks at me as if he must tell me I am going to die. I look at him as if he just told me he is going to kill me.

He turns slowly and sadly toward me. "We have to take it out and put it down the other nostril," he says with a pain uncharacteristic of his profession. I sigh heavily and nod as he moves closer -- incredulous to my luck/fate -- when God intervenes.

"Can I get a shot of Demerol before we do this *again*?"

The doc looks at me with the tube in his hand, looks to the tube, back at me and smiles and shakes his head in a manner that says, 'I am a moron and this man is a genius.' "Let's get 75 milligrams of Demerol IM here stat," and someone is already exiting the room. They return within minutes and I am leaned over, my pants pulled down, my ass swabbed with alcohol and a trip out of the galaxy is administered through a needle. By the time they sit me back up I am a malenky bit slooshy. Within a minute I am fully slooshy.

"Ready to try this again?" the doctor asks happily.

"Go for it," I say from a galaxy far, far away. The doctor grins at my altered perspective and pokes that heinous implement up my nose. It hurts every bit as much as it did before but the view is better. This time it does not curl and I am floated upstairs where I am told that there is a small bowel obstruction and I will need surgery. This obstruction occurred because scar tissue formed since the last surgery and is now preventing the natural processing of food-to-waste. Again, I am asked if I am or have been in pain. I explain that I am not now -- due to the Demerol -- nor was I previously. The doc who will perform the surgery says but for the quadriplegia I would be in excruciating pain and that in all likelihood gangrene has set in in my intestines! I am not thrilled by the trade-off of pain for paralysis *or* the fact that I am about to undergo surgery *again*. But, off I go.... I call Helen -- reading the numbers on my arm -- to tell her the diagnosis and pending treatment. She thanks me for calling; I can hear the tears in her voice and the fact that she is blaming herself for not diagnosing it the first time she held the puke bucket.

In the operating room for the fifth time in five years the anesthesiologist asks if it is okay to use a local, which means I will remain

The Squeaky Wheel

awake for the procedure. I agree. I want to keep my eyes on these people with the fucking knives. He says it won't take much anesthesia because of my paralysis. Big deal.

Various surgical and operating room instruments are laid out on a table as I look on horrorstricken. This is really crashing my buzz. Surgical nurses enter, my belly is bathed in Betadine, monitoring instruments are attached and the surgeon enters. He is funny and we exchange operating room humor. Then a shroud is placed just below my nipples to divide me from the masked bipeds. Conversation and humor continues.

"While I'm down here I'm going to remove your appendix, okay?"

I believe I hear it splat into a tray.

"Didn't leave me much of a choice, did you doc?" I ask him. He peers over the shroud from behind his mask.

"Shall I put it back?" he asks with humor and some anger.

"No, just leave the soul."

He looks away and peers at my splayed guts, shakes his head and looks back.

"You ain't got no soul," he says and returns to the procedure.

"You mean I could get into medical school?"

In a short time I am moved to recovery and then to the post-op floor. Again, I cannot eat or drink and a glass jar and pump are attached to the tube in my nose and the same nasty, viscous, brown substance is sucked out of me. My roommate is a big Japanese man in his thirties. He has been in the hospital for several weeks because of a decubitus ulcer. He is looking at a comic book and informs me that his favorite cartoon will be on TV in a few minutes. Even with a Demerol induced perspective I am not interested. The nurses enter and perform their nursely duties. I ask a gorgeous, slender, longhaired Filipina with loving eyes to call Helen. Helen is nursing a back injury and unable to work so she says she will be down to visit shortly. I call Whining Wayne and tell him I will be here "for about a week."

"And I won't get paid during that time?" is his compassionate response.

Familiar with his priorities and overly sensitive and accommodating to my personal care attendants (due to my perception of being vulnerable and grateful for their services) I tell him to go ahead and bill and that I will ask Helen if she will forego reporting my hospitalization to the nursing agency and thus ensure his being paid for nothing. I wonder why I make this accommodation.

Helen arrives with tomato-red eyes. After she laments and empathizes with the tube in my nose and introduces herself to the other nurses (including the dark goddess) who then depart, I ask why her eyes appear to be bleeding. She runs to the mirror and examines them. She sighs heavily, says she put eye drops in, and comes over to the bed, sits and takes my hand.

"I talked to Shirley (her friend and fellow nurse) because I felt so bad. I thought it was all my fault for not diagnosing this." I scoff. "I know, but you have to understand that I am a *nurse* and we assess all the time. Jesus, I could have killed you." I try to tell her otherwise but she hushes me and continues. "I know, I was telling that to Shirley and she let me know there was NO WAY I could have diagnosed that — it took the *doctors* over half an hour to figure it out with all of their schooling and diagnostic equipment. (Pause) You don't hate me?" I laugh at her statement and the fact that 72 hours ago I was asking the same question. I assure her the emotions I have for her do not include hate.

"Not yet," I say, teasing her. I whisper laments that I have a roommate that precludes us from having sex. She can't believe 1) that I am interested after surgery AND with a tube in my nose and 2) that I would suggest such a thing when she is a nurse at another hospital.

"You don't think that would get back to people I work with?" she asks with bursting eyes.

"No."

Helen remains until late that evening and returns the next day with some of my books. Whining Wayne never comes nor calls. Helen is a frequent and lengthy visitor -- this is not a complaint. Most of the nurses are glad that she is there (although Helen clearly dislikes the dark goddess) but there is one Caucasian LPN who feels compelled to tell her on more than one occasion, "Visiting hours end at eight."

I am about to tell this nurse to take it to the doctor or security or go to hell, when Helen senses this and squeezes my arm. I remain mute. The LPN exits and Helen explains that 1) LPNs have a chip on their shoulder and exercise any opportunity to chastise an RN and 2) "haole nurses tend to be bitches." I laugh at these generalizations and ponder their accuracies.

There is a Japanese middle-aged nurse who is particularly attentive/sympathetic to my needs. She offers Demerol with atomic clock accuracy. As the days progress I become less inclined to partake at

The Squeaky Wheel

regular intervals. Friends from school visit. The dark goddess asks Helen how she can be there so often and work. Helen explains she has an injury. I tell Helen that one of the other nurses said that the dark goddess (not the way I refer to her when speaking to Helen) is Miss Filipina Hawaii. Helen shakes her head and says, "She wouldn't be shit in the Philippines."

This statement and the contempt with which she says it puzzle me. "Why?"

She looks at me with a 'that-is-so-obvious' look that burns.

"Did you see how dark she is?"

"And that's looked down on even in the Philippines?"

"Hell, yes," she says, seemingly perplexed that I would ask the question. I simply shake my head and quietly lament the fact that this hierarchy appears to exist in most cultures on earth. And I wonder why *else* the dark goddess bothers Helen.

On the third day of my internment the tube is still in my nose, the attentive middle-aged nurse has been dispensing Demerol with the freedom of a diner waitress dispensing coffee, my theater friends have been by and Helen arrives before dinnertime -- which is an insignificant time since I cannot eat or drink. She is a welcome guest and it is time well spent. The nurses and health care personnel enter and perform duties that sometimes drive Helen into the hallway. One night after several hours she suddenly glowers and leans forward and in a surprisingly harsh and accusatory tone barks, "Did you want to come in here, or what?"

I am puzzled by her question, her tone and the look on her face. I hear mumbling from the hallway and then Trudy enters. She looks flustered and then slightly recoils when she sees the tube in my nose. I acknowledge her, thank her for coming and ask her how she knew I was in the hospital.

"I called your apartment and Wayne told me so I came down," she says. I offer her a seat and she sits on the left side of the bed while Helen sits on the right. Introductions are made. Trudy has brought cookies that I cannot eat because the tube is still sucking the poison out of my gut. A clear jar holds the daily diminishing vile, nasty, brown bile. She offers a cookie to Helen who sneers and declines.

"Your name is Helen?" Trudy asks.

"Yup," Helen responds tersely without changing expression or looking away from the TV screen.

"You're a nurse," she endeavors further.

"Yes I am," Helen responds in the same manner.

"Are you his girlfriend?" she asks.

I am surprised by this question but Helen now takes her eyes off the TV, pierces Trudy with a laser-gaze and says, "Yes I am," and returns her eyes to the TV.

"Oh," Trudy says without intellection, pauses and adds, "I thought I was."

A second of shock is eclipsed by the implications of this statement.

"Are you fucking *nuts*?" I blurt out as my head snaps in her direction and the tube is yanked and plunges an ice-pick into my brain. "You have a boyfriend, I rarely see you, we don't mm-mm-mm (the universal grunt for coitus) and you think I'm your *boyfriend*? You're nuts."

Neither woman reacts to my tirade. A short time later Trudy exits. I express my shock at her statement. Helen is clearly suspect but lays out the argument.

"I saw her out in the hallway *hours* ago. Every time I got sent out there, she wouldn't look at me. She was *lurking*," she says with a sneer. "I knew she wanted to come in here and I could see that she was cute, so I was not about to leave until I figured out what this black girl was doing here waiting to talk to *my* boyfriend. Finally, I made her come in here. I wasn't surprised by what she said, Brian," she adds in an accusatory manner.

"She's a kook, an empty soup can, nuts! Why would she think she was my girlfriend? I have no idea where she gets that shit."

"I do," Helen says with authority.

"What?"

"Look at our discussion at dinner before you got sick -- the messages I was getting. I know you flirt with her."

I begin to protest this statement, laugh and say, "Even if that's true -- which I don't think it is -- she *has* a boyfriend."

"A boyfriend who she's *bored* with. A boyfriend who doesn't *talk* like you do. A boyfriend who's not in a *wheelchair*, who's not in *graduate school* and doesn't look at her the way you look at her. I should hate you."

"Remind me to thank her for sabotaging this relationship... and the cookies."

"I should go. I should have left hours ago, but I had to find out what was going on here."

"What *is* going on?"

The Squeaky Wheel

"I don't know," she says and kisses me goodbye, "but I will find out. See you tomorrow."

The next day my roommate is moved and my surgeon listens to my belly and announces that there are sufficient bowel sounds to remove the tube and I may now eat and drink. I am glad that the tube is coming out and fearful of the manner, given my last experience. The doctor says that the matronly, middle age nurse will do the deed. He exits and shortly thereafter she enters.

"Bring me a shot of Demerol, please," I tell her. She looks at me with the same look the doctor who placed the tube gave when I made the same request. She administers the intergalactic sojourn, gives me a few minutes to travel beyond Pluto, removes the piece of tape on my face which holds the tube in position and steps back and looks at me sternly.

"You're tensing! Just relax!" I realize that the unpleasant memories have crushed the Demerol and I am as rigid as a railroad track in subzero weather. The Demerol (and my own resolve) reenters the equation and muscles relax to liquid. The tube slides out with minimal pain (but a sick, violate feeling) and I am left to bask in the celestial scenery while this nurse takes away the jar, the pump and the brown nastiness.

I call Helen and tell her that the tube has been removed. She asks me what I would like her to bring me to eat. I inform her that I no longer have a roommate. She arrives later with sandwiches, fruit, cola, reefer and sans panties. I devour the meal and am transferred by hospital personnel to the wheelchair. We leave the room and go out on the nearby lanai to kiss and smoke. There is a chair out there but Helen sits in my lap. There are some plants, a lounge chair, a round plaque on the wall and a metal fence that divides the lanai from empty space and a three-floor drop. Distant machinery makes a watery sound.

"Are you sick of being here?" she asks halfway through the joint.

"Yes, but not at the moment," I say smiling.

"Why not?" she asks anxious for the answer.

"Because the tube is out of my nose, I've eaten for the first time in days, my baby's in my lap -- with no drawers -- and I'm smoking ganja on the back of a boat!"

Helen takes in the surroundings. "It does look like the back of a boat!" she says with awe. "See, that's why that bitch wants you for her boyfriend. You can make an awful hospital stay into a cruise ship vacation. Too bad you're mine. (Pause) I talked to my friend Yvonne in San Francisco," she says and inhales deeply on the joint. "I was talking to her about you and the dinner we had and the fact that a mysterious black girl who looks like Rae Dawn Chong showed up in the hospital thinking she was your girlfriend. Yvonne was quiet for a long time and then said, 'You got a quadriplegic guy juggling you and somebody that looks like Rae Dawn Chong? What's his secret?'"

I laugh -- tremendously flattered by the implication -- and say, "And you told her, 'I don't know, but I'm not wearing panties to the hospital tonight.'" Now, we both laugh. "You're an asshole," she says half joking. This may be the first time she makes this statement but it won't be the last. "I better not see any more nigger bitches showing up thinking they're your girlfriend."

"Whoa!" I say shocked. "Yvonne's black -- does she know you use that word?" I ask expressing my disdain.

"Yvonne uses that word," she responds in a feeble attempt to justify. I scoff.

"Everybody knows that *they* can use that word and only *they* can use that word."

"I don't want to see that lurker again!" she snaps.

Still weak from surgery, horny and not wanting to diminish the effects of the herb -- I say "Fine" and resume kissing. The two of us return to my now private room, where a nurse transfers me back to bed. We close the door, baptize/soil the bed, linger for some time and then Helen must go home. We kiss goodbye and within minutes three nurses enter. One of them is the dark goddess.

"You're going to have three nurses tonight," she announces and smiles warmly. "I am on the other side, but I'll be here," she says. My naughty parts tingle and I feel -- despite all evidence to the contrary -- like one of the luckiest men alive. Then... I sleep.

The next day is Thanksgiving -- my second in Hawaii. Helen and her daughter have three appearances to make in addition to a stop at the hospital. One of the stops is at my friends' who invited me to their soiree. Helen and her daughter bring and feed me turkey and trimmings after their first stop. I have hospital turkey (Real turkey! Not the pressed shit) and trimmings. Trudy appears again -- unannounced -- and feeds me turkey and trimmings. She stops short of apologizing for her stupid statement. She insists that I misled her. I insist she has a boyfriend.

"So, you guys are boyfriend and girlfriend?" she says accusatorially and in disbelief.

"You heard it from Helen," I snap back.

255

The Squeaky Wheel

"You mean like this kind of boyfriend and girlfriend," she says as she puts her right index finger through the okay sign she makes with her left hand -- using the universally understood sign for coitus.

"Yes! Last night, in that bed. "

"Wow," she says ponderously.

"Why does that get a wow?" I ask, anticipating the answer and disgusted.

"I'm impressed," she says earnestly.

"Because I'm a cripple? Why doesn't anybody believe cripples can have sex?"

"No, not because you're a cripple; because she's a babe."

I laugh at myself for rushing to this assumption. I scold her again for her statement from the other night.

"It's your fault," she says as she departs.

Later, several friends from the Thanksgiving Day theatre soiree arrive with more turkey and trimmings. I tell them of my calculated plan for Demerol before the removal of the NG tube. Stacey shakes his head in wonderment.

"If I'm ever in the hospital I want you to be there to counsel me through every minute."

Two days later I am free to return home. The paratransit service takes its usual circuitous route but eventually deposits me at the apartment I share with Whining Wayne. I enter and he informs me that he has smoked all of my dope -- sometimes waking in the middle of the night to do so -- and went for breakfast every day that I was gone. Every morning in Hawaii with him has been an alarm clock going off over his head followed by an alarm clock going off over my head minutes later. He always hits the snooze button on both and this continues until we must rush to get to the cafeteria before it closes and then I must rush to avoid being late to class. I tell him he is a power-tripping asshole and pussy for treating a quadriplegic this way. He laughs. I hate him.

I call my mother. I tell her that I was in the hospital, had surgery again but now am home and fine.

"Why didn't you call me when you went in?" she scolds. I can hear the hurt in her voice.

"I didn't want you to worry or feel like you had to fly over here."

"That's not a good excuse," she responds with many emotions.

Brian Shaughnessy

"No, but you told me a story that my uncle didn't tell Nonnie when he was in the hospital and about my age."
"Just don't do it again, please," she implores.
"I won't," I say through laughter and tears.
"You promise?" she asks, unconvinced.
"Yes, Mamma."

Unexpected Guests

I exit my campus apartment and travel to the University branch bank for a withdrawal. It's Friday. To get to the bank one must pass through the courtyard outside of the campus restaurant/bar, which carries the moniker Manoa Gardens. As I am zipping past concrete tables and students and non-students eating, drinking and relaxing, I hear a voice calmly say my name. I turn to my right and seated at the table immediately next to me are three of my fellow new graduate students. They invite me to join them; after procuring funds, I do.

They are reviewing what they've learned in the first two weeks of the "Theatre of Japan" course we are enrolled in. They share a pitcher of beer. Stacey -- a fellow Caucasian Minnesotan who is tall, slim, bald, bespectacled and a self-professed neurotic -- gets a glass from a waitress. Dale -- a strapping fellow from Maine who has his own theatre company back home -- pours me a glass. Steve -- another Caucasoid who lived in Minnesota for sometime and arrived in Hawaii a year before the rest of us -- struggles to move the concrete bench to allow me near the table.

A straw is placed in a cup of beer for which I give thanks to the group. "Cool," says Stacy, "we were just talking about Okuni, the woman who is acknowledged as the creator/founder of Kabuki Theatre." I nod and the conversation continues with each member volunteering what they know about Noh and Kyogen as well as Kabuki Theatre, something three Minnesotans and a dude from Maine had almost zero exposure to prior to coming to Hawaii. "Was Okuni a priestess or a slut?" I ask seriously and humorously. The group laughs and indeed the textbook (written by my instructor) says that she was both a priestess and a prostitute. The issue is tabled until I can consult the professor. There are lapses in the

The Squeaky Wheel

conversation when we speak of other things, but someone generally brings the discussion back to class materials. Stacy, ever the organizer/director, is adept at this.

"Let's just keep this group happening every Friday about four o'clock and limit it to the four of us cuz we want to have that edge, yeah Brian?" I nod agreement.

"You didn't know we were meeting here today?" Dale asks. "Oh, that was an oversight on Stacy's part. I'm sure glad you stumbled in -- so to speak." There is wincing and laughing. This group is aware that I make and can take such jokes. The Friday meeting becomes a ritual for this semester but Theatre of Japan discussions do not. Beer, however, is still included and some other players sporadically join and miss.

I arrive one Friday several weeks later and no members of my ensemble (now jokingly referred to as the Theatre of Japan study group) are present. I converse with one of the semi-regulars and Dale enters looking sullen. I wave to him, and he grabs a beer and joins me. The semi-regular begs out and departs and the two present core members grab a table outside. Dale informs me that he is fighting with his wife regarding money. Ever since money was invented couples have fought about it. Before there was money they fought about sheep or whatever their article of exchange happened to be. All couples fight about it... often. Even when they think they are fighting about something else, they fight about money. The two of us bond in a way not realized prior to this.

As we connect and have passionate discussions about each other's personal lives, Dale is sitting across the table from me. I see an odd sight. Four unusually and brightly dressed individuals wearing makeup enter the courtyard. Dale does not see them. I realize that this is the opportunity of a lifetime for an Irish/Impish/Theatre Major-who-fancies-himself-funny. I struggle for exactly the right thing to say. It hits me. It is the stuff they put in books and movies. (Ahem.)

"Get a load of these clowns," I say without inflection.

Dale is taking a drink of beer as he turns and sees four people with brightly colored curly wigs -- red, green, orange and purple – polka dotted outfits and BIG shoes. Clowns.

The beer does not explode from his mouth nor pass through his nose. Mercifully. His face lights up and his head drops as he struggles to swallow the beer and *then* roars with laughter. He looks with wonder at the clowns and then at me. "You fucker! You're lucky that beer went down instead of out!" He gestures down and then toward me. "How the hell... you had to have set that up. I don't believe that happened."

Brian Shaughnessy

But it did.

Performing Shakespeare for Professor Noel Cowardly elicits an unexpected offer to play the role of Prospero in *The Tempest* next year. He tells me to learn the lines over the summer. I ask him if he is serious. He says he is. I point out that I have twenty witnesses to this offer in the room. He laughs.

My third semester of graduate school ends and I will be directing my thesis production next semester. Helen and I have already planned to go to the Big Island with whining Wayne who whines about the opportunity. Initially, he demanded that he be allowed to go.
"I'm going to be in a room with two other people. Two other horny people."
I can't argue.

I am less impressed by the Big Island than Oahu because of its lack of beaches. Rocky coastline abounds but there are vast stretches of land where you think you are on another planet.
My mother is moving from New Mexico to Arizona. She would like to visit Hawaii but it's not feasible financially. I lament this to Helen who almost immediately responds, "She can stay at my place. I'm going to San Francisco to see my family for a week so she can stay there."
I'm impressed and can afford the airfare for my mom who arrives with her new companion. They stay at Helen's, a 19th floor luxury condominium in Hawaii Kai. My mother's new partner, Jim, takes pictures of the grounds and the building that impress even Helen. We each have Christmas dinner with our respective mothers.
My mom departs and Helen returns in time for New Year's when Helen and I drink a bottle of champagne. We take the second bottle from the refrigerator and decide to go on an adventure. We travel around campus with champagne glasses as she sits perched on the left armrest of the wheelchair. Her face is close to mine. We travel this way often and we must look disgustingly cute because people always smile and often comment pointlessly.
We wind up on the top level of the parking structure which overlooks the football field. It is very cold for Hawaii and she is bundled in a sweater and a hat. In the middle of a long kiss, Helen pulls away and removes her shoes... and then her jeans.
"Are you crazy?" I ask, uninitiated.

"Yes." She wraps her thighs around my neck and supports herself on the railing of the parking structure. One slight miscalculation of this flying Walenda sex act and she will fall forty feet to the ground. I can only lick, lap, plunge and revel until I hear that symphony of squeals performed for a man who has done the job right. The fireworks are exploding -- literally. Happy New Year.

She climbs down and begins to unzip my fly. Headlights appear in the lot behind us. I turn my head to see, what else, police. Helen pulls her sweater to cover herself as much as possible, sits in my lap, kisses me and commands, "Keep kissing me -- let them do the talking." The voice of experience.

The squad car pulls over and the policeman rolls down his window. With a look of being infinitely bothered and only mildly amused he says, "You can't stay here. Go home."

Whiner

Putting up with my attendant, whining Wayne from Minnesota, is not easy. He does in fact whine about not being in Minnesota, he whines about not being able to drive as far as in Minnesota, he whines I don't spend enough time with him, he whines that I have a girlfriend and he doesn't and he misses duck hunting. I tell him to go back to ducking Minnesota, drive his ducking car as far he wants and go duck himself. He does. So now I have Head-injured Harry performing my cares and an RN girlfriend who is monitoring him. Harry is not a man without goals; he repeatedly attempts to enter the bathroom, sometimes successfully, while my girlfriend Helen is peeing.

Each day, after a suppository has been inserted in my rectum, and the feces are manually extracted; after my feet, legs and arms are stretched through range of motion; after I am bathed and the current wounds bandaged, I am placed in the wheelchair with a rolled up towel in the small of my back. This keeps me from leaning forward all day, thus making me infinitely more comfortable. One day I am rolling across campus, travel down a curb cut and the towel falls out and gets lodged in the belts and gearing that are the wheelchair. I can only travel in a circle. I begin to look for a volunteer to enlist for assistance when a GTE (the Hawaiian phone company) truck slows and the woman driver asks, "Need a hand?"

I nod and she is instantly upon me with a small toolbox. She barely speaks but quickly goes about cutting and extracting the towel from the belts and gear. She struggles to remove the last bit of towel as the job is nearly complete.

"If you disengage the clutch up front --" I begin as she mutters agreement and reaches for the knob to disengage the clutch. I have had to spend many minutes of my life just explaining to an individual *where* that knob is on the wheelchair to disengage the clutch. This woman clearly has some background. We test the wheelchair and it is now moving freely. The large, strong, Caucasian woman wipes the grease from her hands with a towel from her toolbox. I am thanking her profusely.

"I used to work for a group of you guys back in Berkeley," she says matter-of-factly.

Now I understand. I make a mental note of the number on the side of her truck as she is telling me her name is Woodie. Beneath the number is the slogan, "Beyond the call." I travel to KOKUA where one of the lovely Asian girls who assists my every need helps me type a letter to Hawaiian telephone. I begin with my obligatory salutation of, "Sirs," borrowed from every letter to the editor that ever appeared in National Lampoon magazine.

"Talk about beyond the call..." I begin and tell the story of Woodie's rescue. I thank her again and close the letter with a postscript. PS -- Wouldn't this make a great commercial? But it never did.

Head-injured Harry is making me insane. It's hard enough dealing with my disability; I don't have the skills to deal with his disability also. His attempts to see Helen peeing, the numerous misunderstandings because of his disability (often exploited by Harry), the complaints about Helen's overuse of toilet paper and milk, talk of "niggers" and his various 'pieces of professional ass,' tally up to a pink slip.

"I've never been canned from a job in my life," he complains.

"You just lost your cherry," is my unsympathetic response. I have already hired Tyrell to take over the Monday after Easter. Friday evening he is handing me his keys.

"You're supposed to stay here through Sunday!" I remind him.

261

The Squeaky Wheel

He shrugs, then tells me that I told him today was his last day and that he will be leaving by midnight. I immediately have him call Helen and tell him to sit in the living room until midnight. He does. Helen fills in for the next two days.

We hold two nights of auditions for *End Of The World With Symposium To Follow*. Last semester I began designing the set, studying the script, blocking where the characters enter, move, exit, etc., reading reviews and analyzing the play. I now read biography material on the author and immerse myself in my favorite genre -- dark humor. I want the set and play to feel like film noir. The floor of the stage is laid out like a giant home plate. A three-dimensional maze representing the riddle/puzzle/unanswerable questions inherent in a play about nuclear proliferation is painted on the floor. The audience sits on three sides. The costumes are black, white or shades of gray as are the set pieces. There are seven doors where actors make entrances and exit. Over the doors is a screen onto which art deco images are projected for the many locations throughout the play. Over the screen is a New York skyline. Joe, who is the master scenic designer in Hawaii and guided me through this process, honors me with a bottle of champagne and a card. On the front of the card is a line from the play. "What you need to make a play work is a concept."

He tells me I have the right concept for film noir, followed throughout the play by even making sure that the pack of Camels that the lead character smokes are black and white – attention to such details makes for great theater. Unfortunately, the wound on my butt has opened again, so when I am not at the theater directing I must remain in bed. KOKUA graciously sends over to my apartment whatever attractive young coed is available and willing to assist. They help me choose film noir and art deco photographs that I will project onto a screen to suggest the various locales.

Helen walks in one day after one of the angels has left and sees my list of music that will play before the play begins. She sees the pile of photos and the art deco book. "I'm so jealous," she says.

From my trapped position in bed I ask why.

"Because those cute girls get to come over here and help you with THIS. They get to have fun, get paid for it and see your genius at work."

"Thank you, but I think you have an overinflated opinion of me."

I slowly discover that this is true and that Helen suffers from borderline personality disorder. This little malady is characterized by an over-inflated and unrealistic opinion of a loved one -- an opinion that idealizes the object of their love and holds them to such a high standard that that person could never measure up. Then when the loved one does not perform to this idealized standard, the borderline personality disorder individual is devastated. Also characteristic of the condition are low self-esteem, jealousy and a desperate all-consuming need to control. I'm canoeing down a river and ignoring the fact that I hear a roaring waterfall.

One night while we are in bed Helen says, "If I was your mother I would take you to bed."

"I do believe that is the most twisted thing anyone has ever said to me. Jesus! I've heard of an Oedipal complex but not a Jocasta complex."

The play is a hit. I get a big article in the paper and I get paid for doing my thesis production. It's on to graduation! Trudy is at the graduation and Helen makes a scene demanding that she leave. Pat and Kate are in attendance -- they have flown from Minneapolis for the festivities. They are the first to see Helen's bizarre behavior.

I spend another month in Hawaii after my graduation before returning to Minneapolis. Despite graduating I will return to the student apartments next August with help from KOKUA. There is a conference for theater and disability in New York in July that I will be attending. Helen has already announced she would like to visit me in Minneapolis and I invite her to the conference. She will come. She pouts when she discovers that my live-in attendant for the summer will be a woman.

Returning to Minnesota for the summer the airlines loses my batteries. I observe the irony that some are envious of my life in Hawaii. I grudgingly acknowledge to myself that there is much to be celebrated. I take up the challenge of Prospero, and by the end of the summer I can be Prospero.

The girl who is my attendant for the summer, Dorothy, is capable, experienced, unattractive and a nasty bitch to her choke-chained boyfriend. I have always felt obliged/compelled to pleasantly banter with and make these people laugh during the morning routine. She understands that when Helen comes she can continue to do my cares though she should stay at her boyfriend's. Helen and I are discussing the

The Squeaky Wheel

trip one day and she says her 19-year-old daughter is giving her a hard time about leaving.

"Tell her to come to Minneapolis and that we will all go to New York and I will pay for Pasta's ticket."

(Long pause.) "Really?" comes Helen's surprised/pleased response.

It must be explained that "Pasta" is a nickname bestowed on Helen's daughter in infancy. Pasta is shocked at my generosity; I have not been her favorite person since taking more and more of her mother's time. She accepts my offer, travels to Minneapolis and on to New York where cabdrivers have these two small women schlep me in and out of cabs while they watch. Helen is 10 years older than I and Pasta is eleven years younger. They look like sisters. When we are in public and Pasta directs a "Mom" to Helen, strangers often express disbelief. We take the manual wheelchair and leave the electric wheelchair in Minneapolis so no batteries are lost. Mother and daughter bathe me and push me about the Big Apple as we take in play after play.

It is said that if you wait in Times Square long enough you will meet someone you know. As mother and daughter are removing me from a cab, I hear my name called with a question mark. As I am placed in the wheelchair I see one of my sister's friends from Minneapolis. "I guess it's true," I say with a laugh and an explanation.

Back in Minneapolis Dorothy is uncharacteristically loud and talkative during the morning routine. Helen and Pasta are trying to sleep. I figure it is some weird woman thing that I would never even want to try to understand. I simply ask her to respect the fact that there are two people sleeping in the next room. She disrespects.

Before Helen returns to Hawaii she says, "I hope we run into Proletarian Peggy while I'm here because I will beat the shit out of her for ripping you off." She almost gets her wish. We go to a Ringo Starr concert with several friends and family members. Just after we are forced from the general seating area to the wheelchair seating area Proletarian Peggy comes by the row where Pat and others of my friends are seated. Pat begins one of his not uncommon screaming matches with the woman – to no avail.

Brian Shaughnessy

Dancing and the Art of Breaking Boards

I am riding in Patrick's van with the now three children.

"Devlin and Aidan start karate class next week and Mickaylee starts ballet."

"Oh really?" I say somewhat surprised. "Isn't that rather traditional for a granola-eating, former free schooler, co-op working, 'no sugar for my kids' father? Why aren't Devlin and Aidan taking ballet? Or why isn't Mickaylee taking karate? Awfully traditional for me!"

"It's been discussed --" he begins, but Mickaylee interrupts loudly from the bench in the back of the van.

"I don't want to take karate," she begins tragically, "I want to dance," she says, elongating the word dance. "Daddy, I don't have to take karate do I?" she asks with enormous blue-eyed apprehension.

"Of course not, honey." Pat says with a father's love. "If you want to dance, Mommy and Daddy want you to dance, all right?"

She nods her head with relief. My brother looks at me in the rearview mirror. Although I smile, he does not. His look and the little expiration of air says, 'You know nothing of parenthood. You have not tasted it.'

The Thrill Is Gone

I am making my fourth trip from Minnesota to Hawaii. It is my first time flying alone in that direction. I have flown back from Hawaii alone and made other unaccompanied flights. My family assists in getting me to the airport and on the plane. I remember to grab some standard length straws from one of the overpriced vendors at the airport. The airlines only have tiny ones and I have only my two-foot plastic one. In a rare act of courtesy by Continental Airlines they bump me to first class. An attentive, sweet and attractive flight attendant dotes on me. She brings me many beverages and sits and feeds me. She seems to know more of my circumstances than the general population. I query her as to how she has such information and, unsurprisingly, I discover she is studying to be an occupational therapist.

The Squeaky Wheel

"You're doing God's work," I tell her. "I wish the airlines had more like you working for them -- especially in management." She agrees and the flight ends far too soon. I wait while all the passengers depart and the baggage handlers arrive to put me on the modified dolly with the plank nailed to it for my ass and take me to the connecting flight from Denver to Honolulu. Big dudes show up and schlep me out of my seat and onto the degrading contraption with minimal bruising. They take me to the gate from whence my flight to Honolulu will depart. Just then the flight attendant from the previous plane arrives and gives me standard length straws, some airline chocolates and her address. She tells me to write her and she will try to visit Honolulu. The baggage handlers watch quietly and after a few minutes I am the first one on the plane and schlepped into my seat with only a few more bruises. I sit for five minutes while the crew enters. One of the flight attendants asks if I'm traveling alone and if she can help. I thank her and tell her I will let her know.

I wait another 20 minutes as a couple hundred passengers enter, fight with their carry-ons and are seated. A thin young man with dark hair sits next to me in the window seat. I chat and find out he is in the military. Just when it appears that everyone is on the airplane, the gate keeper, in a heinous orange blazer one might wear hunting, enters the front of the plane, speaks to one of the flight attendants, looks in my direction and walks down the aisle and stops next to me.

"Mr. Shaughnessy?" he asks.

"Yes," I respond -- fearing the worst.

"Are you flying alone?"

"Yes," I respond, looking at the other passengers/gawkers paying at least as much attention to this conversation as I.

"How are you going to eat?"

Slightly miffed, I respond, "It's a six-hour flight. If somebody helps me, I'll eat. If not, I won't starve.

"What if you have to go to the bathroom," he presses, infuriating me further as more eyes turn toward us.

I am furious but my skills are still in development. "There is a bag on my leg that I piss into," I snarl through clenched teeth.

"What if you have to..." he begins to ask in a tone that suggests I'm excluding the obvious.

"That's not an issue!" I snap back at this inappropriate moron.

The orange-jacketed oaf nods, puts his tail between his legs and runs away from me down the aisle. 'Good,' I think, 'now Mr. Snappy Dresser will make sure one of the flight attendants pays attention to me.'

As this thought runs through my mind, the thin military man beside me sighs, "God." I turn to him as he shakes his head and looks at his lap.

"A day in the life..." I say. He nods agreement and expresses disdain for the treatment I just endured, and as I look toward him the not-so-nattily-dressed inquisitor returns.

"Mr. Shaughnessy."

I see a puzzled look pass over my fellow traveler and turn toward the airline Lackey -- expecting to see a fluorescent orange coat AND the flight attendant personally assigned to my needs. Instead, I see a fluorescent orange coat with the *baggage handlers* who deposited me into the seat AND the dolly with the plank nailed to it.

"Mr. Shaughnessy, I spoke with the pilot and he says there is an FAA regulation that states that anyone who can't take care of himself cannot fly alone. Clearly, you can't take care of yourself, so the pilot has decided to take you off the plane."

There is nothing in his voice or facial expression to suggest that he disfavors or disagrees with this pilot's decision. I can't believe what I just heard.

"I just flew from Minneapolis to Denver," I say calmly but pointedly.

"I'm sorry, Mr. Shaughnessy, but we're going to have to take you off the plane."

"I've made this flight alone before," I say with growing agitation and emphasis.

"I'm sorry, Mr. Shaughnessy, but we're going to have to take you off the plane."

"I always identify myself as a person with a disability and needing full assistance when I buy the ticket."

"I'm sorry, Mr. Shaughnessy, but we're going to have to take you off the plane."

"This is insane; this has never happened before."

"I'm sorry, Mr. Shaughnessy, but we're going to have to take you off the plane."

At this point the infinite ways this little melodrama might play out go through my mind. I turn to the GI next to me (whose mouth you could put a baseball in at the moment) and ask in my best mock pathetic and sarcastic voice, "Will you fly with me?"

"Of course," he says without blinking. The orange coat nods and turns to flee, almost knocking down the baggage carriers.

"Jesus," I say. As a flight attendant ventures by, I order a drink -- partly because I want to drink and partly to make them as busy as I

The Squeaky Wheel

possibly can. I offer one to my flying companion but he declines as he is not yet 21. I get his name and address. Visions of me being dragged off the plane kicking and screaming and subsequently calling the media dance through my head. But someone is waiting for me at the Honolulu International Airport. I look forward to discussing this with my father and making the airline rue the day...

After several drinks (and what I thought was my last) a flight attendant whom I have not seen asks me if I would like another drink. I decline and she says she would like to buy me a drink. I agree and she returns smiling and kneels in the aisle next to me and introduces herself as Shannon -- a lovely, mid twenties, Caucasian nubile with a story. The story begins, "My brother is quadriplegic."

Shannon tells me that she did not become aware of the situation until after I asked the young man next to me to fly with me. She tells me she chastised the pilots and let them know that the best judge of what a quadriplegic individual can and cannot do is the quadriplegic individual. I applaud her for this and she applauds me for my lifestyle.

"My brother lives in Kansas City, has been a quad for two years longer than you and he barely leaves the house. My mom does everything for him and has become as much of a shut-in as my brother." She shakes her head, "I know you get this question all the time and probably can't answer it but..." she is clearly pained and looks pleadingly into my eyes, "how do you do it?" Her eyes mist.

The effects of the numerous drinks dissipate greatly and I tell her my often-repeated answer to this question. "I don't do it," I say and she gets a puzzled look. "Since the day... it's as if *Brian* has been watching a video of somebody else... somebody manipulates the strings of this guy who looks like me. *I* would be quite content to sit in my apartment and watch videos -- I don't blame your brother, I understand your brother. It's almost harder to understand why I *leave* my apartment. (Pause) But God, my family, and my friends keep me going, keep me accomplishing, keep me glad to be alive and believing that I will walk again and not have to put up with the nonsense I NOW experience when I get on an airplane."

"So, you think it's your faith?" she asks -- missing the big equation.

"And everything else I said."

She nods, apologizes for her airline, thanks me for my time and departs.

Brian Shaughnessy

The plane arrives in Honolulu without further incident. Helen and I greet each other with kisses and mutually inflamed loins. As expected, the airline has lost the batteries for my wheelchair. It is already dark in Hawaii and five hours later for me. Helen drives from the airport to my campus apartment where Tyrell awaits me. We agreed that he would not stay in my apartment this semester. Before he brings in my bags he asks if he can stay the night.

"How many months have I been gone? That means I have not had sex in that many MONTHS. Now, we made this agreement before I left; we agreed again when we talked on the phone; and that's the arrangement. So the short answer to your question is, "No."

He glowers at me as if I am selfish and evil. I know what he is going to say.

"Oh, man, I'd do it for you."

"I doubt it -- not when there is a woman in the equation."

"What about the couch in the living room?"

"Tyrell! Do you have a place to stay?"

He looks at me as if the question is ridiculous... and lies. "Of course, I have a place to stay. I just don't want to go all the way back tonight."

I look out of the bedroom and into the living room where my two new roommates are talking and eating. "Ask them," I instruct Tyrell, but knowing he will just stay. "If they agree, stay TONIGHT. After tonight -- don't ask. You can't sleep in my room, the living room or my van. That's what you agreed to; so don't try to change it now. I'm glad you're here; I want you to keep working for me; so stop trying to get something over on me."

"Man, you're an ingrate! And I ain't like that," he says, staring angrily at Helen and me.

"Aloha. Nice to see you. I'm going to bed."

I am introduced to my roommates -- a local haole, Crybaby, and a Japanese guy, Sillyputty, from Maui. There will be other exchanges with them... and with Tyrell.

But the airline flight is behind me, my batteries are in Kuala Lumpur and those three individuals are in the other room. Helen and I talk, commingle and celebrate ourselves, each other, skin, sniffing and life in the tropics.

My new roommate, Crybaby, comes into my room and tells Tyrell that he cannot smoke in the bathroom. Tyrell has, predictably, already abused staying in the house -- and my roommates.

"I'll get some air freshener," Tyrell says and turns away.

The Squeaky Wheel

"It's not going to help..." Crybaby begins. I intervene.
"It's a non-smoking apartment, Tyrell. You can't smoke in here."
Tyrell looks at me as if I'm a traitor.
"Fine," he says pouting.

I am still having problems with skin breakdown on my butt. I must remain in bed. One day Tyrell is giving me marijuana. Crybaby knocks on the door and enters quickly. "Brian," he begins condescending and sternly, "you can't smoke dope in my apartment."

I'm pissed. "It's not *your* apartment. I live here too."

"Yeah, but it's illegal and it gives me an instantaneous headache when I smell it, so you can't smoke in the apartment. Take it out of here."

"You can see that I can't get out of bed."

"It is a non-smoking apartment, Brian," Tyrell says with a you-deserved-that look.

I continue to smoke dope in the apartment, but I take a small hit and hold it as long as humanly possible and slowly exhale into a pillow. Crybaby never knows.

But Tyrell continues to smoke in the bathroom. One day, Crybaby puts up a "No Smoking" sign in the bathroom. He does this at night while Tyrell is not there. Helen tells me. I never see it. The next day when Tyrell transfers me into the shower chair and brings me to the bathroom there is no sign. Tyrell has me back in the bed, naked, when Crybaby enters the room.

"You took down my fucking sign you fucking asshole!" He rants.

"I don't know nothing about it," I say from the bed, "now get out of my room until I am dressed." Crybaby glowers.

"I don't know nothing either," Tyrell lies.

Crybaby begins screaming, threatening and puling how he is going to have Tyrell thrown off campus. He begins to try to pick a flight with Tyrell. He moves from side to side asking Tyrell if he wants to fight. Tyrell looks amused. He tells Crybaby to stop moving like that and to go ahead and take a punch. Tyrell is a black man who grew up in Detroit and served in the military. Tyrell will kill Crybaby. Tyrell ignores the taunting and rants while I lie naked on the bed. Then Sillyputty comes in.

"You going to mess with the locals," he says moving in the same foolish manner his roommate just demonstrated -- these clods certainly do not know how to fight.

"All right, punks," Tyrell rails and then punches the brick wall with his fist. I feel the wall vibrate. He rips off his shirt and goes toward the two of them. Crybaby wisely says, "Come on Sillyputty, we'll let the office deal with this," he says as they exit.

"I wish one of them would have thrown the first punch, even with the both of them in the room I would have punched Crybaby in the throat and then kicked Sillyputty in the face."

I have no doubt that Tyrell could have accomplished this on the two morons. And that neither one of the idiots would be standing now.

I visit my new physiatrist at the Rehabilitation Hospital of the Pacific Rehab.

"What's the best thing for spasticity, doctor?" I ask him in a tone that suggests he knows the answer. His eyes grow, his brows furrow and he shrugs his shoulders and guesses, "Alcohol?"

"No," I say, "it's marijuana. They prescribe it for glaucoma so why don't we prescribe it for me and my spasms?"

He nods at the flawless logic and says he will check with the pharmacist. He comes back and reports, "I can't get you marijuana. It does however, come in a pill form where the active ingredient is synthesized. Why don't you try that?"

My mind screams, cool, far out, do you write, "reefer," on the script? I wonder how much they sell for on the street, but I say, (slightly over the top) "Thank you, doctor." He gives me a heavy lidded, knowing look and takes out his prescription pad.

I fill the prescription and the little brown balls work like magic. They are unpredictable in that they take effect in anywhere from 15 minutes to more than four hours. I continue to take a single hit and blow it out.

Some nights later I am being fed a tiny hit and blowing it into the pillow. Helen asks if she can smoke some. I ask her to use the tiny pipe but she says, "I'm going to open the window and blow it out."

"Brian!" Crybaby screams as he pounds on the door. "Let me in!"

"Go away," I shout back.

Presently campus police and one of the resident managers are barging into my room. Crybaby tries to enter and I tell him to get out. "You want to put on some clothes?" the resident manager asks Helen. Her eyes brighten and she runs from the room in her towel and comes back in a nurse's uniform. The quadriplegic lies in his special bed and shows the rental police his prescription for marijuana pills.

"I don't need to smoke it. My doctor gives it to me."

The Squeaky Wheel

The intruders leave with their tails between their legs and Crybaby whimpers in the other room.

Auditions for *The Tempest* are set. I see Professor Noel Cowardly in the hallway and begin to speak to him.

"I have to go to class," he snaps at me with a look of contempt. "See me in my office," he commands.

Has this shameful faggot changed his mind? I wonder. Would someone really let me memorize all those lines over the summer only to...?

I am in his office the next day and he is sullen. I perfunctorily ask him how he is. "Well, not well, not well," he says. "You know Laurence Olivier died."

You must be kidding, I think. Professor Noel Cowardly was *maybe* a spear carrier in a play Laurence Olivier was in and he acts like they were long-term live-in companions. And now this old queen is broken into pieces because of his passing after a full, long, ideal and nonhandicapped life. Give me a fucking break, I think.

Suddenly he is asking, "How could you play the part? You're in a wheelchair."

"I was in a wheelchair when you gave me the part."

Professor Cowardly, clearly, it is revealed to me only now for the first time, has no conscience, soul or ability to comprehend how this giving and taking away will affect anyone beyond himself. He, unbelievably, asks me to graciously withdraw. I graciously decline, but I am out the door pondering the injustice and any recourse I may have to expose this bastard.

With the knife still in my back, I go down the hall to the office of Dr. Jim Brandon, an internationally recognized authority on Japanese theatre and an honorable man. By the time the conversation is over, he reaffirms his wish that I co-author his next comedy Kabuki play, which will be produced next year. I feel better. He means it.

The play is a great success and I travel with the cast and crew of fifty to California where the play is presented at the regional college theatre festival. Only because of the forty-five member cast, and at least as many Japanese wigs, it is not invited to be performed in Washington D.C.

Brian Shaughnessy

Payback Can Be Sweet

    I return to Minneapolis from Honolulu alone on the same airline that I flew to Paradise nine months prior -- the flight on which they attempted to bodily remove me from the airplane. Helen sees me off at the airport. Now familiar with the painful complications of air travel encumbered with a wheelchair, I bring tools. Helen deftly unsnaps the modulator (the "brains" of the wheelchair), removes it from the box that holds the batteries, loosens the nuts holding the battery terminals on the two batteries powering the wheelchair, attaches the strap to each terminal and lifts each out of the back of my wheelchair, carefully placing each into its airline issued protective box. It has become my custom to place the modulator box inside the wheelchair's empty battery box. Helen asks where I want the modulator box.

    "Put it in the battery box," I say.

    She peers inside the box with an unpleasant expression. "It's wet," she informs me. I look inside and see water that likely spilled when added to the batteries.

    Helen's efficient packing of suitcases has left the wheelchair backpack almost bare. The backpack has been removed from the wheelchair, which will be going down to baggage... and then off to Greenland. I go off to the gate to be put on a modified dolly with a plank nailed to it for my ass; from that I will then be schlepped into my seat. I look at the empty, red backpack and ask Helen to place the modulator box there. As it disappears into the bag, it strikes me as significant. I dismiss the thought.

    Helen accompanies me to the gate where the barbarians refuse to allow her onto the jetway or to assist with my transfer. On the jetway I forget to remove the watch my mother gave me as a graduation gift from the armrest. I am not bumped to first class for this leg of the journey. After takeoff I take medication for sleep. I sleep soundly for most of the flight. An Australian woman sits with the window on her left and me on her right. She assists me with eating and is flabbergasted that the flight attendant asks four dollars for a Bailey's. The flight attendant explains that the first leg of her journey from Australia to Hawaii was international and ergo drinks were gratis, but now she is on a domestic flight

The Squeaky Wheel

whereupon the airline chooses to exploit drinkers. Over her protestations I purchase her the sweet Irish liqueur.

The Aussie woman awakens me as we descend into Denver. We land, taxi and exchange pleasantries. The other passengers depart and I am left alone on the plane. I lean slightly into the aisle and cock my head to watch for the refrigerator movers who will take me out of my seat, place me on the dolly, roll me to the concourse and place me in another chair or take me directly to my connecting flight... on the dolly. As I peer down the aisle I see a familiar site -- a heinous orange blazer. The same oaf/lackey who uncaringly insisted on removing me from the airplane nine months ago is attached to the jacket. I lean back in my seat and grin -- pondering the musings of the gods. I hear the clang of the dolly and other persons entering the airplane. They walk down the aisle led by Mr. Orange Blazer. He sees me beaming in the seat and reacts like a cartoon. His eyes widen and bug out. His jaw drops to the floor, his head jerks backwards, his head shakes and his cheeks flap. Then, he tries to regain composure.

"Hello, sir. We're here to help get you to your connecting flight," he says smiling.

"Really," I say calmly. "Aren't you here to take me off the plane?"

He now knows that any hope he had for the present exchange to be without reference to the previous exchange has just been bashed on the rocks of my caustic nature and indignation. He plays dumb -- type casting.

"Yes, sir, we are here to take you off the airplane... and get you to your connecting flight."

"Not nearly as much fun as trying to remove me from a plane that's about to take off and keep me from getting to my destination where somebody is waiting for me, is it?"

"Oh, that *was* you," he says, feigning recognition only now. "Sir, I was only doing what the pilot ordered me to do."

"After you waited for *every* passenger to get on the plane, asked me inappropriate questions and then *snitched* to the pilots." I see the two refrigerator movers -- with their dolly -- looking interested and puzzled. "Your buddy here tried to take me off this flight on my way to Hawaii," I say to them. "Because of that, I'm going to own this sorry-ass airline."

"It wasn't my decision!"

"But I believe you enjoyed it... and if you didn't enjoy it, you certainly didn't feel bad about it."

"I was only doing my job!" he insists.

"Yeah, so were the Nazis."

"We're going to take you off the plane now."

"Fine. Just pretend it's the last flight, and you might smile about it *this* time." I know I'm a prick.

Mr. Orange Blazer mumbles to the refrigerator movers and hastily departs. The two "transporters" lift me from the seat, place me on the dolly, tilt the dolly back, roll me down the aisle, bump one of my arms on *at least* every other row, take me onto the jetway, out to the concourse and onto the connecting flight, where they hoist me into another seat. I instruct them to take the three dollars from my breast pocket -- their tip. They take it.

Again, I am bumped to first class for this much shorter flight from Denver to Minneapolis. I am placed on the right side of the plane, and it is just twilight. No one sits beside me. A pleasant female flight attendant sits down and plies me with food and drink. The two businessmen across the aisle from me discuss... business. No sports, no weather, no family, no golf, no women, no wardrobe -- just business.

I struggle to read a book, but because I am not seated in my wheelchair, my body is in an uncomfortable position, and the tray is like ice. Reading is mostly futile. Out of the corner of my eye I sense flickering light. I look out the airplane window, and far off in the distance I see lightning explode in flashes of sinewy, jagged ever-changing art -- more magnificent than anything created by Demerol. I watch in awe as I look *down* on the lightning dancing above the clouds. I turn left and look beyond the businessmen and out their window. I see only darkness. I watch for a few minutes, and with no one next to me to share the experience, I interrupt the businessmen.

"Excuse me, but there is the most *incredible* lightning show going on on this side of the airplane -- you should see it."

The businessman seated next to the window looks at me as if I'm some hippy asking him for spare change, and the businessman in the aisle seat strains his neck, squints out of my window for two seconds, says, "Oh, yeah," and then goes back to his business conversation. Just then I see a passenger from coach walking to the front bathroom.

"Yeah!" he says with dancing eyes, a broad smile and the enthusiasm of a Hare Krishna. "It's amazing! Everybody back there is talking about it! People on the right are letting people on the left side sit in their seats to watch. I've never seen anything like it!"

There lies the difference between first class and coach.

The Squeaky Wheel

I arrive in Minneapolis, and my brother Patrick meets me. His three young children are with him. I give them each the wings I made a flight attendant give me. The powers-that-be allow him onto the plane to assist with my transfer. They actually encourage him to assist. I wait on the jetway for my wheelchair and eventually am sent to baggage in an airline wheelchair -- six sizes too big, horribly uncomfortable and inadequate. The arms do not detach, which makes transfers in and out more difficult.

Finally my wheelchair is delivered -- sans battery, box AND watch. I immediately comment on this and make the appropriate report on the stolen watch. I am never compensated. Suitcases are retrieved, and eventually I am told (is it any surprise now?) that the airline has lost my batteries -- no batteries and no box to house the batteries. The airline lackey responsible for such information tells me that someone will call me when they are located and retrieved from Panama or wherever they are. I growl (mildly), inform him that this happens without exception -- every flight, both directions -- and that invariably the batteries are NOT located and the airline purchases me a new pair. I then go outside with my brother to wait for the paratransit bus.

I arrive at my apartment, and the telephone is ringing. I know it is Helen; she knows the thrice daily or more endless calls make me insane. But I struggle to be polite, and lovingly and gently try to dissuade her from compulsive calling. She whines. I change the subject to tell her that, as usual, the airlines lost my batteries, and this time "some scumbag even took the watch my mother gave me off of my wheelchair."

After a long silence she says, "No."

"Yes," I respond.

"That's the saddest thing I've ever heard."

"It's up there. I always knew if I forgot to take it off that some airline thief would take it..."

The next day I get a call from an agent of the airlines -- a Mr. Smegmabreath.

"Mr. Shaughnessy, we can't locate the batteries and, unfortunately, we destroyed the box that contained them, so we'd like to know who to contact to get new batteries and a replacement for the box. Or, if you would like to get them we can send a voucher for reimbursement."

The ten flights I've made since acquiring a disability flash through my mind in a taunting, tortuous, EVIL montage: the inappropriate employees, the degradation, the bruises, the inane questions, the waiting, the inconvenience, the breaking of wheelchairs, the pilfering of my watch and.... the attempted ejection and subsequent unwillingness to apologize or compensate me for any of it. The seemingly insignificant change of pattern and accompanying experience at the Honolulu Airport explode in a white light and dispel the macabre images. A neon sign lights up that says: PAYBACK TIME.

"What about the modulator box?" I ask.

(Pause) "The what?"

"The modulator box -- it's the brains of the wheelchair, and it rides on top of the battery box. After you people make me take out my batteries and put them in boxes so they are easier for you to lose, I put the modulator box inside of the battery box for transport, safety and SO THAT YOU DON'T LOSE IT."

"Well, I don't know anything about wheelchairs, so I'm going have to check into this. Either my boss or I will get back to you, okay?"

"Fine," I say in a tone of disgust, while I grin and flail about in delight.

I call the company that services my wheelchair in Minneapolis. I ask for my regular service person who I believe to have a nefarious streak as wide as mine and a vigilante sense of justice. I tell him what transpired in the last thirty-six hours and ask what a modulator box costs.

"$2400."

I giggle and think it's not nearly enough compensation for their mistreatment of me -- let alone other wheelchair travelers. I propose he play ball, for which he will be compensated a mere $400. He agrees.

THREE DAYS LATER (Do these people think a wheelchair is a luxury item or that anybody who uses one has several?) Mr. Smegmabreath calls me and tells me that, yes, the modulator box and battery box were destroyed. He says he has no expertise with this and asks me how I would like to handle it.

"You've already left me without a working wheelchair for three days. You inconvenience me *every* time I fly. I've already ordered and received the parts I need. Pay me for them."

Somewhat offended, the delegate asks the name of the company that I purchased the replacement parts from. I give him the name of the company and the individual to contact -- which he does. My nefarious and fair-minded friend is a bit nervous and calls later to tell me that Mr. Smegmabreath from the airlines has contacted him, and that my comrade played along. All the information has matched so far. Mr. Smegmabreath calls me and asks me for a receipt -- which my partner manufactures.

The Squeaky Wheel

The next day my co-conspirator calls and tells me that Mr. Smegmabreath just left their showroom. Luckily, my partner in this payback scam was alone in the showroom and was able to produce the receipt he asked for. I immediately draft a fax to Mr. Smegmabreath asking him why -- in light of consistent incompetence in dealing with wheelchairs by his airline, and the discrimination and degradation directed toward individuals such as myself -- he would treat this as some type of fraud. I point out to him that he acknowledged his company destroyed my equipment and therefore must compensate me for it. I demand that he send a check immediately and not harass me further regarding this. I point out to Mr. Smegmabreath that any perceived ongoing harassment will result in my retaining counsel.

Months later... back in Hawaii... I receive the check.
Helen gets the mail. She opens the envelope. She has already heard the story.
"You know what you just did?" she asks.
"Committed theft?" I guess.
"You've scammed the airlines. Do know that I love scammers," she says and immediately sits on my lap, straddles me, puts her arms around my neck and begins rocking. She kisses the long and hard.
"All chicks do."
She jumps off of me and gives a small shove to my chest.
"You're an asshole," she says and stomps off.

Helen and I travel to the mall. Some fat moron walks directly up to me -- I saw him coming 50 feet off -- and asks, "What happened to you?"
"I don't know. What happened to you?"

Helen invites me to stay at her deluxe condo in prestigious Hawaii Kai for the month of Christmas break. She announces she will do my cares during my stay and take time off of work. This means that I must tell Tyrell he will be unemployed during that time -- as he is when I am gone for the summer -- or can seek other employment. He explodes and demands to be paid during that time. I decline. He immediately calls his good buddy and useless advocate for persons with disabilities, Busywork Juan. I hear him whimper to Busywork but he realizes he really has no choice in the matter. He asks if he can stay in the apartment during Christmas break. I tell him he cannot. I have already stayed at Helen's for several days and Tyrell let himself into the apartment to the wrath of

Crybaby and Sillyputty. Campus police escorted him from the unit... and much unneeded aggravation was brought into my life.

Helen tires easily and we seek someone to come in part-time to perform my morning cares. A fellow quadriplegic recommends someone who previously worked for him. "Totally reliable, excellent worker," are only a few of the glowing descriptive phrases used in his referral. I call Joseph. He is reluctant but Helen holds a pad in her hand and writes down the hourly rate that she and Tyrell are paid by the Minnesota nursing agency to do my cares. His reluctance turns to amazement.

"That's a lot of money," Joseph exclaims as Helen collapses into a relieved position on the couch. Halfway into Joseph's tenure Helen and I have the same idea: Why not replace Tyrell with Joseph, not have him spend the nights and eliminate aggravation? Joseph accepts the offer and I call Tyrell and thank him for his tenure but tell him that his services are no longer needed. He goes ballistic. Minutes later I get a call from Busywork Juan.

"That's fine that you want to terminate Tyrell," he begins beneficently, "You just need to give him two weeks pay."

I laugh. "No, I gave him his two weeks notice."

Busywork Juan says that if I do not give Tyrell two-week severance pay that I will not get Busywork Juan's services again; I will not be able to use any nursing agency in the state; and he will encourage Tyrell to file suit against me and be really, really mean.

"Let's review," I say with a little puff preceding the statement. "The first person you sent to me didn't bathe, caused me to have surgery and spend three weeks in the hospital." Busywork Juan tries to interject. "The next person you sent to me was an ice addict and stole from me. Ramon was fine and Tyrell is a second-rate opportunist who steals my van and anything else he feels he should have. I think *I'll* be pressing the charges and doing the threatening, okay?" Click.

The battle ensues and Busywork Juan loses his job. To quote that incredible actor and sometime reggae singer, Jimmy Cliff, in the unseen blockbuster movie, *The Harder They Come*, "Don't... fuck... with... me!"

The arrangement with Joseph coming three hours in the morning, back for dinner and then returning to put me to bed works out well. Joseph lives in a storage room and has very little human contact but when he is around me he talks incessantly. He is extremely intelligent and can speak to many, many subjects -- many of which I have little to no interest in. His caregiving is exemplary and I endure the avalanche of words, words, words stoically. Although he is a tremendous cook he does not complain about our five nights per week trips to the cafeteria. He refers to it as "fantasyland," given the volumes of food to be consumed.

Screenplay

I'm taking a single writing course to justify my occupancy of the student apartment. It is a screenwriting class and I submit a three-page treatment for *Sarah's Last Waltz*, the title of which has evolved into *Spambulance 4511* as a conjunction for space ambulance and in deference to the Hawaiian fondness for that miserable Minnesota "meat" called Spam. It's feedback time for me in the class.

I'm hearing chuckles around me, getting smiles and thumbs-up when a middle-aged woman begins, "I don't know, I guess it's like *A Boy and His Dog,* which was a movie I hated, but I thought the thing was misogynistic because the girl had to die, but when the captain says, 'If you're going to fuck her, fuck her' -- I couldn't read anymore."

Another woman begins to express similar feelings while half of the women shake their heads and mutter words like, "parody," "black comedy" or "you missed the point." I am surprised by the misinterpretation but the instructor, Stephen Goldsberry, who has already flattered me by circling a line of my prose and writing, "I'm going to steal this," jumps in with open-eyed wonderment.

"I've read the play and not just the treatment and I'm telling you people who find it misogynistic -- you are mistaken. That being said, the greatest thing you can hope for in writing is controversy. You want a controversial book, play or movie because that will equate to sales and fame. Good job, Brian. I want to see this play done here with the new title."

Now I'm even sorrier we never taped the New Mexico version. I tell Darrin of the events of the day and he disapproves of the name change but encourages me to find a way to get it produced.

Brian Shaughnessy

Joseph's father has been diagnosed with emphysema and cancer and will die soon. These are the words told to Joseph in French over the phone. He immediately makes arrangements to return to rural Canada where his father and family wait and ready themselves for death. He sobs for his father and he sobs because he must abandon me. Helen begins to do my daily cares but it becomes too much and she takes me to her apartment. Our understanding at the time is that I will return to the apartment upon Joseph's return. Two months later, after the inevitable for all, Joseph returns but Helen pouts that, If I don't love her, I can go back to the dorm. I know better but I remain. Fortunately, Joseph does not blame me and we remain in contact.

A classmate and dear friend, with the managing director's blessings, asks me to direct the play *12-1-A* for Kumu Kahua Theater. It is the story of and written by a woman whose family was robbed of everything and shipped to a Japanese internment camp during World War II. One of the few actors who auditions is Tomoko, a short, sophisticated and overly groomed woman who was actually in an internment camp as a child. She refuses to learn her lines. That, of course, is my fault and the fault of the disrespectful cast -- according to her. One guy who auditions for the lead is given an eight-word part. He can barely learn the eight words! He walks across the stage like a puppet on Thorazine. The man could not act wet if you threw him into the middle of the Pacific Ocean. I want to replace him days before the play is set to open, but the managing director refuses.
The young man who is playing the lead male is a classmate and very, very angry that Tomoko will not learn her lines. We all are. I'm trying to lead one of the actors to the discovery that the character she plays is gay. There is a scene wherein her character wears a dress and my assistant manager announces, "she wears the dress for Mitch." I say simply, "or for Yoko." My assistant manager stares open mouthed. My assistant director/stage manager, a Chinese woman whom I believe to be gay, is impressed by this choice and discovery. The actress fights me on this interpretation so we costume her to have people question her sexuality and direct around her defiance. I have audience on three sides (a favorite choice of mine as audience and director) and brilliant Joe, the set designer who helped me immensely on my MFA thesis production, hangs four-inch square metal fencing around the stage so that the audience must look through the fence as they see the set, actors and play. It's wonderful.

The Squeaky Wheel

The eight-word actor misses a rehearsal two days after I am not allowed to dismiss him and my assistant director/stage manager gives him the pink slip. The managing director, Darryl Canis understands. Despite Tomoko's refusal to learn lines and the resultant hatred of her by the rest of the cast, we have a full crowd most nights and great reviews. Other victims of internment of the Japanese attend the play. It is reminiscent – in message and tone -- of the concentration camp play I directed with Tim in New Mexico. One of our audience members at that play was a little old Jewish woman from El Paso with a number tattooed on her arm.

Annie, without whom this tale would not be told, and I have stayed in contact and remain fast friends. She calls one day when I am in bed and Helen pouts when I want her to hand me the phone rather that let her listen to our conversation on speakerphone. As I talk with Annie, Helen disrobes and backs her ass and labia into my face. I giggle although I am angered and the conversation ends abruptly. I chastise Helen for insecure behavior.

"Annie was fucking that guy she lives with now before you moved to New Mexico," she says cruelly.

The thought had never occurred to me.

Pasta has accepted my presence in the house and Helen claims that her 20-plus-year-old daughter is becoming more of a behavior problem because of my challenges to Helen's regimen. I apply for more than a dozen jobs but am turned down on all of them. My student loans will come due and I begin filling out the paperwork for deferment -- to no avail. I am in default and jobless. Helen no longer works at the hospital but remains in the house to attend to, serve, feed, make love to but ultimately control me. We have some magical days at the beach or finding places for a tryst on the magnificent grounds of her domicile. When the three of us go to dinner together I'm clearly viewed as, "a lucky guy," despite the fact that there's an electric wheelchair under me.

Helen becomes a vampire -- she sleeps during the day. Her condominium on the 19th floor of the luxury unit is a gilded cage. If a quadriplegic man must be in prison it should be in a gilded cage, on the 19th floor, with two beautiful women to attend him. But I am not allowed out of bed until mid-afternoon because of Helen's odd sleeping pattern. She transfers me to bed, in a manner we dub, "Greg Louganis style." She removes the right armrest from the wheelchair, my feet are unstrapped from the plates and the seatbelt is disengaged. I then fall over into the bed and Helen drags my legs over so that I am on the bed. She must climb onto the bed and move me about to get me positioned. Then ice packs are placed underneath each arm and on my chest and the sheet pulled to my nipples. Her "Iron Curtain" blocks out all light from floor-to-ceiling windows and makes the bedroom cave dark. She then covers herself with an electric blanket topped by a quilt.

I begin working with the Honolulu Improvisational Theater Company -- HITCO. It includes classmates from the theater department and actors from some of my productions as well as new faces. Some of the members are very funny and some are not. The director, despite my protestations, keeps adding new members as the inevitable chaff falls away. We perform at Manoa Valley Theater where I have directed twice now. After rehearsals, Jerry, one of the funny ones and a classmate from the theater, always screams, "Brian Shaughnessy, the ONLY person I have ANY respect for in this group."

Because we both know Jerry is destined for greater things I ask him, after many weeks of this behavior, "Really, why?"

"Only because the director says, 'No drug references, no sex references, no religion references, no naughty part references and no swearing,' and you do 'em all." The tears of laughter and pride flow down my face. "And the amazing thing is," he continues, shaking his head and looking at me with deadly seriousness, "it's always funny." HITCO is a short-lived phenomenon for Jerry and me.

The Squeaky Wheel

Christmas Is for Giving of Yourself

Living in Hawaii Kai with Helen, I awaken mid-afternoon. Actually, I *have been awake* for hours in the hot, dead-aired room waiting for Helen to deem it the appropriate hour for her to move, throw off her two blankets, part the iron curtain that blocks out all light, remove the ice packs from under my armpits and announce that my day may begin.

She rises and fills basins to wash me. I am unable to shower at Helen's but her nursing and loving skills (coupled with the fact that she's the one sniffing me) keep me fragrant as flowers. As she performs this daily routine, I spasm from my bent-knee, spread-leg position onto my right side. Helen apologizes for this inevitability and rolls me onto my left side by grabbing me underneath the knees and moving them to the other side of the bed.

"Oh, no!" she says, with a tone that when coming from a nurse and the person one loves and lives with, bodes disaster.

"What's up?" I ask, attempting to raise my head and look in her direction. As she reaches for the hand mirror, she says, "There is a HUGE blister on your foot." The positioned mirror reveals the truth of her statement. Straining my neck, I can see a blister, three inches by four inches and the indefinite shape of an eastern state extending from the sole of my foot to the top.

"Yup, that's a blister," I say without inflection, as Helen begins to delicately and expertly bandage the wound. I spend weeks in a very, very padded protective boot. Over the next days the liquid in the blister turns crimson as the eruption slowly deflates and metamorphoses into a scab around the edges. I laugh at this development and instruct Helen, "Be careful with that baby, as it will be one of my brother Darrin's Christmas presents."

Helen looks at me from the foot of the bed with shock/disgust and then drops her face onto the bed and laughs. "You're sick!" I agree with her assessment and remind her I come from a sick family. Over the next several weeks the scab slowly curls and begins to free itself from my foot. With each twice-daily dressing change I admonish Helen not to break or otherwise damage Darrin's present. "Don't talk about it," she demands.

"You're making me salivate!" This is what happens to Helen before she vomits.

The scab eventually comes loose, and I place it in a small zip lock bag and then place the bag in a clear cassette case -- for display. For the holidays, I am going to visit my mother in Arizona, and Helen is going to visit her mother in San Francisco.

As always, Helen begs/beseeches/whines/whimpers/pleads/insists that I take her phone calls. I know that this will mean four or five daily -- none of which will be under 15 minutes and may well be over an hour. She packs my suitcases for the journey with clothing and supplies. My mother has arranged for a nurse's aide to perform my daily cares. Darrin, my sister Teri, my mother and I will stay at my mother's friend's home, as access to my mother's tiny trailer in So-Hi Arizona is impossible.

Helen drives to the airport in the van, and I am in the electric wheelchair. I bring the manual wheelchair and check it with the luggage, and proceed to the gate. I transfer from the electric chair to the degrading dolly with the plank nailed to it for one's ass and then into the airline seat. I fly directly to Las Vegas without incident. My mother and her husband, Jim, meet me. There are no batteries to lose. They wheel me to the van he has borrowed to transport me the 100 miles to their home -- or the home of their friend. Jim has a ramp to get me into the van and then places long clamps on the wheelchair to keep me from falling over. We begin the journey from Nevada to Arizona in unbelievable cold for a boy now acclimated to the tropics. A centennial cold spell has gripped the mainland west of the Mississippi for weeks.

"You live in a cold place," I state to my mom who laughs, agrees and assures me that this is unusual. Before we have traveled two miles, before we are on a freeway on-ramp, before reaching a speed greater than twenty-five miles an hour, I watch Jim spin the steering wheel a full turn one direction, and then in the other, and yet the vehicle continues traveling in a straight direction. I watch this a few more times and think this is sheer insanity. He makes no comment. He pulls over and begins to exit the vehicle.

"What's wrong?" Mom asks. Jim tells her that he needs to look at the steering. He spends a few minutes underneath the van and then returns to the vehicle. He explains that something has happened with the ancient directional system on the ancient van. We resume the journey. He must turn the steering wheel one-and-a-half turns before it engages in the direction he is turning. He must then turn the wheel the same

The Squeaky Wheel

distance in the opposite direction before it engages to steer in the other direction.

I'm a terrible passenger anyway, and this does nothing to add to my comfort level. When we venture through the Hoover dam area -- replete with curves/swerves/loops and instantaneous changing of direction in the road -- I think I will die of a heart attack. But Jim deftly, expertly and silently negotiates every turn as if it were ordinary. My eyes are transfixed on the steering wheel for the entire one-and-a-half hour journey. I am amazed and thrilled to arrive at our destination. I meet my mom's friend who has offered my mother her house for the holidays and repeat, "You live in a cold place." She responds -- with 100 percent sincerity -- "Yes, but it's a *dry* cold."

(Pause)

I can't believe the summertime "dry-heat" statement made by desert-dwellers when it's 115 degrees! I certainly can't listen to this, and in a glance this kind woman knows. She -- as someone new does every time I visit my mom -- tells me if it were not for my mother she would not be alive right now. Mom helped her in some emotional way through some horror for which she is eternally grateful. I begin to tear up as I have a half dozen times before when I hear these words and decide to let slide the "dry cold" comment. Mom returns and informs me with a questioning look that Helen has already left a message on her answering machine at home. I grudgingly return the call. Helen tells me that she rode the wheelchair from the gate back to the van and can't believe how people stared at her. She says that some women smiled at her (always an area of conflict), but that when she stood up at the gift store people acted disgusted, as if she were an imposter. She pleads, again, that I take her every phone call. I assure her that my entire family will know she is insane. She claims she *needs* to talk to me almost hourly.

Mom assists in unpacking. She looks at the cassette tape with the broken tabs and zip lock bag and what appears to be a strange leaf inside. She looks at me. "What the hell is this?" she asks, fearing that it's drugs or some other contraband. I see her husband over her shoulder starting to move toward the case, and I say, "It's a scab. It's one of Darrin's Christmas presents." Jim immediately moans, turns 180 degrees and exits the room. Mom laughs, as I explain how I came to possess such a thing. Then she cries. My sister Teri arrives soon after and is delighted with the present for Darrin.

Helen calls incessantly. Mom asks me what her problem is. I say that she is insane, insecure and suffers from other maladies that generally fall under the psychosis known as borderline personality disorders. Mom looks fearful and -- days later -- on Christmas Day, when I tell Helen to "fuck-off," Mom insists that I remain in this cold place. I decline.

We all open gifts. When Darrin gets to his special gift, Jim leaves the house. Darrin looks with puzzlement as Teri and Mom giggle uproariously. Darrin asks the question, and when I tell him what it is, he simply moans, shakes his head and announces, "It's going in your food."

The next day Darrin's girlfriend Bambi arrives. Teri relates the scab story to Bambi. Darrin again states, "It's going in your food." Bambi looks puzzled and looks from me to Darrin and back several times. She begins to speak, stops, starts again and says, *"You* grossed out Darrin," with the disbelief of a person who just watched someone mutate. She repeats it... several times.

Compelled to respond over Darrin's menu announcements, I point out to Bambi that "I *am* the older brother." And the phone rings.

Because I have no job, Helen and I make many trips to the library. I have not owned a television since leaving New Mexico but for my summer lending program in Minneapolis when I usually watch videos. We revel in reading at the beach, poolside or in her apartment. We begin studies of *The Mutiny on the Bounty, The Assassination of JFK, Hawaiian Lifestyle and Mythology* and other topics. Helen cannot read a novel. She prefers facts, facts and more facts over any fiction. She begins taking up books about serial murderers, which helps her sleep habits not a lick.

But Helen has a television and HBO. Every few weeks I pick up a six-pack, and after she has transferred me onto the couch in the sunken living room that my dear friend Dave has built a ramp for, I watch hours of movies. One night Helen brings me out to a seated position after lying down on the couch. I begin to awaken from a deep, deep sleep. It feels wonderful to be asleep when I suddenly remember that I was on the couch. I open my eyes to see Helen inches from my face looking into my eyes. I fainted. I weigh 118 pounds. At the time of my surgery I weighed 150 pounds.

June arrives and I venture back to Minneapolis over Helen's protests. Helen performs a masterful feat of packing and manages to pout the entire time. We travel to the airport. Patrick will meet me at the other side. This year my sister Teri lives upstairs and a Southeast Free

The Squeaky Wheel

School alumnus and friend live in the apartment above me, so I've chosen not to have a live-in attendant. Helen asks that the agency just send men. I tell her I will do the best I can.

The airline loses my batteries. Helen begins a campaign of calling me several times a day. She calls before the nurse's aid arrives and insists that I not hang up on her while they perform the routine. This madness results in her having a $500 telephone bill by the end of the summer, which, naturally, is my fault. I tell her not to visit but she visits anyway.

My niece Mickaylee knows of Helen and keeps asking me when she is coming. When she sees an Asian girl or woman she asks, "Is that Helen?" Helen does arrive and is struck by all of the lakes that she saw flying over. Pat drops us at Lake Calhoun just about a mile from my home. I am thrilled to be sharing my home with Helen for a second and longer time. Helen wants to go out on the sailboat dock. I agree, although there is no railing on this dock and the water is very deep. Helen is in awe of the fish and the activity as my wheelchair begins to misbehave. I push the joystick to go forward and slightly left and nothing happens; it jerks and freezes. Perhaps I whine in frustration and fright.

"Be a man about it," Helen only slightly teases.

But payback is a bitch -- to use the parlance of contemporary modern slang. The wheelchair continues this behavior and after a few blocks the motor on the right side ceases to work at all. Helen must now push and guide me the remaining three-quarters of a mile with only the assistance of the negligible one motor. And there are hills.

"You see, that's God punishing you for making those cracks on the dock when I was in *real* peril! Now, what have we learned from this?"

"What?" Helen asks huffing and puffing and pushing.

"Brian is always right."

Patrick and his three children arrive and enter through the side door where the lift is. Mickaylee immediately opens her arms for a hug and kiss from Helen. Devlin views the stranger cautiously and Aidan, yet to speak, is indifferent. Mickaylee smiles, points to Helen and announces, "That's Helen." She begins to step from one white tile to another white tile. "I like the white ones," she announces as she makes a circle back to Helen. "You're brown," she observes.

Ever conscious of her race Helen slightly dejectedly replies, "Yup, I'm brown."

"I'm pink," Mickaylee observes further and goes back to stepping from white tile to white tile.

"You're pink," Helen says and giggles to me.

Another circle is walked and Mickaylee looks into Helen's eyes. "You have black eyes."

"Brown eyes," Helen corrects her.

"I have blue eyes," Mickaylee states and Helen concurs.

Patrick and I must work on something and Helen takes his children to the park at the beach. Upon their return Helen informs me that Mickaylee announced that they played King Kong at the beach. Helen agreed and Mickaylee announced that Devlin would be King Kong; Aidan would be Fay Wray; and Helen and Mickaylee would be "the brown girls."

"Can't really play a genuine game of King Kong without a couple of brown girls," I observe.

Helen borrows a bicycle from my father and we see the lakes, streams, waterfalls, parks and greenery of Minneapolis with me leading the way in the electric wheelchair and Helen following on a bicycle. One night we see a flock of Canadian geese gathered at Lake Calhoun. We both notice that one of the Canadian geese has different markings than the others. He is smaller and has a pure white neck and head unlike the other members of the flock. He is somewhat apart from the other members of the group.

"Look at that one," Helen exclaims.

"Yup, he's different so he's ostracized by the group. Not just humans do it."

Helen looks at me as if I have said something profound... or familiar. "You're right. Can we go get bread? I want to give it to THAT goose."

I agree and when we return I make a comment about how the mutant goose will one day save the flock because of his differences -- in a goose variation of Rudolph the Red-nose Reindeer. Helen erupts with laughter and this begins *at least* biweekly installments where I must make up tales of the white headed goose. It also begins my habit of honking like a Canadian goose when I want Helen to come to me when I am in bed and cannot go to her. Whenever I honk, Helen immediately stops what she is doing, enters the bedroom, kneels, strokes my contracted arm lovingly and exclaims, "You honked for me!"

I'm always pleased and laugh at her reaction and the fact that she takes such glee in this behavior. She usually wants another installment of the white-headed goose saga, but before she leaves the room I always

The Squeaky Wheel

demand that she drop her drawers, bend over and give me a shot. "That is so gross!" she invariably reacts after dropping her drawers.

First-class passengers would rather talk about business than watch the incredible lightning show; women would rather get the next installment of the white-headed goose saga than look at their partner's naughty parts. That's a universal truth.

We take a road trip to Duluth and the North Shore of Lake Superior. Helen is in awe of the forests and the lakes and the rivers. We stop in a small town that has a banner announcing, "Rutabaga Days." Much as we would love to stay for the festivities we simply take a picture and move on. Helen is smitten with Minnesota charm. We drive into an isolated community of luxury redwood homes on St. Croix River.

"We should live here," she announces, and before I can point out the considerable less charm of the place come January, she continues, "You could write here... and I could sleep."

Back in Minneapolis again we discover that Third World will be performing at First Avenue -- an old favorite bar of mine and the location for much of Prince's movie, *Purple Rain*. Some of the buses in Minneapolis now have lifts and we are able to catch a bus that will take us from near my apartment to almost the front door of our destination. We arrive and are placed on the right extension of the stage. There are no other wheelchair users, but a few bipeds also occupy the area. One woman says to Helen, "Can you give me some room, because I'm a dancer and I'm going to be dancing?" This does not endear the woman to Helen and each time Helen exits or enters the area she bumps the woman who finally lashes out at her. "Do you hate me? Did I do something to offend you? Or do you just not know how to walk? You've passed me like six times and every time you bumped into me. What's your problem?"

Helen stares at her and says, "Really?"

A few minutes later the woman apologizes and leaves the area – possibly for the bar. Ladysmith Black Mumbasa warms up for Third World and the evening is phenomenal. We leave, slightly drunk, to catch our bus. Helen is wearing a very sexy black outfit. We wait for a bus on Nicolette Mall and I make a comment about downtown.

"Downtown? Downtown? This is not downtown," Helen rants, taking in the immaculate condition of this tiny area of the city. "San Francisco has a downtown, and you wouldn't survive two minutes there," she says somewhat boastfully. "This, this is like Disneyland. There's not even a gum wrapper!" We decide to walk eight blocks to avoid having to transfer to a second bus.

There are gum wrappers at our new locale. We see much filth and questionable individuals on Nicolette and Franklin. An Indian male with two Indian females passes us in one direction and then another. A young, white woman approaches us and asks us if we know where a payphone is. We point her in the direction of the convenience store across the street. She later emerges from there and begins to speak to the Indian group. The white girl has a crisis but the Indian male wants nothing to do with her. One of the Indian women presses him to assist and he shrugs and they begin to cross the street. On the other side of the street the white woman taps the arm of one of the Indian women who immediately punches her in the face and drops her to the ground. She then begins to pound the white woman's head against a proximately placed step. The white woman, amazingly, rises and runs back into the convenience store while the three walk toward a terrified Helen and me.

"I'm sorry," the head-basher says to Helen and me. We assure her that there is no apology necessary.

"And if this is Disneyland, they would have been...?" I tease Helen who can barely speak.

Back in my apartment we settle into bed after an eventful evening. Helen lovingly strokes my hair and says, "I could lose you to another girl in a second."

I respond, "I'm flattered by your confidence in me, yourself, another girl and our relationship."

Helen and I see several plays, visit my dear friends Don and Diane, and meet other friends. After keeping her rental car for one month Helen returns to Hawaii. The various nurse's aides on various shifts return until the magnificence of the changing leaves returns, which is fall in Minnesota. When the last red and yellow leaves hit the ground, and before they are raked, I make my reservation to return to Helen and the tropics.

My batteries are lost and the airlines pays to replace them. The leitmotif of this essay.

I call Minneapolis where my brother's youngest son, Aidan, is about to turn four and has yet to say more than a few words. The telephone is picked up by someone who does not speak. I hear music playing in the background and then the breathing of a tiny person... possibly almost four years old.

"Aidan?" Tiny breathing. "Hi, Aidan." Tiny breathing. Hi, Aidan. This is Uncle Brian." Tiny breathing. "Can I talk to your daddy, Aidan?" More tiny breathing. "Is your mommy home?" Tiny, tiny breathing. "Can I talk to one of your siblings, please?" Tiny breathing with music in the background. "Okay, Aidan, Uncle Brian is going to go now. Nice talking to you." I hang up.

I call back a week later. "Did Aidan tell you I called?" I ask Kate jokingly.

"What?" she asks puzzled.

I tell her about the phone call of the previous week. She laughs uproariously and says, "That explains it! All week long he has been picking up the phone and saying, 'Brian.'" Now I laugh uproariously.

Road to Tokyo

On the theater front, productive weekly meetings take place with Kabuki scholar, Dr. James R. Brandon. We have put together a hilarious script we're both pleased with and proud of -- even if it doesn't differ as much as we hoped from his previous production, *The Road to Kyoto*. He will begin the rehearsal process soon. I have been invited to work with high school actors and the playwright for a national VSA project. I accept the opportunity although, as she did with *12-1-A*, Helen demands to be at virtually every rehearsal. She fears I will fall in love with one of the teenage actresses.

But I direct the high school project and enjoy working with the kids, as does the slightly pretentious emissary from Honolulu Theater for Youth, David Snakeskin. The production is fine, although my time devoted to it diminishes my time with *The Road to Tokyo* rehearsals and possible rewrites. It also demands unpredictable paratransit time and that, in turn, lessens my increasingly needed time in bed. Both productions get rave reviews and nobody, to my knowledge, says that I got to work on Dr. Brandon's play "only because he's in a wheelchair."

Brian Shaughnessy

Our anniversary is marked by a trip to a lovely restaurant in her neighborhood. We have a romantic dinner -- complete with chopsticks and wine -- whereupon we travel home. As we lie in bed she gently strokes my head and says (again), "I could lose you to another girl in a second." Helen often and repeatedly states she will lose me to a YOUNGER girl, a darker girl, a lighter girl, a girl in the theater, a disabled girl ("You give them extra points, you know!" I know.) I tell her she is projecting. She asks me if I would like to live on the beach, to which I respond yes, which elicits an, "Oh, no, I could lose you to somebody who lives on the beach." I point out to her that there are no women lining up to steal me from her on or off the beach. It doesn't matter. When we enter grocery stores she points to various women and asks, "Is she cute?" "Do you want her?" This invariably leads to fights that invariably lead to make-up sex -- which is sweaty and noisy and hard and thick and explosive.

"I swear you do this shit just for foreplay," I accuse her more than once.

The idyllic gilded cage is losing its charm. Before I relocated to Helen's she had said, "You think you're so superior because you're white." I had no idea where this comment came from. If ever there was a human being who felt guilty and embarrassed about being white it's me. She often chants, "You're an asshole," and I rarely disagree. She sees women trying to steal me from her EVERYWHERE. Grocery stores, school, beaches, THE THEATER, neighbors and playgrounds. When I ask why she believes this she says, "It's because you're so cute! You talk like nobody else talks; you say what girls want to hear; you're very creative; you love your mom; you cry. Not only do you cry, but you cry cute. A girl would go to bed with you just seeing you cry, and it makes me sick! You're going to be famous and people are going to write books about you. But I'll be able to say, 'yeah, but he's an asshole!'"

I laugh. "Well, honey, that can be the name of your book."

She soon begins to throw and break things, and I am starting to get fearful for the day that some item will be hurled at me instead of against the wall. If one is a woman with a need to control the partner in her relationship the best possible choice would be a quadriplegic. I do remain grateful for the magic, the romance, the caring, the love, and her beauty. But one day, as she is getting me ready, she flies into one of her jealous rages and cracks me in the back of the head with a brush.

"Give me the phone," I say. She panics and demands to know who I am going to call. I assure her that her fears are well founded in that I plan

The Squeaky Wheel

to leave and the police will come. She begs and pleads and apologizes and promises (oh, the fucking promises) and sobs. I decide not to make the call or even to replay a version of the phone call I did on Stench. I threaten to leave many times and she promises to go to therapy, but neither of us keeps our promises or follows through on the threats.

One night I watch the Josephine Baker story -- a figure I've always had an interest in. Helen soon is looming over my shoulders demanding to change the channel, accusing me of infidelities and screaming, "I'm sick of her black tits." After the simultaneous performances... we make love -- incredible, explosive, sweaty, euphoric and better than last time love.

The Road to Tokyo is selected to be performed at the American College Theatre Festival. We will compete against four other plays from our region for the honor to perform at the John F. Kennedy Center in Washington, DC. Darrin will be in attendance at the College Theatre Festival because he is the acting partner for someone in competition for the Irene Ryan acting award. Andrew and his wife Melanie will be in attendance as it is a short way from their home in San Francisco. My friends Tom and Yvette will attend because they are flight attendants and can travel almost at will. Darrin will bring Dawn to the play.

But fate is a cruel dealer. Some viral earwig attacks me and I experience labyrinthitis. This is not the latest video game but a condition wherein the affected perceives his surroundings to be spinning as if he were on a turntable. This, not surprisingly, also creates nausea in the host. I have this condition for the entire time while in Napa Valley. I cannot participate in the happenings of the festival. I lay in my hotel room bed while Helen travels to San Francisco to replenish a percentage of her wardrobe lost in a suitcase that the airlines caused to disappear because I have not brought a wheelchair with batteries for them to lose on this trip.

When Darrin discovers why he cannot reach me at the hotel room he is a frequent visitor and we talk as I lay in bed with my eyes closed. He wins a prize for making fun of the fellow participants. He is overly skilled at this. I recover sufficiently to view the play the night it is performed. Dr. Brandon walks past and I say, "Let me introduce you to my row."

He looks slightly puzzled but as I introduce four friends, two siblings and Helen, he is delighted. The audience is delighted by an art form and intensity rarely experienced on 'the mainland.'

Dawn's review of the play is perfect. At the conclusion and before we exit, Dawn announces with a grin and a big smile, "That play was cuckoo."

I lament that I miss the assistance of KOKUA and that I would like to return to school just to get assistance for writing. "You can write at home. I'll type for you," Helen claims. I see her point. I don't see where she will have the time to type for me, but I look at the mouthstick in my mouthstick holder now mounted to my wheelchair, and I know I can type one letter, one word, one page at a time.

One night I am watching L.A. Law. I decide they should have a lawyer in a wheelchair as a recurring character. I decide I should be playing this character. I decide to write a vehicle for such a character. Andrew has sent me a redacted transcript from the ranting of a mentally ill individual telling the judge that his public defender has requested sex from the accused. The accused also claims to be from another planet so the judge is probably not giving much credence to other words of the man. These become the first pages of what I intend to be my recurring character on L.A. Law. I type one letter, one word, one sentence and one page at a time with a stick in my mouth. Our hero, the lawyer in a wheelchair, is named Ryan Keane and he is wry and keen (which I realize only now)... as well as a thinly veiled version of myself.

Helen shows me an announcement in the paper wherein aspiring screenplay writers may submit the first twenty-five pages of their screenplay to the Honolulu International Film Festival. Ten finalists will be chosen as well as a winner. I am almost up to page twenty-five.

The L.A. Law episode quickly evolves into a screenplay wherein our central character is an adrenaline junkie who likes to bungee jump, scuba dive, parachute, hot air balloon and participate in activities that SANE people *without* spinal cord injuries shy away from. Ryan fled girlfriend, family and friends on the mainland under the pretense of an easier life in the tropics. But duty calls, and he gets a case that sends him back home to L.A. He visits old friends, is scolded for not knowing his dearest friends have been divorced for almost two years and for making himself the island he lives on. There is a lurking passion (in the vein of *Moonlighting* or *Remington Steel* or...) between the lawyer and his aid -- a brown tropical goddess.

In a standout scene Ryan coerces his friend Tommy (who Darrin keeps insisting is my friend Andrew) into a hot air balloon ride. The pilot of the balloon is trying to get divorce advice from the two shysters on board. Tommy, who cares not a lick for heights, screams at the pilot that neither of them are divorce lawyers and don't know or care about the pilot's impending divorce. The pilot responds by turning the gas up high and diving out of the balloon to his death. The two are left in the gondola alone to deal with what they have wrought.

Letterman

But I don't spend all my time writing this screenplay, nor do I limit my television watching to L.A. Law. I decide I will write a letter to David Letterman which will be read. I will give him several to choose from and believe that he will do the hitherto undone and read four letters in one Friday from Brian Shaughnessy. I will need assistance.

I type the letters on the computer Helen has purchased to feed my muse and keep me from the KOKUA girls. I draft, refine and know that all five letters are more than contenders and if David Letterman's writers have the gonads I believe they have, they will ALL be read.

THE LETTERS:

April 15, 1991

Dear Dave:

I see that you no longer wear your highly identifiable athletic shoes and have traded them for loafers (appropriately enough).

Since you're not collecting your fee from the shoe magnate, will there be any other cheesy ways to augment your already over-inflated salary through your wardrobe?

Payola Watchingly Yours,

Brian Shaughnessy
Honolulu Hawaii

April 24, 1991

Dear Dave:

I have noticed lately that at the top of the show, you enter putting on your jacket. Then as soon as you say goodnight you immediately stand and rip off your jacket with such force that one can only imagine you leaving a trail of clothing behind you. What's the deal?

Curiously yours,

Brian Shaughnessy
Honolulu, Hawaii

The Squeaky Wheel

> April 21, 1991
>
> Dear Dave:
>
> Do you ever get any really lame letters? I mean letters that just drag on. I mean letters that just have no point. I mean redundant letters. I mean insipid, vacuous, droning endless letters.
>
> If so, can I have some?
>
> Starved for reading,
>
> Brian Shaughnessy
> Honolulu, Hawaii

> April 15, 1991
>
> Dear Dave:
>
> Just got my degree in drama and thought it would be great for you to bring me out to New York so we can see some Broadway shows, roll some bums, and hang out at your office and your crib. I'll even drive your car.
>
> Just tell me when.
>
> Respectfully yours,
>
> Brian Shaughnessy
> Honolulu Hawaii
> PS -- Can we ditch Paul?

> Dear Dave:
>
> Just got my degree here in Hawaii and thought you might like to come hang out on the beaches, go to some luaus, roll some bums, visit Imelda and catch a Don Ho show.
>
> You can hang out in my beach hut. I'll even let you drive my car. Just tell me when.
>
> Poifully yours,
>
> Brian Shaughnessy
> Honolulu, Hawaii
> PS -- Can we ditch Paul?

I have Helen purchase tacky Hawaiian tourist stationery. She transcribes what I have written on the tacky stationery with her magnificent handwriting and signs my name. One of the letters will not go on this stationary. It reads:

> Dear Dave,
>
> Stop doing the late-night bookmobile bits... or else.
>
> Psychotically yours,
>
> A Bibliophobe

The Squeaky Wheel

I have Helen get out many, many magazines. I have her clip out the letters and portions of words that will make up this missive to Dave. She lays it all out and it looks, as is intended, to be a ransom note. She just needs the piece of paper to glue the bits of magazine to the paper.

On the computer Helen has purchased I create a letterhead that reads:

Aloha
from
Brian Shaughnessy
Honolulu, Hawaii

Helen places the five letters into an envelope addressed to Rockefeller Plaza. "Wait," I say before she closes the envelope. I have her write one more.

I dictate:

Dear Dave:

Does anyone ever write to you more than once? Why?

Just wondering,

Brian Shaughnessy
Honolulu, Hawaii

The mail goes out and I am parked at the TV the next Friday. My smile fades as my letters are not read, but I figure it is too soon for them to properly respond to my treasures. The next Friday my smile fades again. The next Friday is a repeat. More Fridays come and go and I fear I may have overestimated the gonadal size of Mr. Letterman's writers. I'm getting threatening letters from the student loan people.

Again over Helen's protestations I return to Minneapolis. The airline loses my batteries. Darrin also returns and is having a play he wrote produced at California State Fullerton. I have become tragically able to type with the mouthstick at the computer. I decide to buy a laptop and visit my cousin who works at the University of Minnesota bookstore -- selling computers. When I was hit by a car at 14 and spent a month in the hospital she came almost daily to visit and read to me.

"I never sell to family members because it's a prescription for hell." This from a woman who has not even spoken to her mother in a decade.

She sells me the laptop anyway. I continue on my lawyer-in-a-wheelchair screenplay story typing one key at a time with a stick in my mouth. The computer explodes. It is replaced and the next one explodes. This is replaced by yet another smoking and exploding computer. I'm getting apologies from the local representative for the computer company as well as the regional manager in another state. My cousin simply laments breaking her rule.

"You don't need me anymore," is Helen's response to my announcement that I purchased my own computer.

Helen visits despite my protestations, and we travel to Mount Rushmore State Park. We rent a vehicle and Helen bravely transfers me into the front seat. I label the outing the, "Ping Wa And Her Majesty Go on a Crime Spree through the Dakotas," trip. Every day is 100 degrees and South Dakota is flat. We stop halfway for rest at the Corn Palace but have no corn. We stop to get gas and Helen fuels the vehicle and goes into the rural Dakota station/store. She charges the gas and when asked for identification she produces her Hawaii driver's license.

"Hawaii, huh? You look just like one of them Hawaiian girls. Just like on TV!"

Mount Rushmore is amazing -- even more amazing than the four giant faces carved into a mountain are the forests, the buffalo, the elk and the other majestic flora and fauna -- including wild horses. Helen feeds the wild horses through the passenger-side window while I try to retreat from the giant teeth in my face. When the equines come to her side of the car she rolls up the window and departs. We watch a buffalo play chicken with a motorcyclist. But every day it's over 100 degrees and that is just plain wrong.

The Squeaky Wheel

Huffisms

The ever-recurring sore on my butt is back again with a vengeance. This, again, forces me to spend days and weeks in bed. The nursing agency calls and tells me that Shawn Hall will be coming mornings and afternoons, five days a week. I give my standard directions to my apartment and say Shawn Hall should come to the side door of the building instead of the front door, as I have no way to answer that door. As happens consistently when I give these instructions to the agency, the next day the world's most obnoxious buzzer sounds and startles me. Shawn Hall is late. After the initial shock, I shake my head and futilely try to scream. There are three doors, two rooms, a hallway and a flight of stairs between Shawn Hall and me. The buzzing continues... and continues... and continues. After 20 minutes he comes through the door to the hallway -- not the door from the outside he could have entered without incident. He calls from the kitchen, and I yell from the back room for him to enter. He is a tall, thin, black man in his 20's who wears the rapper's uniform of the day -- expensive sneakers, nylon workout pants and a black cloth cap with the White Sox logo. Today he wears a T-shirt several sizes too big with a photograph on it of Malcolm X holding an automatic weapon. Underneath Mr. X it reads, "By whatever means necessary." Shawn Hall is apologetic in explaining that a black man cannot "just walk into" an apartment in this neighborhood. He had buzzed ALL of the apartments and showed one of the other white tenants his paperwork and nametag. They let him in without blinking.

He is pleasant and funny and takes my direction easily -- I am his first adult client. For the last few weeks he has been the companion to some profoundly disabled children. Shawn Hall is *very* conscious of his blackness and speaks of the "black thing" at length. He agrees with me that *all* of the shows with black characters -- with the exception of the Cosby Show -- amount to nothing more than shuffling.

The two of us discuss an Eddie Murphy stand up comedy special. I relate one of the stories -- attempting to affect the voice and attitude of an angry black man like Eddie Murphy did. Shawn Hall's mood changes slightly, and he tells of a similar routine on *In Living Color*. He makes my angry black man sound like an eight-year-old white girl. He tells me that the stereotype that all black people *can* dance does not apply to one of his friends. "Brother gets out on the dance floor, the NAACP come around asking him for ID and shit."

Because we are men, the conversation eventually turns to women and sex. He has a girlfriend. He speaks of his other friends and their claim they don't eat pussy. "It's not a black thing," he says. This phrase is often repeated over the summer. He says that although one of his friends denies engaging in cunnilingus EVER, the women he has dated claim: "He's busier down there than a ghetto Dairy Queen in the summer."

His pager sounds and he spends too long explaining he needs it for work. He went through a similar lengthy explanation with the clerk when acquiring the pager. He showed his nametag and paperwork from the agency, which he felt he had to do because the assumption is that any black man wanting a pager must be a dope dealer.

"What *do* you sell?" I ask.

He is initially shocked and then laughs and says weed. Only weed. His mom smokes it. She hates rap music. She calls it "that bump, bump thump shit." I tell him his mother has excellent taste.

I tell him there are some supplies in the outer closet he needs and he responds, "Okey-dokey." I point out that this phrase is not really a "black thing." He chooses not to respond.

Some days later I run into Howard -- another black man who worked for me some weeks during the previous summer. I tell him of the initial meeting with Shawn Hall and his reluctance to enter the apartment in this white neighborhood. He laughs. When I later relay this story to Shawn Hall he tells me, "The brother not really black then."

Shawn Hall supplies my marijuana over the summer and is late in both the a.m. and p.m. I try to explain to him that this is not cool even when I remain in bed for the day. He tries to explain that the black man cannot *be* on time. Time is a notion created by white people to fuck with black folk, he says, and that I will have to live with "CP time"(colored people time) for the summer. He assures me this will give me soul.

One day when he arrives late the conversation drifts toward pornography. "I got no time for that shit," he says. "I don't wanna watch nobody fuckin' that ain't me." He tells me I should put a block on my telephone so long distance calls can only be made with an access code. "With all the people you got comin' in here, you gonna have calls to Alaska and Jupiter and shit."

I leave that morning for a medical appointment, and Shawn follows me out and locks the door. The van has already arrived to take me to the doctor. As I am loading, the two of us exchange last-minute instructions and the meaningless agreed-upon time that he will return in the evening.

The Squeaky Wheel

The white driver says, "Your friend looks like a rapper." That night Shawn returns very late and very drunk. It's payday. I scold him for being late, and he tells me his hat flew off by the lake and he was looking for it, as it was an expensive hat. I tell him not to insult me, and he continues for a short time until he realizes he won't get this one over. His girlfriend calls, and the three of us talk on the speakerphone. She talks of what they will do with his paycheck. They will go to Kmart and put some more money down on a quilt they are buying on layaway. "I want some Kentucky Fried Chicken," she says. I laugh and say, "Live the myth, man -- live the myth." Shawn understands and laughs as he helps me eat Kentucky Fried Chicken.

The next day he arrives hung over and -- as always -- Helen is on the phone. She calls even more often when she knows I am on bed rest. Every summer when I return to Minnesota she complains of her $500 in long distance charges. After she finally hangs up, Shawn again comments that the picture of her in the room and the voice on the phone are incongruous to him.

"The brown skin and the California accent?"

"Yeah," he says adamantly.

I am up and in the wheelchair making final arrangements when a police siren blasts outside. He initially ducks and reels about and slowly comes up and watches the squad car pass. I have not flinched.

"See? That the difference between black folk and white folk," he says, staring at me. "Black folk hear the police and they jump. White folk hear the police and just figure they're goin' after black folk."

We are off to the grocery store. "Oh, we goin' to the *white* grocery store?" he says, beaming. "Gotta stock up on the mayonnaise and tuna fish, do you, Brian?"

"No," I say, nonplussed. "I thought I'd try some soul food. So we're buying baloney and Kool-Aid -- okey-dokey?" Shawn often brings baloney sandwiches to my house.

As we enter the upscale grocery store Shawn comments, "Damn! Ain't carpeting in the ghetto grocery stores cuz black folk will just fuck it up." He sees an attractive black woman bagging groceries and another young black male doing the same. The cashiers are all white. "See, they'll let black folk *work* here, but don't none of 'em touch the money."

His tardiness continues and worsens. I talk to Stewart, the supervising nurse, looking to him for advice and asking him not to say anything to the staffing people. I explain that I like Shawn's work and his company, but the lateness is becoming intolerable and abusive. When

Shawn arrives late, Stewart speaks to him. Stewart knows of the lateness from other clients and implores Shawn to be timely or he will lose his job. Shawn understands and agrees.

Later that week, in some drunk and reckless incident with his friends and an automobile, he is arrested. Because he is in jail he cannot come to my house that evening. Nor the next day. Nor the next. This is the last straw; I ask staffing to begin sending someone else. Shawn apologizes and promises to visit Hawaii and to do a better job next summer. In the eight-month interval he becomes an exemplary employee and in great demand. He never makes it to Hawaii.

I make my annual visit to 3D, M.D., Ph.D. -- not just because I make annual visits -- but because there are always medical issues to be dealt with. Chronic urinary tract infections, open sores and now the chronic, chronic, chronic decubitus ulcer on my butt that keeps me in bed half my life demand that I see 3D, M.D., Ph.D. He gives me the Marinol (marijuana in a pill form) without problem. He peers into my ear with one of his doctor gadgets and mutters, "Oh, my God! This is bad. Oh, God Brian... I don't know."

I'm terrified. I think it's partly because I am altered by the Marinol. I suddenly remember who I am dealing with and know that there is nothing to be terrified by.

"How long do I have, Doctor?" I ask with soap opera earnest.

He drops his doctor gadget but it does not hit the floor as it is on a coil connected to the wall. He laughs and looks up my nose expressing disgust.

He refers me to Susan, one of the occupational therapists who has been there since my first trip to the occupational therapy department of the University of Minnesota Hospitals. I tell her of the chronic breakdown on my butt. She smiles.

"I have just the place for your bony butt. They do wonders."

I travel to Tamarac Habilitation and they do wonders. They make a seating system molded to my back and heinie and put me in a brace/corset that straightens and compensates for my scoliosis. The brace/corset is fabric but is nonetheless made from the inside of a lamp -- a lower watt lamp than the previous plastic braces but nonetheless a lamp. I have ordered a wheelchair that this one-piece seating system will not fit into.

The Squeaky Wheel

Mission Control to Houston -- Send a Daiquiri

While Tamarack Habilitations is building me a one-piece seating system, custom molded to my butt and back, I realize it will not work in the wheelchair they are ordering in Honolulu. I ask Parker, the primary technician working on the seating system, how to resolve this dilemma.

"Call your vendor in Hawaii and tell them you want a tilt-in-space system rather than a reclining system. It's a better system anyway, since the seat and feet come up as the back goes down."

I have been trying hard to get this wheelchair and spending many months in bed, concerned... about rocking the boat. But I call the long-winded salesperson -- no problem. Within days I pick a color. I choose teal, uncertain of what the color teal is. My previous two electric wheelchairs only came in two different colors -- black or brown. I return to Hawaii, and after complications with the new wheelchair, I am eventually delivered a teal wheelchair with the tilt-in-space feature. Once the seating system is mounted in the new chair, and the headrest is in place, I recline the wheelchair. Helen immediately lunges in the direction of my head as it goes in the direction of the floor. The process gives the uninitiated observer the appearance that I will tilt over backward and crack my previously opened cranium. The safety balance bars prevent this from happening. Strangers lunge when I perform this function at the beach, park, movie theater or anywhere I encounter other humans. When they see the process begin, the uninitiated are transfixed like a hypersensitive hypnosis victim to a shiny object. Though when the headrest reaches a certain point in the process, the uninitiated inevitably dive in my direction and then embarrassedly run their fingers through their hair as if they never even noticed my presence.

Once in the position of total recline, I look like an Apollo astronaut strapped into his tiny seat ready for lift off and/or a tourist awaiting libations in a kitsch glass they get to take home. I ask Helen for sunglasses and Tang... with vodka and the paper umbrella. The hours, the days, the weeks and the months I have spent confined to bed because of the sores on my ass have just ended.

Brian Shaughnessy

The Fight With Very Special Arts

    VSA arts Hawaii, an arts organization for persons with disabilities, has a new director. The old director, Harvey, and I had procured funding for two theater projects for persons with disabilities. Until now, I was unable to meet my commitment to launch the first two projects. The new director explains that a production must be performed before January or the money must go back from whence it came. I explain to him that I now have a wheelchair and seating system that will allow me to perform the job. I enlist Jerry and another friend, Buddy, from the theater department and HITCO to perform *Sarah's Last Waltz,* which has been renamed *Spambulance 4311.* I ask a couple of directing friends to direct me in David Mamet's children's tale told to adults, *The Frog Prince.* My friend Joehn (who goes by Jo) makes the commitment. As I search for other actors with disabilities (Jerry has a disability) I rediscover a local blind storyteller who was banished to the Molokai leper colony as a child. Primo's stories are celebratory and funny. Leprosy, or Hanson's disease to use the little-known but politically correct term, has eaten away at Leroy's face; his fingers from the nails to the knuckles are gone. One night at a rehearsal I watch him playing the piano deftly. I wonder how he can feel the keys; I know he can't see them.

    The next day I ask, "Primo, I saw you playing the piano -- can you feel the keys?" He and his wife shake their heads and he explains that he plays only with the "sense" of where his fingers are in relation to the keys.

    "So, you don't have sensation in your fingers," I invite him to respond.

    "No, no sensation," he responds incorrectly.

    "Oh, Primo," I begin disappointingly, when I ask you, 'Do you have sensation in your fingers?' you're supposed to say, 'Sensation? I barely have fingers!'"

    Primo and Brian laugh uproariously as Helen and Primo's wife grimace.

    I quickly find out three small projects are three times more work than one large project. Helen plays two parts in *The Frog Prince* and, simply because an actor bags on us, she must play Sarah in *Spambulance 4311.* Sadly, Buddy never learns his lines for *Spambulance 4311* but Helen and Harry try to carry him. I only want to see him carried out... in a

The Squeaky Wheel

body bag. Notwithstanding, *Spambulance 4311* is some people's favorite. We get great crowds and I am invited to direct another play at Kumu Kahua Theater.

As I close the VSA art projects, I am holding auditions for the Kumu Kahua show, *Christmas Cake*. (It sounds glamorous but the pay sucks. Yet I wouldn't trade it for anything!) Getting actors will be tougher than usual, as it demands rehearsal over Christmas when many travel to the mainland. One, large, apish oaf enters in the middle of a scene, tries to talk to me while people are auditioning and when I shoo him away he continues to raise his hand and make eye contact with me. The sad thing is he might get a part. But he doesn't. The play does demand one elderly Japanese woman and the same person who hired me to direct *12-1-A* recommends Tomoko. My first reaction is to kill him, but as I think about it and review the lines I decide I might be able to use her without killing her or myself. I cast two of the other actors that I used in *12-1-A*. They want to kill me but are committed to the production. I cast Helen again.

Tomoko can't/won't/doesn't learn her lines. Again it's my fault as well as the other cast members. I give as many of her lines as I can to other characters. Darryl Canis, managing director, former artistic director and founder/father of Kumu Kahua theater comes, as is his custom, to view the rehearsal process. The fucking playwright has not come to view the rehearsal process. It is abysmal. Darryl loses his mind. He shrieks and carries on as only an Aussie intellectual can.

We perform in a 200-seat theater for four weekends. The show gets better every night. Each night there are more tickets sold. One night I tease a high school girl -- telling her she does not want to enter late and miss part of the show.

"I know, this is my second time coming to see it. I love it!" She gushes.

I have to know. "What makes someone in high school GO to a play… let alone go to it *twice*?" I ask in disbelief.

"I had to see it for my acting class but I liked it so much I came back a second time. It's the first time I've *ever* gone to a play twice!"

Higher praise has not been heaped on Steven Spielberg. And I doubt she knew she was talking to the director, and if she did she would not have cared or understood what that person's job was.

"I see Open Door Theater is doing another show," Larry says to me that night matter-of-factly but clearly wondering why he wasn't involved.

"No, we're not," I say with a scoff and a scowl.

Brian Shaughnessy

Now Larry looks frightened. "Yeah, Brian, they are. There's an article in tonight's paper. David Snakeskin is doing it." He hands me the paper open to the article. He is speaking the truth. Open Door Theater, which I named, created, and procured funds for, has been usurped from me and is doing a production. I lose my mind. I think of Jimmy Cliff's line... but then …

Sometimes I grow weary of being quadriplegic for so long. Every February second is the black anniversary of my surgery. I wonder how I made it another year. I wonder if I will make it yet another or if I will initiate plan B and take the 100 Valium I have stashed away for checkout time. No one would blame me. I would be missed by some, but the act would be understood. I am growing not just to dislike Helen and my living situation but I dream of ways of escaping. I hate myself for feeling this way. I have begun to see a therapist and she stops just short of slapping me across the face and saying, 'Get the fuck out of there, Brian!' I keep in close contact with my former attendant and devoted friend Joseph as I know him to be a man of honor and that he will assist me when I finally flee. The sadness of hating this person that I also love/loved only compounds my sadness and insanity. She gives generously but conditionally and neither I, nor anyone else, can meet the terms.

But I choose to focus on the fact that a project I initiated has been taken from me without an explanation. I call the new director for VSA arts and calmly, sternly explain my disappointment at being excluded from the Open Door Theater project I named, procured funds for and initiated. "For God sakes, I didn't even get an announcement!"
"We told you when we began that it was our hope and intention to involve other people, Brian," he says with a tone that lets me know he takes glee at this fact and that it was absolutely deliberate, malicious and undeserved that I was excluded. I point out to him that including other people never meant to the exclusion of me. He says they were under no compulsion to use me on the project this time or any time in the future. I ask, "Isn't it the creed of Very Special Arts to 'Enrich the lives of persons with disabilities?'"
"Well, yes it is." He concedes. "But it's not to enrich the life of Brian Shaughnessy."
"Okay, I understand that this conversation is futile and I will find another way to deal with your actions... and inactions."
"I'm sorry you didn't get an invitation," he taunts sarcastically.

The Squeaky Wheel

But he has taunted the wrong cripple.

I draft the letter on the computer that will go out to all the members of the Board of Directors and various key members of the arts and disability community... and, of course, the media. This puffster new director may not hear the footsteps but they are coming.

The first letter is to Darryl Canis -- managing director of Kumu Kahua Theater, favored professor, person of integrity and... he saw the show. Darryl is a David Mamet published scholar and has invited me AGAIN to direct at his theater.

The Board removes the puffster new director from his position at the next meeting. They replace him with the assistant director, Ruthless. I later find out Ruthless is fucking David Snakeskin -- the able-bodied person who took over Open Door Theater.

Later, the kindly old ladies who are the Board and have worked tirelessly, devotedly and without compensation for years are told by the new director that they have all been Board members too long and must quit. The national office endorses Ruthless's actions. She, with help, empties the coffers, absconds and Very Special Arts Hawaii ceases to exist.

I begin writing *Damn Gravity* a play about a red-headed alien, Talzar, who is a trapeze performer on his home planet, but on earth, where the gravity is greater, is confined to a wheelchair. He first insults a black man, Tyrone, who is applying for the position of live-in attendant and then informs him of his secret and hires him. Our visitor can also control minds. We learn that on his home planet the blondes have been fighting the redheads for centuries. Talzar was to fly his small spacecraft to the appropriate distance and unleash a bomb that will destroy only the blondes on the planet. At the last minute he cannot kill half the humans on the planet. Because he makes this choice he cannot return as a traitor to his planet. He leaves his wife and infant daughter for the "water planet," Earth.

Talzar ditches his spacecraft in the waters off Oahu because on his planet there are only two "races," whereas in Hawaii there is an infinite number. Oahu is also ideal because he can stash his craft in the sea just off a very deep ocean shelf. Talzar and his aid have a wacky neighbor who insists she has contact with "space people." She suspects Tyrone is a space person.

Talzar fights off the love and advances of his nurse, Leilani, and his love for her. Through a sophisticated linkup that only an alien would have the knowledge to perform, Talzar is able to send messages to his home planet. More importantly he receives them -- six days later. It takes six days for a message to travel from here to his home planet, Woden.

In the final scene Talzar discovers that all life on his home planet has been destroyed. It is unclear and unimportant whose fault it is. Talzar crumples into a ball and into the arms of Leilani. His wife and daughter are dead, the planet destroyed, he will live the rest of his life in a wheelchair... on a different planet -- never to walk a tight wire again.... but he has the love of a woman, the balm of the babe. Not a crash landing.

Darrin has won the American College Theater Festival award for his one-act play, *The Manager*. This is the same competition that *The Road to Tokyo* was entered in. *The Manager* is performed at the Kennedy Center in Washington D.C.. My father and his wife travel to see it. It will also be published by Samuel French. Darrin has "o'er topped my toppings" -- Shakespearean for "done me one better." He is staying upstairs with Teri and I tell them of my screenplay I have been typing. I have set aside *Damn Gravity* and am working on *The Squeaky Wheel*. I tell Darrin that I have submitted the first 25 pages to the Hawaii International Film Festival. I get a call that I'm one of the 10 finalists. Now, he asks to read it. As he loves to do, Darrin asks me questions, analyzes and attempts to prod me into making it into a better screenplay. It's not done yet.

The Squeaky Wheel

Strange Brew

Home from Hawaii I renew contact with family, friends, my apartment, my neighborhood, the postman and the agency sending nurses aides to assist me. This year I resolve to live in the apartment by myself, which will require more effort on my part to make sure everything I need for the day is situated so that I have ready access to it. Someone will come to feed me, someone will come to clean and -- most importantly -- make sure that I am properly positioned and equipped to make it through the night. One of my previous nurse's aides extolled the virtue of a new product on the market. It was a clear beer.
"It will get you tanked," he informs me.

Armed with this information and my own innate curiosity about such a product, I travel to the nearby liquor store and purchase a six-pack of clear beer. I return home and with assistance from the nurse's aide, who has been cleaning and is about to leave, I enjoy one of the clear beers while listening to music. A friend comes by to welcome me home, and I consume a few more clear beers. He passes on a clear beer offer. As he is leaving, I instruct him to place a clear beer on the table with a long straw so that I can drink yet another. I see a look from him questioning the prudence of this request. I smile drunkenly as he grants my request and exits through the outside door, being careful not to knock his head on the lift.
Before finishing the next beer, my sister Teri arrives to welcome me home. We chat as I finish clear beer number four and move on to clear beer number five. Teri also declines my offer. She departs, and in a few moments my brother, Patrick, arrives through the inside door of the apartment as a new evening attendant arrives and knocks on the outside door.
I live in an area of Minneapolis difficult to find. As stated, most people who visit are impressed by the fact that it is not only a beautiful neighborhood but also one that is well hidden. The novices arrive and praise me for my meticulous directions. Some, however, arrive and go into a rant about how difficult my place is to find. "I was driving around in circles!" or, "I was going back and forth on Lake Street!" are not uncommon statements in my home. This is invariably because the nursing agency gave poor instructions.

I holler for the person at the door to come in. Lynn enters with a timid but complete introduction. Lynn -- a 6 ft. 3 in., bald, bespectacled Norwegian man with a recessed chin in his late 40s -- enters. "Hello, I'm Lynn," he says sheepishly, looking at the floor. "I was sent by Badland's Home Health Care. I'll be your aide tonight and for some nights to come -- maybe all summer. I have several years of experience working with quadriplegics... and blah blah blah," I hear, as the peripherals of my vision begin to turn gray. Soon, the gray is moving toward the center and everything is disappearing into the same dull, sparkling that is like static from the TV when the station is not broadcasting.

"Hang on," I say matter-of-factly, as I begin to recline my chair. My brother and Lynn watch me cautiously as my legs come up and my head moves toward the floor. Four of the five empty bottles sit on the kitchen counter. Once I am fully reclined, I begin to see a tiny circle through the gray. It is the ceiling. The circle grows, and once again my vision is back. "I'm feeling kind of light-headed, so lemme stay like this for a couple of minutes, okay?" They nod and talk. Actually, Pat does most of the talking until I announce, "All right, I think I can get up and go to bed." I press the switch that will bring me back up to the sitting position. Before I am vertical the grayness returns. A gray blanket drops like a black hole, and I am unconscious.

I slowly become aware I am sleeping, and it feels like a deep, wondrous sleep. It feels right. But I realize I should not yet be asleep. I remember I am in the living room with my brother and Lynn. My eyelids slowly crack to reveal my brother's face inches from my nose with the telephone pressed to his ear. "What the fuck was that? Are you all right? Or should I stay on hold to 911?"

"Yeah, I guess you can hang up. I feel weak but okay," I say. "911 put you on *hold*?"

"Yes!" he blares. Lynn stands by grinning emptily. "You were bringing up your chair," he begins with terror and urgency, "and you got a couple inches and like," he searches for the word, "snorted like a pig and then went out like a light. You didn't feel me shaking you?"

I am already laughing at this description as I shake my head.

"Yeah, ha ha, very fucking funny. You scared the shit out of me! So I call 911 and it rings about 20 times and somebody answers and says, 'Hold please.' I mean, what the fuck is that? And then she just goes away for forever!"

"Forever?" I say through the laughter. "How long was I out?"

Pat tilts his head and looks wide-eyed at Lynn who remains statuesque. No, he remains statue-like. "I think eight to ten minutes, ya' think?" He asks Lynn.

Lynn is shaken from his trance. "What? Oh, no, not that long. It was under five minutes -- probably three."

Pat scoffs his disagreement at him and begins to dispute this with him, and I interrupt. "This pig snorting -- was it like snoring or convulsions?"

Pat is looking downward as he ponders the question. He raises his head, eyes me and says, "Yes," indicating that it was a combination of both. This sends me into another fit of laughter. "And what was Lynn doing during this time that you are shaking me and calling 911 and waiting on hold?"

My brother shakes his head as he rolls his eyes and turns toward Lynn. "I was asking him if he had any idea what the fuck was going on, and he just said, 'uh.'" He affects a voice that sounds nothing like Lynn and is not flattering. "I know when people drink alcohol that can happen. I see my wife do it..."

I cut off my laughter to say I should go to bed before the incident repeats itself. I want to end this before one of us asks Lynn if his wife is a lush. Patrick, who does not drink, says, "What is that shit you were drinking, anyway?"

I look at the bottle with the long straw and half the clear, sparkling liquid remaining. "Poor it down the drain," I say, as I head toward the bedroom so that Lynn can put me in bed for the drunken slumber I am likely to pay dearly for tomorrow. "And pour that last one out! G'night."

The Rainbow Coalition

My friend Diane is playing with her new bohemian band at the very hip club, the Trés Trendy Café. I haven't been there. I naturally agree to the soiree and take Metro Mobility.

My friend Andrew is also in Minneapolis. He and his wife Melanie visit. I call him to see if he is interested in joining this outing. He is very enthusiastic and queries has wife, who agrees. I then call another friend since high school, Tom, to see if he and his wife would like to join us. They agree. I tell them I'll get there early to get us a table up front.

This is very pleasing to me, not only because I'll be seeing rarely seen, *good* friends, but also because it reminds me of my 18th year on this planet, which means I was walking. These are sacred memories. Diane was then performing at various venues. More than a few times I showed up with many friends/audience members -- to Diane's horror and delight. I am disappointed I only bring four others tonight.

I arrive at the Trés Trendy Café to stairs -- lots of stairs. Diane called ahead and, yes, there is a handicapped entrance in this ancient edifice, but I don't see it. There are outside tables where a waitress with purple hair, a ring through the center of her nose, cat's-eye glasses, black lipstick and LARGE, barely-covered mammaries serves patrons mutton, gruel and mead. She eyes me as I eye her, and she walks over. "Can I help you?"

"You have another entrance," I tell her.

"Okay, let me go get the manager, and he'll help you," she says smiling, nodding and turning to walk up the many stairs she must ascend and descend every time she takes, brings or places an order.

Momentarily she emerges with the manager. He is unkempt, about six feet tall, starvation thin, sheepish and sporting the saddest attempt at dreadlocks I have ever seen. I wonder why white people attempt this hairstyle when it is almost invariably pathetic looking. Confused Bob sporting this hairstyle and the reminder does not endear me to this individual either. I understand him to be the owner of this highly successful club. He mumbles something about following him and leads me nearly a block to a dingy-looking door. He removes a ring of keys, sorting through them while shaking his head and mumbling inaudible speech. The six pathetic dreadlocks of fine, dishwater-blonde hair and dirt don't move.

He inserts a key and, naturally, it does not unlock the door. He makes a few more attempts, and the door is opened, revealing a dusty storage/construction area. There is a lift inside. The manager removes buckets, long planks and other sundries from the lift and opens the gate, signaling me to board it. I do so as he presses the button to bring the lift up, and nothing happens.

By now my friend Don is inside the establishment peering down at the two of us from the area where the lift will ascend. The lift is next to more (but fewer) stairs. The manager checks switches, plugs, safety

The Squeaky Wheel

latches and even tries kicking the device to get it to ascend. Unsuccessfully. I eyeball the planks.

Diane has joined Don at the top of the stairs and is looking upset and disappointed. I do not want her experiencing these emotions before her performance. "Aloha," I say. They smile and respond but remain concerned. I covet the planks through further unsuccessful attempts by the manager and his lackey to get the device working.

"I think we can take those two planks and lay them on the stairs, and with the two of you behind me and Don in front, I can just roll up."

The manager and his employee ponder, mutter and acquiesce. The planks are placed, the two assume their position behind me and Don delicately holds the front of the wheelchair as I "climb" the stairs and enter the Trés Trendy Café.

Don and Diane give hugs, greetings and direct me to a table down front. It is the first time I have seen them this summer. Diane and the other members of The Café Bohemian *Orchestra* -- all five of them -- are setting up. Immediately Marilyn and Jack arrive. They are good friends of Don and Diane and were my teachers at the Southeast Free School, which three of my siblings and I attended. I share a comfortable bond with this couple despite infrequent encounters.

I tell them I have four friends coming, and they give a thumbs up, as they push two tables together. Andrew and Melanie arrive, as do others, in time for the music to begin. Soon Tom and Yvette are seated at the table. The band is wonderful, and we all are catching up when Marilyn says, "She's talking to you."

I come out of my conversation to realize that Diane is looking at me and saying, "The next song is for my friend, Brian, who lives in Hawaii -- which we all hate him for and are jealous of -- but he made it here tonight. Thank you, Brian." At which point the Café Bohemian Orchestra renders their version of, *On the Beach in Waikiki,* as my chin trembles and my eyes mist.

The evening goes too quickly and it is time for me to leave. After backing down the planks, I say my goodbyes to all and because it is a wonderfully cool Minnesota night I roll along the bus route in the direction of my apartment. No bus appears as I travel the three plus miles from the Trés Trendy Café to home. Just as I am turning off the main street for the final two blocks of my journey, a bus breezes past. No loss.

The next day Diane calls and thanks me for coming and "forcing your other friends to come." She knows better and I correct her. They've been listening for over 15 years. "I gotta tell you, it was a little weird looking out at my table -- at the Rainbow Coalition." I am lost for a moment as she proceeds. "We had Marilyn -- Jewish, Jack -- Filipino, Tom and Don -- white dudes, Yvette -- black, Andrew -- Chinese, Melanie -- Japanese, and Brian -- the dude in a wheelchair. Jesse Jackson couldn't match those demographics."

I am laughing before the list is complete. "Not a very common sight here in the land of 10,000 loaves of white bread." Diane cackles. "But in the land of poi it's not that uncommon. Hell, I believe I *know* someone who is a member of each of those groups."

"What happened to you?" A Metro Mobility driver asks me the next day.

"What's my name? (Pause) Perhaps you should ask me that question before we get intimate."

Helen has resumed her regular calls. One morning I lose my mind and I scream and tell her to never call again and she sobs hysterically. I do not hear from her for a week. I think that she has seen the ridiculousness of her actions and I call her. She tells me that I'm not welcome back in her house, that she might throw my stuff out, and that I can see whoever I want and she can date whoever she wants.

"Who are you fucking?"

She claims no one. I review all of my threats, including the last one, and know that I have to go through with it, but I still try to negotiate... pathetically. She has participated in her first theater production without me and is "seeing" the unmannerly, apelike oaf with the prehensile forehead (how else would you expect me to describe him) who tried to interrupt me when I was holding auditions for *Christmas Cake*. He is Pasta's age. I discover this because I go to Target and find her model of answering machine and get the access code off of the manual. Sue me.

Helen visits Minneapolis despite my being banished from her apartment. I allow her to visit. I access her answering machine at home and find she is calling the unmannerly, apelike oaf *from my house*. I tell her to leave -- I am not polite. She responds by breaking Mark's Mickey Mouse telephone. She writes a check for several hundred dollars to pay for the phone and to placate Mark's whining that the apartment is overcrowded. Mark rented the apartment while I was gone to Hawaii with the knowledge that we would cohabitate upon my return in the spring. He was unprepared for the infantry of people that come through my door daily. Helen leaves a sarcastic letter for Mark, which Darrin and I tear up.

The Squeaky Wheel

The Greatest

The phone rings, and I answer. It is the nursing agency staffing person. "We're sending out a new nurse's aid tomorrow. Mohammed Ali will be there at seven in the morning."

"The greatest?" I respond. "I guess I couldn't be in better hands!"

"Yeah, yeah -- I've heard it all since he started working for us."

I know from his name that Mohammed Ali is Muslim. I am fairly sure from the recent influx of immigrants that he will hail from another country. When he walks into my apartment, I immediately know what country.

"You're Ethiopian," I announce, as he enters my bedroom and attempts to introduce himself through not just broken, but demolished English. Helen has already called and is on the phone. "Yes," he says, surprised. "How know this?"

"You look Ethiopian. You look at least as Ethiopian as I look Irish." Mohammed has no idea what I said in the second sentence and grunts "eh" as I shake my head. I know it's going to be a long morning.

"You very smart, Brian Shaughnessy," he says and claps his hands. "What, what, what," he says and holds his hand out and moves his fingers in a "come here or give me" gesture. I interpret this as his way of asking what to do first. I struggle -- nearly futilely -- to explain each stretch involved in each portion of my range of motion -- toes, feet, knees, hips, legs, arms, elbows, fingers and the various movements involved in stretching and exercising those parts of my anatomy. At times, I wish I had a gun. Each utterance from me provokes the "eh" question from... the greatest. One thing Mohammed Ali says very clearly is "I have to go." He says this after each portion of the range of motion.

"Are you here for three hours?" I yell at him.

"Eh?" comes the predictable monosyllabic response.

I eventually communicate my question to Mr. Ali.

"Yes, yes, yes -- seven to ten, three hours, yeah yes. That is right, Brian Shaughnessy."

"Then shut up about having to leave until 9:50, okay?"

"Eh?"

Somehow I communicate the procedures for the transfer to the shower chair, showering, returning to bed, connecting the leg bag, dressing wounds, dressing me and returning the chair. He still says, "I have to go" repeatedly and makes the motion with his hand, but I have decided to be amused and not enraged. He wants to leave before I have been fed, but I impress upon him that part of the job is to feed me. He agrees. About the time my head is ready to explode, my abbreviated list of morning tasks (abbreviated because there is no way I can communicate and have Mohammed perform all the duties in three hours) is complete, and I send Mohammad out the door.

When Mohammed puts the brace on me and tightens the belts I discover I must have him loosen the lower ones if I am to breathe. I don't realize that this means I am putting on weight because I cannot step onto a scale every day.

Darrin has been sleeping in the middle room. He emerges shortly after the slam of the door by Mohammed. "Fuck!" He blasts the word. "What the hell was that?" he asks as he lights a cigarette and moves toward the coffeepot.

"That was... the greatest."

I explain the reference to him and he nods.

"*I* wanted to kill him; *you* must have..." he shakes his head leaving the statement unfinished.

"Just another day in the life, brother."

"Yeah, I guess so," he says, pondering and pouring. "Did you tell the clown that he could actually accomplish things *quicker* if he didn't run back and forth like a midway bear?" He shouts the expletive again and mimics Mohammad running five feet in one direction and back with hands flailing while he says, "I have to go."

"Will he be back?"

I ponder the horror of this. "At this point we don't know." He laughs because this was his oft-repeated line from *Sexual Perversity in Chicago*.

Mohammed returns that evening to put me to bed. I need Darrin to show him where the paper adhesive tape is and how to start it.

"You should really look into some community education classes in English if you're going to continue in this line of work, don't ya think, Mohammed?" he says as he hands Mohammed the tape, pats him on the back and nods. Mohammed responds in kind.

"Eh?"

This begins Mohammed helping/working/tormenting me six mornings and two evenings a week. This continues for at least a month -- as does his favorite saying and manner of delivering services. One evening while he is rushing about for no reason I say to Darrin, "Can you grab my rubberstamp out of the side bag on my armrest? If I have to explain it to him we'll be here til tomorrow."

Darrin nods a knowing nod and walks to my armrest. Mohammed looks at me and says, "What is that, Brian Shaughnessy?"

I giggle like a five-year-old who's been caught.

Mohammed laughs and nods, "Aah, ha, ha! See? I understand, Brian Shaughnessy."

"Not much, and only when it suits you," I respond.

"Eh?"

Over the weeks he somehow informs me that his Ethiopian wife has left him again because he beats her. She has taken their daughter with her.

"America great country, Brian Shaughnessy. I am glad to be in America but, why, why, why give rights to women? That is crazy. Women like children -- stupid. They no should have rights. In my country..."

This is the first of many "my country" stories. The stories are as frequent as his fictional conquests of women that he attempts to share. Darrin sometimes allows him to speak for five minutes while he keeps his arms crossed, his head tilted and nods in feigned interest. Mohammed makes it very clear that cunnilingus (although he could never say this word) is not engaged in "in my country."

"You're missing out," I tell him.

"You do this, Brian Shaughnessy?" he asks with horror and alarm.

"Every chance I get," I say with zeal.

He laughs and wretches and seeks assurances. I assure him.

"I hear white Americans do this, but I don't believe it."

"The brothers do it, too. They just lie about it."

"Eh?"

Mohammed goes on to explain that "in my country" when little girls are born, the clitoris is cut out of them. This is my first exposure to this practice, and I am in denial. He insists, and I am disgusted and ask him if he would do this to his daughter.

"Eh?"

He chooses not to respond.

I again make forays to the video store to rent smut tapes. One morning as Mohammed performs my cares Darrin sneaks in and cues up a tape to a double... accommodation scene. He giggles and dances and makes sure the volume is all the way down. Eventually, Mohammed sees me fighting back laughter and turns around. Within seconds he realizes what he is watching. "What is this, Brian Shaughnessy? Oh my God!" With that said he sits down in the chair and watches... intently. His hand is to his chin, and he leans forward as the copulation continues.

"Never, never, never do I think of fucking like this. People do this? That way? In the butt?"

"Yup, yup, and yup," I respond.

"You do this, Brian Shaughnessy?" he asks, seemingly terrified.

"Every chance I get."

"Eh?"

A few days later he says he picked up two girls hitchhiking who insisted they be taken back to his apartment. I know he is lying, but I listen. "We go my house and dis, dat, den one say, 'Eat my fur-burger.' I say, 'No! I cannot. Get out!'"

"You expect me to believe that story, Mohammed?"

"Eh?"

Joehn -- the wheelchair using woman I knew from the University of Minnesota Theatre department who visited me in the hospital and announced she would be exploiting our conversation -- has returned from England where she earned *her* master's degree in theater. She has been asked to put together a performance for an Americans with Disabilities Act conference in Minneapolis. She has located two other actors with disabilities -- Hope, an attractive, short haired, fair skinned, thin but spoiled young paraplegic woman earning her bachelor's degree in theater who uses more dramatic pauses in her speech than William Shatner would even dare to -- and Karl, a young man with a mild form of CP that leaves one hand contracted and causes him to use a four poster or "quad" cane to ambulate but has no acting instruction.

Joehn asks me to direct about 30 minutes of scenes these actors have chosen dealing with disability. I keep putting off answering her. When Helen returns home I agree to direct the endeavor.

We begin to meet nightly. The first night I arrive Joehn is slumped over a table looking exhausted and terrified. Hope looks like a deer in the headlights and Karl is expressionless (as is his acting) but manifests his fears with jerky movements of his head and body. I ask them to begin with the scene that they are all in. They run through with very little movement or performance. We work on this piece for most of the evening, and I can see they are delighted with my suggestions/direction and the fun I have brought to the process. But they do whine.

The Squeaky Wheel

We rehearse nightly for what will be little monetary compensation but a wealth of personal satisfaction. Hope feels that Joehn is criticizing and antagonizing her in the rehearsal process. She goes right to the line of blaming Joehn because Hope can't memorize her lines. Joehn feels compelled to over-explain my directions to Hope to the point that when I tell Hope to laugh at the end of a sentence, Joehn will say, "You see, Hope, when Brian tells you to laugh, he wants you to smile, open your mouth and go ha ha ha ha."

Hope fancies herself a sophisticated, militant disability advocate. She feels walking is overrated. Her marriage is disintegrating and she has had an affair. Her husband lives in her apartment for another few months until she deems he has had enough time to accept the inevitable separation. She calls me and complains of Joehn daily. Because she is attractive, because she is a woman with a disability and because my own relationship is over I listen. She understands the conundrum of moving into Helen's without ever wanting to move into Helen's. "You never got to choose," she laments on my behalf. Her empathy impresses me but the rest of her tiny world is only focused on Hope. I am attracted to her but find her immature. She is attracted to me but feels the age difference. She points out to me that she is the same age as Pasta.

Our performance is well received. We are immediately invited to perform at the University of Minnesota and other venues. Together we begin the Open Door Theater with me as the artistic director. We agree to keep in contact while I am in Hawaii and that we will mount a production the following summer.

As always I have kept my contact with Joseph. I invite him to cohabitate with me again and work as my aid. He is in Canada staying with his brother. He agrees and will travel to Minneapolis to rendezvous with me at which point I will return to Honolulu. He is delayed at the border yet again because he has not gotten the U.S. citizenship he has been entitled to since his discharge from the U.S. Army more than 30 years previously. He finally arrives. Since he does not want to pay the airfare from Minneapolis to San Francisco, he decides to take a Greyhound from Minneapolis to San Francisco at which point he will join me on the airplane from San Francisco to Honolulu. Pat gives him some of his homegrown marijuana for which Joseph is infinitely grateful. Joseph fears that a fellow traveler on a Greyhound will stick themselves with a needle and then poke it into Joseph in an attempt to infect Joseph with the HIV virus. I tell him to concern himself with more likely scenarios.

I fly from Minneapolis to San Francisco. Joseph enters the plane and we travel on together. Helen is at the airport with my van. A woman with a disability rights organization in Hawaii had told me that we could stay with her until Joseph and I found a place. Upon arrival I call her and she tells me, "My landlord won't allow you to stay with me -- you need to go to the shelter." I call the shelter and they tell me that the clients sleep on mats on the floor and that it is not a fit place for a quadriplegic. We deliver Helen to her home and she winds up naked and spread-legged on her kitchen counter -- a common spot for oral coitus for us. As I am about to plunge my tongue into her the phone rings. I know it is the unmannerly, apelike oaf, and I want to tell him that I am readying her for his arrival, but I don't. Joseph and I leave and stay at the YMCA. They do not want to allow him to stay in the room with me.

We begin looking for a domicile the next day. Each day is an exercise in futility, and the woman who had yanked the invitation out from under me is no help. She wants to blame Helen but also suggests that I go to the hospital, claim that I am dizzy, get admitted and force the hospital to deal with me because they cannot discharge me until I have a place to go. I am not ready to do this ... yet. I pay money to an agency to assist us in finding an apartment.

I call the KOKUA office and Ann suggests that I remain at the Y until the next semester and return to student apartments at that time. We continue our daily scouring of the newspapers for ten days until one day Joseph sees an ad for a "One bedroom apartment for wheelchair." We immediately call and make an appointment to see the unit. There is a tub -- which means I cannot roll into the shower in my waterproof wheelchair. I take the unit. I get a loan on my credit card to come up with the first month's rent and security deposit. I have also applied for the Section 8 housing assistance. Helen always stated while I lived with her, "If you want to leave me you can apply for Section 8." I allowed myself to be bullied and let my application lapse.

When I tell Helen my new address she shrieks. (Interestingly enough, the street, Wilder, bears the same name as the street I lived on until I was five years old.) She has just applied for and accepted a job two blocks away at a nursing home. She tells me of the interview. The supervisor asks why her employment ended almost three years ago.

"I told her that I had met a patient who was quadriplegic and that we began dating and eventually moved in together. The woman's mouth opened and she said, 'So you're the one.'"

"What does that mean?" I ask.

The Squeaky Wheel

"That's what I asked her," Helen continues. "My supervisor said that she had heard of a nurse at Kuakini who fell in love with her patient and took him home." She asks me for the access code to my voicemail. I tell her, "No fucking way." She insists, since I have been accessing her answering machine. I again decline. Click.

The apartment has a huge living room/dining room/kitchen that all blend together. This is followed by a long narrow hallway, which leads to the bedroom. To get to the bathroom one must walk through the bedroom. Joseph sleeps on an egg-crate mattress he rolls up each morning. We are on the third floor and quickly meet my quadriplegic neighbor who lives below me. His name is Drake and he is a heroin junkie. Not surprisingly he also has a penchant for participatory delusions.

Joseph and I exit my van when a neighbor leans over the railing and comments, "What's up with you guys? You," he says pointing to me, "are always smiling and he," he says pointing to Joseph, "is always frowning." I never noticed but Joseph agrees that I am often smiling and that humans owe it to other humans to try to smile when they encounter each other.

The ten finalists in the Hawaii International Film Festival screenplay writing competition gather in a room on campus for feedback from "Hollywood experts" and the revelation of the top three winners. I enter the room and see a man who is clearly flattered to be there. Each of the finalists will speak with one of five individuals with positions in the film industry. We receive five written critiques from these individuals. Each of the five is scathing. But all five do acknowledge the verbal acumen and humor of Ryan Kean. One expert comments that although the screenplay is unsatisfactory the backstory is very interesting and worthy of a screenplay. She comments that Ryan's "wicked wit" is outstanding writing. Naturally, the Hollywood expert who pulled the short straw and is assigned to me (I believe his job was tour guide at Universal Studios) does not believe that a 90- to 120-minute movie could have a quadriplegic central character. I grin knowingly and look forward to proving him wrong.

We travel downstairs for the award presentations and the man who was clearly flattered to be there is railing to his wife. "They shouldn't be that cruel! They're industry experts and we are just hobbyists!"

"I'm sure I have the same five pieces of paper you have," I tell him with my years of experience of rejection and a masters degree in the area. And I'm sure whoever wins this competition has virtually the same five pieces of paper and reviews we have. "

"Okay, we'd like to begin the award presentations. We will do the runners up in no particular order. They announce the flattered angry man first and he picks up his bookstore gift certificate. My name is called next. They work through seven more names and then the presenter announces, "This is somewhat anticlimactic because our winner is not here..."

When I later meet the winner he informs me that this was the highest achievement his screenplay reached and no studio showed interest in his script. My script however becomes a pilot movie of the week and a series that runs for seven years -- seen only on the Parallel Universe Network (PUN).

No longer incommunicado, I actually see friends. I run into Alex and Tokio Kahn who invite me to return as one of their annual Thanksgiving guests. I accept. They also invite Helen. She arrives late and -- as all are just finishing dessert -- when she walks into the dining room everyone *happens to* depart. She is certain that I have said something to besmirch her character to the group. Alex, characteristically, hits on Helen when the two are alone in the kitchen.

After this newly re-established annual Thanksgiving dinner at the Kahns and as the crowd dissipates I remain -- waiting for the Paratransit system. I am happy to be the last guest, as I do not get to see these people enough (and have not seen them for years during my internment in the cellblock of passion, incredible lovemaking and even more incredible fighting and insanity that was my cohabitation & relationship with Helen). The dynamics change when the masses are gone. The Kahns and I share the room with Helen. The Kahns are seated (as am I) as Helen stands and circles the chair she occasionally sits in. We all hear the sound of a car pulling into the driveway. Alex parts the curtains and peers out the window.

"It's Rodney!" (known as Professor Fragilego to you) Alex says to Tokio with eyes widened in a tone that suggests this is extremely important.

Tokio runs to the door and looks out. "He's with his mom, the mother and the baby!"

"Well," Alex says with calmness *and* urgency, "go greet them."

The Squeaky Wheel

Alex has confessed more than once with pride, "I have my nose so far up that man's ass, I know how his shit smells before he does." Tokio runs out the door and greetings are heard as she ushers the crowd in and introductions are made. Professor Fragilego and I each politely set aside any contempt for the other. As Helen is about to sit in the chair she has been circling (and using) Tokio snatches and offers it to Rodney (A.K.A. Professor Fragilego). Helen looks at me incredulously, and I shrug.

The young boy is about nine months old and looks more Caucasian than the undetermined Asian ethnicity of his mother. There is, as always, much theatre and movie discussion among the men. Tonight it focuses on David Mammet, because Rodney (A.K.A. Professor Fragilego) has just directed a production of *Sexual Perversity in Chicago* (my production in New Mexico with Darrin was, naturally, far superior to his adolescent rendering), and I played the lead in the same author's version of *The Frog Prince*. The author's movie version of *Glengary Glen Ross* has been released, and both Alex and Professor Fragilego directed *Laundry and Bourbon* which Darrin directed. I told Alex, honestly, that his production (casting three native Japanese speakers with no acting experience) was infinitely superior to his mentor's. Amazingly, Professor Fragilego and I *agree* that Al Pacino's best performance ever was in the film version of *Glengary Glen Ross*. Conversation continues and shifts to the baby.

"You know," Professor Fragilego comments," (unnamed child) has the same shade of red hair as you do, Brian." It is too much for me to resist.

"I've never seen this woman before in my life!"

Only Helen laughs and then immediately leaves the room.

I come home and roll into my bedroom where the telephone I can use sits on my desk. It's Friday. I check my voice mail.

"No, no, this is not Brian Shaughnessy," a voice I don't recognize states. "I happen to know this because I know that the real Brian Shaughnessy is dead. I know that because I know that Paul Schaefer killed him. Brian, this is Vernon, Hope's husband. You were on David Letterman tonight. They read your letter."

I let out a big "whoop," and hear my cousin Roxann. I love her. She has been supportive and hopeful since the surgery. She showers me with gifts and cards on every possible occasion -- Christmas, birthday, St. Patrick's Day, Thanksgiving, Easter, cloudy Thursdays or no reason at all. When DC comics decides to kill Superman, Roxann purchases a copy --

no small feat as it is an immediate collectors item -- and sends it to me because, "You're a writer."

"I really hoped you would be watching David Letterman tonight without my having to call. But I want to make sure that you watch it and don't miss it. Okay, I hope nobody gave away any more than that."

I don't have a television so I call my good friend Dave to tape this wondrous event.

"Cool," is his response. "Tonight I will do what I never do and watch it as it is broadcast instead of taping it and then watching it."

The next day he arrives with a tape labeled, "Late Night with Brian Shaughnessy." I travel to the University of Hawaii Sinclair library -- as I have no TV -- and enter through the wheelchair-user swinging gate, cross the foyer, wedge myself into the ancient and tiny elevator, elevate to the third floor, enter the Wong audiovisual library, am assigned a television and VCR and the librarian pops in the videocassette. David Letterman reads from the tacky tourist stationary Helen penned my missive on:

Letter number four:

Dear Dave,

Does anyone ever write to you more than once? Why?

Just wondering,

Brian Shaughnessy
Honolulu, Hawaii

"I don't know, Brian, if anyone writes us more than once. Paul, does anyone ever write us more than once?"

The camera shows the piano sans Paul.

"Paul? Where the heck is Paul?"

We see a plane in flight and then Paul steps into a "tropical" apartment. A man in a bad aloha shirt sits in a wicker chair.

"Are you Brian Shaughnessy?" Paul Schaefer asks.

The Squeaky Wheel

"Yes," the actor portraying Brian Shaughnessy responds.
"Mr. Viewer Mail. Love your show, Dave. Love your stuff, Dave. Love you, Dave. Did you ever once think to write me?"

The camera zooms in on Paul as we see for the first time the chainsaw he carries. The motor roars and the chain spins as Paul smiles broadly and lets out a maniacal laugh. The camera then zooms in on a conch shell sitting next to a telephone. We hear a scream as the telephone and shell are spattered with blood and the chainsaw buzzes. The audience laughs, shouts, and applauds their approval of the scene as Paul reenters the studio cleaning his glasses. It is lost on me at the moment that this was an acknowledgment of the accompanying letters asking -- "P.S. -- Can we ditch Paul?" I am seeking a librarian to assist me when the power goes out. Thirty minutes later the fire department is called to schlep me down the stairs. Several muscular men arrive wearing yellow fireman overalls. They ask if they can take me out of the chair to carry me down. I decline. They put my chair in neutral and four of them nearly effortlessly carry me down two flights of stairs.
"Is there anything else we can do for you?" the man with the Captain's badge asks.
"Can I ride on the back of the truck?" I ask raising my eyebrows.
Six fireman stare at me blankly.
"No," the Captain says, unsure of who he is dealing with.
My disappointed look is followed by, "Then, can I pet the spotty dog?"

I go home with the sacred tape in my backpack and pen the following.

Top Five Ways my life has changed since having my letter read on the David Letterman show.
5. Only have to pay for a Gulp when I get a Super Big Gulp at 7-11.
4. Constant, haranguing, calls from Oprah asking me to write to her.
3. My barber calls me "Letter-boy."
2. Free cheese.
1. People asking, "Was that really you who Paul killed on the show?"
   To my knowledge, they never acknowledge.

I am listening to Jimmy Buffett sing, *"Mermaid in the Night"* from his album, Off to See the Lizard. It is the tale of a man who goes fishing, catches a mermaid and falls in love with her. It provokes me to begin to write a play about a man on Kauai who catches a mermaid after a hurricane. I am determined to write it and be true to Hawaiian mythology and mermaid mythology. I research Hawaiian methodology, hurricane Iniki, mermaids, fishing and fish. The title changes from *Siren's Song* to *The Lawahine* (Fish Woman). I aim for the humor of *Splash* without stealing the words. I am checking with one of the Hawaiian KOKUA girls to see if I'm on the right track, and she says, "I love the part where you say he turned into a fish and swam up the inside of her -- that is *so* Hawaiian."

Welcome Back, Clark

I return to Minneapolis after wintering in Hawaii (yes, the airline loses my batteries) and begin to rehearse for an August show with Open Door Theatre. We name our production, *for gimps who have considered homicide when enuf is enuf.* This is a catchy adaptation of a well-known poem, "for colored girls who have considered suicide when the rainbow is enuf." I almost come up with the title but the woman who will be ESL interpreting for us (who is a wheelchair user) suggests homicide to substitute for suicide. We all like it. We rehearse daily in the common room of a government subsidized building especially intended for persons with disabilities. This "Gimp Ghetto" is the site of too frequent rapes and robberies. Cowards.

Midway through our six-week rehearsal process Hope wants to quit. *All* these fucking cripples have cried and whimpered about learning their lines since the beginning, but I can't believe when Joehn says she too doesn't believe we will be ready in time. I tell them if they quit now I won't be involved next year and we compromise by printing on the program and flyers that the production is, "a work in progress."

"It's gutless and if we get review words they will tell you that," I admonish.

One night after rehearsal, as I roll in the direction of the liquor store at the strip mall that replaced the lumberyard, someone calls my name. I turn and see a person I have not seen in years. It is Clark Simeon --

The Squeaky Wheel

Pam's gay friend who would drive her from Grand Forks to Minneapolis to enable us (Pam and I) to engage in torrid weekends. He smiles a smile that fills the years we have been incommunicado. He last saw me at the Rehabilitation Department of the University of Minnesota Hospital. The two of us hug, and he introduces me to his partner, Barry. Clark is a *very* funny man who affects many voices and characters. I ask him how the two of us got out of touch, and he tells me that shortly after he last saw me, he was shot.

"Whoa, this is not parking lot conversation. Do you have time to go over to the coffee shop or to the bar or... would you like to come over to my apartment? I'm just a couple of blocks from here."

Clark and Barry agree to take care of their business at the strip mall and then meet me at my apartment. Errands are run, and I roll back to my apartment to await their arrival. Clark informs me that soon after I last saw him -- as he was driving a cab -- he picked up a fare one evening in South Minneapolis and drove the man to his requested destination. Clark turned off the meter and was reaching for the logbook when he heard what he thought was the cab backfiring and silently cursed the vehicle. But then he felt a sharp pain in his shoulder as the cab backfired again... and again. He realized he was being shot and dove for the floor of the cab as his assailant emptied out the clip and ran.

Clark then lifted himself from the floor of the taxi and the pool of blood that was now on the front floor and knew that four of the seven bullets found their target. The cab was still running. Clark began to drive to a hospital six blocks away. The humerus bone in his upper left arm had been shattered but he was able to control the steering wheel with his left hand and his leg. With a finger he plugged one of the bullet holes to stem the flow of the bleeding. As he drove the few blocks he worried that he would black out and lose control of the cab. That could hurt or kill someone else. Finally, he spotted the hospital and followed the signs directing him to the emergency room. He pulled up to a darkened hospital. It had ceased to exist days before due to mergers and HMO's -- another victim. He now raced three miles to another hospital still worrying about the possibility of harming others. He pulled into the emergency room parking lot of the Fairview Riverside Hospital and an officious security guard immediately barked, "You can't park here."

"I've been shot!" Clark screamed at security guard, Fife.

"Where?" security guard Fife asked in a manner/stance suggesting he will apprehend the shooter and/or dive under a car for self-protection.

"Just get a fucking gurney out here before I bleed to death!"

Clark tells of the incidents which follow -- instructing the emergency room personnel on how to treat him, his hospital stay, the police informing him that the unknown assailant surfaces yearly, kills someone and then resumes his usual life selling Flair pens or working as a security guard or living in a cave or.... The police never find the man. He has killed four people before Clark. Clark is the first to survive. This does little to facilitate Clark's healing.

The nightmares that began in the hospital with a police guard outside of his door have continued for years. Mark dreams that his assailant returns. For the first two years after getting out of the hospital he was afraid to leave the house. He would then see the man on the street, at the bar, at the shopping center, at the park, the lakes, at the grocery store, in church or any other place where people gathered.

Just then there is a knock at the inside door of my apartment. All three of us jump at this as I hear the door open. "It's him," I whisper as the door creaks open and I see my brother, Darrin, entering. My back is to the outside door directly across from the inside door by 20-plus feet. "What's up?" he asks, as he approaches and sees the other two people in my apartment. He greets them, realizing vaguely that he has met Clark. "What are you do --" he stops abruptly in mid-word and tilts, pulls back his head, squints and walks slowly toward me.

"Why are you so *pale*?"

"Am I?" I ask and look to the other two men in my apartment. They nod and smile. A much abbreviated version of Clark's shooting is related to Darrin who is, naturally, horrified.

"I forgot what I came down here for," Darrin says at the close.

"I'm not surprised," I say and add, "Why are *you* so pale?"

Pam comes to town and we meet with Clark and his partner. Clark has been working as a personal care attendant since getting fired at as a cab driver. For five years he has worked with elderly clients, persons with disabilities and mainly gay men dying of AIDS.

Pam cannot make it to town during the run of, *"for gimps who have considered homicide when enuf is enuf."* But plenty of people do, including Clark Simeon and his partner Barry. After the show, as has become custom, the members of Open Door Theatre, whatever Shaughnessys are in attendance, volunteer ushers and members of the audience so inclined, travel one block to the bar for bottles of Grain Belt Beer served up in buckets with ice. Several buckets into the revelry, Hope asks, "So, Clark, how do you know Brian?"

The Squeaky Wheel

I know his response before she can even finish the question. I know his response right down to the verbiage, cadence and where he will pause.

"I met Brian when he was having an affair with a married woman from Grand Forks. I would drive her to Minneapolis every weekend so they could have hot and constant sex and continue their illicit affair, much to the horror of her husband." But Clark says it all with less inflection than Steven Wright on his best day. He says it as if he just looked in his wallet and reported he had $23. There is laughter and gasps and wide eyes all around. Burke, the tall, motorcycle riding, personal care attendant who works weekday mornings, will accompany me to Hawaii this fall, recommends clear beer, is a second-rate opportunist and sucks face with his unbathed girlfriend stops and laughs loudest and hardest.

Hope regains her chin, and when the laughter nearly subsides she says, "I can't believe you never told me that, Brian," with an et tu Brute look and tone.

"Yeah, yeah," I croak, my voice dropping several octaves, "that *would* be a story I *would* tell often... but I could never capture it the way Clark has."

"What happened to you?" The giant biker dude asks me on a crowded bus.

"That is an inappropriate question, which I'm not going to answer."

Brian Shaughnessy

Greg As Emissary of Payback

for gimp's who have considered homicide when enuf is enuf has closed after a successful, well-received run. Family, friends, the theater community, a reviewer, the disability community and the curious came, and most were *more* thrilled by the production than I or the other members of the Open Door Theatre. The public came, paid a modest amount by theater standards, were entertained (and instructed), told their friends, came again, complimented the production, asked to be involved in future shows and hired us for future performances. We achieved the nearly impossible by making a small amount of money on the production without grants or subsidies of any kind. We auditioned for and will be performing at the international VSA parts festival in Brussels next year -- sponsored by *Minnesota* VSA.

I am meeting Greg -- the director of Minnesota VSA -- who has asked me to join him to evaluate the downtown theater venues for accessibility. There are three grand, old-style, newly remodeled theater halls in downtown Minneapolis. I meet Greg outside the first theater, exchange greetings and enter to meet the manager for the tour and assessment. The entrance doors are wheelchair friendly, the lobby is fine and one of the ticket windows is accessible, as is the entrance to the house. The manager is very proud of the newly refurbished theater and the work done to make it accessible.

"Let me take you to the stage," the manager says.

The manager shows us the entrances to the stage -- easily negotiable for a wheelchair user from a few directions -- and takes me center stage. Alone on stage, I look about the massive stage and think about the many musicians and plays I have seen here -- from the audience. It feels natural and wonderful to sit down-stage-center and look out at the hundreds of seats (and potential audience members). I belong here. I look up at the balcony and the additional seating and think, I'm home. The manager and Greg grin at my indulgence as I see myself telling Cosby-Wildean stories to a smiling, laughing, applauding audience.

"Can I take you to the dressing room now?" the house manager asks.

The Squeaky Wheel

I sigh heavily. "I guess, but per our contract, the caviar better be fresh, the wine better be old and if there is one purple Skittle in the dressing room, I refuse to go on!"

Greg laughs at this, but the house manager reacts as if he's seen this played out -- for real -- more than once.

The doorway to the first dressing room has the appropriate levered doorknob, as opposed to a round doorknob, and the door pushes open easily. Inside is a *massive* room with many, many mirrors surrounded by many, many lights. There are sinks at a level that I can roll under. A bed, closets, a small kitchen and nearly as much room as my apartment taunts me. The manager apologizes because one of the four sinks is dirty. Greg is checking things off on the checklist, and there are no empty boxes. The manager asks if we have any suggestions or questions.

"I have a question," I say, and he raises his eyebrows. "When can I move in?" The manager is nearly devoid of humor.

We go on to the other two theaters. As I travel to the next one Greg says the manager of the first one asked him about *for gimps*... "So, what was that... a bunch of persons with disabilities complaining on stage?" We laugh. "No, I told him that it was a very professional, very funny and very honest production." I'm flattered.

The two of us review the next two theaters, which are adequate but not nearly as extravagant as the first. There are a few items at each theater that can be fixed or implemented to help patrons with disabilities. The managers of each theater promise to implement the suggestions soon. Greg offers to buy me a beer, and we proceed to a bar that he frequents.

"I just came from a conference for the directors of all of the state VSA's," Greg begins innocently enough. "While I was there I met Ruthless -- the VSA director from Hawaii." The mention of her name makes me queasy. "Anyway, there were about, oh twenty -- no, more -- directors from the different states, and Ruthless was talking about *all* the programs that VSA Hawaii had implemented. She talked about -- well, mainly she talked about national programs that all of the states do -- the Young Playwrights program, a puppet program, visual arts for persons with developmental disabilities, Start with the Arts, whatever -- but she's bragging about all of their programs and then says, 'But we just haven't been able to get a theatre company going for persons with disabilities.'"

My head jerks in Greg's direction, and I open my mouth to protest but see Greg's smile as he sips his beer with one finger raised to let me know there is more to the story. He sets the beer down and continues.

"I said, 'Ruthless, what about Brian Shaughnessy?'"

I am already pleased. Greg continues.

"So, this woman said . . . " (I can tell by the way he says, 'this woman,' that he shares my contempt for her.) ". . . she said, 'Oh, I just don't think he could do it.' I said, 'Ruthless, he has a Masters degree in theater *and a* disability.' Then, as more national directors are gathering around and listening, she said the same thing again, 'I just don't think he could do it.' So, I said, 'Ruthless, he did it for you *once*!'"

I couldn't be any happier.

"She said, 'I know, but we almost *lost* the grant before he got to it.' I said, 'Yes, but he helped *get* the grant before you were even involved and was in the hospital and was limited in the amount of time he could spend out of bed, right? And when he did do the job, you took it away from him!' She said they wanted to give others the opportunity so I said, 'By taking it away from the person who *named* the theatre company *and* came to VSA Hawaii with the idea *and* helped get the grant BEFORE you ever worked there?"

I *thought* I couldn't be any happier. All of these factors had not even occurred to me. I'm ready to kiss Greg.

"So, AGAIN, she started with the, 'I just don't think'... shit and I kind of lost my patience and said, 'Ruthless, I just came from Minneapolis where Brian did what you keep saying, 'I don't think he can do,' and already did for you! He put together a theater company of persons with disabilities -- which he calls Open Door Theatre, by the way -- staged a play that got a HUGE audience, great reviews and support from the community -- with no funding from VSA Minnesota or any other source, made money off it and is planning to do it again next summer in Minneapolis! (Pause) -- after he spends the winter in Hawaii. Now, I want you to tell me AGAIN that you don't think he can do it!"

Finally I realize the hugeness of what Open Door Theatre accomplished. I thank Greg for telling this story.

"Believe me, it was my pleasure."

I signal toward my beer with the straw in it, and we toast. As the glasses clink I say, "Revenge is a dish best served by someone else in the presence of many of her colleagues."

Open Door Theater catches on. We perform in schools, universities, shopping malls, corporate venues and established theatres. People with disabilities express their appreciation. I write and perform the following -- and more.

The Squeaky Wheel

ERNEST: Good evening and welcome to our show. I'm Ernest Guy.
PAT: And I'm Pat Tronizing.
ERNEST: As always this program is sponsored by Paradise Products Hawaiian Style Popcorn -- which includes macadamia nut, coconut, kona coffee, pineapple ...
PAT: Paradise Popcorn is not just a taste treat; it's a tropical vacation.
ERNEST: Aloha to that, Pat. The only problem with this stuff is trying to decide which flavor to eat.
PAT: You can say that again, Ern. There's a luau in every bag. It's hula-icious!
ERNEST: This week's installment is entitled NO MORE STARES/stairs.
PAT: And concerns itself with the issues of the handicapped. The handicapped ...
ERNEST: Excuse me, Pat, but I believe that term has fallen out of favor....
PAT: How's that?
ERNEST: We're no longer using that title to describe... them.
PAT: No more stairs?
ERNEST: No, handicapped.
PAT: Then what's the show about?
ERNEST: The ha- those people whom you just referred to as the handicapped.
PAT: Oh, we can't call them that anymore?
ERNEST: Correct.
PAT: How come?
ERNEST: Because it's politically incorrect.
PAT: It's politically incorrect?
ERNEST: That's correct.
PAT: Oh! Well I... I didn't know that. I just... well, I certainly hope I didn't offend anyone.
ERNEST: I do too, Pat.
PAT: What's wrong with that word?
ERNEST: Handicapped?
PAT: Correct.
ERNEST: Well, you see Pat, the term handicapped was originally coined back in the time when *the poor misfortunates in*

	society were forced to beg for money with their caps in their hands; ergo: HANDICAPPED.
PAT:	Are you sure?
ERNEST:	Sure I'm sure.
PAT:	Sure, sure...
ERNEST:	Look it up.
PAT:	I think I will.
ERNEST:	Feel free.
PAT:	I will.
ERNEST:	I know you will.
PAT:	What? You don't think I will? I will.
ERNEST:	Where are you going?
PAT:	To get a dictionary.
ERNEST:	What for?
PAT:	To look it up -- see, I knew you didn't think I'd look it up.
ERNEST:	I didn't think you would look it up NOW! We're doing a show!
PAT:	About what?
ERNEST:	Ah, wha, ..ah, we... look it up.
PAT:	I will.
ERNEST:	I know you will.
PAT:	What? You don't think I will?
ERNEST:	Look it up!
PAT	I'm looking it up.

-------------------------------- (FADE OUT) --------------------------
-------------------------------- (FADE UP) ---------------------------

PAT:	..... hair raiser, half penny ... (sound of pages turning) hand...handcraft, handcuff,... handicap! From "hand in cap." You were right!
ERNEST:	Told ya.
PAT:	Well, but actually it says it's ... huh? A race or contest in which an advantage is given or a disadvantage is imposed in the form of points, strokes, weight to be carried, or distance from the target or goal. 2) A disadvantage that makes achievement unusually difficult; esp: a physical disability. HANDICAPPED: A physical or mental disability substantially limiting activity; esp: in relation to employment or education...

The Squeaky Wheel

So what do we call them then? Disabled?
ERNEST: Look it up.
(SOUND OF PAGES)
PAT: DISABLED OR DISABILITY?
ERNEST: Well, they'll both be there.
PAT: Right.
(AS PAGES TURN)

---------------------------------- (FADE OUT) ----------------------------
---------------------------------- (FADE UP) ----------------------------

ERNEST: ...I...L...I...T...Y
PAT: Okay, here it is. DISABLE: To make incapable or ineffective...ew!...
ERNEST: That's disability?
PAT: No, that's disable. Disability is...Damn!...
ERNEST: What?
PAT: Inability to pursue an occupation because of physical or mental impairment.
ERNEST: How awful for them.
PAT: The condition of being disabled.
ERNEST: What's disabled?
PAT: Umm...incapacitated by illness, injury or wounds.
ERNEST: Well, that might not be so bad. What was disable again?
PAT (To make) incapable or ineffective; esp: to deprive of physical, moral, or intellectual strength. CRIPPLE syn: see weaken.
PAT: Remember that one?
ERNEST: Weaken?
PAT: Cripple?
ERNEST: Sure.
PAT: That's one you don't hear much anymore.
ERNEST: It's become taboo.
PAT Why?
ERNEST: It's completely unacceptable.
PAT: Because?
ERNEST: Of its negative connotations.
PAT: Which are?
ERNEST: Inherent in the word.
PAT: Which means?

---------------------------- (FADE OUT) --------------------------
---------------------------- (FADE UP) ---------------------------

PAT: Cripple. Being a cripple.
ERNEST: That's it!
PAT: LAME.
ERNEST: I'll say.
PAT: A LAME or partly disabled person (or animal).
ERNEST: Oh, that lame.
PAT: Something flawed or imperfect.
ERNEST: I know what it means. I just thought you said the definition was LAME.
PAT: I did. CREEP.
ERNEST: Creep?
PAT: Yeah, creep.
ERNEST: What's that supposed to mean?
(QUICK PAGE TURN)
PAT: Annoyingly unpleasant.
ERNEST: Huh?
PAT: An irritating or obnoxious person.
ERNEST: I hear ya.
PAT: Producing a nervous, shivery apprehension or horror.
ERNEST: All right, knock it off.
PAT: Huh?
ERNEST: I won't stand for that.
PAT: What?
ERNEST: Name-calling.
PAT: Who's calling you names?
ERNEST: You got a mouse in my pocket?
PAT: What are you smoking?

---------------------------- (FADE OUT) --------------------------
---------------------------- (FADE UP) ---------------------------

ERNEST: Did you or did you not just call me a creep?
PAT: I did not; I was reading from the dictionary.
ERNEST: Creep? Why would you be looking up creep?
PAT: (page turn) From cripple ... derived from CREEP. Remember?
ERNEST: Huh? Oh...no, I don't.
Pat: Turn up your hearing aid.
ERNEST: You never... Let me see that.. CRIPPLE... LAME... OK. Derived from Creopan: CREEP.

The Squeaky Wheel

PAT: All right?
ERNEST: I think they mean the verb.
PAT: The what?
ERNEST: (pages turn) Listen. CREEP. VERB. To move slowly on hands and knees ....
PAT: Yeah...
ERNEST: ... To go timidly or cautiously...
PAT: ... uh huh...
ERNEST: ... To enter or advance gradually so as to be almost unnoticed...
PAT: .... I gotcha, I gotcha...
ERNEST: Well... ?
PAT: What?
ERNEST: Am I right or not?
PAT: You're probably right.
ERNEST: Probably?
PAT: Maybe so...
ERNEST: Maybe so? Come on, I don't really think it's...um... an unpleasant or obnoxious... ah... who produces a nervous or shivery sen...
PAT: .... Well, some of them can make ya kinda, ya know, sort of ...what?...uncomfortable, sometimes...
ERNEST: Oh, for crying out loud, stop it! Why can't you just once admit that I'm right?
PAT: Why do you always have to be right?
ERNEST: I don't always have...
PAT: ... I think you're fixated, if ya ask me....
ERNEST: .... Fixated? Now I'm ...
PAT: You really ought to have it looked into...
ERNEST: Fixated.
PAT: Ernie.
ERNEST: I've told you not to call me Ernie. (pause) Haven't I?

------------------------------ (FADE OUT) --------------------------
------------------------------ (FADE UP) --------------------------

Disadvantaged...
Physically limited...
or mentally...
Incapable....

Brian Shaughnessy

Impairment...
Impaired, incapacitated....
Feeble...
What's feeble mean...
I'm sitting next to it...
All right now...
Infirm...
Invalid...
Shut-in, shut-in, that's a good one...
Physically challenged...
Bedridden...
Sickly...
Handicappable...
Special...
Differently abled...
Confined to a wheelchair...
Helpless...
Gimp...
Abnormal...
Ill...
Sick, sickly, sickish...

Pat: So, what do we call them...?
(Music Up)
Ernest: Oh, we're out of time. Thanks for tuning in. I'm Ernest Guy...
Pat: and I'm Pat Tronizing. See you next time...
(Music Fades)
--------------------------------- (OUT) ---------------------------------

This scene I write for Hope. I write others for Joehn and Karl.

New P.S.A.

SCENE: Woman in wheelchair in leather jacket, sunglasses, looking seedy and dozing. Her head jerks; she wakes and addresses the audience.

The Squeaky Wheel

'Bout time you people showed up. What chu think, jus cuz I can't walk I ain't got THINGS to do? Wake up! Look, anyway, here's the scene. (HEAVY SIGH.) I wanna thank you for your time and listenin' to my crippled ass and all that trash -- now let's cut through the bull. I need some money!

See, see, I know what you're thinking and it ain't like that. See we . . . *(Points around, realizes she's alone and gives dismissal gesture.)* okay, I am collecting for (Pause) . . . oh man, what we called again? *(Starts checking pockets.)* I got it here somewhere. Hey, I knew it before, but you had to get your walkin' around self here late! What's the excuse? Wanted to *jog* an extra mile or some lame story like that. *(Wipes nose on sleeve and finds card in pocket.)* All right, here it is. (Reads.) I am seeking donations for the "Make 'em Stand Foundation." *(Takes out cigarette.)* See, that's a bunch of scientists in white coats hookin' up computers and jumper cables or injecting raisins or whatever into people like me's spinal cord to get our butts up and workin' at a 7-11 or the cleaners or some damn place. Now I know you *fine* people don't want to see my rear stuck in this till I die. I know you mens want me up so you can get a look at my booty. Some of you sisters, too. Hey, that's cool. Whatever.

What was I saying? *(Sees card in hand.)* Oh yeah. Send donations to me, Sally, at Box 655 Mpls. MN 55408. You might as well send cash 'cause a cripple with a check is a bother. I gotta get on the sorry bus, go to the *sorrier* bank, have 'em ask me if I got an account --. Just send cash, and if you got to send a check, make it out to me and I'll get it to the dudes with the lab coats. *(Pause.)* I see how you lookin' at me. You think I would try to scam you? Now you sound like my worker. You know how little junk I can buy with a disability check? You think I'd rip off my brothers and sisters in wheelchairs? Man, be for real. I ain't like that. You can trust me. So send whatever you can cause I am tired of pushing this thing around, and you're tired of seeing me in it. Be cool. Oh, oh - and buy some of that funky popcorn, too 'cause I - we get a piece of that. Thanks.

TOP TEN REASONS FOR BEING DISABLED
10. Pharmaceuticals.
9. All the rubber gloves you could ever need.
8. Crotch-sniffing guide dogs.
7. Free government cheese.

6. Condescending looks from attractive members of the opposite sex.
5. Needles, needles, needles.
4. Incredibly long-winded gimp stories from temporarily able-bodied strangers.
3. No irritating daytime job.
2. Parking privileges.
1. Big fat disability checks.

Abhorring winter, I return to Hawaii with Burke who makes Tyrell look conscientious and respectful. He takes my van incessantly until I take the keys from him. One day when I call him to pick me up he says, "I don't have any keys." I direct him to the first hiding place where I have left his set of keys. He cackles when he picks me up then says, "You're going to have to find another hiding place now." Second rate opportunist. His moron friend Beavis is quickly followed by his unbathed girlfriend Stardust who eats my food and wears my clothes until I throw them out. Mercifully, Darrin arrives and will remain lest these losers try to gain access again.

I believe that my company will welcome me in the spring. I write grants for the company and get them. Our ASL interpreter, Gwen, is pushing to get us in more venues and amazingly lands us an evening at the prestigious Tyrone Guthrie Theatre -- the premier preparatory theatre company outside of New York and inside of Minneapolis. Production plans are made for the spring.

But suddenly I'm receiving communications from Gwen regarding, "my continuing involvement with Open Door Theatre." I receive press communications that do not even mention the existence of another member let alone an absentee artistic director.

Darrin and I stare holes into each other.

"Are these filthy little animals trying to rip off your theatre company, brother?" Darrin asks.

A blast of breath explodes from me. "It wouldn't be the first time!"

Joehn is totally noncommittal as to her own role in this coup d'etat but Hope tells me that their performances suck, that Gwen is a megalomaniac (she uses the word correctly) who smells of fecies and that I will be welcomed back with open arms. I have my doubts and make sure that I will be allowed to perform David Mamet's *The Frog Prince* on the Guthrie stage if I do nothing else.

The Squeaky Wheel

I receive more ultimatums from Gwen but have a commitment on *The Frog Prince*. Darrin will direct me. We must return in March to rehearse in time for the Guthrie show. I contact David Mamet's agent who informs me that Mr. Mamet wants our company to be allowed to perform the play without having to pay royalties.

"Can I thank Mr. Mamet personally?" I ask, never wanting to miss an opportunity.

Darrin has always joked that Gwen may not actually be using American Sign Language but is making it up. We arrive back in Minneapolis on the day Open Door Theatre has a show at the University of Minnesota. We watch the play and Gwen is a fixture down stage center. The cover of the program announces, "Featuring Gwen Stinkslikeshit." At intermission we hear a woman complaining that the interpreter stinks -- not literally.

"How did you think the show went tonight?" Darrin and I ask the actors afterwards.

Karl thinks its okay. Hope is embarrassed by it and Joehn thinks it sucks. Gwen and some flunky she has spouting her politics think the show is great and are surprised by Joehn and Hope. They are even more surprised when Karl changes his opinion. (One does not need the Vulcan mindmeld to change Karl's opinion -- the wind will do.) If one is going to strike the king they must kill the king and now Gwen is without power. Darrin and I write, rehearse and pound away until performance day. One of our friends with whom I played Einstein to his Johnny in *Arsenic and Old Lace* is a technical director at a theater and a recent amputee. He is an official member of Open Door Theatre and helps us get competent, professional, free artists and technicians for this major show. He plays the serving man to my Frog Prince.

One day I am talking to friends uptown at Hennepin and Lake and I see a girl and think she looks like Lisa from New Mexico. I look again and I think she *really* looks like Lisa from New Mexico. When I look a third time and she is staring at me I say, "Lisa?" It is the girl from *Sarah's Last Waltz*. She plays the milkmaid in the Frog Prince. Darrin has her stroke my flippers.

It turns out Gwen does do a terrible job at interpreting -- the deaf hate her. But the Guthrie show is a huge hit and family, friends and community, as well as the Guthrie Theatre, sing our praises.

Darrin pulls his arms inside of his T-shirt and stands at the microphone. "Hello, I'm Darrin Shaughnessy and I'm with Open Door

Theatre," he says as he twists and flails the empty sleeves. Hope is looking horrified and doubled over laughing at the same time. "We're not looking for a handout... just a hand."
    O'er topped again.

    Open Door Theatre -- sans Gwen -- travels to the International Arts Festival in Brussels and wows them. My wheelchair is destroyed by Northwest Airlines. I must use a European behemoth manual chair and Bobblehead Brad (so named because he constantly nods while talking or listening) is my attendant. He pushes me around Brussels and then on to Amsterdam. We arrive in Amsterdam and after checking into the hotel we go in search of coffee shops.
    "Now remember where the car is, because I won't," I say. I will be sampling the fabled wares of the Amsterdam coffee shops and Bobblehead will not because he chooses to believe the dogma of the Kingdom Hall. I like the wares and it is very cold (compared to Honolulu) in Amsterdam. I make an altered exit as Bobblehead pushes me, I believe, in the direction of the car. After 15 minutes I am asking, "Are you lost?" and assured that my helmsman is not. After 30 minutes I seek further assurances. After thirty-five I see a statue we passed earlier but after thirty-eight we find our car. Just before boarding the plane back to Minneapolis I ingest hashish. I giddily watch icebergs bounce about the sea over Greenland.

    Dawn is graduating from high school. Daniel has returned from England and no longer finds his family unfit. The Shaughnessy's travel to Kingman Arizona to watch our sister receive her diploma. She looks great in her square hat and short legs.
    I send a letter to Northwestern Airlines outlining the damages to my wheelchair on my vacation/business trip to Brussels and demand $3600 and another trip to Europe. They offer me $800.
    "See you in court."
    Through my new friends at the Guthrie I am put in contact with local columnist Jim Klobuchar who writes three articles outlining the injustices of air travel to me specifically and wheelchair users as a group. The first article basically says you wouldn't expect a pansy artistic director of some invalid theatre company to be a squeaky wheel -- but here he is. On the eve of the court hearing the brainless corporate lackeys finally offer me everything I have asked for. They have not just endured humiliation from the newspaper but also utilized their own in-house attorneys' time and

The Squeaky Wheel

paid outside counsel. Morons. My father's wife assists in lawyering the deal. I get the $3800 and a voucher to go to Europe. Darrin wants me to go to "Fancyland."

"What happened to you?" From a drunk at a bar.
"Have you ever been sodomized? DON'T ... answer that question. But your question is equally inappropriate to the one I asked ... unless you buy me a beer."

Lifts!

I return to Hawaii and for the first time they do not lose my batteries. This is merely because I now have gel batteries which do not require special packaging and handling. (I'll take a win any way I can!) Bobblehead Brad has accompanied me -- having tasted travel on his European sojourn.

Buses have lifts. I left the frozen tundra of Minnesota for the palm trees and cool breeze of Hawaii, but the charm of the tropics cannot measure up to the thrill of being back on public transportation. I have become expert at a bus ride. More than a decade of waiting and waiting for paratransit and being locked out of city buses have made a bus ride an ecstasy -- usually.

My friend Dave asks how I pay my fare.
"The bus is free for persons with disabilities."
He nods knowingly and says, "Membership has its privileges."
I want to kill him.
I ride. I press the special signal for wheelchair users, which dings twice instead of once, and the driver goes right past my stop.
"Driver, that was my stop."
He seems indifferent.
"You usually get off at Dole."
"Yes, I know," I say. "Today I needed to get off there."
"You can get off at the next stop and roll back, yeah? I see you rolling all over town."
"Yes," I say, "I *can* roll back from the next stop."
By now I am almost to the next stop. It is a freeway overpass.

"Yeah, yeah." He snickers, seemingly enjoying this power trip. "You're one of the good ones."

I am already pissed. I ponder the possible implications of that statement. One of the good... cripples?... Caucasians? I should have challenged him on the statement, but if I challenged every statement made -- obviously or seemingly inappropriate -- I would have little time for other endeavors.

By now he is releasing me from the safety straps, and the lift is up. I roll onto the lift. I am a few feet above the safety railing, keeping pedestrians from dropping 50 feet into a stream of cars traveling 50-plus miles per hour. The view is disturbing. I am lowered to a narrow sidewalk -- certainly not Americans with Disabilities Act compliant -- exit the lift and shake my head over the incident and the narrow sidewalk. It's been four years since the Americans With Disabilities Act was passed, and four years since city sidewalks *should* have been wide enough for me to travel without the fear of dumping myself into the street. I head slowly in the direction of my destination. On my left, the terror of the freeway. On my right, the horror of a very high curb.

Curbs are frightening for a person in an electric wheelchair. I have experienced firsthand an electric wheelchair develop its own personality and go in a direction and at a rate of speed undesired by the occupant. I have watched Rochele -- at the mercy of one of these assistive devices -- go plummeting off a curb and spill into the street while I sat by unable to render help. Paralyzed. Later, she foolishly plummeted off another curb in her wheelchair. I have seen the bruises, black eyes and broken bones of other quadriplegics who have experienced this... what? Stripping away of something they dared to actually think they had control over in their lives and the subsequent punishments for it? And I have heard many similar stories from those who lived it. Curbs are frightening.

I get to the corner to discover no curb cut. I giggle, shake my head, cautiously turn around so as not to dump myself into this street as previously described, and proceed toward the other corner, trying to keep my eyes fixed at the concrete directly in front of my feet. If I look right, I see the terror of the freeway and if I look left, the horror of the curb. But, as stated, it is a narrow sidewalk and my peripherals take in both unpleasant options. I reach the other end and -- tell me you didn't see this one coming -- no curb cut.

I shriek. I laugh. I wonder what the hell to do about this situation. I look about for a volunteer to enlist. It had better be a big one because this is a high curb and between me and the wheelchair 300+ pounds are

The Squeaky Wheel

involved in easing both down the curb. Cars whizz past, but not even a skinny third grader shows up to help resolve this dilemma. I begin the sojourn back to the other corner -- ever watchful for someone to assist. I pray I only *imagined* a curb and in actuality there is a perfectly graded curb cut to ease me into the street and to the other side, like the chicken, but alas -- across the street -- you guessed it -- a curb cut taunts me from the mountain I am on.

The irony of this situation is not wasted. Here is a man *confined* to a wheelchair (let me apologize right here to my militant wheelchair user friends for this terminology, but given the present situation, it applies); the wheelchair and its user are *confined* to a concrete "island" with terror to the left and horror to the right on an *actual* island with no one to lend assistance. It is -- *seemingly* -- an allegory for my present life. Stuck. Stuck. Stuck. Going back and forth like a proverbial duck in the shooting gallery between the various inept, uninformed, insensitive bureaucracies and individuals I encounter in daily life!

There is no rhyme nor reason to the present situation. There is no justice. It makes no sense. But there I am. Now deal with it.

But wait. Do I really see what I think I see, or is this just my mind replacing the imaginary curb cut I want so desperately to see with an alternative mirage? A squad car? And the officer is looking with an expression that says, what's the problem? Just wait for the next time someone says there is never a cop around.

This *is* an allegory for my life. The problem is resolved. I dealt with it. I identified the problem. Stuck. I checked to see if I had the resources to deal with it. Can I get out of this wheelchair, off this curb or off this island? Nope. What are my options? Enlist a volunteer. I found an organization -- the police -- whose job is to protect and serve. The officer stops the car, gets out and asks me what she can do to help. I explain the procedure of getting down the curb. She groans under the strain. I am free -- sort of. At least not stuck on that scary overpass. Now I can get on with what I am doing.

I could have sat on the sidewalk on the overpass in the wheelchair and cried. Certainly, there was a time I would have. Nobody would blame me for it. I could have stayed home. For sixteen years. Watching videos. I could have killed myself long ago. But I didn't. I try to allow some credit for that -- and maybe even some of the other accomplishments in my full and difficult life -- instead of dismissing it as some dinky "thing" everybody has to do everyday.

Brian Shaughnessy

Bongo

I roll to my usual restaurant on campus. I spy David seated at an outside table with his back to me. As I approach David I see the person seated and talking with him is someone I met at this place years ago. He is thin, Caucasian, mid-'20s and wears the same mustache and haircut he did when last we met. I was slightly intoxicated, and he was drunk and being very friendly and only mildly annoying. He told me at the time that he was going into the Peace Corps. I saw him one more time.

I recognize him. He sees and recognizes me. He speaks first as our eyes lock.

"Hey, Dude. How's it going?" He does not wait for a response. "You remember me?" he asks, quivering slightly with a break in his voice characteristic of a busted schoolboy.

David has turned, and we exchange eyebrow waves. "Yes! You're the scumbag who was hitting on my girlfriend behind my back at the Third World concert." David erupts with laughter. He knows me to be the same dog as 98% of the penised population on this planet. I turn to David. "He a friend of yours?" David nods through his laughter. He knows I will seize this opportunity to pull the wings off this fly.

"Oh, I guess you do remember," he says, dejected and embarrassed.

I scoff. "Yeah, that's one people tend to remember."

The poor bastard is so shaken at the reminder of hitting on a guy in a wheelchair's girlfriend that he has turned pale and struggles for something to say.

"So... how are you doing?" he asks, lost.

"Fine, motherfucker -- how you doin'?" I ask, wide-eyed, open-mouthed and with a lack of sincerity mirrored only by the moon's lack of atmosphere.

"I'm married now!" he says, as a naive and futile prayer that this will make me stop. The prayer goes unanswered.

"Cool! Introduce me to your wife."

David is doubled over with tears running down his face. I know the poor, unsuspecting Peace Corps volunteer has suffered enough, and

The Squeaky Wheel

David will explain to him my caustic nature, fondness for and ability to verbally pounce on a weak member of the herd... *or* the alpha male.

"I gotta get a beverage and go to class," I announce to the relief of the prey. David is still laughing. "I'll talk to you later." I reach for the joystick on the wheelchair and shoot my prey one last glance. "Take it easy, man," I say emptily as I begin to roll toward the door. I know I shouldn't but... "You open the door for me?"

Bongo -- as I later find out is a handle the fellow goes by -- clumsily rises and opens the door 15 feet away. As I go past him I repeat what I say to everyone who opens the door for me. "Thank you."

I continue to apply for grants and write material for my theatre company. One day, I am in the KOKUA office and I see my friend Kevin waiting patiently, as always, for someone to walk him to his next class. Kevin is blind. I know he has been trying to get into law school for some time. Suddenly, a strange sense of clarity and purpose embraces me.

"Kevin, are you in law school?" I ask.

Kevin grins ear to ear. "Yes, I am," he responds.

The epiphany is complete.

Advocate for persons with disabilities;

Middle class income;

Freedom from poverty and dependence;

Expert status in dealing with the bureaucrats who torment me and my brothers and sisters in disability;

I go upstairs and get the application to take the Law School Entrance Exam.

The *Ia Wahine*, my mermaid play, comes in third in the Diamondhead Theater Playwriting Competition. Sadly, they only perform the first and second place plays.

"If you cut out 98 percent of the fish puns you would have won," Oscar, the individual in charge of the competition, tells me. "Do that and resubmit next year."

Done.

Brian Shaughnessy

Don Knotts vs. Mohammed Ali

My mother sends her annual treats for Christmas. This is always looked forward to by whomever I live with, as well as myself. This year she has sent lemon bars (my favorite), Christmas cookies, chocolate chip and miraculous white chocolate, milk chocolate and peanut butter fudge that she has added to her motherly repertoire. Bobblehead Brad and I indulge in several and place them in the refrigerator. Another day goes by, and we indulge further, when it occurs to me to share the treats with my neighbors, Sharon and Kimo. I ask Bobblehead Brad to place the parcel in my lap as I am going next door to share the treats. The shocked looked on his face suggests I just removed a kidney... from him.

"Really?" he says, as if I just told him I am giving them my own kidney. I laugh.

"Yes, really."

"Oh," he says, with a look that says I am taking his paycheck, violating our relationship, making fun of his mom and breaking his heart. The fudge *is* good. He slowly opens the refrigerator and removes the parcel. He looks down on it with a look usually reserved for one's own offspring. Slowly, he moves and delicately places it in my lap. "You're sure?" he asks, pleading with me not to do this insane act. I assure him of my sureness and try to mask my amusement.

"That's really generous," he says in a manner that says, 'That's overly generous, you fucking moron. Leave them here! Please, please please!'

"I know," I respond, as I exit through the doorway and two doors down. "Tis the season." Bobblehead Brad is a Jehovah's Witness, so the season is void to him.

I look through my neighbors' doorway and see my neighbors and their two daughters. "Knock, knock," I say and make an offering of the holiday treats. I extol the virtues of the baked goods as the box is opened and distributed. The parents sample them and emphatically agree, as the young girls gnaw at their treats with dancing eyes.

Sharon looks with amazement at the fudge that is being gobbled. Another neighbor enters and samples -- soon she is making sounds usually heard only during coitus. The young girls have come close to me, and their heart-warming brown eyes volley from the box to my eyes solicitously. Their mother shoos them away as Kimo's co-worker arrives to give him a ride to work. The treats are offered to her and -- although *everything* has been sampled and raved about -- she reaches for the three-toned fudge. She thanks me profusely and turns it over examining and admiring this gift as she raises it to her mouth. Now everyone is making orgasmic sounds.

"Better than sex," the visitor says, seeking agreement.

My brow immediately frowns as I ponder this statement. "No," I say after serious consideration. "But I've been getting a lot of chocolate lately."

My mermaid play has been selected to be performed at Diamondhead Theater in a "staged reading." This means that we will rehearse and rewrite for four weeks and perform the show with scripts in hand if necessary. Darrin comes to Hawaii to direct and assist on the rewrites.

As we begin revisions Darrin offers what becomes the play's title -- *Jimmy's Tail* (the tail being the mermaid). In the play, Hurricane Iniki has just ravaged Kauai. Jimmy -- an out of work disc jockey -- feels bad because his house is left standing and because he can't keep a girlfriend. He fishes with his buddy who departs and Jimmy lands Momi -- a mermaid. But mermaids are immortal and -- although capable of love -- soulless creatures. And therein lies conflict. Jimmy's ex (a beautiful but hopelessly insecure sylph) is now dating Jimmy's criminal half-brother.

Soon, Momi does not want to leave and therefore must spend nights in the bathtub. We get Brian's Hawaiian mythology version of mermaids and I keep my fingers crossed that no Polynesian wants to kill me for it. I make sure by constantly checking with the Hawaiian studies professor and fellow quadriplegics as well as the KOKUA expert on Hawaiiana, Ilima. Manning, one of the KOKUA staff who supports me totally and drinks beer with me frequently, assists me in implementing and training the speech recognition software and creating commands that will allow me to write in the proper form infinitely more easily than with a stick in my mouth.

I cast Manning and Ilima in the play. Ilima has never acted before nor has Ikaika, my neighbor, who begs Darrin to use him in the play. My good friend Richard plays Jimmy and Alexandra is the perfect, sensuous, beautiful and funny fish woman. She even sews her own tail.

We rehearse nightly and all but one cast member (there's always one) work until they sweat blood. Darrin and I are again working late into the night, printing revisions the next day and torturing Bobblehead Brad with Darrin smoking in my room. He was warned.

My KOKUA family attends as do many of my theater family members. The play is reviewed and Ikaika and Ilima are singled out for their outstanding performances in small roles. The reviewer raves about Alexandra and her steamy sexuality and (accurately) describes Richard as a "cipher."

At the close of the play all characters are relieved that the tuna cans contain tuna and not Momi.

At the cast party everyone is given a can of tuna with a bow on it.

I now begin submitting *Jimmy's Tail* to myriad potential producers and again it becomes the pilot movie for a seven-year series (a variation on *I Dream of Jeannie*) on the Parallel Universe Network (PUN). I forget to send a copy to David Mamet's agent.

The Squeaky Wheel

Part III -- LAW AND DISORDER

The Squeaky Wheel

I'm in.

I have delayed telling my father about law school for fear he will try to talk me out of it. I was sure he would say, "Brian, do not complicate your life with that much work! Stick with your plays and your theatre."

I am surprised; he thinks it is a great idea. "I would never discourage any of my kids from doing anything they wanted to do," he says with the obvious unspoken tag of... unless it was stupid.

My mother is concerned. She worries that it will be too hard on my body. She worries about what I might become. She makes me promise not to practice criminal law. I tell her I don't want those people in my office.

My father tells me myths of law school. In the first year, they scare you to death; in the second year they work you to death; and in the third year, they bore you to death. Having dealt with unimaginable fear, work and tedium, I scoff at this oft-repeated myth. Later, I discover this myth is true.

But What Lovely Decorations

I return to Minneapolis. The airline loses my footrests since losing the batteries is now too difficult. My ankle looks like shit -- again. I call the doctor's office and give the report. I tell the answering machine, "Hi, this is Brian. Well, the wound on my right ankle looks bigger, angrier and possibly infected. Let me know if you want me to come in or do something different. Okay. Thanks."

A few minutes later my phone rings and it's Shannon -- the nurse from the big, sweaty, (but very, very nice) genius doctor's office. She tells me she's on her way. This is at least the fifth time she has come to my home. She might have been required to come once or twice, but she *keeps* coming (beyond job responsibility or compensation), either because she is that caring, compassionate and determined to see I heal this damn thing, or because I have affected her (by who I am) enough to raise the bar on her caring, compassion and determination level, or maybe because she wants me or some combination thereof.

Shannon arrives and shouts a greeting from outside the entrance to the stairs and lift. She is wearing a nursing uniform and is without her two enormous dogs. I greet her and thank her for coming. I hear the unavoidable sound of wood-to-wood friction as she pushes the door to the steps open. She deftly descends the stairs and ducks to avoid the unforgiving angle iron of the lift. She enters bowing -- as she must to avoid banging her head on the lift. She is clearly pleased to see me and displeased by the circumstances.

"What's going on?" she asks, sounding concerned.

"Have a look for yourself," I answer, motioning in the direction of the boot on my right foot.

Shannon has a look about the apartment and spies the stool she has used before when assessing and treating my ankles. She retrieves it and carries it over to where I sit. The stool keeps her heinie a foot off the floor. I recline my wheelchair, thus raising my foot another foot from the floor. Shannon removes the strap holding my foot to the footrest of the wheelchair. She then removes my foot from the footrest and swings the footrest out of her way, placing my foot in her lap -- squarely against her pudenda. She removes the boot and returns my foot to its previous (coveted) position and removes the dressing, revealing a round, raw, bloody wound the size of a half dollar. She peers at the wound while she strokes my leg.

"Yes, it looks angry, but it's not bigger or infected... but it's no smaller." She looks up at me with her hands intermeshed, resting on my leg with my heel increasingly pressed against her love shack. "You need to be concerned about that. You need to be concerned about that because..." Her hand moves up to my knee and down to my foot. "How long have you had this? -- two -- four years? One day, you will go see a VASCULAR SURGEON, and because vascular surgeons perform SURGERY -- and because it will be reality -- that doctor is going to say, 'You're not walking on these feet. You're never going to walk on these feet. They're just decorations. They're giving you too much trouble so we're going to take them,' and then they will take them.

"So... you can do the time and get them healed up now, or you can wait for a vascular surgeon to tell you what I just told you. I just wanted you to hear it from me, so you can either avoid that eventuality or be ready for it. Okay?" She says this as she slaps me on the thigh and begins covering the offending area and replacing the boot.

I am grateful for Shannon's honesty, yet I am terrified by it.

But I nail her anyway.

The Squeaky Wheel

"Brian Shaughnessy, this is Beverly Hatfield. I'm the associate dean of the William S. Richardson school of law. Please call me."

I return the call and again get her voice mail. "I know you're calling because you don't have the grade for the class I was enrolled in last fall," I begin. "My grandma ate it, aliens took it, I forgot, and my dog died."

"I was calling," Dean Hatfield begins, "and now I know the answer, to see if you needed a microphone in class."

I tell her I will need an accessible desk and I would like to be in the front. She asks if I am excited, prepared and scared to go to law school. I tell her that I'm not frightened. There is a long pause.

"Well, I'm glad that you are excited and prepared for law school... but you should be a little scared,"

My father and his wife assure me I will be scared and the prudent thing is to be scared already. I laugh.

"Call me in four weeks and let's see if you're laughing," by father says.

Arriving for William S. Richardson School of Law orientation, I see fellow aspiring lawyers walk through the front door. I am directed to the back door of the classroom -- to the CP entrance (crippled people). The associate dean introduces herself. The seventy-five students begin introductions. After twenty-five of them I discover that these people are funny. After fifty it strikes me they are hilarious. I must go last. My infinite ego dictates I have to top them all as my mind races.

The microphone is placed in my face. "Hello, I'm John Grisham, and I'm here to write a book." Laughter. "And after hearing those seventy-four introductions, I think I have enough material, so goodbye." More laughter. I give a quick bio and conclude with: "I acquired a disability ten years ago, and in that time I have experienced discrimination, degradation and indifference from individuals, businesses and government. Now I'm going to get even."

We adjourn to groups of fifteen where over the course of the week we meet and prepare for a mock legislative hearing wherein myself and one of my classmates (as well as two individuals each from the other four groups) will be allowed to argue the merits of and then the necessity of gambling in Hawaii.

Brian Shaughnessy

One of the presenters/students regales us with the scholastic and recreational benefits of HIS legal fraternity (as opposed to the other McCoy legal fraternity). He is as funny as and similar in build to a Hawaiian John Belushi. He comes into our group of 15.

"How many times *have* you seen *Animal House*," I ask him.

"Not enough," he says with the look of the alpha funnyman who has bested an opponent but invites him to spar again. He talks about the diversity of the school population in regards to previous occupations. "We have teachers, policemen, laborers, accountants -- and a guy who was a DEA agent who is the coolist guy in the world."

"Could you point out the DEA agent to me," I ask to a stony silence. When I later repeat this to Stacy and a friend both erupt with laughter.

Each year, twelve are admitted and given four years to complete law school instead of three. In addition, these twelve individuals are provided with tutors to assist them in studying for finals. Depending on your perspective, these twelve are either the ones who have been deemed most needed in the legal community or the future special education lawyers who need this extra assistance to be in the legal community. I choose the former view. These twelve belong to minority groups underrepresented in the Hawaii bar. That includes me. My classmates in this group are Hawaiian and/or Filipino.

In the mock legislature, my classmates present well after four other law students are filleted while they flail about foolishly and see lawyers and politicians bombard them with accusatory questions regardless of their position on gambling. I stop them in their tracks. My classmates are smitten.

"You slayed them," one classmate states incredulously. "And they killed just about everybody else." I know I am in the right place.

I talk with one of my classmates in the library. She is concerned (jokingly) that her six-year-old son enjoys putting on her clothes too much. I tell her that my nephew once slipped on the stairs in his mother's high heels and never dabbled in cross-dressing again. I tell her she needs negative reinforcement to deter him.

I purchase my legal textbooks and the volumes of study aids without which law school would be impossible. I have the spines cut from the books and the new beauteous Asian angels at KOKUA punch holes in the loose pages and place them in binders for me. This way I need only take the week's pages from each text and, more importantly, I can hold these few pages in the bookstand which rests over my chest while I am in

The Squeaky Wheel

bed. Each night I read my assignment, my notes from the day and the study guides. I have note takers who are second and third year law students -- they know what to pay attention to and what to ignore.

The regular instructor for the sessions for the twelve chosen has taken the semester off to be treated for cancer. Julie was a notoriously maternal teacher and the "mother" of the twelve. She has been replaced by a dictator with a sense of humor. This is fortunate as we are a rowdy bunch and I am often the lead behavior problem.

On a particularly insolent day Julie's replacement, Mark, barks, "Are they adjusting your medication? Let me give the doctor some advice -- MORE!"

On another day when the other ten (there are only eleven chosen this year) are being particularly "lively" during a tutor led study section, Brenda (my classmate with the worrisome son and closest friend in law school) observes, "the natives are restless today," to which I fall forward with laughter. "You're laughing because we are all brown," she observes. I acknowledge her statement and the fact that I am the white guy, but as I tell them, "I'll stack my marginalized status up against any of you. Besides, my soul is brown."

Christopher Reeve has broken his neck. "Nobody wants him to get up more than I do," the other redheaded quadriplegic in the universe, Keoki, tells me. "Except me," I finish. This, however, does not stop me from donning a Superman costume on Halloween to go to the law school party. Bobblehead Brad snickers as he puts a blue T-shirt with a red and yellow "S" on the chest on me and ties the cape around my neck.

"Smart law students are going to get the reference, aren't they?" I ask, uncertain.

Bobblehead nods, as he does so well. "This is better than last year's costume," he says, reminding me that last year there was no World Series. I suited up in my Twins Kirby Puckett Jersey and hung a sign around my neck that said, "WILL BUNT FOR FOOD OR MONEY."

But when I turn the corner to enter the courtyard of the law school I see one of the eleven chosen in a child's Superman costume. The faculty members present understand my costume, but my classmates do not. When I explain it to them they are initially horrified and then laugh hysterically (while wincing) and then go get beer.

In Contracts class (taught by Beverly Hatfield) we discuss the significance of a seal on the contract. This always elicits a seal's bark from myself which causes some classmates to laugh and others to tense even more. One day in the same class, Beverly (as she insists on being called) asks a student, "If I come to you and ask you to sign this birthday card for Dean Grant and tell you it's his birthday --which it is by the way--"

"Did he get the pony I sent him?" I ask to the delight of some and the horror of others.

When I later ask Dean Grant if he received this equine gift his eyes widen and he responds, "Pony? No, I didn't receive a pony, although in the course of any given day I receive a lot of pony byproducts."

But the rigors of law school and the rigors of quadriplegia are not the only rigors in my life NOW. Helen has never returned a single item of mine that was in her house at the time of my banishment and steadfastly declines to do so despite occasional conjugal maintenance visits. In the days and years since my liberation/eviction she has borrowed two CDs which were never returned. When she asks to borrow a third I tell her "No," because she is a bad risk. She dares to take umbrage although she has volumes of my childhood pictures, Pam's love letters (taken from my apartment without my permission), tapes of my productions, various "gifts" she had given to me (her favorite act was to take gifts back) along with my own personal items left behind.

"You're no fucking better than Proletarian Peggy," has no effect on this woman. It is the last shred of control she holds and she will never let go even if it means stealing from the quadriplegic boyfriend she once loved -- or thought she loved in some twisted, protracted, parasitic, psychological way. I think she planned all along only to steal my stuff and throw me out. Not really. But this is pathetic and the stuff of soap operas.

The royal scam has been in effect from 1986 through 1995. In that time I have maintained my Minnesota domicile and the accompanying medical assistance benefits. That's all over. Leslie from New Mexico, who acted in *The Frog Prince*, is my first tenant to really fuck up to the system. The letters from the state medical assistance office say, "DO NOT FORWARD," in very big letters with no indication of subtext. Leslie forwards them anyway rather than stick them in the envelope and let my father pay the postage as he has done since 1986. Minnesota discovers that I have a vehicle in Hawaii, I pay resident tuition, and I receive non duplicative services from them. The show's over.

The Squeaky Wheel

Luckily, I thought, my eight years on the waiting list to receive Hawaii Medicaid and be allowed to live independently had ended and I was placed on the Hawaii program that will pay Bobblehead and others to tend to my needs.

"We terminated you from the program when you went to Minnesota last summer," a vicious Japanese woman from the program informs me. I ask to speak to her supervisor who is even more vicious. "I want to tell you with all the aloha I can muster," she begins, "to go back to Minnesota or move to Michigan where the services are better." I explain that I have been in Hawaii since 1987 and I am in law school and have no intention of returning to the mainland. She tells me to make my own arrangements then. Click. It smells like racism, but being a white guy, I am unfamiliar with the stench. I am removed from federally mandated entitlement programs by the State of Hawaii, without notice or opportunity to respond.

I try to negotiate with these lemmings. I try to get legal aid to assist me. I contact the local Hawaii Disability Rights Center and am turned down for assistance in this matter. The law school has no idea what to do. I finish my second final examination of law school and go to Queen's Hospital where I am admitted for tests my doctor has ordered. He offers to release me the next day. I explain that I have no services and therefore cannot be discharged. He is slightly miffed at the prospect that he has been played but refuses to discharge me to the streets. The social workers are not so kind. I am forced to engage in a "civil disability strike" and armed with my new knowledge of the law, I spend eighteen days in a hospital, over Christmas break, refusing to comply with the illegal demands of small-minded, malicious, bureaucrats.

"Isn't your father a lawyer? Don't you have five brothers and sisters who could help you pay for your care?" two soulless Caucasian women bark from the foot of my bed.

"I'm 36 years old and I'm not asking my family for money."

"We have discharged people to the street," the elder bitch says to her understudy.

"Is that a threat?"

"I wasn't talking to you," she says snidely.

"O. K., but we both know it was said for my benefit."

They depart and another hospital stay is underway. Diagnosis: red tape. I call lawyers, politicians, the media, government agencies and the governor. Finally the director of the agency that cut me off without notice or opportunity calls to inform me I will be placed back on the program. Beverly Hatfield was a social worker before she became a lawyer and is horrified, so tries to figure out how to help me -- other instructors and my KOKUA family exhibit similar responses.

"So have the representatives stop calling, have the law professors stop calling, have the lawyers and politicians stop calling," she attempts to demand.

"They will stop calling when I am back in my apartment."

Bobblehead has discovered the Internet. He is a Jehovah's Witness and has discovered Jehovah's Witnesses chat rooms. He has found a love interest on the Internet. He flies her to Hawaii. They are married the next day. He has tendered his resignation and Joseph returns for the third time as my aid in my second semester of law school. Bobblehead is off to live in his new wife's big trailer. The Hawaii program will send someone in the AM and PM to get me out of bed in the morning and return me to bed in the evening. They will also send vicious supervisors to attempt to taunt me. I receive a B- in my Contracts class and friends and tutors are shocked when I receive a D in civil procedure. Any lower grade would have meant probation.

So I spend Christmas in the hospital and the next semester I am inundated with an endless parade of nurses aides who call themselves nurses but can't wash their hands. They are late. They don't show up. The supervising nurse visits one day and I listen to classical music on public radio. Another day she returns and Prince shouts expletives. "I can't believe I'm in the same house."

"I'm eclectic."

My friend Dave enters the house one day and announces, "You need a microwave." The next day I have one. Dave is a washing machine cowboy. He drives around in his truck and finds old washers, dryers, microwaves and housewares that have blown a fuse and been set outside to be toted away. He fixes them and resells them. He enters this day and my 500 CD player is playing the same two seconds of one of the 5000 songs endlessly.

"You're in hell!" he exclaims.

"You're only figuring that out now? That, that, is nothing."

He nods pained agreement.

The Squeaky Wheel

Getting supplies from the antichrists at the agency is futile and degrading. One of my aides tells me I need to utilize my acting classes and act crippled and pathetic. I refuse.

"What the fuck am I in law school for if I do that?"

Finally and exasperatedly the agency calls me one night to tell me yet another aide will be arriving in the morning at 7 AM.

"What is this person's name?"

"Demitrius Jones."

Joseph stands next to the bed as I speak on the speakerphone. He sees me shake my head.

"Have Demitrius call me."

Demitrius Jones calls me and assures me he will be at my home at 7 AM.

"Do you imagine that Demitrius Jones is... black?" I ask Joseph.

He doesn't know. He doesn't know from the conversation or from the voice he just heard on the phone.

"Of course he's black. Which means he'll never be on time."

At 7:25 AM Joseph is beginning my routine; Demitrius is not present. Five minutes later the phone rings and we buzz him in from downstairs.

"I'm sorry," the tall muscular black man informs me.

But he comes regularly -- tardily but regularly. We become fast friends. We share the same appreciation for Prince. He asks how I know so much about black folk.

"You been sneaking into the meetings. The revolution will not be televised."

He opens a container of my vitamins and looks away disgustedly.

"Hell, know," he retorts, "they just put cotton in these things to fuck with black people. Always trying to make black people take cotton."

"Heard it. Hurry up. And please be on time tomorrow."

"I'm a black man in Hawaii. I got two strikes against me. I'll never be on time."

"I had this discussion with Joseph two days ago."

"See, you're black. You say, 'shit yeah,' just like my Dad, who is black."

"Yes, I'm an octoroon," I say testing.

"What is that?"

"1/8 black. My grandmother's blacker than you."

"Now it makes sense! Really?"

"No. I am whiter than bleached snow. But my soul is brown."

Joseph has no concept of bleach. Apparently on laundry day he takes the clothing, grabs the bottle of bleach, places it on top of the clothing and goes to the laundry room. Items begin to return with negative Rorschach ink blocks.

"You're no longer allowed to use bleach," I tell him.

I tell my brother Patrick of my near probation.

"Take gingko balboa every day and I guarantee your grades will go up."

I take it and my grades do go up. They continue to go up every semester. I return to Minnesota for the summer and Northwest Airlines loses my footrests. I will use the voucher I received for the last European debacle to travel to Italy with Pam this summer.

Clarence from Jamaica, who worked for me last summer, agrees to accompany us to Italy as my aid. Fancyland is booked. He calls me "Boss" and often says, "You should be rich, Boss." He comes two hours late and is drunk.

"I'm sorry I'm so late, Boss," he says reeking.

"No, you're not or you wouldn't have blown me off to get drunk," I point out.

After Clarence announces that he won't be going to Italy, (he would have been a bigger liability than asset), the agency, unsurprisingly, finds someone immediately.

Darrin and Shelli are getting married. Actually, they have already eloped some months ago and are doing the sanctioned version in the church. They make preparations. I am in bed and they visit as my mother calls on the phone. Shelli speaks to her.

"Dawn has picked out your wedding gown," my mom tells Shelli who wonders if she is serious for half a second. Both are laughing.

"It will probably be red," my mother says.

"Well, Mickaylee will like that because that's Chinese style," Shelli states.

"Why would Mickaylee like that?" I ask unenlightened.

Darrin rolls his eyes. "She likes everything Chinese -- not just Chinese, anything Asian.

"Oh," I say flatly and pause. "She's like me, huh?"

The Squeaky Wheel

The wedding is festive and the reception, as so many parties have been, is in the backyard of Xerxes and the adjoining parks. Parks Siding Park -- better known to me and mine as Brian's Park.

Days later we are off to Italy. We arrive in Amsterdam and my aid, Raul, says, "My goal is to see one Filipino here." He is one of six Filipinos in Minnesota. He does not meet his goal. We travel to Milan where we discover my wheelchair is in the reclined mode. We discover that there are many Filipinos here. It's like little Manila. We travel to the hotel where an illness keeps me bedridden. We discover that Italy is closed in August and nobody bothered to tell us -- although I was dealing with a travel agent for travelers with disabilities -- and we cannot get the chair repaired.

My father and his wife offer to fight on but I surrender to the indignities of Northwest Airlines. "They win," I tell them sadly. "I got no more fight for this one." They understand.

I return to Hawaii for my second year of law school. Something is broken on the wheelchair and I am delayed returning home. Upon arrival Joseph unbandages my ankle that has been open and wounded now for years. It looks as if the leg was put through a meat slicer and a three-inch circle was cut from my ankle. It's ugly.

"Whatever you're doing isn't working," my doctor informs me. I spend the first week of my second year of law school in the hospital. The next week I am a week behind in law school and stressing. When I see the doctor again he insists that I return to the hospital for another week. After that week I am three weeks behind in law school.

Being so far behind, I have an anxiety attack that would kill a rhino on angel dust. I leave law school and go home because I cannot function. I call Demitrius Rebound to put me to bed. I am planning that I will go to North Dakota and banish myself to live with the shame of failing law school. Demitrius laughs.

"You do more than six people do in a day. You got to go to the hospital. Then you'll finish law school." We're talking about sharing an apartment.

At the end of the fourth week my doctor demands that I enter the hospital for at least five weeks. I am devastated but accept my sentence. Five weeks. That night I drink to excess and see a movie. The movie sucks and I turn myself in to the hospital authorities. I am stripped of clothing, weighed (I am back up to 140 pounds). The nurses cannot get an IV into me and a resident tries. He later tells me he stuck himself with the needle; I assure him I am not HIV-positive.

My reading stand and various home items are brought and I flirt with nurses. I must take a primary physician. One of the social workers is showing a catalog of potential doctors. "Dr. Bradley sings," the woman informs me.

"Bring me the singing doc," I instruct her. When I meet Dr. Bradley it turns out we know mutual people in the theater community and he often performs in musicals.

Mostly I'm in bed. Occasionally I am allowed to sit in the wheelchair. None of the bathrooms are accessible, so the bean-counters are terrified by the prospect of a quadriplegic law student. The word is to give me what I ask for. I ask for transfers into the tub to be scrubbed down by young, brown nurses.

Classmates and friends visit. My friend Dave and I have beer and dinner across the street. My nurse comes in to tell me I can't be there... drinking beer. Patrick O'Brien is fascinated with the idea that I have smoked dope in the hospital before. He dares to try. Since even cigarette smoking is no longer allowed in the hospital we decide to cross to Thomas Square Park. It is drizzling and I suggest we go to the bathroom. As we cross the Park, I say, "This is a gay hangout, you know."

"Really?" he asks.

We enter the bathroom door and the spacious wheelchair accessible stall, close the door and on the floor is a copy of HUGE magazine.

"Really."

"Before you were injured, did you have a girlfriend?" Michelle, the Filipina poem with graceful fingers and the classic nose of her people asks in broken English and with the subtext of, you can't get one now.

I scoff. "Before, during and after. I snap back at her. "Hell, if you weren't married, I would make you mine." Later, when a Hawaiian born nurses aid asks I am disappointed. But I get along well with nurses, although one morning when one of them is changing the bandages she screams at me while I sleep.

"Brian, stop moving your leg."

"I don't control that!" I shout. "It's called paralysis. Those are spasms."

The Squeaky Wheel

"If you concentrate you can make it stop," she insists.

"Fuck you, you don't know what you're talking about. I do. I have experienced it for 12 years. You don't get it."

The other nurses and aides spoil me. There is a Chinese girl, Amy, who spends increasing time in my room on her infrequent days working. On Halloween she dresses me and braids my long red hair. We exit my hospital room and she introduces me to a nurse from another floor. There is equipment in the way and Amy strokes my tied hair unknowingly as she speaks to the other nurse. Electrical charges radiate from the back of my head throughout my body like never before. She confides a painful experience in a foreign land.

"Why am I talking to you this way?" she asks puzzled, somewhat frightened and with the innocence and magic of a child but the pain of an adult.

She and others bring me bags of salts. "All chips and snack food are just vehicles for my salts," I tell nurses.

I ask to call Amy and she agrees. I will not see her for several days and then I will at long last be allowed to leave. The ankle looks more like an ankle.

Brian Shaughnessy

You're Going To Put That Where?

Five weeks have almost expired. Hints of my release are beginning to solidify into talk of my going home, although the official date has not been set. Dr. Bradley makes his regular visit to my bedside. "Because of the anemia I want you to have a colonoscopy and endoscopy or upper and lower G I -- as we discussed."

This utterance transports me back to just after my surgery when Dr. Liar entered the room and said the same three words. Immediately muscles tense, my neck-hairs stand on end and a chill runs from my coccyx to my hair follicles. The doctor does not see this and continues, "It's not a pleasant procedure, but I feel it is a necessary one. If my father had had it done he might still be with us today. I've had it done, and they found a small tumor, which they were able to excise immediately. I would like to find out if there's some internal bleeding or other irregularities that may be causing the anemia. In the procedure they take twelve feet of flexible tubing with a camera attached to the end and go in through your anus and up into the intestines to have a look around." He is grinning. "If everything is okay, they'll go down your throat twelve feet and check it from that end."

"I hope they rinse that thing first!" I blurt out. The doctor guffaws his usual loud laugh and assures me that the tubing and camera will be rinsed.

I ask if there is an option or alternative to this procedure.

"Nothing short of surgery," the doctor tells me.

I ponder this and say, "Given a choice between being prodded and surgery... I'm mooing."

The singing doctor doubles over onto the bed. He regains himself. "This is set up for tomorrow morning, and if Dr. Chang and Yamamoto give the green light you should be able to go home the next day."

"Great!" Let's make sure they do." He nods and bids aloha.

Later that night I am studying tort law. The book is held in place on the reading stand with clamps, brackets and elastic to keep the pages of

The Squeaky Wheel

the book open. The reading stand is attached to the over-the-bed hospital table with bungee cords, and the hospital table is positioned at the right height and distance from my face to allow me to turn the pages with my mouthstick. I must be delicate in turning the pages and tucking them under the elastic, or I will have to hold the stick in my mouth and against the page as I read each word. A nurse I have not met before enters the room.

"Hi, I'm Bev. I'll be your nurse tonight. You didn't have dinner, right?"

"Right."

"You're going down for a colonoscopy tomorrow morning. You're supposed to -- " she says, as she slings and slams a gallon jug on the corner of my hospital table, " -- drink this." I look at the bottle and the label. It is familiar.

"Go-Litely?! That's seawater!"

The nurse laughs a not-at-you-but-with-you laugh. "I know. It's awful stuff. The doctors should have to drink it. I know there are easier ways to clean you out -- and they wind up giving you enemas and everything else anyway."

"So, you've had the pleasure?" I ask, already bonding with this person.

"Oh, yes."

"Then you know that nobody would drink this stuff willingly?"

"And they shouldn't have to, but you know I have to come in here every twenty minutes and push this shit on you, and I know you're going to give it your best shot."

"Has any patient you've had ever drunk all four liters?"

She hesitates. "I'll tell you that when you're done. Deal?"

"Deal."

She begins to open the cask of amontillado. "Let's see how much you can drink right now." She looks about the room for one of the hospital's feeble, plastic, eight-ounce cups.

"Okay," I agree. "Why don't we use that purple container by the sink. I'll bet it holds a quart."

She sees the container, nods, and returns to the gallon from hell. She opens it and I listen to the gurgling sound as the heinous beverage defiles my beverage container. I can smell the ocean already.

"Here we go," she says, as she brings the container and the long plastic straw to my lips. I begin to drink. I taste salt. I taste what strikes me again as dead, decaying fish. As I drink, my eyebrows move down, my cheeks move up, the corners of my mouth move down, my eyes narrow and I shake my head. "God! Just like I remember it."

Beverly laughs again. "I'll be right back." She exits the room and is right back carrying a clipboard. This is the release for the procedure tomorrow." I can tell she is wondering how I will sign it. "Why don't you just sign it?"

I laugh loudly -- with her, not at her. "See all these books piled around here?" She looks about the room and sees boxes of books, stacks of notebooks and three books in front of me. "These are all law books. And they all say, 'never, never, never *just* sign anything.'" She grins sheepishly but becomes defensive. "How are you going to read this? I can't stand here and hold it for you -- I don't have time."

I let out a small laugh. "Well, let's see. I need something that will hold a paper in front of me... hmmm -- " I see her looking about the room. "What can we use?" I stop moving my head and look straightforward. "Oh, look! Check out this thing in front of me!" She looks at it and picks up my sarcasm and mutters "all right, all right," as I continue. "I'll bet you could clip that paper to this thing and then I could read it! Hooray! The crisis is passed!"

She grins, but looks out of the corner of her eye at me. "Funny, I heard good things about you in report. Nobody told me you were a smart-ass," she adds as she leaves the room. "Hit the call light when you want me to turn the page."

I read the lengthy release form. I have seen many of these, but now I see it for the first time as a student of law. It strikes me how much more complete this document is than the first one I read. As I read, Bev returns. "See this section here?" I say, as I point with my mouthstick to one paragraph. "I don't like it. Can we cross that out?" She laughs and shakes her head. "Here's the one I'm really concerned about, though. See here," I say, pointing and speaking with the stick in my mouth. "See here where it says that they can use the video for educational or other purposes?" She nods. "Does this mean that someday I could be watching the surgery channel..." she grins knowing where this is heading, "... and say, 'Hey, I know that asshole!'" It was more than she expected, and she crumples. "I guess so," she says struggling. "Sign the damn thing!"

"Yup."

"And how is that done?"

"Oh, I need you to open that black bag attached to the armrest of that wheelchair in the corner of the room."

The Squeaky Wheel

She looks about and walks directly to the bag and brings it back to the bed. She places it next to the gallon jug she has been force-feeding me and raises her eyebrows as if to ask 'what next?'

"I need you to unzip the bag," I say, "and take out the gray rubber-stamp in there." She rummages through the bag and removes the stamp. Again, she raises her eyebrows. The phone rings. "Hang on," I say, as I bite the mouthstick and press the button on the speakerphone to answer.

"Hello, Brian, my darling," comes a known -- but unrecognized -- accented voice.

I am totally caught off-guard. I instruct Bev to hand me the handset, which she does and then departs.

"How are you?" I ask, hoping more words, words, words will reveal who I am talking to.

"I'm fine... I just wanted to call to see how you are doing." It's Amy. I recognize the sweet, soft, almost cartoonish (in a good way) voice. I wonder how this sweet, naive, innocent, unbelievably compassionate Chinese girl ever manifested the boldness to call me. I already know I have not misjudged her.

"I know that you're going for the procedure tomorrow," she says.

"Yes, and they're making me drink a gallon of Go-Litely --"

"Oh, no!" she says, giggling and feeling my pain. "I hate to give that to patients. Everyone hates it!"

"It is awful, salty stuff."

"But I think you like salt," she says mischievously.

"Not in this form!"

"Try to drink as much as you can. I am happy you are getting out soon, and I wanted to wish you good luck in school.... and in life."

I laugh. "You can't get rid of me that easily. I told you I would call you, and I'm a man of my word."

"I would like that. Was someone in the room just now, when I called?" She sounds concerned.

"A nurse I haven't seen before. Her name is Bev."

"Bev?!" she shrieks. "The haole Bev?"

"I guess... blond hair, about my age..."

"Did she know it was me on the phone -- were you on speakerphone?"

"I don't think so. I didn't know it was you. I was on speakerphone at first. Then I had her hand it to me."

"Oh, how embarrassing. I'll talk to you later," she says and quickly hangs up. I can see her blushing at the other end.

Bev re-enters, stamps the consent form and delivers the bag to its previous position.

"They're going to give you some *really* good drugs tomorrow for this procedure," she says, as I ponder the implications of Amy's call. Bev now has my attention. "Really?" I ask, as I wonder what tipped her to the notion that I would want and appreciate this information.

"Oh, yes," she says, nodding, smiling, reliving and staggering the vowels in the two words. "And be sure to ask for more," she says with piercing eyes. I understand.

"Can I get them to give me a doggie bag?"

She laughs and tells me that won't happen and offers more of the vile substance. By now I have drunk more than three liters and am feeling bloated and uncomfortable. I decline and tell her to take it away. She agrees and tells me no one has ever finished all four liters. The rest of the night is peaceful save for the visits by the nurse's aides to clean up the shit the Go-Litely has caused me to expel endlessly.

The next day there are nursing students present on the floor. The head nurse asks if a nursing student can give me the enema. "I hate to do that to the poor girl, but bring her in." Only because this girl has been so friendly over the last five weeks and because she honestly *wants* to (sick yeah?) give me the enema, I agree. When her instructor and the head nurse are out of the room, I tell her she doesn't have to and I *know* she doesn't want to. She disagrees. I tell her I can tell the higher ups 'no' and then she can just take temperatures and give bed baths. She declines my reprieve. The phone rings.

Today, I instruct the student nurse to pick up the handset and place it to my ear. It's Amy. I am flattered and tell her that there is a parade of people who will be coming in and out of the room since it is Student Nurse Day, and I am full of shit still. She understands -- seemingly. The phone rings often as I am repeatedly placed on my side; a hose is stuck in my anus, water pumped in (with much discomfort); and then I am probed by feminine fingers. The student nurse attempts this procedure. Then one of the hospital nurses attempts it. Then the head nurse, then the instructor, then another student, then the whole group attempts it again! The phone rings... and rings... and rings! I am certain I will lose my mind between the discomfort, the smell, the fucking phone and the degradation.

The Squeaky Wheel

This violation/humiliation/discomfort continues. Four women are in the room and a fifth one enters. "They called for him; the transporters are on their way," one nurse remarks. "He's still not clean," says another. "They'll check him again down there," says yet another, this time with finality, and all scurry to clean both me and the room. Just as they finish, the transporters arrive, and the plastic board is placed under me to slide me onto the gurney. I am wheeled out of the room, to the elevator, down five floors, down a hallway and into a room with two nurses, lots of medical equipment and the infamous flexible pipe and camera. I am greeted by one of two female nurses. The non-greeting nurse says to the other, "He needs an enema," as if it is my fault. "Okay," the greeting nurse says with near enthusiasm, "we can do that." The other nurse sneers at me.

The greeting nurse sticks a tube up my ass, forces water into my bowels and catches it in a clear plastic container as it is expelled. She apologizes with each step. The sneering nurse readies the already readied equipment. The smiling nurse holds the water up to the light and examines it. "You're clean!" she says. She looks admiringly at the water and says, "I could drink this."

"Some people would pay to watch that," I say, as the greeting nurse laughs and the sneering nurse sneers.

The gastrointestinal specialist enters, grunts a greeting, puts on gloves, takes the endoscope (twelve feet of pipe with the camera on the end), sits, adjusts the monitor and looks up at the nurses. The greeting nurse briefly explains the procedure to me, and the sneering nurse injects the touted substance into the IV port. I am instantly on board the Enterprise traveling at warp speed. I no longer care what they stick up my ass, or if they rinse it before they stick it down my throat. I keep my head turned away from the monitor and my eyes closed, as visions of psychedelic sugar plumbs dance through my head. After a reasonable amount of time I am reminded of Bev from the night before and a line from Dickens.

"Please, could I have more?"

The sneering nurse looks at me with surprise. "You're still feeling discomfort?" she asks.

"Definitely," I respond quickly.

She responds by pumping another ampule into the port on the IV, and the mother ship has new dilithium crystals, has doubled its speed, and is now blasting beyond the edges of the universe. I sit in the lounge sipping a celestial mai tai and looking out the window. Paisley, Disney,

Brian Shaughnessy

Peter Max, M. C. Escher, Salvador Dali and Dream Works collaborate on the scenery. This continues indefinitely, but as the vibrant hues begin to dim, I open my eyes and request enhancement. The sneering nurse simply shakes her head, and I close my eyes and enjoy the rest of the journey.

Back in the room (not clear on how I got there) I silently thank Bev for her input. Dr. Bradley enters and informs me everything is fine. "They did see something atypical with the esophageal view, but they cut it out and sent it for biopsy. I wouldn't worry, although it does mean we'll need to do this again in six weeks." He grins at me, but the mother ship is still in the landing area and has not yet finished commission.
"You must still be feeling some of the effects of the medication they gave you down there," he says, smiling. "Most people react very strongly to the suggestion of EVER having that procedure done to them again."
"Sorry to disappoint you," I smile.
"No problem, there will be other opportunities. You just keep doing what you're doing so that we can send you home. I'll see you in my office in a couple weeks."
I thank him for his help and friendship, and he does the same as he gushes over me. I, of course, dismiss it as he exits. In my mind I have gone home -- to my food, my bed, my hours, my friends, my furniture, my limitations, my school, my clothes, my books, my life and to the possibility of Amy entering that life.

I return to school and Professor Ippoliti spies me in the back row. Because of my absences I have abandoned the front row this year.
"Brian's here," she says, and my classmates applaud.
"If I got applause for just showing up I wouldn't have left my theater job," I complain.
The annual Ete Bowl is held. This is a game wherein the alumni women (those would be lawyers), pummel the hell out of the women law students. My civil procedure professor buys me a T-shirt and I nearly cry. I find time to call Amy and we have our first picnic/date at Waikiki Beach. One of the nurses from Amy's floor approaches, to my discomfort and Amy's horror.
"Now, everyone on the floor will know of this," she laments. I am relieved that it was not arranged. A bird shits on my head in a classic first date moment. By Christmas break we are spending much time together. My grades continue to go up. Amy gives gifts to Joseph and Demitrius for

The Squeaky Wheel

Christmas and I manage to send many, many T-shirts with Hawaiian themes to family members.

The next semester I use my classmates as note takers. Darline (one of the eleven chosen) takes meticulous notes and draws Hawaiiana drawings in the margins with her palate of pastel pens. Kevin and I share similar classes and I now am paid by the KOKUA program (where more than half of my studying takes place) to read my homework into a tape recorder for Kevin's benefit. It is truly wondrous.

The enormous, tattooed and mohawked Polynesian man asks me, "What happened?" I look directly at him, terrified, and tell him that I am not going to answer that question.

"What's wrong with you?" another asks.

"I don't know. What's wrong with you -- besides being rude?"

I learn the mental gymnastics of law and my grades improve, although I am tremendously overworked. But the support of my peers, friends, family and faculty is overwhelming. I forget what the beach looks like, smells like and feels like. Many, many hours are spent on my back turning pages with a mouthstick. I learn what a tort is.

The first day of law school we were told to be ready for lawyer bashing. It is Easter and I have been invited to a brunch/picnic at Kaimana Beach Park (just to remind me). Stacey and the Kahns have orchestrated this. Stacey introduces me to a middle-aged and an elderly woman. "Brian is in law school."

"There're too many lawyers. All these people go into law school thinking they're going to make a fortune," the elderly one begins.

"Yup," the middle-aged woman choruses, "and then all their money goes to malpractice insurance."

"And the poor doctors are being driven out of their practices because they're afraid of being sued and because their malpractice insurance is so high!" The old one concludes.

I was caught off guard and I feel tennis ball battered.

"What type of law are you going to practice, Brian?" the old bat asks.

"I'm gonna sue doctors," I say in my best oafish voice as Stacey tries to grin and apologize.

Amy would like to visit me in Minneapolis. I agree. I travel from Hawaii to the land of my birth but the complications of having a disability and the indignity of Medicare and Medicaid have left me without the crucial coverage for nurses aide services in Minneapolis. Minnesota points a finger to Hawaii and Hawaii holds up a mirror. I cannot get an agency to send a nurse. I enter the hospital. I try to force their hand again as Amy is arriving in days. One night I hear my brother Patrick coming down the hall to my hospital room. He sings and talks to nurses.

It is about 11 PM. "Did you hear about the Tyson fight?" He asks. I tell him that I haven't but that I'm very tired.
"I'll go if you want but you will hear about it. You should watch the tape now."
I watch Mike Tyson bite a piece of ear off of Evander Holyfield.
Somehow I am liberated and Amy spends only one night with me at the hospital and we are discharged late, late the next day. The beneficent hospital personnel offer to let me spend another night but, unsurprisingly, I crave freedom. We travel by bus on a cold night and we roll through the dark around Lake Calhoun, shivering, to get to my apartment. That night, many blankets are piled on me as I have not yet acclimated to the Minnesota cold. After three weeks we will travel back to Hawaii together. While she visits Minneapolis, Hong Kong, her birthplace, returns jurisdiction and ownership to the Communist Chinese from the imperialist British. It was out of the uncertainty of this day that caused Amy to relocate to Hawaii only a few years ago.

The Squeaky Wheel

Feral Children and Adults

One of our regularly occurring summer picnic barbecues is held to acknowledge my imminent return to Hawaii. Mike and Annie (former Across-the-hall Mike and Annie) and their children, three other couples with their children, Darrin and Shelli and Pat and his three children have gathered with Amy and me in the backyard for summer foods and brief forays into Park Siding Park for diversion. As more beer is consumed, the men exhaust the supplies of various types of food by pitching it up into the air to be caught in the mouth of another man several feet away. As the evening begins, grapes are lobbed about. When the grapes are exhausted, cantaloupe pieces volley back and forth in badminton arches. By the time darkness descends the men have begun hurling hamburgers and hotdogs with considerably less arch than cantaloupe pieces flew. These are ENTIRE hotdogs and burger patties -- not broken pieces.

As one of the Mikes catches a Wendy's size burger with a slight turn of the head, amidst the cheers and applause of many men, Darrin calmly asks, "So, Amy, do you do this in Hong Kong at your picnics?"

Amy looks slightly puzzled but mostly amused by this question, and soon she is following Mickaylee and the other four girls into Park Siding Park for an after-dark adventure. As I talk with these friends I don't see often enough, one of the wives invites me to be a member of *their* group -- instead of the men's group -- The Spider Bitches. Flattered as I am, I decline. Just then I see Amy come back from Park Siding Park... alone. She stays away from the adult crowd, and the girls remain in Park Siding Park. She shakes her head when I call her to come over or ask her what's wrong. Pat beckons to his triad of children that they must get into the van. It is time to leave and soon they are gone.

I manage to squeeze out of Amy that one of the children asked, "Why don't you speak English?" Mickaylee responded that Amy *is* speaking English, and not to be mean. Too late. I know which little girl made this comment without being told. Amy is pouting until the girls come over and make her the new leader of their group. Amy is such a child herself that she quickly accepts her responsibilities and leads the girls around the building with a flashlight and more skill than any Piper from Hamlin.

We return to Hawaii but are delayed while Continental Airline contacts the local wheelchair repair company to remedy the latest damage to my chair. I begin studying constitutional law this semester. We are up to freedom of speech and the definition of pornography -- without any artistic value and appeals solely to the prurient interest. The Professor is on the left side of the room asking various class members the definition of prurient. Several students do not know. I turn to the woman classmate next to me and say, "Makes your naughty parts all tingly and engorged." I turn back toward the Professor and more classmates unable to define prurient, then back to the woman next to me who has tears of laughter coming down her face.

"Professor," I begin uncharacteristically from the far side of the room as the scholar recovers from his surprise and turns toward me with a raised eyebrow. "I believe we have a working definition over here, don't we, Tracey?" She shakes her head, still laughing.

I repeat my definition to laughter and approval.

Mr. Cheat

I receive my monthly newsletter from the Office on Persons with Disabilities. As I look through the "want ads" I see an advertisement for a modified minivan. The price is $16,000 -- not an outrageous price for such a vehicle. New modified minivans at the time cost as much as $35,000. I call the number listed in the ad to inquire further.

"Good evening," the saccharine voice at the other end answers, and I immediately remember this individual. He is another wheelchair user I met at an exposition of products for persons with disabilities. Amy and I attended, and when I got to this man's booth (he sells medical supplies, as well as renting and selling adaptive minivans), I was immediately put off by him. I am not usually a jealous person (and jealousy is probably not the emotion I was feeling), but this man (twenty years older than Amy) grasps my girlfriend's arm, says hello to her, and begins speaking with her, seemingly very deliberately ignoring me and touching her way too much. (The emotions I am feeling are both repugnance and pity.)

The Squeaky Wheel

At her first available opportunity Amy introduces me to this cretin. I see her make the effort a couple times, while this man paws her. I search for an opportunity to assist -- while gritting my teeth -- and am about to rudely tell the moron to desist when Amy is finally able to make the entrée. I make no effort to hide my contempt. Nor does he. A brief perfunctory exchange ensues between us and we exit.

"I will never do business with that letch," I announce.

"Mr. Cheat..." I explain, "I saw your ad and am interested in the van." He goes on to tell me of the tender loving care that he has administered to this *rental* van. I know that it does not matter how much tender loving care the mechanics (which Mr. Cheat is not) administered to the rental vehicle, because those who pay money to drive the vehicle treat it with indifference at best. Outright abuse is the norm.

I arrange for a time when he will come by to show me the vehicle and allow me to ride in it. I remind him we met at the products exposition, and my soon-to-be wife is a nurse he knows. He remembers my soon-to-be wife but, unsurprisingly, does not remember me.

At this time I am not *just* in law school, but I'm also making preparations for my upcoming nuptials. When the proverbial question was popped (there is some argument between myself and my betrothed as to when and how this occurred) and the details discussed, Amy asked "when" I want the ceremony to occur. I suggest it occur after the bar exam, at which point the two of us could beat a hasty retreat and go on a honeymoon and relax from the ordeal of law school, bar exam preparation and planning of the wedding. My ever-practical Chinese fiancée points out that my entire family will meet in Oahu in May for my graduation. Her fiscal acumen points out that having the wedding in May would save Minnesota residents the trouble and expense of returning.

I sigh a heavy sigh and say, "Okay, but if we get married in May, I am asking you to give me the time and the place, because I won't be able to help at all." I say this knowing that the rigors of the final semester of law school, as well as making arrangements for accommodations to take the bar exam *and* arrangements to get the materials for the bar preparation courses in a form I can use, will be a huge time demand.

"All right," my lovely and intelligent betrothed says, and we laugh out loud. We know this will never happen. I will be making phone calls, decisions, picking out invitations etc., both with and without her.

I call an agency that rents houses for nuptials and other celebrations. Amy and I arrange to meet with the woman, Barbara, who shows us a portfolio of the various venues available. She shows us lovely palatial homes and one that is not too pretty but has a huge yard on the beach. We attended a perfect wedding there not so very long ago. The two of us reduce the portfolio to four potential pieces of property and set a date to look at them. I again point out my time and travel limitations and ask Amy if I can have two of my female classmates go with her instead of myself to view these properties. She agrees, as do they.

But if Robert Burns tells us the best laid plans of mice and men often go astray, I'm telling you my plans really don't have an ants chance at an aardvark dance. My classmates ask to reschedule. Time is slipping away and the dates of graduation and marriage are no longer creeping -- they are hurtling. There really is no time to reschedule. Amy is going through the not uncommon "pre-wedding hysteria," which is fueled by heartrending outside pressures. Someone from her Chinese Christian Church has called and scolded Amy for 45 minutes because she is marrying, "a non-Christian." She challenges and offends Amy. This same girl's mother calls Amy's mother and scolds her for the same reasons. "I would say congratulations but I can't because you have failed your daughter," the intermeddler closes the phone call and hangs up. This woman's son – and one of my classmates -- is asked by the pastor what he knows of Brian Shaughnessy. He allegedly tells the Pastor, "I think Brian Shaughnessy looks down on Chinese."

"Only Andrew," is my comment when I am over the shock of hearing this story. Amy is ready to call it off and elope. She asks if there is some way that I can go and see the houses with her.

I remember Mr. Cheat. I remember that not only is selling a van part of his business, but also so is renting that van. I call him to inquire as to whether I might rent it for a day. Before I can get to that question I must listen to him as he tells me what a good person he is, and how he is in service to persons with disabilities, as he has been a wheelchair user for forty-plus years. Finally the self-serving sermon ends, and I am permitted to make my query. I explain that Amy and I are looking at houses to rent for the wedding. I tell him I have no van at this time. I tell him I would like to rent the van for a day so I can view the houses with her.

"Well, listen Brian, why don't you call me that day, in the morning, and I'll come over. Then Amy can drive me home and drop me off, and the two of you can go look at the houses. This way you won't have to pay me to rent the vehicle. Would that be ok? Would that help you?"

The Squeaky Wheel

I gush profusely and tell him that this would be ideal, and would certainly be most HELPFUL. I wonder if perhaps I may have misjudged this man, or if this could be just one of his sales tactics.

"I have to do it, Brian. I have to help people." There is something painfully insincere in all of this.

I review the plan with him one more time. I explain to him that I am to meet the woman showing us the houses at noon. I am to meet her at a shopping center approximately thirty minutes from my apartment. Therefore Mr. Cheat needs to be at my apartment around 10:30 in order for Amy to return him home and get back to pick me up so that we can proceed to the shopping center.

"Yeah, yeah, yeah -- I'll be there. It's what I do," he responds.

The day of the appointment arrives. I place a call to Mr. Cheat shortly after 9 a.m.

"I'm in the van now, Brian. I need to stop by the office and then go over to the airport post office. After that I will come over to your apartment," he informs me matter of factly. I remind him that I have an appointment, but he dismisses my concern.

10:30 comes and goes. 11:00 comes and goes. I leave messages with Sharon, the woman who will show us the house, telling her that we will be late. It is 11:30 and neither Mr. Cheat nor the van is in sight. I call Sharon to tell her that we must cancel. This is now the fifth call I have left on her voice mail. Five minutes later my soon-to-be wife rushes back into the apartment to tell me that he has arrived. I call the agent one more time and inform her that we are on our way.

"So, how do you like the van, Brian?" he asks cheerily. His left eye twitches like a lying whore.

I, however, am not so cheery. "I don't know, yet. Right now I'm wondering how Amy is to get you home and then back here so that we can be at Aina Haina in 20 minutes," I say through clenched teeth.

The man looks puzzled and perhaps miffed. "I didn't know you were *using* the van," he says almost under his breath. His left eye twitches like a guilty felon.

I am shocked. I think back to our conversation when I asked to *rent* the van. I wonder how I could have made it clearer, and wonder if there was something lacking in my communication that misled him.

"I told you when we talked that I wanted to RENT the van! I told you we had an appointment at 12:00 to look at houses for our *wedding*. You are the one that offered to let us *use* the van, even though I offered you money. Am I mistaken?" I seethe.

Consciously ignoring my question he blurts out, "I'll take you to Aina Haina. That's no problem."

There is a quick discussion about my taking a bus home from Aina Haina and Amy continuing on to look at the two pieces of property not in that area. This was the plan we hatched while waiting for this salesman to show up with the vehicle. We realize I could have taken the bus to begin with. We get into the van and are on the freeway and pointed in the direction of Aina Haina. Mr. Cheat extols the virtues of the van and attempts a conversation with Amy. He fails on both counts.

We reach the first turn to the Aina Haina shopping center, and our driver blows right past it. Amy is signaling me that he should have turned. I nod and interrupt Mr. Cheat -- who has been prattling on about the virtues of the van and himself since departure -- to inform him that he missed it."

"Missed what?" he asks.

"Aina Haina Shopping Center," I respond.

"No I didn't!" He says indignantly.

I look at my soon-to-be wife, who is looking puzzled and adamantly shaking her head. She points out the shopping center on our left.

"Where?" he asks, as he looks around.

"It's behind you on the left. If you turn here we can go in the back way."

He turns and looks. "That's not Aina Haina Shopping Center."

I am beginning to wonder if I have a brain disorder.

"That's Niu Valley," he says with finality.

I am wondering, but Amy is shaking her head violently. Her mouth has curled downward into a frown.

I see the grocery store where we are to meet the agent.

"Ok, but I believe this is the place where we are to meet her. If we're wrong, I'll deal with it."

"All right, but that's not Aina Haina Shopping Center," he says (with more than a grain of arrogance). I direct him to circle the block and let us out in the massive parking lot.

As Amy helps me out of the van she whispers that I can ask someone if this is Aina Haina Shopping Center, although she is certain it is. Once out of the van, Amy walks toward the grocery store. I thank Mr. Cheat and, although I doubt it is my doing, I apologize for the confusion.

The Squeaky Wheel

"Do you *really* want to buy the van?" he asks.

My immediate reaction is rage. The implication of this statement is that I somehow scammed him into giving me a ride. I quickly calm myself, let out a puff of air, and say, "Yes, I'm still interested in purchasing the van."

"Then should I tell the other people who want it that it's sold?" Another puff of air comes from me. I am certain there are no other people interested in the van, and that this is just another of his typical salesman's ploys.

"If you have people interested in the van who are ready to turn over the money, then you should sell it to them. I still need to look into financing, tax credit, etc., before I can commit to this."

"Ok, because I *really* want you to have the van. I told other people more, but I can let you have it for $18,000."

Now I am certain I have a brain disorder. Given the circumstances of the morning, I plan to have a CAT scan. I gaze down at the blacktop, and my feet, thinking that the advertisement was *asking* $16,000.

I join Amy who is walking toward the grocery store. It is now 10 minutes after noon, which means the agent, if she has arrived yet, is waiting for us. I ask a clerk if indeed this is Aina Haina Shopping Center. It is. I am immediately reassured that it is not me who has the mental defect. I announce to Amy, "I know I have said it before, but I will never do business with that feeble excuse for a man."

The agent arrives. She is Japanese, thin, middle-aged, attractive and cheery. She has a young Caucasian male with her who is also looking at property for his wedding.

"Did you check your voice mail on your cell phone?"

"No," she responds with a puzzled and concerned look.

"Not to worry," I say. "You have about five messages from me that range from informative to panic stricken. Some guy was torturing Amy and me."

Barbara now looks even more concerned. I shake my head and say, "Just some smarmy salesman telling us "white" when we're looking at black. You can delete all five messages because the point is moot now that we're here!"

I roll across the street and view the grounds where my friends were married some months ago. There is a large green lawn and a rickety house with a lovely wood lanai that function perfectly as a stage for the reception. The view of the ocean is magnificent. The sea is turquoise blue with white waves, and off to the left is the Kokohead Volcano. We can use the house for dressing, heating up the food and for the two bathrooms. This is fine, as we anticipate the guests remaining outside in the hope of a perfect day.

From here we travel to an unmemorable and unacceptable house. One last stop in the neighborhood brings us to a large ornate house. The door opens, and we are greeted by the landlord. She is a large, blonde woman with too much makeup, and a giant poodle wearing a pink Rhinestone collar. This breed of dog is perhaps my least favorite creature on the planet with the possible exception of a cockroach.

The house is as massive and gaudy as are the landlord and her dog. The yard has a beautiful view of Diamondhead crater, but there is no way to get 100 human beings back there comfortably. And, we are not allowed to have food or drink in the house! This strikes me as an absurd limitation given the purpose for which the house is being offered. The four of us exit.

Amy will continue with the others to look at other potential properties. Amy, Barbara and I agree that, for our purposes, the same yard in which Josh and Julie were married will be best. I take a bus home, and when Amy returns she announces that the other locales were unacceptable. I fume, again, about Mr. Cheat, and she listens quietly. I am amazed at how nonjudgmental and truly Christian this woman is.

The deal is closed on the house. Several days go by before one day, as I exit the house, the phone rings. Amy presses the button for the speakerphone, and I give the customary greeting.

"Hello, Brian, this is Mr. Cheat. How are you?" he asks in what has ALWAYS struck me as an ingratiating tone.

"Fair," I respond tersely.

"Only fair?" he says, feigning concern.

"Yup. We're on our way out the door, so I'm rather busy."

"So am I!" he says defensively. "I'm wondering if you are interested in the van."

I want to respond, 'I'm wondering if you have a drinking problem or a brain disorder,' but instead I say, "Not after the run-around you gave me."

"What run-around?" he asks solemnly.

"Well," I begin with a laugh, "I asked to rent the van for the day -- I know I made that very clear -- and you, in your infinite goodness, said you would allow Amy and me to *use* the van. I was very specific about how that was to occur. I was very specific about a commitment and the time

The Squeaky Wheel

constraints I had that day. I called you in the morning per your request, and you chose to run errands and arrive an hour and a half later than we had agreed. Upon arrival, you announced that you did not know we wanted to 'use' the van. At Aina Haina Shopping Center you insisted that it was not the Aina Haina Shopping Center -- which it was -- but the Niu Valley Shopping Center. You then implied that I had somehow 'scammed' you into giving us a ride by asking me, 'Do you *really* want to purchase the van?' When I stated I did, you insulted me further by saying that you *really* wanted me to have the van, and therefore you would let me have it for $18,000. Your ad in the Commission on Persons with Disabilities Newsletter listed the *asking* price as $16,000. For these reasons, and more, I will *never* do business with you."

"Ok." Click.

Four years of law school go by.
I propose to Amy, the future Mrs. Shaughnessy.
I plan my wedding, which will take place four days after graduation.
I am scared, tired and bored to death.
I prevail.
I find out I'm not a bad orator.
I sweat through twenty law school final exams.

"So, how'd you fuck yourself up, man?"
Again with the jaw dropping!
"Bet nobody ever asked like that before?"
"You're right! Nobody's ever been that ignorant before."
"So? Are you going to tell me or not?"
"... or not."

I am asked by my classmates to be the speaker at graduation.

Honored to tears, I resolve to overcome my fear and deliver a speech worthy of their confidence. I call my family to tell them of this added honor. "Dad's been telling everybody," Darrin informs me.

Wedding plans are finalized. The phone rings. Shaughnessys and non-Shaughnessys arrive. A friend comes from Thailand to be there. The phone rings. My mom and sister check into their hotel. Brothers arrive. In-laws arrive. The phone rings. Nieces. Nephews. Cousins. Aunties. My father, his wife and their son Billy Bubba arrive. They all lend their assistance. My Chinese in-laws are openly exuberant. The cake for the wedding is ordered. The rings arrive. The graduation speech is written. The preacher is booked. The phone rings. The bride-to-be returns daily with bags of stuffed bunnies.

Graduation day arrives. It's pouring. My attendant bathes, dresses, grooms and feeds me. The rain stops. I roll to the law school for graduation rehearsal at the Andrews Amphitheater. Graduation pictures are taken. Rehearsal begins. It rains. Rehearsal is moved indoors. Contingency plans are made in the event the rain continues. The reports say it will rain for the next two days. Flood warnings are issued. Rehearsal ends and I return home in the rain.
The gathering begins in my Hawaiian-sized apartment. A festive mood arrives with the guests. It rains. More people arrive. It rains some more. More wet people arrive. Damp food and drinks are served. Unexpected but welcome guests arrive. The festive mood grows and is unaffected by the weather. Stories are shared and years of catching up take place in an afternoon.
We depart for the ceremony. My soon-to-be wife helps me into my cap and gown. My classmates enter through the front and I am directed to the back door. I am backed down the very steep driveway to the massive and ancient stone Andrews Amphitheater and down to the grass where the ceremony will be held. I join my classmates on the lawn. We proceed to our seats. The ceremony begins.

Finally, the master of ceremonies says, "Now we will be hearing from our class speaker." I move into position. The microphone is adjusted and I say:

Hello. I'm John Grisham and I'm going to write a book.

I want to acknowledge all of the persons who asked me to mention them during my speech.
Hi.
Ladies and gentlemen of the class of '99:
Wear sunscreen.
If I could offer you only one tip for the future, sunscreen would be it. The benefits of sunscreen have been proven, whereas ...
(interrupted by MC, Patrick, whispering in my ear)
Kurt Vonnegut?

Trust me about the sunscreen.... okay?
Four score and seven years ago our fathers...
(interrupted by Patrick again)
Wow -- I'm in trouble...
Okay.
Section 1: Scope of agreement
WHEREAS: This speech delivered this 17th day of May, 1999 by myself (hereinafter referred to as I or me or speaker or myself) having been elected by the graduating class of '99 (hereinafter referred to as you or them or the class of '99) does contain the following agreement:

I or me agree to the following consideration for this speech.
Nothing.
Section 2: Conditions
In exchange for this consideration I or me agree to the following conditions:
To limit said speech to five minutes. ... Fat chance.
Any irreverence will be the joint and several responsibilities of speaker's parents or therapist.
The speaker agrees to at some point talk about the law and the future, but will refrain from any references to the next millennium.
Any litigation arising from said speech will be indemnified by class of '99 jointly and severally.
(My classmates groan in disagreement.)
Perhaps we need a lawyer to review the contract?
Section 3: Warranties
Brian represents and warrants that he has the experience and ability to perform said speech in a professional, competent and timely manner -- (*I laugh uproariously.*) -- and that such performance shall not infringe upon or violate any federal, state, municipal, law ... unless deemed necessary. Class of '99 and audience shall not determine or exercise control over speaker (pause) nor could they.
Section 4: Liability

The class of '99 shall purchase insurance. Life, term, accident, legal, natural disaster, acts of God, worker's compensation, motor vehicle, comprehensive, general liability and protection from circus animal insurance.

Section 5: Confidentiality

The speaker shall not disclose anyone being too dumb to be an attorney (or breathe for that matter) either in class, faculty, or audience (except for himself).

Footnote No. 1

-- What I really want to do is direct. My agent called today and offered me a part on *Baywatch Hawaii*. But there's a catch... I have to have Pamela Anderson's implants put in. End footnote 1.

Section 6: Apology

Said speaker apologizes for the previous statement and hopes all take it in the spirit in which it was intended.

Section 7: Governing law

Said speech will be construed and enforced in accordance with the UCC, UBC, UPC, MBC, Uniform Speech Code, federal rules of evidence, Model Penal Code, all restatements, international law, Hawaii Revised Statute, Code of Military Justice, and (*a la Darth Vader*) the rules of the Empire.

Section 8: Royalties

All royalties derived from the sale, auction, gift or Internet commerce of said speech will be payable to Kurt Vonnegut.

Permission to reuse the speech at another commencement address is at the sole discretion of Mr. Vonnegut.

It's now time to do the top 10 list. From the home office in Ishpeming, Michigan, today's topic is -- appropriately enough -- top 10 reasons for going to law school and becoming a lawyer.

10. Couldn't get into medical school. (Well, that was fairly predictable.)

9. Wanted to develop a deeper understanding of *Ally McBeal, the Practice* and *Law and Order*.
8. Giggled at thought of working in the penal system and digging through briefs.
7. Babes, Babes, Babes or, in the alternative, Dudes, Dudes, Dudes.
6. Don't have enough stress in life just worrying about the depleting ozone, Hawaii economy, Y2K, AIDS and – well, you get the picture.
5. Thought it would be really cool to say, "Objection, Your Honor."
4. Desire to wear black and send people to jail.
3. Desire to be regarded by society on the same level as used car salesmen.
2. Shyster.

And the #1 reason for going to law school and becoming a lawyer?

1. To zealously represent individuals unable to do so for themselves. Discriminated persons. Politically powerless persons. Poor persons. Exploited persons. Persons who didn't have the opportunity or drive you had. Persons who thought they had no legal recourse. Severely disadvantaged persons. The discrete and insular minorities subjected to a history of purposeful unequal treatment.

When I was 18 years old, my father, a longtime member of the bar, told me I wouldn't like being a lawyer. He was right... then. But after acquiring a disability and enduring 12 years of discrimination, degradation, injustice, ignorance and inquisition by individuals, businesses and government because of having a disability, I was driven into law school.

And now, I'm going to get even.

Almost on the eve of the greatest injustice in my life, my father said, If you want justice, don't look in a court of law. It's our job to change that.

Choose a hero and always ask yourself what would he or she do. I have many. One is Ann Ito. And when you're asked to represent someone or to do something, make sure to ask yourself what your role model would do.

May God bless and keep you always.
May your wishes all come true.
May you always do for others.
And let others do for you.
May you build a ladder to the stars and climb on every rung
And may you stay
Forever young.

Being of semi-sound mind, I declare this to be my graduation speech for the class of '99 and revoke any and all other class of '99 speeches. IN WITNESS WHEREOF the parties present set their signatures and seals
(Class of 99 barks and claps like seals.)
This 17th day of May 1999.

The reaction is overwhelming. Nearly everyone stands and applauds. I take my position. I am called to the podium first, receive my diploma and return. As my classmates pass by, they say that they're glad they chose me to represent them. They call me shyster. They touch me. They hug me. They kiss me. They thank me. They cry. They say they don't know how I did it. I cry. I don't know how I did it either. This all continues as each of my classmates pass by. Then Kevin, my blind brother and the classmate who sparked the revelation that I must go to law school, walks by to accept his diploma.

The William S. Richardson School of Law, class of '99, is presented to the audience. We are piled with leis so high, I can't see who's giving the next one. The man for whom the Law School is named comes to my side. "You're going to be disbarred before you're *admitted!*"

The Squeaky Wheel

I laugh and look to my father. "I'll be in good company."

Four days later, my wedding takes place -- oceanside. 120 friends arrive. They arrive to tables full of stuffed bunnies as their pictures are taken and glued in a book where they sign wishes for the couple. The music begins. Guests are seated. I stand at the ocean's edge with the preacher, and with my sister who is the best man. From the house, down the grassy hill, march five of the cutest little mixed race girls the world has ever seen. They wear the cutest pink dresses the world has ever seen. They each carry a large stuffed bunny. They take their place. The harpist and flutist change tune.

From the house comes my bride. She is wearing a *haku* lei made by a friend. Her long black hair cascades down the front of her bridal gown. She is a gift from God. Everyone stands and smiles. In lieu of a bouquet of flowers, she carries a stuffed pink bunny. It is the year of the rabbit.

She comes to me as we both fight back tears of joy. The guests face each other. The preacher tells everyone to sit. The preacher expresses what everyone is feeling and he asks me if I take Amy to be my wife.

"I do," I say.

He turns to Amy and asks if she takes me to be her lawful husband. She remains silent. There is a pause. The audience shifts uncomfortably, just as we had planned.

On cue, the musicians play the theme from *Jeopardy!* -- do, do , do, do. do, do, do, do, do, do. Now the relieved wedding guests feel free to laugh. The preacher asks again, and Amy says, "I do."

The preacher then asks Amy, " -- and what was your wager?"

On cue, one of the little girls unfurls a large banner that says:

EVERYTHING!!